THE HARRAP
OPERA GUIDE

THE HARRAP OPERA GUIDE

by Sir Alexander F. Morley

HARRAP LONDON

FOR ROSALIND

First published in Great Britain 1970
by GEORGE G. HARRAP & CO. LTD
182 High Holborn, London, WC1V 7AX

Reprinted 1977; 1979

ISBN 0 245 50509 1

Printed in Great Britain by offset lithography by
Billing & Sons Ltd, Guildford, London and Worcester

Preface

Music and words are brother and sister", says the composer in Richard Strauss's *Capriccio*, and in outlining the stage action in the operas described in this book I have had in mind that in only a few works of the older school—if indeed in them—can the music be fully enjoyed without a fairly close understanding of what is being said and done, from moment to moment. In summarizing, therefore, as much of the significant dialogue and action as is practicable within a modest compass, I have tried both to illumine passages which I know from experience are apt to be obscure (even when the opera is performed in English) and to retain the order in which the situation is unfolded. A précis in logical narrative form or a general situation report would often be more readable and more concise, but is usually much less helpful to the opera-goer. It follows that the length of the outline bears no necessary relation to the time needed to perform a work and has been partly determined by the kind of libretto and the way it has been set.

It would be impossible in a book of this size to attempt any elaborate description or analysis of the music. But I have, where practicable, inserted a few musical signposts; and in the introductory notes have attempted to say something about the music as a whole, as well as to assess and place the work.

The choice of operas must be taken to represent not the author's taste but his judgment of those which a reader whose opera-going is confined to English-speaking countries is likely most frequently to encounter. The repertory has almost everywhere, happily, been so broadened in recent years, that it is not possible to include everything that will be given; and from this standpoint, if there prove to be important omissions from this book, it will even be a matter for satisfaction.

I take this opportunity to express my deep gratitude to Mr David Matthews for reading the text of the Guide and for making some valuable suggestions.

A.F.M.

Contents

Aida

Opera in four acts. Music by G. Verdi. Libretto by A. Ghislanzoni based on C. de Locle. First produced at Cairo, December 24th, 1871.

SCENE: Memphis and Thebes (Egypt).

TIME: Egyptian antiquity.

PRINCIPAL CHARACTERS:

THE KING OF EGYPT		(Bass)
RADAMES	*Captain of the Guard*	(Tenor)
RAMPHIS	*High Priest*	(Bass)
AMNERIS	*Daughter of the King*	(Contralto)
AMONASRO	*King of Ethiopia*	(Baritone)
AIDA	*His daughter, slave of Amneris*	(Soprano)

This is the last of Verdi's operas prior to his late flowering. As befitted a work commissioned by the Khedive for the opening of a new opera house in Cairo (though not in fact used on that occasion) it is on a "grand" scale with spectacle, a crowd scene à la Meyerbeer, and ballet. The characters are heroic and only Amneris is presented in any psychological depth. The work is distinguished by a wealth of flexibly moulded melody, the clarity and unbroken tension of its action, the growing freedom of its form and a very telling conciseness in its recitative (cf. the part of Ramphis). But even more remarkable are the elaborate orchestration, far more sophisticated than anything Verdi had previously done, and the way the whole vibrant score is saturated with exotic colour—though only in the temple music and some of the dances as a result of deliberate devices.

The short Prelude is based mainly on the motive associated with Aida, together with a descending motive associated with the priests.

ACT I

Scene 1. A hall in the King's palace at Memphis. Ramphis informs Radames of an Ethiopian invasion. Isis has pronounced who shall lead the defending

army and he is taking the name to the King. Alone, Radames expresses
the hope that the honour may be his. His thoughts turn to his love for
Aida and the prospect of being allowed to marry her, in the familiar
romanza "Celeste Aida". The jealous Amneris asks the reason for his look
of joy, in the hope of extracting some admission of his love for her slave,
but he replies that it is due to a dream of proud ambition. The duet
becomes a trio as Aida enters and Amneris inquires ingratiatingly about the
cause of her tears. Aida replies that she dreads war and trembles for her
country. Radames fears that Amneris may have read what is in his heart.
The King and his court enter. After hearing from a messenger of the
advance of Amonasro on Thebes the King announces that Radames is to
lead the Egyptian army. All take up the martial patriotic strain announced
by the King, except Aida. At the climax Amneris hands Radames the
standard before he departs for the temple, with the words "return
victorious." Aida, left alone, takes up these words and, in a famous scena,
expresses the conflict in her heart, ending with a beautiful prayer for pity
in her secret agony; for no-one knows that she is Amonasro's daughter.
Scene 2. Interior of the Temple of Ptah. Radames and priestesses invoke
the God in an exotic chant. As the latter dance to soft flute measures,
Radames goes up to the altar and participates with Ramphis in a rite of
dedication. The first prayer is repeated, ending with a mighty cry to the
God.

ACT II

Scene 1. A hall in Amneris's apartment. Female slaves sing to Amneris,
while she is being attired for the festival of victory, of Radames' glory
and her love, Amneris echoing each verse. A light dance of Moorish
slaves forms a middle section to this song. Seeing Aida approach (to
her usual motive) Amneris enjoins a tactful silence and resolves to test
Aida's feelings for Radames. She begins their great duet by expressing
sympathy at the defeat of Aida's people and suggesting that in time love
will heal her feelings. Aida rises to the mention of love and Amneris
tells her that Radames is dead. When Aida's grief is apparent she tells her
that it was a lie and, seeing Aida's rapture, openly declares herself a rival.
Aida checks herself from revealing her identity and begs for mercy at the
feet of the exultant and threatening Amneris. As the approaching sound
of the patriotic march is heard, Amneris orders Aida to follow her and
take her place in the dust at the foot of the throne. After a climax the
scene closes with the soft return of Aida's prayer which ended Act I.
Scene 2. Outside Thebes. The King and his court take their places before
a popular throng, to a chorus of triumph and praise to which priests later
add the motive heard in the Prelude. The victorious troops pass the throne
to the well-known march (in which the sudden key-change among the

stage trumpets is the feature of interest). Then follows a group of dancing girls. The chorus is resumed, in praise now of Radames who, on his arrival, is embraced by the King and receives the laurel of victory from Amneris (to a reminiscence of the Act I Scene 1 duet). At his request the prisoners, including Amonasro, are led on. Aida cries out in recognition of her father but he whispers to her not to betray his rank. He leads the captives and slaves in a prayer for mercy, to a new phrase, against which the priests are heard calling for their death, to the motive already heard, while Radames is transfixed by the beauty of Aida in her grief. After a big climax Radames asks for the boon of life and liberty for the prisoners; Ramphis resists this and the King compromises by keeping Aida's father as a hostage. He bestows Amneris's hand upon Radames to the former's triumphant joy and the latter's confusion. The chorus is resumed once more, with the principals voicing their emotions above it and, after another mighty ensemble, the scene ends with a repetition of the first phrase of the march.

ACT III

Shores of the Nile, near a temple of Isis. Moonlight night. The orchestra paints the scene and a chorus of invocation of the goddess is heard. Amneris and Ramphis alight from a boat. He conducts her to the temple for a night of prayer before her marriage. Aida enters cautiously for a tryst with Radames, fearful that it will prove their last meeting. She sings the famous romanza "O patria mia" in which she expresses her fear that she will never again see her beloved country. Suddenly Amonasro encounters her, having fathomed why she is there. In the opening strain of a big duet he plays on her love of her country. Then he tells her that the Ethiopians are ready to fall upon the Egyptian army if only she can find out from Radames the path they will be taking. He underlines that the responsibility will be hers if the Egyptians again sack their country and threatens to lay his curse upon her. In the final section he exacts her reluctant promise to do what he asks and withdraws among the palm trees. Radames arrives, proclaiming his love in a rhapsodic phrase, to be met by Aida's question how he can avoid marrying Amneris. Over staccato trumpets he explains that after another victory he plans to lay bare his heart to the King and claim her hand as his reward. Aida fears the vengeance of Amneris (motive from trio in Act I Scene 1). She proposes in a new section of the duet that he should flee with her to her native land where they can live in bliss together. Radames is at first reluctant but when she taunts him with not loving her, eventually agrees. The duet ends with a unison repetition of the rhapsodic phrase. As they are leaving she asks him how they will avoid the Egyptian army. He replies that their route will be clear till the morrow. It is the pass of Napata. Amonasro repeats this and emerging proclaims that he is the

King of Ethiopia. Radames realizes that he has betrayed his country but when, after a short trio, they seek to depart with him, Amneris comes out with Ramphis from the temple and, having overheard, denounces him. Amonasro tries to stab her but Radames comes between them. He bids Aida and Amonasro fly while he gives himself up to Ramphis.

ACT IV

Scene 1. A hall in the royal palace, above the subterranean justice chamber. After a short Prelude, which recalls a motive of Amneris's vengeance heard in Act I Scene 1, she is discovered torn by conflicting emotions. To a repetition of the opening of her duet with Radames in Act I Scene 1, she decides that she loves him so much that she must try and save him. She orders him to be brought to her. She offers to save him and to give up all for him, but he is not interested in living now that Aida is dead. Amneris tells him that, though Amonasro has been killed, Aida escaped. He prays that she may reach her country but still wishes to die for her sake. Amneris promises him vengeance for this insult, but when Radames has been led away and the priests are assembling below (to a major version of the motive from the Prelude) she is overcome by despair and remorse. The prayers of the priests below and the unanswered threefold charge of Ramphis (a semi-tone higher each time) are punctuated by her cries to the gods to save Radames. The priests declare him a traitor and Ramphis condemns him to be interred beneath the temple. She curses the priests when they emerge in procession.

Scene 2. Above, the interior of the Temple of Ptah. Below, the dark crypt, the entrance to which is being closed by a heavy stone. Radames, below, has just voiced the hope that Aida will never learn his fate, when he finds her exhausted, having entered secretly in anticipation of his fate. Their final duet is rapt and soft. After a stanza for each the chanting of the chorus above is heard. During the third stanza, which they share, Amneris appears in mourning above and adds a prayer for peace. She and the chorus are left softly intoning as Aida dies in Radames' arms.

Albert Herring

Comic opera in three acts. Music by Benjamin Britten. Libretto by E. Crozier after G. de Maupassant. First produced at Glyndebourne, June 20th, 1947.

SCENE: Loxford (a small market town in East Suffolk).

TIME: April-May 1900.

CHARACTERS:

LADY BILLOWS *An elderly autocrat*		(Soprano)
FLORENCE PIKE *Her housekeeper*		(Contralto)
MISS WORDSWORTH *Head-teacher at the Church School*		(Soprano)
MR GEDGE *The vicar*		(Baritone)
MR UPFOLD *The mayor*		(Tenor)
SUPERINTENDENT BUDD		(Bass)
SID *A butcher's shophand*		(Baritone)
ALBERT HERRING *From the greengrocer's*		(Tenor)
NANCY *From the bakery*		(Mezzo-soprano)
MRS HERRING *Albert's mother*		(Mezzo-soprano)
EMMIE ⎫		(Soprano)
CIS ⎬ *Village children*		(Soprano)
HARRY ⎭		(Treble)

In this, the third of his operas, Britten returned to his native Suffolk for subject. Eric Crozier's libretto is a satirical but recognizable picture of English village life not so long ago, with firmly drawn characters and amusing dialogue, colloquial in style. Much of this is set to a free recitative which can differentiate the characters or underline the points (like the solemn cadence to the words "a piece of best English beef"). From time to time there are formal pieces, often parodying the solemnities of other operas. Lady Billows is given some coloratura to mark her old-fashioned zeal; Mr Gedge has melodies of a decidedly clerical cut; Sid and Nancy have what comes nearest to a straight lyrical style. The texture of the music is light and it moves fast, as it must if it is to sustain wit and be witty in itself. Everywhere Britten's special gift of finding just the musical equivalent for a particular character or situation is strongly in evidence.

ACT I

Scene 1. Breakfast-room in Lady Billows' house. Florence is trying to keep track of Lady Billows' innumerable instructions. The four village functionaries arrive, somewhat nervously, for a meeting at which the business is to elect a May Queen who is to receive from Lady Billows a prize of twenty-five sovereigns. But Florence has something against the morals of each girl suggested and the meeting is baffled, while Lady Billows rails against the shameful state of affairs to which Loxford has sunk. The Superintendent at this point suggests a King of the May and proposes the simple Albert Herring. This is received with surprised indignation. But the vicar feels that virtue should be the test and Lady Billows agrees to the proposal in order to teach the girls a lesson. It is taken up with enthusiasm and the scene ends with a formal sextet. An orchestral Interlude looks forward to

Scene 2. Mrs Herring's greengrocery shop. The three children are playing ball outside to a jaunty little action song. The ball rolls in and Harry, coming after it, steals some apples. Sid catches him and throws him out. The children run away. Albert Herring comes into the shop (backwards) and Sid tries to get him to break away from his mother's apron strings by a recital of pleasures which could await him. Nancy comes into the shop. She and Sid arrange a rendezvous for that evening and go out, leaving Albert to meditate on what Sid has said to him. Florence arrives and warns Mrs Herring that Lady Billows and her committee are on their way. They arrive and Lady Billows pompously announces that Albert is to be May King. When the deputation has left Mrs Herring is jubilant at the prospect (especially of the £25) but Albert is in rebellious mood, till she sends him upstairs, to the delight of the three children looking in at the window (and still singing their jaunty tune).

ACT II

Scene 1. May Day. A marquee with a long table set with refreshments. Florence bustles in and out. Sid describes the special church service to Nancy and then takes her off to tell her about a secret scheme. Miss Wordsworth rehearses the three children in the song to be sung in praise of Albert. Sid and Nancy return and Sid pours rum into what will be Albert's lemonade glass (to the opening of the *Tristan and Isolde* Prelude) "to loosen him up and make him feel bright". The official party arrives; the children sing their anthem and bouquets are presented. There are speeches from the members of the committee and presentations are made to Albert, who can only mumble his thanks. After all have sung an anthem in praise of "Albert the Good", a toast is drunk. Albert drains his glass (more *Tristan*) and at once has his glass refilled by Nancy. He gets hiccups (each time to the *Tristan* chord, played staccato). The company falls noisily upon the refreshments.

The orchestral Interlude begins with a fugato passage on the tune of "Albert the Good" but slows down to a quotation from the lullaby in Britten's *The Rape of Lucretia*, leading into
Scene 2. The shop. Evening. Albert enters gaily, with the sound of "Albert the Good" still in his head, too tipsy to light the gas. He thinks of Nancy but realizes that "girls don't care for chaps like me". Just then Sid and Nancy are heard outside, Nancy saying that she would like to help Albert sow a few wild oats. They go off happily together. Albert has been stung by what he has overheard. He tosses up. It is "heads" for "Yes" and he goes off whistling into the night. Mrs Herring returns (the *Lucretia* tune again) and goes sleepily off to bed, thinking Albert to be already asleep himself.

ACT III

The shop. Afternoon of May 2nd. Everyone is hunting for Albert. Nancy in her contrition sings a sad little song; but Sid says that he is fed up with hearing nothing but "Albert". The Superintendent is baffled. Mrs Herring gives him, for identification, her only photograph of Albert, taken on the pier at Felixstowe. She is convinced that he is dead and starts what proves to be a quartet of lamentation. The atmosphere grows even tenser when Albert's crown is solemnly borne in, found crushed on the road by a cart. A big ensemble on the words "in the midst of life is death" begins softly and has built up to a great climax when Albert hesitantly comes in from the street. They pile recriminations and questions upon him and he coolly tells them a horrifying tale of his night out. When they reproach him he tells them frankly that it was because his mother "did up my instincts with safety pins", and then politely but firmly asks them all to let him get on with his work (to a phrase that might have come out of Verdi's *Falstaff*). Left alone with Sid and Nancy he asks if he has laid it on too thick and Nancy gives him a big kiss. The children are outside and he invites them in and gives them peaches. They burst into their jaunty song (with new words in praise of Albert) and, just before the curtain comes down, Albert chucks the crown into the audience, to the words "jolly good riddance".

Alceste

(Alcestis). Opera in three acts. Music by C. W. von Gluck. Libretto by R. da Calzabigi, revised by the Marquis G. le B. du Rollet. First performed at the Burgtheater, Vienna, December 26th, 1767. (Revised version in Paris, April 23rd, 1776.)

SCENE: Thessaly.

TIME: Antiquity.

CHARACTERS:

ADMETUS	(Tenor)
ALCESTE	(Soprano)
HIGH PRIEST	(Baritone)
HERCULES	(Baritone)
EVANDER	(Tenor)
HERALD	(Baritone)
THANATOS (Death)	(Baritone)
APOLLO	(Baritone)

Gluck introduced this opera with a famous preface in which he called for a balanced blend of music and poetry and proclaimed his ideal of a "beautiful simplicity". His operatic ideals are well exemplified in "Alceste" and particularly in the solemn Overture and Act I, in which an atmosphere of high tragedy is established by music of which the refinement and sensitivity counterbalance the limited vocabulary. The feeling is, of course, classical throughout. The language was originally Italian but nowadays the Paris version (in French) is most likely to be encountered.

ACT I

Scene 1. A square before the palace of Admetus. The people are lamenting the illness of Admetus whom the Herald tells them is near to death. Alceste comes out with her children, for whose future she despairs. She prays to heaven (in a short aria) and the people are deeply moved. She bids them follow her to the temple to offer sacrifices and the people resume the chorus with which the scene opened.

Scene 2. Temple of Apollo. After a short orchestral piece, while the people assemble, the High Priest calls on the god to avert Admetus's fate. Alceste enters and adds her own prayer. The sacrifice follows to another orchestral air. It is successful and the High Priest calls for silence for the Oracle, whose message is that the King must die that day, unless another can be found to take his place. The crowd abandon hope and depart. Alone with the High Priest Alceste resolves on death. He replies that to save Admetus she must die that day. In a famous aria she passionately defies the "divinités du Styx"; she will die for her love and does not need their cruel pity.

ACT II

A great hall in the Palace. Admetus receives the congratulations of his people on his recovery. There are dances in his honour. Evander tells him how he was saved, but not by whom. Alceste enters and all share their joy at being reunited. But she cannot conceal her grief, not even when Admetus seeks, in a full-length aria, to comfort her. She assures him that she still loves him and eventually admits that she is the unknown hero who is to die for him. Admetus declares that he cannot live without her. Alceste is left alone with the grieving chorus and laments with them her unhappy fate.

ACT III

Scene 1. A forecourt of the palace. As the people mourn the loss of Admetus and Alceste, Hercules who is a friend of Admetus arrives, rejoicing at the completion of his labours. Learning the sad news from Evander he vows, in a rather jaunty aria, to restore Alceste to them.
Scene 2. The gates of Hades. Alceste struggles on through the horrors of the scene (an accompanied recitative seems to anticipate the Wolf's Glen in *Der Freischütz*) and pleads with a chorus of unseen spirits for quick admittance. (A beautiful aria here.) Admetus overtakes her and begs to be allowed to die with, or in place of, Alceste. Alceste seeks to dissuade him and the argument is carried into a duet which is interrupted by the voice of Thanatos calling for one of them to offer himself up; it is for Alceste to choose. Alceste is still inflexibly resolved when Hercules arrives. He and Admetus struggle with the Infernal Powers and rescue Alceste. Apollo appears, confers immortality on Hercules and restores both Admetus and Alceste to life.
Scene 3. As in Scene 1. Apollo bids the people rejoice. Hercules, Admetus, and Alceste join in a short trio of thanksgiving and the people sing a joyful chorus. The opera ends with a divertissement.

Arabella

Lyrical comedy in three (two) acts. Music by Richard Strauss. Libretto by H. von Hofmannsthal. First produced at Dresden, July 1st, 1933.

SCENE: Vienna.

TIME: 1860.

CHARACTERS:

COUNT WALDNER	*A retired Major*	(Bass)
ADELAIDE	*His wife*	(Mezzo-soprano)
ARABELLA } *His daughters*		(Soprano)
ZDENKA }		(Soprano)
MANDRYKA		(Baritone)
MATTEO	*An officer*	(Tenor)
COUNT ELEMER }		(Tenor)
COUNT DOMINIK } *Suitors of Arabella*		(Baritone)
COUNT LAMORAL }		(Bass)
THE FIAKERMILLI	*A grisette*	(Soprano)
A FORTUNE-TELLER		(Soprano)

It would be futile to look in this opera, the last of the Strauss-Hofmannsthal partnership, for the grand manner of some of its predecessors. This is a comedy of sentiment, set to music which is in parts almost the junior partner. Though always responsive to the inflexions of the spoken word, it takes charge of and amplifies only the more emotional and introspective moments. The picture of a self-assured young woman, immersed in the social world and unable to make up her mind to marry any of her suitors, whose latent romanticism and strength of character are aroused by a rough stranger from another milieu, offers Strauss the opportunity to create another of those female rôles at which he excelled; while he surrounds Mandryka with an earthy, Slavonic atmosphere. Both have glorious singing parts and the lion's share of the passages where the conversational style soars, in the Straussian manner, into lyrical heights. But there are some subtle character sketches among the smaller parts and Act II provides a characteristic Viennese background, with waltzes which are only lightly sketched in and do not dominate the scene as in "Der Rosenkavalier".

The last two acts are sometimes joined, in which case the Prelude to Act III covers the change of scene.

ACT I

A salon in a hotel where the Waldner family live. Adelaide is having her fortune told while Zdenka, in boy's clothes, deals with a series of visits from tradesmen with unpaid bills. We learn from the conversation that the family is hard up and that Waldner, a prematurely retired Army officer, is a compulsive gambler. Adelaide is anxious to see Arabella, who "sees through men like glass", married off. Zdenka, who adores her elder sister, is kept dressed as a boy because her parents cannot afford to acknowledge two marriageable daughters. Left alone, Zdenka prays that they will not have to leave Vienna. She wants Arabella to accept Matteo, a young officer deeply in love with her, though she herself, whom he thinks a boy, is in love with him. Matteo comes in, asks for news of Arabella and threatens to shoot himself. He cannot understand her indifference after receiving from her so wonderful a letter (really written by Zdenka). When he has gone Arabella comes home and it is clear that she is indifferent towards her many suitors including Matteo. When Zdenka taunts her with being a proud and cold coquette she replies (in the opera's best-known passage) that when the right man comes she will recognize him at once and love him devotedly. Zdenka says she will help her to find such happiness. The soaring duet, in which these confidences are exchanged, is based on a Slavonic folk-song which frequently recurs later. Elemer, an ardent and favoured suitor, calls and presses Arabella to ride with him in his sleigh. After some hesitation she agrees to go with him in half an hour, but her "brother" must go too. Their parents come in and send the girls away. Waldner tells his wife that he has written to Mandryka, an old regimental crony, rich and eccentric, enclosing Arabella's photograph, in the hope that he might turn up. But there are only bills. Just then Mandryka is announced but it turns out to be his nephew with the same name. In a superb monologue he explains that his uncle is dead; he opened the letter; he fell passionately in love with the photograph; and has come to ask for Arabella's hand. He is a gauche country squire and has inherited his uncle's estates in Slavonia. He has sold a wood to finance his journey and holds out a full purse to Waldner, remarking "Teschék, bedien' dich" (pray, help yourself). The incredulous Waldner keeps repeating this (or hearing the musical phrase in the same rhythm). Mandryka withdraws ceremoniously. Zdenka, who comes in, is quite bewildered at her father's condition. When he has left Matteo returns, anxiously seeking a letter from Arabella. Zdenka replies that Arabella hopes to have one for her to deliver that evening. He leaves and Arabella enters, ready for her sleigh-drive. She muses on the idea of marrying Elemer or Matteo, but her thoughts turn to an attractive stranger she has seen from the window. Then she remembers that it is Shrove Tuesday and that she is to be Queen of the evening's cabbies' ball and goes out gaily with Zdenka for her drive. This final scene for Arabella is another outstanding passage.

ACT II

A room leading out of a ball-room. Arabella is introduced to Mandryka by her parents and recognizes the attractive stranger. The intensity of his declaration of love frightens her a little but she sees in him the right man. He tells her that, had she been a girl in his part of the country she would tonight have brought him, symbolically, a glass of clear water from the spring behind her father's house. They pledge themselves to each other to another South Slavonic folk-tune of touching simplicity which serves to mark the total surrender of the worldly and sophisticated young woman. She then asks for, and is granted, an hour at the ball to say goodbye to her girlhood. At that moment the Fiakermilli appears and presents Arabella with a bouquet on behalf of all the revellers. Arabella goes off to dance with Dominik. Zdenka tries to encourage Matteo, who is disconsolate that Arabella has ignored him. Mandryka, in the seventh heaven, orders champagne and flowers all round. Arabella takes sentimental leave of each of her three suitors in turn, including a last dance with Lamoral, before going home to reflect on her happiness. Zdenka and Matteo meet again. She gives him a letter which she says is from Arabella and contains the key of Arabella's room where her sister will be in a quarter of an hour. Mandryka overhears this and at first can hardly believe that it can be his Arabella. But when everyone begins to look for the Queen of the Ball and a note from her is brought him saying goodnight, he is greatly upset and flirts with the Fiakermilli who responds in coloratura strains. He is heavily sarcastic with Arabella's parents when they ask him where she is. All three go off to the hotel to find her. The party continues at Mandryka's expense.

ACT III

A lounge in the hotel with a staircase. After a Prelude, which seems from the motives used to refer to what is happening in the room upstairs, Matteo is seen about to come down but, hearing a bell, he hides. Arabella comes in happily from the ball, her head full of waltzes and of her future life with Mandryka. Matteo appears. She greets him coolly and with surprise and cannot follow his allusions; and he is puzzled to find her downstairs in her cloak. In the middle of all this her parents and Mandryka arrive. Mandryka recognizes Matteo as the man with the key and, in a rage announces his departure from Vienna. Arabella's explanations satisfy her father but not Mandryka. Arabella tells the baffled Matteo, who now intervenes, that the latter is her betrothed and that he is compromising her. He does not know what to say. Arabella cannot understand why Mandryka will not believe her and is insulting her. A duel threatens and hotel guests gather. Suddenly Zdenka, in a négligé and with her hair down, rushes down stairs, threatening to throw herself into the Danube for shame. She confesses that it was she who sent Matteo the key and that it is she who was just now with Matteo in the darkened room. Arabella forgives her at once. Mandryka could sink through the floor. He humbly begs Arabella's forgiveness, but she turns to Zdenka and thanks her for teaching her to follow single-mindedly the heart's promptings. She cuts Mandryka's apologies short and bids him forget the recent scene. They win Waldner's consent to give Zdenka's hand to Matteo. The hotel guests disperse to bed. Mandryka and Arabella are left alone. She refuses to talk about it any more but asks for a glass of cold water from the hotel fountain to refresh herself and goes upstairs, leaving Mandryka feeling that he has only got what he deserved. Arabella appears again at the top of the stairs and slowly descends with the glass of water on a tray. She hands him the glass untouched. He drinks from it and then smashes it on the floor. They are united in a short duet based on now familiar musical material.

Ariadne auf Naxos

(Ariadne on Naxos). Opera in one act with a prologue. Music by Richard Strauss. Libretto by H. von Hofmannsthal. Original version first produced at Stuttgart, October 25th, 1912. Revised version first produced at the Hofoper, Vienna, October 4th, 1916.

SCENE: Vienna (prologue); Naxos (the opera).

TIME: Early eighteenth century (prologue); Antiquity (the opera).

PRINCIPAL CHARACTERS:

In the prologue:		*In the opera:*	
THE MAJOR-DOMO			(Speaking part)
A MUSIC MASTER			(Baritone)
THE COMPOSER			(Soprano)
THE TENOR		BACCHUS	(Tenor)
THE DANCING MASTER			(Tenor)
A LACKEY			(Bass)
PRIMA DONNA		ARIADNE	(Soprano)
ZERBINETTA		ZERBINETTA	(Soprano)
HARLEQUIN	*Members of a*	HARLEQUIN	(Baritone)
SCARAMUCCIO	*Commedia dell'Arte*	SCARAMUCCIO	(Tenor)
TRUFFALDINO	*troupe of players*	TRUFFALDINO	(Bass)
BRIGHELLA		BRIGHELLA	(Tenor)
		NAIAD	(Soprano)
		DRYAD	(Contralto)
		ECHO	(Soprano)

The original conception was of an entertainment consisting of an abridged version of Molière's "Le Bourgeois Gentilhomme" with incidental music and the opera as the "divertissement" for the end of the play, the whole to be produced by Max Reinhardt. Such a production is hardly practicable except under special conditions and the second version was therefore written, with a musical Prologue, which explains the juxtaposition of legendary and Commedia dell'Arte figures, replacing Molière's play, but the opera proper being left virtually unchanged. It is this second version which is usually performed and is discussed below, the incidental music to the play remaining familiar as a concert suite.

The whole work requires only a chamber orchestra (with piano) and Hofmannsthal's imaginative plan evoked some of Strauss's most delicate and unforced music, free from all the extravagances of his early operas. The witty Prologue is largely in the conversational style reproduced in "Arabella" and "Capriccio" and consists of free recitative broken by thematic anticipations of the opera proper but with a few longer lyrical passages, notably for the Composer (a grateful breeches rôle sometimes taken by a mezzo) and the Dancing Master. All the characters are strongly delineated and the Major-domo's part deserves an actor of substance. The special features of the opera are first the way in which music in Strauss's normal style has been poured into classical moulds (e.g., Zerbinetta's rondo) and manages to convey an eighteenth century atmosphere; second, the happy blend of the heroic style with the lighter but stylized touch required for the comedy troupe. Indeed, the two dancing quintets are perhaps the most original sections of the score, though Zerbinetta's long and difficult recitative and aria display her character to perfection. The final rhapsodical duet is of great but more orthodox beauty.

PROLOGUE

A large room in a rich man's mansion, where preparations are afoot for a theatrical performance. The Prelude successively alludes to motives associated with the Composer, Ariadne, and Zerbinetta and to the closing scene of the opera. The Music Master obtains confirmation from the haughty Major-domo that his pupil's opera seria is indeed to be followed by an Italian opera buffa. An officer enters Zerbinetta's dressing-room. The anxious Composer tries to get his fiddlers and his Prima Donna to rehearse but an insolent and pedantic Lackey explains why neither is available. A snatch of melody is forming in his head; but he must try to speak about the part of Bacchus to the Tenor, who proves to be too deep in altercation with the Wig-maker. Zerbinetta emerges with the officer, whom she is telling of her fear that the audience will have been bored stiff by the opera *Ariadne auf Naxos* before her turn comes. (The Prima Donna emerges for a moment from her room, half-dressed as Ariadne, with the Music Master.) The Dancing Master reassures her. The Composer, attracted by Zerbinetta, is told by the Music Master that she and her four partners will be singing and dancing in a light piece after his opera. He rages against the suffocating philistinism of patrons. And yet only a few minutes ago he had thought of a beautiful melody. This time a beautiful song to Cupid takes shape and he writes it down. The Music Master advises him to come to terms with the world, but he tears up his manuscript in a fury. The Prima Donna and Zerbinetta make spiteful remarks about each other's performances. The Dancing Master assures the latter (in a delightful passage taken from the incidental music to the Molière) that it is much better to be second on the programme, while the Music Master assures the former that Ariadne is all that will be remembered. A message is brought that the company is rising from table. Amid the commotion the Major-domo reappears with the information that his master now wants both pieces performed simultaneously, exactly as ordered and paid for but still ending punctually in time for the fireworks. The audience will be arriving at any minute. He leaves general consternation behind him. Only the Dancing Master is complacent because the opera will now have to be cut; the Music Master would comply if only he knew how; the Composer is uncompromising at first but is forced to sit down with a red pencil while the Prima Donna and Tenor each try and secure that it is the other's part which is cut. The action of the opera—Ariadne abandoned by Theseus on a desert island, awaiting death but visited by Bacchus—is explained to Zerbinetta who brushes aside all the Composer's profound inner meaning and interprets it in her own way. She and her partners are to be a cheerful band who are on the island by chance and will find an opening to join in the action. The Composer is horrified. But coquettishly she tells him, in a soaring passage with a beautiful motive of its own, that though she plays light parts her heart is lonely and longing for a man to whom she can be faithful. The Composer in ecstasy thinks he has found a kindred soul and is reconciled to having her in his opera. After this scene (which Strauss called "particularly pretty") she runs off and the music returns to a conversational level as the Music Master returns with his company. He has some difficulty in coaxing the Prima Donna onto a stage where Zerbinetta is also to appear. The Composer's mood is now transformed and full of new courage. In exaltation he proclaims in another soaring passage that, good as may be the words which poets write for music, music is the most holy of all the arts. But when Zerbinetta's partners, as well as herself, take their places on the stage, he feels betrayed and rushes off in despair; and the Act closes with a tragic minor cadence.

THE OPERA

Naxos. The Overture introduces motives of Ariadne's lament in a mood of classical restraint. As the curtain rises she is seen asleep at the mouth of a cave, while Naiad, Dryad, and Echo are watching over her in her unending sorrow. Their voices blend in a trio of dispassionate charm. Ariadne awakes with a sigh and in a preliminary recitative asks herself whether she still lives. Zerbinetta and her partners comment briefly from the wings on the depth of her despair. Now, after an arpeggio-like motive on the horn, begins her great lament. She contrasts her former happiness with Theseus with her present state and looks forward to death. Harlequin interpolates that she seems out of her mind and, encouraged by Zerbinetta, tries to soothe her with a tender little song (a typical Strauss lied) of which the first and last phrases are wordlessly repeated by Echo. Ariadne pays no heed and, rising, meditates in a new strain on the Kingdom of the Dead, and ecstatically looks forward to the arrival of Hermes, death's messenger, to take her soul away and free it from the burden of life. The comedians try to dry her tears by dancing and by singing a quintet but she pays no attention and Zerbinetta dismisses her four partners and addresses her direct in an elaborate coloratura scena. In the recitative she respectfully tries a woman-to-woman approach and goes on to point out that it is the lot of women to encounter the faithlessness of men. Ariadne retreats into her cave. In the first part of the aria Zerbinetta speaks of the difficulty of remaining constant; in a scherzando section she illustrates this by enumerating some past flames; and finally she begins a formal but florid rondo at the words "each one arrived like a god". Harlequin bounds out and unsuccessfully tries a little love-making himself. Then follows a second quintet in which Zerbinetta dances around and flirts with each of her partners in turn to music in Strauss's "Viennese" manner. At one point she slips off with Harlequin, while the other three are clowning around. (It is a vocal version of the conventional Commedia dell'Arte mime.) All at length disappear.

The music now becomes more serious as the three nymphs reappear with tidings of the approach of a youthful god, Bacchus, who has just escaped from the wiles of Circe, his first adventure. (His motives are heard in the excited orchestra.) They call to Ariadne. Bacchus becomes visible on a rock exulting that he has been able to escape from Circe. Ariadne comes out of the cave listening, though she cannot yet see him. She thinks him the long-awaited messenger of death. Twice Bacchus is interrupted by the trio of nymphs urging him in a simple melody, reminiscent of Schubert's *Wiegenlied*, to sing on. The remainder of the opera is virtually a long, though unusual love duet. When Bacchus descends from the rock and confronts Ariadne she cries out "Theseus" in fear but thereafter continues to welcome him as the god come to carry her off, transformed, to a place of forgetfulness and peace. Bacchus however is struck by her beauty and fears at first that she may be a sorceress, like Circe. He cannot understand her wish to die and vows, as he is a god, that this shall not be. She sinks into his arms, thinking this the moment of death and he embraces her. The stars come out and she feels herself, freed from all her sorrow, already in Elysium, while Bacchus feels himself filled with god-like rapture. To a surging passionate phrase he declares that the cave of her sorrow must be a bower of love for them. A canopy descends over them and the nymphs join in with the Schubertian melody. Zerbinetta appears for a moment, softly singing "Each one arrived like a god", underlining that, as Hofmannsthal put it, the two worlds of a faithfulness redeemed only by a miracle and of light emotion are in the end "connected ironically by non-comprehension". The music rises to one last climax and the passionate phrase is heard again before Bacchus and Ariadne disappear from view.

Un Ballo in Maschera

(A Masked Ball). Opera in three acts by G. Verdi. Libretto by A. Somma after A. E. Scribe. First produced at the Teatro Apollo, Rome, February 17th, 1859.

SCENE: Boston (Sweden).

TIME: Late seventeenth century (1792).

CHARACTERS:

RICCARDO	*Earl of Warwick and Governor of Boston (Gustavus III, King of Sweden)*	(Tenor)
RENATO	*His Creole secretary (Anckarstroem)*	(Baritone)
AMELIA	*His wife*	(Soprano)
SAMUELE	*(Count Ribbing)* ⎱ *Enemies of*	(Bass)
TOMASO	*(Count Horn)* ⎰ *Riccardo*	(Bass)
ULRICA	*A Negro fortune-teller (Mlle Arvidson)*	(Contralto)
OSCAR	*Riccardo's page*	(Soprano)
SILVANO	*A sailor (Cristian)*	(Baritone)

The scene of this opera was laid in Sweden and it was called "Gustavo III" (with the date and characters as indicated in brackets). It suffered a last-minute switch in place and time to appease the censor, with some absurdities as a result. It needs only small textual changes to return it to its original historical setting and this is often done, though Ulrica is best left. Indeed it is not uncommon for all the Italian names to survive a restoration of the scene to Sweden. Apart from this difficulty the libretto is a good one and evoked one of the best of Verdi's "middle period" scores. It contains some famous arias in which the winding cantilena of Verdi's maturity is much in evidence and some splendid ensembles, in which the dramatic rôles of the characters are sharply delineated and there is clever use of irony. (The final scene for instance, takes place against the brilliant background of music for the ball.) The opera is almost free of those patches of vulgarity or the commonplace which mar some of Verdi's earlier works. The part of Oscar, for a high soprano, is most original and is often taken by famous coloratura stars. The two conspirators, whose motive combines well in counterpoint, cling vocally to each other in an effective way.

The Prelude is based on motives to be heard when the curtain has risen, assigned to the main chorus, the conspirators, and Riccardo, in that order.

ACT I

Scene 1. Reception hall in the palace. Officials and nobles sing Riccardo's praises but Samuele, Tomaso, and their followers are plotting against him. Oscar brings Riccardo the list of guests for a ball and he expresses his delight at seeing Amelia's name, in a beautiful solo. But he is troubled because she is the wife of his faithful secretary, Renato, who is uneasily aware that Riccardo's enemies are plotting against him. A judge asks for Ulrica to be outlawed, but Oscar intercedes for her. To Renato's dismay, Riccardo decides to see her for himself and, to Oscar's delight, bids his followers to assemble that afternoon in disguise to visit her abode.
Scene 2. Ulrica's hut. Ulrica is engaged on her magic rites as Riccardo, disguised as a fisherman, joins the spectators. Silvano, a sailor has his fortune told. Amelia arrives and everyone is sent away except Riccardo who hides. To his joy he overhears her tell Ulrica of her love for himself: she asks for a magic herb to cure herself of it. In a striking passage Ulrica tells her she must pick it herself at midnight at the place where the gallows stand. Amelia prays for strength for the ordeal in another fine strain which leads into a short trio. When she has gone Riccardo emerges and is joined by his court, all disguised. He consults Ulrica in a delightful, if slightly unexpected barcarolle. She prophesies that he will die by the hand of a friend. Riccardo laughs at the idea and, joined by Oscar, Samuele, and Tomaso, leads a quintet in which the reactions of the characters are skilfully distinguished. Ulrica then adds that the first to shake his hand will be the assassin. All shrink from him but Renato enters at that moment and shakes him warmly by the hand. There is general relief, as it is unthinkable that he should betray Riccardo. The latter is recognized by Ulrica to whom he gives money. The Act ends with an ensemble in which the crowd sing Riccardo's praises.

ACT II

A lonely place outside the city beneath a steep hill. A Prelude, which quotes Amelia's phrase from the trio in Act I Scene 2, sets the grisly scene. Amelia presses on with trepidation (recitative and aria in which the cor anglais is prominent). Riccardo appears and passionately seeks to overcome her already failing resolve in a fine duet. Renato approaches; the conspirators are on Riccardo's trail and he is anxious for his safety. Exhorted by both Amelia and Renato to escape, Riccardo first exacts a promise from Renato to escort the veiled Amelia back to the city without seeking to learn her identity. The conspirators are heard approaching (still singing their opening motive.) They want to know with whom Riccardo's assignation was and tear her veil from her. When they see that it is Renato's wife they burst into a tune of mocking laughter while, after dark mutterings, Renato bids them assemble at his house the next day. Faithful to his promise he brusquely leads Amelia to the city, while the laughter of Samuele, Tomaso, and their followers is heard in the distance.

ACT III

Scene 1. Room in Renato's house. Renato intends to kill Amelia but after hearing her plea (a wonderful passage in E flat minor with cello solo) spares her life and reflects that it is rather Riccardo who deserves to die. (The familiar vigorous aria "Eri tu".) Samuele and Tomaso present themselves (to their usual motive) and, after some incredulity, are persuaded that Renato wishes to join the conspiracy. After some argument about who shall do the deed, Amelia is made to draw the name from an urn. It is Renato. (All this in a quartet which contains a splendid "oath of vengeance" passage, anticipating that in *Otello*.) Oscar arrives with an invitation to a masked ball at the palace that evening. It is accepted and followed by a quintet in which all look forward to the occasion with different feelings, Oscar's being that of excitement at the prospect of a brilliant party.

Scene 2. Hall in the palace. Riccardo, to a strain from his Act I Scene 1 solo, feels in honour bound to sign a paper ordering Renato and his wife to England. He expresses his feeling that this is the end of it all in a sad aria. As the ball begins Oscar brings a warning from an unknown woman which Riccardo, anxious for a last sight of Amelia, spurns. Oscar points out to Renato which of the masked revellers is his master, after at first refusing in a brilliant little song. Riccardo recognizes Amelia who tries desperately to persuade him to leave at once; but he will not go, overcome by the thought that he will not see her again. He tells her she is to go to England and they bid each other farewell. Renato, overhearing, stabs him. With his last breath, Riccardo tells Renato that the love between Amelia and himself was innocent and forgives everyone.

The Barber of Seville

(Il Barbiere di Siviglia). Opera buffa in two acts. Music by G. Rossini. Libretto by C. Sterbini after P. A. C. de Beaumarchais. First produced at the Teatro Argentina, Rome, February 20th, 1816.

SCENE: Seville.

TIME: Second half of the eighteenth century.

PRINCIPAL CHARACTERS:

COUNT ALMAVIVA		(Tenor)
DOCTOR BARTOLO		(Bass)
ROSINA	*His ward*	(Soprano)
FIGARO	*A barber*	(Baritone)
BASILIO	*A singing teacher*	(Bass)
BERTA	*Rosina's duenna*	(Mezzo-soprano)
FIORELLO	*The Count's servant*	(Baritone)

"The Barber of Seville" is the best known of the whole Italianate species commonly called "opera buffa", which stands to opera somewhat as farce to theatre. Delightful tunes succeed each other in profusion, grateful opportunities for the singers abound and the craftsmanship is admirable, despite the speed of its composition. (The Overture is an earlier work, originally written for another purpose.) Between the set pieces there is a good deal of recitative which should be taken fast. The former comprise not only familiar arias but some sparkling ensembles—notably the elaborate finale to Act I—and, in the last scene, one of the most graphic orchestral storms in the whole range of music. No less than three of the male parts may be regarded as "buffo"—i.e., comic roles demanding facility in the rapid "patter" associated in Britain with the name of Sullivan.

ACT I

Scene 1. A street outside Bartolo's house. Towards dawn. The Count, with Fiorello and a band of musicians, sings an aubade beneath the balcony of Rosina, but is disconcerted by their noisy gratitude when he pays them off. Just then Figaro, no mere barber, appears, singing the famous "Largo al factotum". He agrees to help the Count contact Rosina. She is closely watched over by her guardian who covets her fortune. She contrives however to drop a note from the balcony, asking her suitor's name. In a short song the Count says his name is Lindoro. Stimulated by the promise of a reward, Figaro proposes that the Count gain entrance to the house by disguising himself as a drunken soldier with a billetting-order. They part, each pleased with the deal.

Scene 2. A room in Bartolo's house. Rosina, in a familiar aria, indicates that she has been touched by Lindoro's voice and no-one shall thwart her. When the suspicious Bartolo asks her if she has seen Figaro she does not tell him that he has just entered the house. Bartolo speaks to Basilio of his plan to marry Rosina and his suspicion that the Count loves her. Basilio advises him to start a scandal about the Count, graphically describing how scandal can grow in an aria famous for its own crescendi. They withdraw to draw up the marriage contract. Figaro tells Rosina that Lindoro is his cousin and much in love with her. She entrusts him, during a sparkling duet, with a letter to him. Knocking is now heard and the Count, disguised as a drunken soldier, forces an entrance and makes a scene when Bartolo tries to eject him, but manages to pass a note to Rosina. The noise brings gendarmes and the Count is arrested but, when he shows the officer his papers, he is at once released. The Act ends in the discomfiture of Bartolo and general confusion.

ACT II

Scene 1. Music room in Bartolo's house. The Count revisits the house disguised as a sanctimonious music-teacher. He explains that Basilio is ill and has sent him in his place. He wins Bartolo's confidence by a ruse and obtains permission to give Rosina a singing-lesson, during which they manage to exchange confidences. (The soprano customarily inserts a song of her own choice for the lesson.) Figaro appears and insists on shaving Bartolo, but first succeeds in obtaining the key to the balcony. Just then Basilio arrives. The lovers and Figaro try to persuade him that he is ill but it is only after he has been slipped a purse during an amusing quintet that they succeed in getting rid of him. While Figaro shaves Bartolo the lovers plan an elopement. Bartolo overhears them and the others vainly try to allay his suspicions. The aged Berta is left alone for a moment of peace in all this confusion, and muses, in a charming aria, on the follies universally induced by love.

Scene 2. As in Act I Scene 2. Bartolo sends Basilio, whom he has summoned, to fetch a notary so that he can marry Rosina at once. He arouses Rosina's jealousy by pretending that Lindoro has another lady-love and she tells him of the elopement plot. A storm breaks. When it has subsided, the Count and Figaro steal in by the balcony. Rosina meets them and the misunderstanding between the lovers is quickly resolved. With difficulty Figaro cuts short their raptures and they are just about to leave when they find that the ladder has been removed from the balcony. Basilio arrives with the notary but the Count gets them to substitute his own name in the marriage contract. Bartolo enters with a magistrate and tries again to have the Count arrested. But the Count reveals his identity and claims Rosina as his bride. Bartolo is appeased by being allowed to keep Rosina's dowry for himself and all ends happily.

The Bartered Bride

(Prodaná Nevěsta). Opera in three acts. Music by B. Smetana. Libretto by K. Sabrina. First produced at the National Theatre, Prague, May 30th, 1866.

SCENE: A Czech village.

TIME: Early nineteenth century.

CHARACTERS:

KRUŠINA	*A peasant*	(Baritone)
LUDMILA	*His wife*	(Soprano)
MAŘENKA	*Their daughter*	(Soprano)
MICHA	*A rich peasant*	(Bass)
HATA	*His wife*	(Mezzo-soprano)
VAŠEK	*Their son*	(Tenor)
JENÍK	*Micha's son by his first wife*	(Tenor)
KEČAL	*A marriage broker*	(Bass)
THE MANAGER OF A STROLLING TROUPE		(Tenor)
ESMERALDA	*A dancer*	(Soprano)

"The Bartered Bride" enjoys somewhat the same place in Czech opera as "Der Freischütz" in German, with additional nationalistic overtones deriving from Czech history over the last century. It has at the same time an assured place in the international repertory. It is folk opera, full of Czech rhythms, dances, and cadences which give a delightful tang to what is, in essence, a simple score. The music consists of straightforward, lyrical numbers joined by formal recitatives. Kečal is strongly delineated, and is a first-class comic role for a rich bass voice, while Vašek's is an excellent character rôle for a light tenor. The other parts are, from the musical standpoint, less interesting, though Mařenka and Jeník offer grateful opportunities to the singers. It is all very tuneful and the work's world-wide popularity is well deserved, even though the total effect nowadays seems a trifle conventional and lacking in subtlety.

The familiar, bustling Overture is based on two themes from the finale of Act II.

ACT I

A village, with an inn on one side. Carefree villagers are looking forward to a fair. But Jeník, who has been driven from home by his stepmother and is thought to be dead, and his beloved Mařenka are anxious because she has heard that her father wants her to marry Jeník's half-witted stepbrother Vašek. (The final section of this duet recurs elsewhere as a kind of love motive.) When they have gone Kečal and Mařenka's parents arrive. In an amusing trio Kečal holds Mařenka's father to his promise to marry her to Vašek in return for a large sum from the latter's wealthy father, though Mařenka's mother thinks they are going too fast. Mařenka joins them and, in the quartet which follows, says that she has sworn not to forsake her lover. She is quite unmoved by the contract which Kečal produces. The villagers now assemble and the Act ends with a gay polka danced by the younger ones.

ACT II

Inside the inn. There is drinking and the chorus sing the praises of beer. Jeník is for love, but Kečal is against love without money. A furiant is danced and they all leave. The stammering Vašek makes a timid appearance. He has been sent by his mother to woo his bride. Mařenka, whom he does not know, finds him and warns him that Mařenka will be unfaithful; she tells him that she knows just the girl for him, one who is already pining for him. She makes him swear never to see Mařenka. Vašek tries to kiss her. When they have gone Kečal comes in with Jeník and tries to persuade him to give up Mařenka for a girl from Moravia, where Jeník says his home is. He knows of a rich match for him, but Jeník is unimpressed. Finally he offers Jeník three hundred crowns to give up Mařenka. Jeník accepts but only on condition that Mařenka marries the elder son of Micha and that, if so, all her father's debts to Micha shall be forgone. Kečal goes off well content with the bargain, while Jeník remains to sing a short aria of steadfast love for Mařenka. Kečal returns with the villagers and calls on them to witness the contract. When they hear that Jeník is to receive money for renouncing his beloved all denounce him as a mercenary rascal, as he signs the bond.

ACT III

Same as Act I. Vašek, in despair that he cannot find the girl he recently met, sings, still stuttering, a sad little aria in F minor faintly reminiscent of Barbarina's in the same key in Act IV of *The Marriage of Figaro*. A strolling troupe arrives but the Manager is told that one of the company

is too drunk to play the bear. Vašek has been admiring the dancing of
Esmeralda who persuades him to take the man's place in return for
promises of her love. His parents and Kečal now arrive, but he flatly
refuses to sign a promise to marry Mařenka against whom the unknown
girl has warned him. He leaves amid consternation as Mařenka arrives with
her parents. They have just told her of Jeník's bargain and she is upset and
miserable, but refuses to marry Vašek, who returns at that moment and
recognizes her as his ravishing counsellor. Mařenka asks for time to think
and the others agree to this in a reflective sextet. Mařenka is left to sing a
melancholy aria. When Jeník joins her she repulses him indignantly in a
duet with the rhythmic snap of a local dance (one of the best numbers in
the opera). Kečal appears and promises his money as soon as Mařenka has
signed the contract to marry "Micha's son". When Jeník presses her to
sign she is the more indignant. The villagers return and she announces that
she will marry Vašek. But Jeník is recognized by his parents and when he
asks Mařenka to choose between Micha's two sons she chooses him at once.
Kečal, who has been outwitted, departs wrathfully. Just then the bear
trots in and Vašek emerges from the skin, to be taken home by his mother.
Jeník is reconciled to his parents and there is general rejoicing at the
betrothal, to the same chorus as had opened the opera.

La Belle Hélène

(Beautiful Helen). Opéra bouffe in three acts. Music by J. Offenbach. Libretto by H. Meilhac and L. Halévy. First produced at the Théâtre des Variétés, Paris, December 17th, 1864.

SCENE: Sparta and Nauplia.

TIME: Antiquity.

CHARACTERS:

PARIS	*Son of King Priam*	(Tenor)
MENELAUS	*King of Sparta*	(Tenor)
AGAMEMNON	*King of Kings*	(Baritone)
CALCHAS	*High priest of Jupiter*	(Bass)
ACHILLES	*King of Phthiotis*	(Tenor)
AJAX I	*King of Salamis*	(Tenor)
AJAX II	*King of Locris*	(Tenor)
ORESTES	*Son of Agamemnon*	(Tenor)
HELEN	*Queen of Sparta*	(Soprano)
BACCHIS	*Her lady-in-waiting*	(Soprano)
LEOENA	} *Demi-mondaines*	(Mezzo-soprano)
PARTHOENIS		(Soprano)

This is the most firmly established of Offenbach's many operettas. The concept of treating the personages of Greek legend as contemporary Parisian bourgeois retains its humour, even if some of the satirical allusions to Third Empire society do not. The long stretches of dialogue are still amusing in the theatre. The music is naturally in "numbers", some of them simple, most of them tuneful and nearly all with the characteristic Offenbach sparkle and tang. But there are some of more elaborate construction which tend to drop into almost unconscious parody of the "opera seria" tradition still very much alive at the Paris Opera of the day. The rôles of Helen and Paris require accomplished singers. The other royal personages and Calchas are buffo parts in which good comic acting need only be supplemented by an ability to sustain the vocal line accurately and clearly.

The short introduction consists of suggestions of the tune of the Kings' Entry varied by the refrain of the ballad of the Judgment of Paris, both to be heard during Act I.

ACT I

Sparta. A public square before the temple of Jupiter. People present offerings at the temple and depart. Calchas and an attendant gather them up complaining of the proportion of flowers. A blacksmith brings them the newly repaired zinc sheet which will be needed for thunder for the day's festival of Adonis. A chorus of girl mourners for Adonis arrives, followed by Helen. The former sing of the day's business; the latter adds a plea to Venus to send them a little love and passion. Before entering the temple Helen discusses with Calchas the "affair of Mount Ida", in which Venus is said to have bribed Paris to award her the prize by promising him the love of the most beautiful woman in the world. The gay young spark Orestes arrives, with Parthoenis and Leoena and other girls, singing a couplet with a polka rhythm. He prevails on Calchas to let his lady friends enter the temple. Paris, disguised as a shepherd, enters simultaneously with a dove carrying a letter from Venus to Calchas, asking him to introduce Helen to Paris. Paris tells him of the recent beauty contest between the three goddesses, in a ballad with a charming refrain, and asks to meet Helen incognito. The mourners and Helen emerge from the temple. Helen is greatly struck with the beauty of the shepherd and, dismissing Calchas, begins to flirt with him. They are interrupted by the arrival of a procession of Greek kings gathered for the festival, followed by a great throng. Ajax I, Ajax II, Achilles, Menelaus, and Agamemnon successively introduce themselves, to an irresistibly cheeky tune, and take their seats in a circle. Agamemnon announces a literary contest to celebrate the festival. Paris wins every event and is acclaimed. (The finale begins here.) He reveals his identity. "Heavens! the apple man" exclaims Helen, in a coloratura passage, before she crowns him. Menelaus, relieved to find that the winner is a nobleman, invites Paris to dinner. Paris whispers to Calchas that he would be happier without Menelaus, and Calchas is obligingly inspired, to a peal of thunder, to announce, in a parodistic passage that Jupiter decrees that Menelaus should pass a month in the Cretan mountains. Menelaus obeys and takes leave of Helen. The elaborate finale ends with a reprise of the tune of the Kings' Entry.

ACT II

Helen's apartments. After an introduction which anticipates the Act's finale Bacchis and Helen's maids urge her to look her most gorgeous for the evening's programme, but she insists on a simple toilette in Menelaus's absence. She addresses her mother Venus in a charming song, asking why she gave her this fatal beauty. Paris is admitted and after failing, as he has for the past month, to overcome her hesitations, goes off threatening to win her by trickery. The Kings enter, to a gay little march, to play a gambling game, in which Calchas is caught cheating and makes a hasty exit with the Kings in pursuit. Helen decides that she cannot trust herself to attend the supper. She goes to bed and asks Calchas (who has returned after arranging a compromise with the Kings he has cheated) to ask the Gods to send her dreams of Paris. When she is asleep Paris enters disguised as one of the slaves guarding her. An unaccompanied chorus of revellers led by Orestes is heard in the distance. Helen wakes and assumes that she is seeing Paris in a dream. They sing an extended duet which is the lyrical high point of the whole work, in the course of which Paris overcomes her resistance by telling her that on Mount Ida (the ballad tune on the oboe) he had found Venus not more beautiful but more forthcoming than her. Their embrace is interrupted by the sudden return of Menelaus who, set on a big scandal worthy of an epic husband, summons the Kings. They arrive, a little tipsy and still singing the revellers' chorus. There is a mock tragic passage ending in a humorous cadenza while Menelaus speaks of his injured honour, followed by couplets for Helen in which she reproaches her husband with his bad taste in returning unannounced. But the Kings are scandalized and throw Paris out and, to the strains of the famous waltz which dominate the rest of the finale, Helen tells Paris that it would be wiser to leave. This, after some fast-moving ensemble, he does.

ACT III

Nauplia. By the seaside. Orestes and his lady friends are enjoying themselves. (The opening chorus is followed by a song in a siciliano rhythm.) Agamemnon and Calchas, mixing incognito with the crowd, have become aware of the general laxity of morals—Venus's revenge. Helen has come to recuperate after the terrible scene of a week ago, and to try to forget it. Menelaus presses her to explain what she means by saying that it was all a dream. In couplets she maintains that it *was* a dream, but if Paris was so attractive in a dream, could she resist him in reality? Agamemnon and Calchas now round on Menelaus. The country is going to the dogs because Venus has not been propitiated by the sacrifice of his wife. (An extended trio.) Menelaus announces that he has written to Venus to send her own High Priest to advise. Just then a vessel arrives with Paris disguised as the High Priest on board. The people greet him with supplication but their mood soon changes when Paris complains and points out that the cult of Venus is a joyous one. He promises that Venus will pardon them if Menelaus will do what is proper and send his wife on a short journey with him to Cythera. Menelaus consents. The journey is arranged and Helen embarks to a finale which gradually works round to the tune of the Kings' Entry from Act I. At the last moment Paris reveals himself and tells Menelaus that he is taking Helen to Troy. The people assure Menelaus of their support for a war of revenge!

Billy Budd

Opera in two acts. Music by Benjamin Britten. Libretto by E. M. Forster and E. Crozier after H. Melville. First produced at the Royal Opera House, Covent Garden, December 1st, 1951.

SCENE: H.M.S. *Indomitable.*

TIME: 1797.

PRINCIPAL CHARACTERS:

CAPTAIN VERE	*In command of H.M.S. Indomitable*	(Tenor)
BILLY BUDD		(Baritone)
RED WHISKERS	*Impressed men*	(Tenor)
ARTHUR JONES		(Baritone)
JOHN CLAGGART	*Master at arms*	(Bass)
MR REDBURN	*First lieutenant*	(Baritone)
MR FLINT	*Sailing master*	(Bass baritone)
LIEUTENANT RATCLIFFE		(Bass)
DANSKER	*An old seaman*	(Bass)
THE NOVICE		(Tenor)
SQUEAK	*A ship's corporal*	(Tenor)
THE NOVICE'S FRIEND		(Baritone)
DONALD	*A sailor*	(Baritone)

Originally in 4 acts, "Billy Budd" was revised in 1961. Most of the text is in prose and set in a declamatory style, often with a briskness befitting the naval types who comprise the all-male cast. The orchestra therefore bears more weight and the music is more complex than in most of Britten's operas. Close analysis can show how it reflects by bitonality and other means the dilemma confronting Vere, which is the work's core. But the opera can also be enjoyed as a well-written tale with its overtones brilliantly emphasized by music which vividly conveys the atmosphere of a British warship at sea in the Napoleonic Wars—or of Herman Melville's conception of it—even down to details like the wind in the rigging, the piping, and the bugle calls. There are several passages which make an immediate impact such as the action song early in Act I Scene 1, the sea shanties in Act I Scene 3, and Billy Budd's ballad at the opening of Act II Scene 3, this last affording a point of diatonic repose in a strenuous

*and darkly coloured score. The splendid orchestral interludes are
sometimes symphonic in style.*

ACT I

Prologue. After a few bars of string quavers in contrasting keys, which
illustrate both doubt and old age, broken (on the brass) by a motive to be
associated with Claggart, we see Vere at the end of his life spotlit and
musing on the confusion between good and evil, the former always with
some imperfection in it. The words "Oh what have I done" are sung to a
basic motive of a rising fifth and the semitone above it which will be heard
in countless versions throughout the opera. At the words "Who has
blessed me? Who saved me?" his mind goes back to the difficult days of
1797 after the mutiny at the Nore and the lights go up on
Scene 1. The main deck and quarter-deck of H.M.S. *Indomitable.* Sailors
are "holy stoning" the deck to an action song contrived from the basic
motive interrupted by several incidents illustrating the harsh discipline
which they suffer. The Novice slips and is ordered twenty strokes of the
cat. Flint is left alone on the quarter-deck for an expressive moment of
solitude with a hint of Billy Budd's ballad to come. The cutter comes
alongside with Ratcliffe and three men impressed from the homeward
bound *Rights o'Man.* Claggart is sent for, reports (to his motive) and
assists the officers to question and allocate the recruits—the complaining
Red Whiskers, the meek Arthur Jones, and the keen, extrovert Billy Budd
(stammering in moments of excitement), who is at once made foretopman.
In his enthusiasm for his new life he sings farewell to the *Rights o'Man*
(to the basic motive). The officers read a political meaning into this, have
the decks cleared, and instruct Claggart to keep an eye on so dangerous a
man. Claggart, full of hatred of life, tells Squeak to "play his tricks" on
Billy and encourages him to steal his things. The Novice is dragged on
deck (to a lachrymose motive on the saxophone) by his Friend and a small
group who sing in unison. His flogging has broken him in spirit as well as
body and a sad little tune follows before they go below. There follows a
conversation in which Dansker and Donald rag Billy and Red Whiskers and
warn them to keep clear of Jemmy-legs, as the men call Claggart. But
Starry Vere the Captain is, they all agree, brave and good and the salt of
the earth. The bosun sends them all below and a reflective orchestral
passage leads to
Scene 2. Captain Vere's cabin. Evening, a week later. Vere, who is reading
the classics, sends for Redburn and Flint to take a glass of wine with him.
They talk about the imminence of action and Redburn and Flint sing a
jaunty little anti-French duet. They go on to touch on the danger of
mutiny and Flint speaks of the disgrace and sorrow of "The Nore, the
floating Republic" (basic motive) while Vere calls for vigilance against

"the infamous spirit of France...the tyrant who wears the cap of liberty."
This leads to mention by Flint of that "young chap who shouted out
Rights o' Man", but Vere is sure there is no danger there. The sound of
shanties is now heard from below decks as Redburn's entry to announce
land on the port bow breaks up the gathering. Two sea shanties dominate
the orchestral transition to
Scene 3. The boat-deck. The sailors sing the first of the shanties and then
Donald starts another with amusing words. Dansker tells the recruits that
he is too old to join in the tune. All he needs is 'bacca and Billy, who is
now regarded by all as a good fellow, at once goes off to fetch some from
his kit-bag. But his stammer is heard and he reappears dragging the
protesting Squeak, who draws a knife. The ensuing fight brings in Claggart
who, on hearing the facts from Dansker, has Squeak put in irons and
gagged. He congratulates Billy and orders the men to turn in. (The
second shanty from the Intermezzo is heard softly.) Alone he launches,
over a solo trombone, into a tremendous Iago-like Credo in which he
proclaims that he has no choice but to annihilate the beauty, handsome-
ness, and goodness which disrupt the order of his world; for what hope
remains if love can escape? The Novice comes down and Claggart bullies
and bribes him into the reluctant rôle of agent-provocateur of Billy. The
Novice wakes Billy, who is "fathoms down" over a hint of his ballad, and,
to a staccato version of the basic theme, offers him Claggart's guineas to
lead a discontented gang. Billy stammers in rage and the Novice flees.
Dansker emerges from his hammock to inquire what it is all about. When
Billy tells him he understands at once. In a superb duet, Billy recalls
Claggart's congratulations and speaks of his happiness and prospects of
promotion but Dansker repeats with chaconne-like insistence, to Claggart's
motive, "Jemmy-legs is down on you."

ACT II

Scene 1. As for Act I, Scene 1. Some days later. The officers dislike the
look of the mist. Claggart asks to see Vere and (to trombone chords)
starts, long-windedly and to Vere's impatience, to bring a charge, when a
French frigate is sighted and the mist lifts. Instantly all is life as the ship's
company rush to action stations, delighted that their moment has come
at last, and more sail is made. Billy, climbing down the rigging, is among
the volunteers for a boarding-party. The lively ensemble is broken for a
moment as all utter a quiet prayer for wind. A shot is fired but it falls
short. The wind drops and the mist closes in. The men are dismissed and
the officers fear for discipline. Claggart ascends to the quarter-deck again
and accuses a seaman of fomenting mutiny by offering a novice guineas.
When he names Billy Vere refuses to believe him and in a short duet warns
him against false evidence. But he orders Billy to be brought to his cabin.

There is a brief quartet of the officers railing against the mist, Vere speaking of "confusion without and within". The orchestral Interlude is clearly concerned with Vere's state of mind and leads to
Scene 2. As in Act I Scene 2. Vere's opening monologue makes it plain that he has seen through Claggart. Billy comes in and, against a horn solo, prattles of his expectation of promotion and his hopes of another encounter with the French, while Vere, in an aside, is surer than ever of his innocence. However, he calls him to attention and has Claggart brought in to make his accusation to Billy's face. But when Billy is called on to reply he stammers with indignation and strikes Claggart who falls dead. Vere sends Billy into his state-room and sends in agitation for his officers. He feels that it is he, not Billy, who is on trial. A quartet brings out the mental confusion of the officers. Vere calls a drumhead court martial over which Redburn presides. There is an expressive cello and viola recitative as they take their places and during the court. Vere testifies as to the facts. Billy accepts them but indignantly denies Claggart's accusations and calls on Vere to save him. He is taken back to the state-room. The three officers debate their verdict, but decide that the Regulations leave them no choice and, after Vere has refused to help them, declare that Billy is guilty and must hang. Vere fixes the execution for the next morning and undertakes to inform the prisoner. In a soliloquy he says that he has seen iniquity overthrown and now he himself must be the messenger of death and destroy goodness. He goes in to Billy, the curtain falls, and the interview is represented by an extraordinary Interlude of 34 slow semibreves each a common chord, with varying scoring and dynamics but finally becoming pianissimo. When the curtain rises we are in F major.
Scene 3. A bay of the gun-deck. Before dawn. Muted, swaying violas alternate with piccolo triplets and Billy, in irons, sings Melville's pathetic ballad called "Billy in the Darbies" to a simple diatonic melody. Dansker steals in with a mug of grog, which cheers him, and says that there is trouble in the ship. Billy insists that there be no mutiny and Dansker leaves. It is fate and Captain Vere is in as much trouble as he, Billy exclaims to himself, and takes leave courageously of the world in a broad melody over arpeggios. "Don't matter now being hanged....I'm strong and I know it." (At the end 23 bars of the semibreves recur in the orchestra.) Another Interlude leads to
Scene 4. As in Scene 1. Dawn. To muffled drums the ship's company slowly assemble, each section being accompanied by its now familiar motives. When Billy has been brought on between marines Flint reads the sentence and Billy greets it with a cry of "Starry Vere, God bless you!" which the crew repeat. He is then led off and hung from the yard-arm, Vere removing his hat. Immediately the crew turn upon the quarter-deck in mutiny, singing a quick, wordless fugue on the basic motive. All hands are swiftly sent down below by the officers. The light fades and we come to

The Epilogue. The aged Vere is again spotlit and the quavers of the Prologue return. He knows that he could have saved Billy. But he answers his own question in the Prologue by saying that Billy has saved him and proclaims that he "has seen where she's bound for" in a triumphant version of Billy's melody at the end of Scene 3. As the orchestra and the light fade, he is heard muttering that his mind can go back in peace to the summer of 1797.

Bluebeard's Castle

(A Kékszakállú Herceg Vára). Opera in one act. Music by B. Bartók. Libretto by B. Balász. First produced at Budapest, May 24th, 1918.

SCENE: A castle with doors but no windows.

TIME: Not specified.

CHARACTERS:

BLUEBEARD	(Baritone)
JUDITH *His wife*	(Soprano)

This is Bartók's only opera though not his only stage work. The influence of Wagner and of the Debussy-Maeterlinck "Pelléas and Mélisande" upon the young composer are obvious. The symbolism of the work, the atmosphere of which remains misty and unfocused, suggests a warning that a woman who seeks to possess a man's mind too thoroughly, risks losing him.

The music is in the form of Wagnerian unending melody for the orchestra, colourfully scored, with passages of graphic scene-painting; on this is superimposed an expressive recitative. Melodies are sometimes of a typical Hungarian cast—e.g., that first heard on the clarinet shortly after the shutting of the outer door. Other recurring motives are the chords (followed by a rhythmic phrase) with which the work opens and ends, the chords derived from the rhythmic phrase which mark the shutting of the outer door, and particularly the piercing minor seconds associated throughout the work with the idea of blood. Bartók displays in the vocal line his sensitive feeling for the rhythm of Hungarian speech with its heavy initial accent on each word. A satisfactory translation is therefore particularly difficult and the "Hiawatha" metre imposed by the music can sound monotonous.

A spoken Prologue (usually omitted) tells us that the scene is as much within ourselves as on the stage. Bluebeard and Judith enter through a small iron door. He asks her whether she wants to leave her family and follow him into such a place. She is sure. He shuts the door. She notices the darkness and the dampness. She wants to bring light and warmth, but

Bluebeard replies that it can never be. She sees seven large black doors (string chords) which she wants opened. She bangs on the first and a sigh is heard. He gives her the key and another sigh is heard as she opens it. It is the torture-chamber and the walls run with blood. With the second key she reveals the armoury (trumpet solo), with blood on the weapons. The third key opens the door to the Treasury, where there is blood on the crown and robes. The fourth reveals a flower-garden, with blood on the roots of roses and lilies. Through the fifth door she sees a wide view of all Bluebeard's lands (solemn chords), but the clouds are red with blood. Bluebeard tries to stop her going further, but she insists. The sixth door reveals a waste of water (harp and clarinet arpeggios). It is all tears. He passionately kisses her to distract her from the last door, but will not answer her question concerning whom he has loved before her. She fears that in the last chamber are his murdered wives. There is a climax as she forces him to give her the seventh key. Three beautiful, richly clad women, his former wives, appear. The first he saw at dawn, the second at midday, the third at dusk. She is the fourth. He found her at night. She is the most beautiful of all. He puts a crown and robes upon her. She goes unwillingly after the other women through the seventh door. The stage grows dark and Bluebeard's last words are that eternal night awaits him.

La Bohème

(Bohemian Life). Opera in four acts. Music by G. Puccini. Libretto by G. Giacosa and L. Illica after H. Mürger. First produced at the Teatro Reggio, Turin, February 1st, 1896.

SCENE: Paris.

TIME: About 1830.

PRINCIPAL CHARACTERS:

RODOLFO	*A poet*	(Tenor)
MARCELLO	*A painter*	(Baritone)
COLLINE	*A philosopher*	(Bass)
SCHAUNARD	*A musician*	(Baritone)
BENOIT	*A landlord*	(Bass)
ALCINDORO	*A Councillor of State*	(Bass)
MIMI	*A maker of artificial flowers*	(Soprano)
MUSETTA	*A grisette*	(Soprano)

"La Bohème" owes its position as perhaps the most popular of all operas to a number of inspired melodies and the great vocal opportunities which they offer. If, however, a cool assessment of so hot a favourite is permissible, it is the latter which make it difficult to see the work as it is. A light, impressionistic, sentimental "opéra comique" after the French manner, with the merest wisp of plot, calling for a delicate touch in performance, it has been a magnet to generations of "great" singers, many of whom have brought to it a heavy and insensitive manner which has tended to obscure its overall merits and to emphasize the contrast between the "juicy" passages and the sometimes rather thin material between them. But, despite some scenes which no-one remembers, the work as a whole, though far from offering a "saturated" score, does paint a vivid picture of the Latin Quarter, as Mürger saw it in his "Scènes de la vie de Bohème". Act II is full of atmosphere and life, skilfully handled, while the work abounds in details which show Puccini's craftsmanship, like the orchestral description of a snowy morning which opens Act III. The well-made libretto forced the composer to explore moods other than "despairing passion" without making demands outside the range of his talents at this stage of their development.

ACT I

A garret with a view of snow-covered roofs. The motive in the introductory bars recurs constantly and seems to stand for Bohemian life. Rodolfo gazes out of the window; Marcello is working on his picture of the Red Sea. Both are cold as the fire is low. They decide to sacrifice the manuscript of Rodolfo's play to gain some momentary warmth (which the orchestra reflects). Colline enters with a bundle of books which he has failed to pawn. The flames die down. Two boys enter to a gay melody, with provisions and fuel, followed by Schaunard with some coins. He explains, though no-one listens, that he has been giving music lessons to an Englishman. But they agree to his proposal that they should go out to eat, as it is Christmas Eve (suggestion of a carol). Benoit calls for the rent, is given wine and is reassured by the sight of Schaunard's money. He is encouraged to boast of his exploits with women whereupon, pretending to be scandalized, the young men push him out without paying anything and share out the money. The others go off to the Café Momus, leaving Rodolfo to finish an article and follow in five minutes. There is a knock at the door and Mimi comes shyly in to get a light for her candle. She coughs from the effort of climbing the stairs and faints, dropping her candle and her key. After reviving her Rodolfo lights the candle again and she leaves, but quickly returns for her key. The wind blows out both her candle and his and he gropes for her key in the dark. Finding it, he puts it in his pocket and goes on searching. Their hands meet in the darkness. At this point begins the famous aria "Che gelida manina" which falls into two parts, in the first of which he announces that he is a poet, and in the second ardently declares the love which she has awakened in him. She replies with the equally famous "Mi chiamano Mimi" in which, with touching simplicity, she contrasts her lonely life, making artificial flowers, with her romantic dreams of spring. Rodolfo's friends call to him from below. He opens the window, letting in the moonlight, and tells them that he has company and will follow shortly. The couple then embrace, singing together (to the melody of the second part of Rodolfo's aria) of their new-found love. At the end she shyly suggests, over the opening phrase of her aria, that she accompany him to the café and they go off arm in arm, to the opening phrases of his, Mimi soaring in happiness to a soft top C (and the tenor too, if the conductor is weak enough to allow him to move in unison!)

ACT II

A square in the Latin Quarter, with the Café Momus on one side. Gay Christmas Eve throng. Trumpets introduce the lively scene with a marcato version of the carol hinted in Act I. Amid the cries of vendors, children, and the rest of the crowd, we have a glimpse of Schaunard buying a horn, Colline collecting a coat after repairs and buying a rare book, and Rodolfo taking Mimi to buy a hat. The friends take their places in the café, Rodolfo introducing Mimi, and, while children pursue a toy-seller, order a fine meal and begin to converse. A diversion is caused by the entry of the coquettish Musetta, a former flame of Marcello, followed by Alcindoro, an elderly admirer, whom she is leading a dance. Marcello, pale, pretends not to see her, while she behaves worse and worse to attract his attention. The others are much amused at the scene. Musetta, addressing herself mainly to Marcello, now launches into her well-known waltz aria in which she preens herself on her irresistible charms. The comments of the others and the protestations of Alcindoro blend with her to make an amusing little sextet. Marcello is vanquished. To get rid of Alcindoro she pretends that her shoe hurts her and sends him to buy another pair, while Marcello takes up the waltz melody which ends in a mutual embrace. The waiter brings the young men the bill which they find that they cannot meet. But, as a military tattoo approaches, playing an authentic French march of the period and distracting attention, Musetta arranges for their bill, as well as his own, to be put in Alcindoro's place. The young men and Mimi quickly withdraw through the crowd, Marcello and Colline carrying the shoeless Musetta, who receives an ovation. The march dominates the scene as Alcindoro returns, with new shoes in a parcel, sees the two bills and collapses with shock.

ACT III

Outside the toll-gate on the Orleans road. A snowy dawn in February. Bare consecutive fifths on flutes and harp paint the cold scene, as successive groups of sweepers, milkmaids, carters, and peasants are admitted by the octroi official, and revellers, including Musetta singing her waltz, are heard from a nearby inn. Mimi's motive marks her arrival from the city, coughing and inquiring for Marcello who comes out of the inn where he is living with Musetta. Mimi will not enter and join Rodolfo who is also there. Weeping she tells Marcello of Rodolfo's jealousy in anguished phrases and begs him to help them to separate. Marcello bids her hide while he wakes Rodolfo. The latter comes out and confides his mixed emotions about Mimi— jealousy at her flirtatiousness, the tortures of love, pity, and guilt at her perhaps mortal illness which needs more care than love alone can give. The listening Mimi's coughing and sobs betray her presence. Rodolfo embraces her while at the sound of Musetta's laughter Marcello runs inside. Mimi tells her lover sadly that they must part. She will return to her former lonely life. She will send for her few possessions, but if he wishes he may keep the hat as a memento. They sing a regretful farewell, the second verse of which becomes a quartet as Marcello and Musetta emerge in a jealous quarrel over a conversation with a stranger, and part in anger. Rodolfo and Mimi however go off together, reluctantly resolved to separate.

ACT IV

As in Act I. Spring. Rodolfo and Marcello are trying to work, but each eagerly listens when the other speaks of seeing his mistress with her latest flame. Rodolfo contemplates Mimi's hat and Marcello a ribbon of Musetta's, as they sing a duet expressing their longing, and a violin solo underlines the sentimentality. Schaunard and Colline enter (to the "gay" melody of Act I) with modest supplies which all pretend are a feast. Then they affect to be at a ball at which Colline challenges Schaunard to a duel. But this hectic gaiety is interrupted by the sudden entrance of Musetta in agitation, who has with her Mimi, now very ill. She whispers to the others that she had heard that Mimi had left her Viscount and had found her, asking to die near Rodolfo. Rodolfo bends over the bed where Mimi feels better, though drowsy, but needs a muff for her cold hands. Musetta takes off her ear-rings and goes out with Marcello to buy her one from the proceeds; Colline takes off his coat and says goodbye to it in a familiar passage before going off to pawn it, taking Schaunard with him, to a reflective version of the "gay" melody. Alone with Rodolfo, Mimi speaks, in a touching melody, of her boundless love for him and recalls, in both words and music, their first meeting, while he produces the hat which she insists on putting on. But at the end of this tender scene she falls back in a spasm of coughing. Musetta and Marcello steal in, with a muff and medicine. Mimi eagerly snatches the former and Musetta lets her think it a present from Rodolfo. She appears to fall asleep but an abrupt change of key in the orchestra tells us that all is over. While Musetta prays for her, Schaunard, who has also returned, sees that Mimi is dead and whispers to Marcello. Rodolfo, in a speaking voice, asks why their manner is so strange and then guessing the truth, falls sobbing on the bed. The orchestra plays Mimi's last touching melody and then, as the curtain falls, the cadence of Colline's farewell to his coat.

Boris Godunov

Opera in a prologue and four acts. Music by M. Mussorgsky. Libretto after A. S. Pushkin and N. M. Karamzin. First produced (in complete form) at the Maryinsky Theatre, St Petersburg, January 27th, 1874.

SCENE: Russia and Poland.

TIME: 1598-1605.

PRINCIPAL CHARACTERS:

BORIS GODUNOV	(Bass)
FEODOR } *His children*	(Mezzo-soprano)
XENIA }	(Soprano)
THE NURSE	(Contralto)
PRINCE SHUISKY	(Tenor)
PIMEN *A monk and chronicler*	(Bass)
THE PRETENDER DMITRI *Called Grigory*	(Tenor)
VARLAAM } *Vagabonds*	(Bass)
MISSAIL }	(Tenor)
MARINA MNYSHEK *A Polish Princess*	(Soprano)
RANGONI *A Jesuit in disguise*	(Bass-baritone)
THE HOSTESS OF AN INN	(Mezzo-soprano)
AN IDIOT	(Tenor)

There are four versions of this opera, two of which are posthumous revisions by Rimsky-Korsakov who refined the ruggedness in the score which especially commends it to modern taste. The other point of importance to the listener is the order of the scenes in Act IV. If the death of Boris ends this series of episodes from history à la russe, then indubitably he is the protagonist. If it ends with the Revolution scene, as in Mussorgsky's second and definitive version, it becomes an opera about the Russian people. The former is good, orthodox theatre; to end with the Idiot is the more imaginative.

In addition to the orchestration and the strong choral writing, one should note the superb declamation given to the voices, which even in translation comes over as exactly matching words, character, and situation. Motives associated with the leading characters are mainly heard in the orchestra. Boris has three great monologues; but there are otherwise only a few passages which stand out as detachable from the work's continuous fabric.

PROLOGUE

Scene 1. Courtyard of the Norodievicky monastery, near Moscow. Urged on by police with whips, a crowd appeals to Boris for protection. The clerk of the Boyars' Council announces that Boris has not yet agreed to become Tsar. Pilgrims pass into the monastery. The crowd are ordered to reappear at the Kremlin the next day.

Scene 2. A square in the Kremlin. Boris has just been crowned and is hailed by the crowd in a fine chorus. He appears in full regalia and utters a short prayer for heavenly guidance. The chorus is resumed.

ACT I

Scene 1. A cell in the Chudov monastery. The aged Pimen is at work at night on the final chapter of his chronicle. (A running figure in semiquavers seems to represent his busy pen.) Chanting is heard. The young Grigory wakens from a dream. He is restive at spending his youth as a novice in a monastery; but Pimen advises him that the peace of the cloister is better than political strife. A reference to Boris as a regicide leads to reminiscences of the murder, at Boris' instigation, of Dmitri the young Tsarevitch, the episode that is to conclude his chronicle. Grigory is excited by Pimen's account.

Scene 2. An inn near the Lithuanian frontier. The Hostess sits darning and singing a folk-song. Two drunken, vagabond friars enter, followed by Grigory, who sits moodily apart. He is anxious to cross into Lithuania. The two vagabonds drink and Varlaam sings a rollicking song about the victory of Ivan over the Tartars. Grigory elicits from the Hostess that sentries are searching all travellers on the road to the frontier but that there are other routes. Police arrive looking for a monk called Grigory and are suspicious of the identity of Varlaam. Their officer asks Grigory to read aloud the warrant and he does so, but substituting a description of Varlaam. Then Varlaam, with difficulty, reads out what is really written; but, just as they all realize that Grigory is the wanted man, he escapes through the window.

ACT II

Imperial apartments in the Kremlin. Xenia sits weeping before a portrait of her dead betrothed. The Nurse sings a folk song to cheer her and then she and Xenia's young brother, Feodor, sing a clapping song together. Boris comes in, comforts his daughter and sends her and the Nurse away. Feodor explains to him the map of Russia which he has been studying and Boris bids him study his inheritance well. He then muses sadly, in the first great monologue, which concentrates much of the opera's thematic material, on the failure of his rule and the misery and unrest in his kingdom. He is haunted by the memory of the murdered child. There is a commotion outside. Feodor is sent to investigate. A Boyar announces that Shuisky is seeking an audience. He adds that there are rumours of the disaffection of Shuisky and other Boyars. Feodor returns with a tale of a parrot which had attacked a nurse. Shuisky enters and is abused by Boris for being the leader of the seditious Boyars. He has come with news of a rising in Poland in favour of the false Dmitri, who has been recognized by the King and the Pope. He feels bound to add a warning that if the Pretender were to cross the frontier, he might gain a popular following. Feodor is sent out of the room. With mounting emotion Boris asks Shuisky to confirm that Dmitri was killed. Shuisky replies that he saw the body of the child himself, still sweetly smiling after five days' exposure. At this Boris waves him away and collapses. He mistakes a striking cuckoo clock for the dead child and falls hysterically to his knees in prayer. (This is the famous "Mad Scene".)

ACT III

Scene 1. Marina's room in Sandomir Castle in Poland. Marina is dressing. Girls sing a romantic, flattering song, but she prefers songs of martial heroism and dismisses them. In a song with the lilt of a mazurka she muses on the Pretender Dmitri and her ambition to be the Tsar's wife. The Jesuit Rangoni appears and fans her ambition. He tells her that it is her heavenly duty to convert the Russians to the true Church.

Scene 2. The castle garden. Moonlight by a fountain. Dmitri is waiting anxiously for Marina. Rangoni joins him and, to an insinuating figure in triplets, tells him that Marina is yearning for him despite the envious gossip of the court. He promises to lead Dmitri to her and asks only in return to be allowed to stay at his side. When they have gone, a brilliant company comes out, to a polonaise, with Marina on an elderly gentleman's arm. They sing of the coming expedition to Moscow and drink a toast to Marina before re-entering the castle. Dmitri, who has been watching, resolves to set forth at their head. When Marina joins him she at first replies sarcastically to his protestations of love; it is the throne she wants and Dmitri is lost in love-sickness for herself. He reacts to her taunts by declaring his purpose to march on Moscow. Then suddenly, assured of this, she throws herself upon him, to a luscious melody and, as they embrace, Rangoni emerges in triumphant contempt.

ACT IV

Scene 1. Great chamber in the Kremlin. The Council of Boyars is in session to endorse their support of Boris in the face of the Pretender's invasion. Shuisky joins them and tells them of the strange state of the Tsar who imagines he is haunted by visions of the child. Boris enters distraught but pulls himself together. He agrees to receive Pimen who tells of the miracle of a shepherd healed of his blindness at the tomb of the young Dmitri. At this Boris falls swooning and then calls for Feodor. In another superb monologue he gives the boy his final counsel and prays for blessings on his children and forgiveness for himself. With his last breath he names Feodor as the new Tsar and, amid chanting and the funeral knell, falls back dead.

Scene 2. A forest clearing near Kromy. (This scene is sometimes called the "Revolution Scene".) A crowd ties up a Boyar and baits him. An Idiot wearing an iron hat is mocked by urchins and robbed of a kopeck. (There is an ironical echo of the coronation chorus here.) Missail and Varlaam incite the crowd to greet the liberator, Dmitri, and to hang two passing Jesuits. Dmitri rides in and the crowd obeys his call to follow him. The Idiot is left alone, singing an infinitely pathetic song, of which the last words call on the poor, starving Russian folk to weep as darkness nears.

Capriccio

Conversation-piece for music in one act.   Music by Richard Strauss.
Libretto by C. Krauss.   First produced at Munich, October 28th, 1942.

SCENE: A château near Paris.

TIME: About 1775 (when Gluck was beginning his operatic reforms).

CHARACTERS:

THE COUNTESS	(Soprano)
THE COUNT *Her brother*	(Baritone)
FLAMAND *A musician*	(Tenor)
OLIVIER *A poet*	(Baritone)
LA ROCHE *The theatre-director*	(Bass)
THE ACTRESS CLAIRON	(Contralto)
MONSIEUR TAUPE	(Tenor)
TWO ITALIAN SINGERS	(Soprano and tenor)
THE MAJOR-DOMO	(Bass)
EIGHT SERVANTS	(Four tenors and four basses)

*Strauss's last opera is in essence a sophisticated debate, almost on a chamber
scale, about the perennial question of the primacy of words or music in
opera, symbolized by the rivalry of a poet and a composer for a lady's
favours.   The answer may be taken as "both are equally compelling."
Strauss's own practice in "Salome" and "Elektra" had been heavily on the
side of music.   But here he practises what he now preaches and his later
feeling for lighter textures and greater scope for words to be audible
reaches its logical conclusion.   During the conversational passages, often
amusing, the orchestra is usually sparingly used, mainly to illustrate or
underline points in the argument or situation.   But he seizes every
opportunity to provide variety by music of a more expansive or lyrical
cast whenever it can be plausibly introduced into the play.   Some of this
is as beautiful as anything he wrote—e.g., the setting of Olivier's sonnet,
the moonlit interlude before the final scene, and the final scene itself.
Indeed the impact of the last quarter of the opera, after the house-party
has broken up, is immediate.   But the fullest enjoyment of this charming,
original, and ingeniously written piece demands familiarity with the words
or ability to follow them.*

The introduction is the movement of a string sextet of which the first three bars contain two important motives. After the curtain has risen on the salon of the château, with La Roche asleep in an armchair, it is continued from behind the scenes and we learn from a short conversation between Flamand and Olivier that it is a composition by the former which is being rehearsed for the celebration of the widowed Countess's birthday, for which Olivier has written a poem. They are rivals for her favours. Words before music or music before words? They are "brother and sister". La Roche wakes up when the music stops. Music and poetry both bore him; neither can exist without his art ("Poor Gluck" comments Flamand and two bars from the Overture to Gluck's *Iphigenia in Aulis* are heard). He has no use for the reforms and is all for the Italian opera—Maestro Piccini knows his job. All then go off to prepare for a rehearsal, as the Count and Countess enter. The Count, who does not like music, banters his sister on her inability to choose between music or poetry. Or is it between their exponents? She returns his thrust by hinting that his love of poetry may have some connection with Clairon, who is expected. La Roche and the other two return. Clairon arrives in her carriage, is gushingly greeted by the Count and asks whether Olivier has finished the play in which she is to appear. He has. She and the Count, run, reciting, through part of a love-scene ending with a sonnet (a translation from Ronsard). Together with La Roche they go off to start rehearsing.

Olivier remarks that the sonnet was intended for the Countess and recites it again for her while Flamand improvises at the clavichord. He snatches the manuscript from Olivier and hurries off into the next room. Olivier is much distressed at the thought of what music will do to his poem. He declares his love for the Countess who is unwilling to commit herself. Flamand returns and sings the song to which he has just set the sonnet. A trio follows in which the Countess muses on what the music has done to the words, Flamand continues to sing his song, and Olivier jealously says to himself that his poetry is ruined, while it is at the same time the instrument of his rival's victory. Is it now his own or Flamand's? The Countess replies that it is her birthday present and belongs to her. La Roche bustles in to fetch Olivier for the rehearsal. Alone with the Countess Flamand describes the birth of his love for her and, in a passage in which the music grows in intensity, presses her to declare herself for Olivier or for himself. She promises to give her answer in the library the next day at eleven o'clock. He presses a kiss on her arm and hurries out. The Countess sits reflectively, the orchestra voicing her thoughts for a while, while the sounds of the rehearsal are heard from the next room.

The Count enters full of praise for Clairon and his sister rallies him. As for herself, she confesses that it is Olivier's sonnet and Flamand's music for it which together are capturing her heart. Perhaps an opera will be the outcome! The others now join them for chocolate after their rehearsal. To divert them La Roche produces his latest discovery, a dancer who dances a passepied, a gigue, and a gavotte, to music in the style of the period played by the musicians on the stage. Meanwhile Clairon tells Olivier, who has sat down at her side, that there is no longer anything between them. The Count remarks to Flamand that music is servant of the dance to which Flamand retorts that no-one would move a limb without music. This provokes Olivier to pronounce that both dance and music are governed by rhythm and with these words to enunciate the theme of a fugue during which an argument takes place about the respective rôles of words and music with La Roche claiming that the theatrical arts are the key to both. They are on the brink of opera, a prospect welcomed by the Countess, though to her brother an opera is an absurdity. The Countess's mention of Gluck has the party divided for and against the new style. (At the mention of opera the fugue is interrupted while the horn plays a lovely melody taken from a little known song by Strauss.) La Roche backs up his support for the old bel canto by producing two Italian singers who sing a duet from an Italian opera. Refreshments are brought for the singers while the Count flirts with Clairon.

La Roche is now pressed to disclose his plans for the birthday and speaks of a "Birth of Pallas Athene". The others mock his ideas and there follows a lively octet, a "laughing ensemble", in which the Italian singers join, she praising the refreshments and he anxious about their fee. La Roche outlines a grand spectacle, "The Fall of Carthage", as the second part of the entertainment. This leads to the second part of the octet, a "quarrelling ensemble" in which Flamand and Olivier attack his sensational ideas and the Italian singers resume their duet. Finally La Roche is goaded into a great outburst, on Wagnerian lines, in which he pours withering scorn on the young aesthetes and sees himself as the guardian of beauty and the theatrical tradition. He ends by foretelling his epitaph—"The gods loved him, men marvelled at him. Amen." The company is impressed and, to the Count's disgust, the Countess proposes, as a symbol of general reconciliation, that Flamand and Olivier compose an opera. They agree and La Roche is enthusiastic. "Ariadne on Naxos" or "Daphne" are considered as subjects (to quotations from the operas by Strauss) but rejected. The Count wickedly suggests that the opera should be about the day's events and, after some hesitation on the part of La Roche, all take up the idea with enthusiasm. Clairon now takes her leave with exaggerated courtesy accompanied by the Count, as do Flamand and Olivier, each politely telling the other that the other's task comes first, and La Roche asking for a good rôle as Marshall of the Stage. The Countess withdraws.

Now follow three delightful episodes in lighter vein. Eight servants comment on the day's events from their point of view and exchange their own views on the theatre. When the Major-domo tells them that after they have laid for supper they can have the evening off, they go off rejoicing.

T023396

Then Monsieur Taupe, the prompter, emerges dazed, having fallen asleep and been left behind. He tells the Major-domo that it is really he who makes the theatre go round. The Major-domo promises to get him back to Paris. Moonlight now floods the terrace on which the Countess lingers in thought. The stage is empty and the orchestra, led by a solo horn, plays a more elaborate version of the song by Strauss which was heard at the first mention of an opera. This intermezzo is one of the most luscious passages in the whole of Strauss's oeuvre. The Countess returns and the Major-domo brings her a message from Olivier that he too will await her in the library at eleven the next day to be told the end of the opera. She takes the manuscript of the sonnet and sings it through. But she cannot, as she quizzically looks at herself in the glass, decide between her two lovers—cannot find an ending for the opera that will not be trivial. When supper is announced she goes out with the question unanswered and the orchestra brings the opera to a quiet close. This last scene is one of Strauss's great monologues for female voice and, for all the many overtones of the situation, may be enjoyed quite simply as a sympathetic picture of a woman who cannot make up her mind.

Carmen

Opera in four acts. Music by G. Bizet. Libretto by H. Meilhac and L. Halévy, after P. Merimée. First produced at the Opéra Comique, Paris, March 3rd, 1875.

SCENE: Seville and surroundings.

TIME: Early nineteenth century.

CHARACTERS:

DON JOSÉ	*A sergeant*	(Tenor)
ESCAMILLO	*A toreador*	(Baritone)
DANCAIRE	*Smugglers*	(Baritone)
REMENDADO		(Tenor)
CARMEN	*Gypsies*	(Mezzo-soprano)
FRASQUITA		(Soprano)
MERCÉDÈS		(Soprano)
MICAËLA	*A peasant girl*	(Soprano)
MORALES	*A sergeant*	(Bass)
ZUNIGA	*A lieutenant*	(Bass)

The immense popularity of "Carmen" is doubtless due to its appeal to every taste. It offers a simple and readily followed libretto with strong situations; scope for elaborate stage spectacle; a tremendous rôle for a prima donna of any voice with strong low notes, though preferably one with a dark timbre over the whole range; tuneful music which all can enjoy, especially the Spanish colouring associated with Carmen in Acts I and II and the third entr'acte. The more experienced will admire the clear Mediterranean light which pervades the whole score, the brilliant orchestration, and the clever construction. The three entr'actes, an unusual feature, stand apart from the main fabric but help to establish the atmosphere. There is a little spoken dialogue—which makes the piece "opéra comique" in the French classification—but sung recitative is sometimes substituted. The character of every personage is clearly delineated both in the action and the music.

The short Overture plunges straight into the brilliant Toreador's March, follows it with a snatch of Escamillo's song, and ends with the brooding theme associated with fate.

ACT I

A square in Seville, outside the cigarette factory. Morales and the guard
are watching the comings and goings. Micaëla is looking for José but is too
shy to wait for him. The relieving guard, which includes José, arrives
preceded by urchins with a trumpet and fife band. José, told that
Micaëla has been looking for him, does not conceal his love for her. The
cigarette girls emerge from the factory, followed by Carmen, and the
soldiers and men in the crowd press round, eager to flirt with them, except
for José who sits apart, indifferent. Carmen sings the famous habañera
about the capricious nature of love, seeking to attract the attention of
José at whom she finally flings a flower before leaving. The crowd
disperses. José picks up the flower, saying that the woman is a sorceress.
Micaëla now finds him and gives him a message and a kiss from his
mother in their village, which momentarily breaks Carmen's spell. But
after her departure girls come running out of the factory with a story of a
violent quarrel between Carmen and another girl. José is ordered by
Zuniga to enter the factory with two men and arrest her. She answers
Zuniga's questions with a mocking snatch of a song and so he leaves José
in charge of her while he makes out a warrant for her arrest. She plays the
coquette with him and sings, in a seguidilla, of the wine and dance to be
enjoyed in her company at Lillas Pastia's inn near the ramparts. José,
unable to resist, loosens the cord which ties her wrist so that when
Zuniga emerges with the warrant (to a little fugato) and she is marched off
to prison after insolently reminding Zuniga of the habañera, she succeeds
in making her escape.
  There is a tuneful little entr'acte.

ACT II

Tavern of Lillas Pastia. Carmen and her gypsy friends are carousing with
Zuniga and other officers. There is singing and dancing and Carmen joins
in. Zuniga whispers to Carmen that José, after being imprisoned for his
part in her escape, has been set free. Escamillo, followed by his train,
arrives fresh from triumphs in the ring at Granada and sings the familiar
"couplets du toréador" about the bullfighter's life. He makes unsuccessful
advances to Carmen. All leave except Carmen, Frasquita, and Mercédès,
who are joined by Dancaire and Remendado. There follows a lively quintet
in which the two smugglers request the services of the women as cover for
some business but Carmen refuses to accompany them as she is in love and
for once love must take precedence over duty. They leave without her,
just as José is heard singing in the distance the melody of the entr'acte.
Carmen sings and dances for him. But when bugles are heard sounding
retreat and José prepares to leave Carmen taunts him with his military

discipline. As the fate motive sounds in the orchestra he draws the faded flower from his breast and sings the Flower Song, describing how it had consoled him in prison till he could see her again. She tries with a lilting melody to persuade him to desert and join their mountain band, but he hesitates, even if it means a final parting from her. At that moment Zuniga returns hoping to find Carmen alone, and the two men draw swords in a jealous quarrel. Carmen calls in the gypsies and the two smugglers escort Zuniga out. This act of insubordination to an officer settles matters for José. He agrees to join the band and all praise the life of freedom in an ensemble based on the lilting melody.

The entr'acte is based on a pretty theme.

ACT III

A wild mountain place. Smugglers assemble to a march-like tune, which turns into a sextet (for the leading gypsies and José) with chorus, about the smuggler's life. José is thinking of Micaëla (suggestion of Act I duet) and another life than this; Carmen replies that he is free to leave (fate motive). After all, fate is master. The three gypsy women proceed to tell their fortunes with cards in a splendid trio in which the frivolity of Frasquita and Mercédès contrasts with a grave middle section in which Carmen, having foreseen the successive deaths of José and herself, speaks of the inevitability of the cards' message. The smugglers set out on their operations, leaving José on guard. Micaëla now appears, fearful but determined to extricate José from Carmen's grasp. She expresses these feelings in a tender aria and disappears behind the rocks, just as José fires at, and narrowly misses, an intruder who proves to be Escamillo, come in search of Carmen. A fight breaks out between them but the gypsies and smugglers, who have heard the shot, separate them and Escamillo insolently departs with an invitation to all to see him in the bullring at Seville. Micaëla is seen and brought in. She begs José (the Act I duet) to return to his mother. Carmen urges him to go, but he jealously declares that he will never leave her. However, when Micaëla adds that his mother is dying, he decides to leave, telling Carmen (to the fate motive) that they will meet again. Escamillo is heard singing the refrain of his "couplets" in the distance. Carmen starts to run towards him but José bars the way.

The third entr'acte is a brilliant piece, with a strong Spanish colour, in preparation for what is to come.

ACT IV

A square in Seville outside the bullring. An animated crowd, Zuniga among them in attendance on Frasquita and Mercédès, await the bullfighters' procession. Soon they approach, to the march heard in the Overture, and are rapturously greeted by their aficionados, especially Escamillo who is accompanied by Carmen. They sing a short love duet with a surprising note of sincerity before he enters the ring. Carmen refuses to heed the warnings of Frasquita and Mercédès that José is looking for her. He finds her and pleads for a return to their former life, but Carmen is fearless and inflexible. When the crowd is heard acclaiming Escamillo she struggles with José to enter the arena and join her lover. At last she gets past him but he catches her just at the entrance and stabs her to death while the crowd are heard singing the "couplets". As they emerge the fate motive is again heard and José cries out that he is ready to be arrested for his deed.

Cavalleria Rusticana

*(Rustic Chivalry). Opera in one act. Music by P. Mascagni. Libretto by
G. Targioni-Tozzetti and G. Menasci after G. Verga. First produced at the
Teatro Costanzi, Rome, May 17th, 1890.*

SCENE: A village in Sicily.

TIME: Late nineteenth century.

CHARACTERS:

SANTUZZA	*A peasant girl*	(Soprano)
TURIDDU	*A peasant*	(Tenor)
LUCIA	*His mother*	(Contralto)
ALFIO	*A carter*	(Baritone)
LOLA	*His wife*	(Mezzo-soprano)

*This universally popular slice of Sicilian village life was produced when
Mascagni was 27. (He continued composing for a further 55 years but no
other opera of his has ever looked like establishing itself outside Italy.) It
is in distinct numbers and written with a direct simplicity which aims at
matching the stark "verismo" of Verga's play. Perhaps its success has been
due in part to the strong "theatre" of the latter, as well as the opportunities
afforded to the producer and by the part of Santuzza, to whom the best
music falls. The remainder indeed is somewhat thin. The composer was
adept in making passages of inspiration go a long way. It would of course
be foolish to look for great refinement or subtlety of execution in a work
of this kind, but some of the numbers seem out of key with the passionate
concentration and intensity which are intended to be its hallmark.*

There is an Introduction of some length consisting of repetitions of
phrases of Santuzza's music into which is inserted a Siciliano sung by
Turiddu from behind the curtain as an aubade to Lola. The curtain rises,
amid the chiming of church bells, to disclose the empty village square
across which peasants pass on their way to Easter service. There is a chorus
in a triple rhythm in which women, at first unseen, sing of spring, and
men, at first unseen, sing of women. Santuzza crosses to Lucia's wineshop
and insistently asks where Turiddu is. When Lucia replies that he went the

previous night to Francofonte to fetch wine Santuzza tells her that he was seen in the village. She refuses to enter Lucia's house. The carter Alfio arrives, to the sound of whip and bells, and sings (with chorus) a couplet about his carefree life and his love for his faithful wife, a number which could have come straight from an Offenbach operetta. He asks Lucia for some of her old wine. When she says that Turiddu has gone to buy some more Alfio remarks that he saw him outside his own house that morning. Santuzza quickly silences Lucia as the congregation in church are heard singing the "Regina coeli". People outside the church join in a big devotional ensemble led by Santuzza, at the end of which all but Santuzza and Lucia go inside. When Lucia asks why Santuzza had silenced her Santuzza tells her the whole story. When Turiddu returned from military service he found Lola, his old sweetheart, married, and turned instead to herself. Now Lola has snatched him back and she herself is left dishonoured. She begs Lucia to go into church and pray for her. There follows her scene with Turiddu which is the core of the work. Santuzza first reproaches him for visiting Lola, then pleads with him, but Turiddu, with brutal frankness, says that her jealousy is useless. Just then Lola is heard singing a light-hearted song. She enters and spiteful remarks are exchanged with Santuzza before she goes into church. Santuzza restrains Turiddu from following her and breaks into a passionate outburst, the melody of which has already been heard in the Introduction. When he still spurns her and enters the church she curses him and tells the whole story to Alfio who comes upon her. Alfio vows to have his revenge. The stage remains empty while the orchestra (joined by the organ within) play the famous intermezzo, which is perhaps best regarded as a moment of tranquillity amid these torrid events, and a transition to the light-weight chorus to which the villagers emerge from church. Turiddu invites his friends to a glass of wine and sings with them a drinking-song, another number with an operetta flavour. Alfio arrives but refuses the drink offered by Turiddu. In the sudden hush Lola is escorted out. The two men embrace and Turiddu bites Alfio's ear as a challenge in Sicilian fashion. Turiddu has a moment of compunction about the fate of Santuzza if he shoud die in the coming fight. He commends her to the care of his troubled mother, from whom he takes a tender farewell. When he has gone, Santuzza tries to comfort her. An excited crowd gathers (to a phrase from Santuzza's plea). A woman in the distance is heard shouting that Turiddu has been killed. People rush in; Santuzza and Lucia faint; and the curtain quickly falls.

La Cenerentola

(Cinderella). Opera buffa in two acts. Music by G. Rossini. Libretto by J. Ferretti. First produced at the Teatro Valle, Rome, January 25th, 1817.

SCENE: Salerno.

TIME: Eighteenth century (?).

CHARACTERS:

DON MAGNIFICO	*Baron de Montefiascone*	(Bass)
CLORINDA	} *His daughters*	(Soprano)
TISBE		(Mezzo-soprano)
ANGELINA	*Known as La Cenerentola, his stepdaughter*	(Contralto)
DON RAMIRO	*Prince of Salerno*	(Tenor)
DANDINI	*His valet*	(Bass)
ALIDORO	*His tutor, a philosopher*	(Bass)

This is a farcical opera buffa, with some pathos surrounding Cenerentola, but no element of fairy-tale or magic. The music is effervescent, with passages of comic patter and of florid, "old-fashioned" writing for all the singers. The name part requires that modern rarity, a coloratura contralto. The most striking feature of a gay and frivolous score is the many ensembles with which each new turn of the plot is greeted, especially the finale of Act I and the sextet in Act II Scene 2. Cenerentola's final rondo, with its intricate fioriture, is the best known solo number.

The Overture, after the usual solemn opening section, has three elements— a) a sparkling violin tune, b) a cheeky tune first heard on the clarinet, and c) the inevitable Rossini crescendo, here anticipating those in the final section of Act I.

ACT I

Scene 1. A room in Don Magnifico's dilapidated mansion. Cenerentola is making coffee at the fire. Her two sisters are admiring themselves. Cenerentola sings to herself a ballad about a king who preferred an innocent and good-hearted bride. Her sisters are trying to silence her when a knock at the door reveals Alidoro disguised as a mendicant pilgrim. The sisters send him away but Cenerentola slips him a cup of coffee and some bread for which, he says to her, heaven may reward her before nightfall (quartet). Retainers of Prince Ramiro's suite announce his impending arrival to conduct the sisters to a party in his palace, at which the most beautiful girl will become his bride. The sisters are in haste to dress for this, shouting orders at Cenerentola. They give the retainers a small tip, which Cenerentola says to the departing Alidoro she would rather have given to him, eliciting another mysterious promise of happiness. (All this in an ensemble.) The sisters are quarrelling as to which should tell their father when he enters, complaining in an aria that they have spoiled a dream about a flying ass, which signified that he would have, through their marriages, royal grandchildren. They tell him of Ramiro's impending visit and all three go off to make ready. Ramiro enters hesitantly, disguised as his own equerry, to see quietly for himself. His eye falls on Cenerentola; they are mutually attracted. His is captivated by her confused explanation that she is Magnifico's stepdauthter (duet). Magnifico bustles in, just as Dandini, disguised as the Prince, arrives with an escort. He sings a mock-poetic passage about "his" search for a bride and when the sisters enter pretends to be overwhelmed by their beauty. All meditate on the situation in a fast ensemble. Dandini continues to play his part exuberantly and is about to escort the three of them to his carriage when Cenerentola re-enters and pleads with Magnifico in touchingly florid phrases to be taken too, only to meet with a storm of contemptuous abuse which enrages Ramiro and shocks even Dandini. But Alidoro has returned, this time not in disguise, and asks for the third sister whose name is on his list. Magnifico says she is dead and when Cenerentola ingenuously tries to contradict him, pushes her away. This leads to a furiously fast ensemble, after which all except Cenerentola leave the house. Alidoro returns as a pilgrim, summons Cenerentola and takes the astonished girl off to the party. (The concluding aria about the swift changes in life's theatre exists in two versions, one not by Rossini, and is sometimes omitted.)

Scene 2. An apartment in the Prince's palace. Dandini rewards Magnifico for a learned dissertation on wine by making him Chief Vintner and sending him off to the cellar, while making himself pleasant to the two now competing sisters. Retainers celebrate Magnifico's capacity for drink in a gay chorus. He reappears and dictates a comic proclamation forbidding all dilution of wine with water. All leave to prepare for dinner. The extended finale now begins. Over a busy violin accompaniment Ramiro quietly asks Dandini what the two sisters are like and is told they are a mixture of insolence and caprice. He decides therefore to keep up the pretence. When the sisters enter Dandini says that he can only marry one and the other will have to be given to Ramiro. But they say the latter is beneath them. At this moment a veiled lady is announced. No one knows her identity but the sisters at once evince jealousy. Cenerentola enters and, in a florid passage with a touch of parody, says that he who wishes to marry her must offer respect, love, and kindness. When she unveils all are struck by her resemblance to Cenerentola (and Alidoro notes that Ramiro seems to be in love with her already). Magnifico comes in to summon them to table and blurts out what all are thinking. Dandini tries to get them in to dinner. There follows an ensemble in a very fast tempo, with huge crescendi, while all speculate on the situation in some alarm.

ACT II

Scene 1. Another room in the Prince's palace. In a comic aria with much patter Magnifico's imagination again soars and he pictures the influence he will have as father of the Princess. Ramiro overhears Dandini making advances to Cenerentola and is delighted to hear her rebuff him as she is in love with his equerry. He steps forward and offers himself, but she replies that he must first find out who she really is. She gives him a bracelet, promises him its fellow if he still likes her when he has found out, and departs. Ramiro tells Dandini that the masquerade is over and bids him harness horses so that they can go in search. In a big aria he expresses his love and determination to find her. Alone, Alidoro, delighted with the way his plan is working out, announces his intention of causing the carriage to overturn near Magnifico's house. A long duet follows, in which Dandini, with portentous solemnity, breaks to the first incredulous and then furious Magnifico that he is only the valet. Alidoro re-enters, his mind on the accident which the dark and stormy night will make credible.
Scene 2. A room in Don Magnifico's house. Cenerentola, in rags again, is singing her ballad and dreaming of the equerry when the family return and cast black looks at her for her resemblance to a "certain witch". A storm blows up in the orchestra, ending with a pastoral passage (as in Beethoven's sixth symphony). Dandini and Ramiro enter for shelter. When Dandini indicates that the latter is the Prince, Magnifico's hopes rise again; but as Cenerentola brings a chair for him, Ramiro recognizes the bracelet and Cenerentola is stunned to find out who her lover is. There is a sextet in which all express their amazement. This is continued by a passage in which Magnifico and Clorinda seek to dismiss Cenerentola to the kitchen, Ramiro turns his anger on them, and Cenerentola intercedes for them. Ramiro declares his intention of marrying her and mocks the sisters ironically. A rapid ensemble follows before Ramiro leaves with Cenerentola. Alidoro, who has been a silent spectator, expresses his satisfaction.
Scene 3. Ramiro's throne room. Cenerentola can hardly believe the change in her fortunes; her father kneels before her; and when Ramiro speaks contemptuously of her sisters, she proclaims that her revenge is to forgive them. In a final immensely florid rondo she embraces her sisters kindly and dwells rapturously on her new happiness. All join in towards the close.

Cosi fan Tutte

(Women are all alike). Opera buffa in two acts. Music by W. A. Mozart. Libretto by L. Da Ponte. First produced at the Burgtheater, Vienna, January 26th, 1790.

SCENE: Naples.

TIME: Late eighteenth century.

CHARACTERS:

FIORDILIGI	*Two sisters from Ferrara*	(Soprano)
DORABELLA		(Soprano)
DESPINA	*Their maid*	(Soprano)
FERRANDO	*An officer in love with Dorabella*	(Tenor)
GUGLIELMO	*An officer in love with Fiordiligi*	(Baritone)
DON ALFONSO	*An elderly philosopher*	(Baritone)

This work, commissioned by the Emperor Josef II and subtitled "The School for Lovers" was composed at the height of Mozart's powers. The artificial comedy, verging at times on the farcical, is set to apt and witty music, with a strong element of parody but also of a sentimentality which is constantly spilling over into genuine and touching sentiment. Such ambivalence of mood has always been a challenge to producers, especially when what is almost a "chamber-opera" is given in a large house. The music consists of an Overture (introducing almost at once the phrase which occurs later to the words "Così fan tutte"), formal arias, symmetrical ensembles of various combinations of the characters which carry the action forward, lively recitatives, and two full-fledged finales. The part of Fiordiligi calls for a soprano of great range, power, and agility, that of Dorabella for a softer-grained voice; Despina's is a soubrette rôle.

ACT I

Scene 1. A hot quarrel in a café between the two officers and the cynical old Don Alfonso about the ability of their lady-loves to resist any test of their constancy ends with their acceptance of a wager upon it and agreement to place themselves under his orders.

Scene 2. In a garden by the seashore the two ladies rhapsodize over miniatures of their lovers in exaggeratedly ornamental phrases (in which at one point the bassoons mockingly join them). Don Alfonso enters hurriedly and breaks to them that their lovers have been ordered to the war. The lovers appear and after mutual protestations of fidelity and a martial chorus, embark, to a tender quintet in which they promise to write daily, while Don Alfonso splits with laughter. As they sail away he and the ladies wish them a calm voyage in a little trio full of the sweet sorrow of parting lovers.

Scene 3. Interior of the sisters' house. The sisters are inconsolable (tragic aria for Dorabella) and flounce out at the pert Despina's suggestion that they might find distraction with other men. Don Alfonso enters and persuades Despina, with a tip, to admit two suitors. The officers enter disguised as Albanians and the sisters return, indignant at the sound of strange men in the house who ardently protest their love (all this in a lively sextet). Fiordiligi affirms the sisters' constancy in an immense, florid, parodistic aria and they depart in disgust, leaving the officers crowing over Don Alfonso, who reminds them that the joke is not yet finished.

Scene 4. Finale. As the ladies luxuriate in sorrow in their garden, to the delicate accompaniment of flutes and bassoons, their lovers rush in, drink poison and appear to be on the point of death. Despina arrives, disguised as a doctor, to find the ladies giving first aid. The learned doctor passes a large magnet—an allusion to Dr Mesmer, the hypnotist—over the patients' limbs; they come round, thinking they are in heaven and attempt to embrace their "goddesses", to the laides' high indignation.

ACT II

Scene 1. A room in the house. The sisters, impressed by further advice from Despina, decide that a little flirtation would be harmless, Fiordiligi taking the blond Ferrando and Dorabella the dark Guglielmo. Don Alfonso urges them excitedly to come into the garden.

Scene 2. The garden by the sea. The officers, in a flower-decked barge with a band of musicians, sing them a ravishing serenade. The officers feign shyness. Don Alfonso and Despina help them out in a brisk quartet and then slip away. After some awkward small talk between the two couples Guglielmo gets Dorabella to accept a heart and wear it round her neck in place of Ferrando's portrait which he puts round his own neck, in the course of a charming duet expressing the emotion which she (and perhaps he too) begins to feel. Ferrando has less success with Fiordiligi, but he has made an impression and she gives voice to the confusion of her feelings in another tremendous aria (a rondo with florid horn parts). Ferrando's delight at his lack of success turns to rage when Guglielmo shows him the portrait given him by Dorabella. Guglielmo sings a quizzical aria about the fickleness of women while preening himself on the constancy of his own lady. But Don Alfonso warns him not to count his chickens too soon. *Scene 3.* A room in the house. Dorabella is quite complacent, but Fiordiligi still torn with doubt, suddenly decides that, to avoid temptation, they must put on old uniforms of their lovers and join them at the war. Ferrando however rushes in and begs her not to leave him, threatening to stab himself. Their duet becomes romantically serious and Fiordiligi yields, to a touching oboe phrase. This is too much for the watching Guglielmo, but Don Alfonso soothes the two men with a philosophic little song and makes them join in the refrain "Così fan tutte". Despina announces that the ladies wish to marry them and that she has orders to find a notary. The men agree to this. *Scene 4.* A brightly lit hall. Finale. The wedding party begins. The two couples toast each other to a mellifluous round. The notary is called in and the contract is on the point of signature, when the martial chorus of Act I Scene 2 is heard in the distance. Don Alfonso returns with the news that the officers are just disembarking. The Albanians and the notary hide. The officers in their uniforms enter joyfully, and are duly taken aback by the confusion of the ladies. Guglielmo pulls out the notary from hiding and he is revealed as Despina claiming to have just returned from a fancy-dress ball. When the officers see the contract their fiancées confess and they go off in search of the Albanians. They return with their Albanian disguises half on and with musical quotations from previous scenes. All is cleared up; Don Alfonso accepts responsibility, wins his wager, and bids them make it up. This they do, the ladies (in thirds, as usual) seeking forgiveness in a melting phrase. The opera ends with a gay sextet pointing the moral.

Don Carlos

Opera in five acts. Music by G. Verdi. Libretto in French by G. Méry and C. du Locle, after Schiller (later revised by A. Ghislanzoni). First produced at the Opéra, Paris, March 11th, 1867 (revised version at La Scala, Milan, in 1884).

SCENE: Fontainebleau and Spain.

TIME: Sixteenth century.

CHARACTERS:

PHILIP II *King of Spain*		(Bass)
DON CARLOS *His son and heir*		(Tenor)
RODRIGO *Marquis of Posa*		(Baritone)
THE GRAND INQUISITOR		(Bass)
ELISABETTA DI VALOIS		(Soprano)
PRINCESS EBOLI *Her lady-in-waiting*		(Contralto)
TEBALDO *Elisabetta's page*		(Soprano)
A MONK		(Bass)

"Don Carlos" marks the transition from Verdi's middle period to the full glory of "Aida" and of his later work. As such it abounds in splendid numbers in both styles. Its weakness is its length, written as it was for the mid-century Parisian taste. Verdi was aware of this and later tried unsuccessfully to shorten it. It is indeed difficult to know what other than the ballet in Act III Scene 1 can be cut; only the auto-da-fé scene (which owes nothing to Schiller) falls markedly below the general musical level and this encloses essential dramatic action. Act IV Scene 1 is as good as any single scene that Verdi wrote. All the music associated with King Philip is in Verdi's later manner, grave and powerful and concerned with political subjects. On the lyrical side there are three beautiful love duets while Eboli and Rodrigo have fine "middle period" solos.

ACT I

The Forest of Fontainebleau. Winter. Don Carlos muses on the love awakened in him by the sight, during a hunt, of Elisabetta whom he is to marry as one of the conditions for peace between France and Spain. She and her page, lost and cold, encounter him. He says that he is one of the Spanish Ambassador's officers and offers to escort her home. The page leaves and he lights a fire. Elisabetta speaks of her fear at leaving France to marry a strange Prince. Don Carlos, to reassure her, shows her a portrait which is of course of himself and declares his love. She returns it. (All this in a duet of great beauty.) But her page returns with the news that she is to marry King Philip himself. Courtiers assemble and when the Spanish Ambassador formally offers his sovereign's hand, she sadly accepts, amid the rejoicing of all but the desperate Carlos.

ACT II

Scene 1. Cloister of the Convent of San Giusto. Monks pray at the tomb of Charles V; Carlos has taken refuge there from the world. His friend, Rodrigo, just returned from Flanders, seeks him out and tells him that the cause of Flemish liberty is in need of him. Carlos confides in him that he is troubled by a guilty love for his stepmother. They swear eternal friendship in a typical Verdi "oath" duet which is interrupted by the arrival, to Carlos's consternation, of the King and Queen to pray at the tomb. *Scene 2.* A garden outside the monastery. The Queen's ladies await her and Eboli sings the florid Veil Song, describing a Moorish romance. When the Queen arrives Rodrigo contrives to give her a note from Carlos, together with a letter from her mother, in return for which she offers to do him a favour. Rodrigo asks her to receive Carlos. With trepidation she agrees and Rodrigo manages to get her suite out of earshot. Carlos at first asks her to persuade the King to send him to Flanders. When she replies formally he accuses her of indifference to him and to his ardour. She replies with a reminder of her duty to his father and seeks to dismiss him. At this he falls senseless at her feet and then, recovering, tries to embrace her before rushing disconsolately away. The King comes out and, in anger at finding the Queen unattended, orders a lady-in-waiting to return to France. The Queen consoles her. The King orders Rodrigo to remain and encourages him to speak freely. Rodrigo pleads for a more liberal policy in Flanders. The King regards this as a youthful dream. He warns him to beware of the Grand Inquisitor. As a mark of his own favour he confides his suspicion about Carlos and the Queen and asks him to keep a watchful eye. This duet between the two men is one of the opera's finest passages.

ACT III

Scene 1. Gardens of the Queen's Palace. Night, during a masked ball in the Palace. After a short Prelude, Carlos, having received a note making a rendezvous, makes love to a masked figure whom he takes for Elisabetta but who proves, to his unconcealed dismay, to be Eboli. (She has persuaded herself that Carlos is interested in her.) In honeyed tones she tells him that she knows of his love for the Queen and utters dark threats. Rodrigo who has appeared tries to explain the situation away and, when this fails, has to be restrained by Carlos from stabbing her before, after an excited trio, she storms off. At Rodrigo's suggestion Carlos promises to hand his friend documents which might prove damaging and the scene ends with a reminder in the orchestra of the melody of eternal friendship. *Scene 2.* A great square in Madrid. The people are assembled for the auto-da-fé. A chorus alternates with a march as, first, monks conduct the heretics to be burned at the stake and then grandees and officers of state take their places. The King, crowned, comes ceremoniously from the church. Flemish deputies, led by Carlos, beg for mercy for their country. The King dismisses them as rebels but in the ensuing ensemble they have the sympathy of the majority. He refuses a request of Carlos to be made Viceroy of Flanders, as training for the Crown. Carlos defies the King by drawing his sword and swearing to save the Flemish. When the King orders that he be disarmed it is Rodrigo who takes the sword (to a snatch of the friendship motive). The march is resumed and a heavenly voice floats down as the procession moves forward.

ACT IV

Scene 1. The King's apartment. After an introduction in which the cello has a moving solo Philip broods in a famous monologue on his loveless marriage and the watch which, as King, he must keep until the time comes for his long sleep beneath the Escorial. The aged and blind Grand Inquisitor, for whom he has sent, now enters. In a tremendous scene between two basses the King ascertains that he will have the support of the Church if he decides to punish Carlos with death. The Inquisitor goes on to denounce Rodrigo as even more dangerous. When the King hesitates the Inquisitor upbraids him as a man failing in his duty. As he leaves the King asks, in a great phrase spanning two octaves, whether the throne must always give way to the altar. Elisabetta breaks in, complaining of the theft of a jewel-casket. The King points to it on the table; she opens it to discover a portrait of Carlos. He accuses her of adultery and she faints. He calls for help and Eboli and Rodrigo enter. Eboli is stricken with contrition at her betrayal of the Queen; the King regrets his suspicions; and Rodrigo feels that only his self-sacrifice can now save his friend. (A fine quartet.) When Eboli is alone with the Queen she confesses that it was her jealousy that had actuated the suspicions of the King and, further, that she had been his mistress. The Queen says that, as penalty, she must choose between exile and the veil. Left alone, Eboli has a magnificent aria, cursing her fatal beauty. But she has still one day in which to save Carlos.

Scene 2. Carlos's prison cell. As Carlos broods gloomily, thinking of Elisabetta, Rodrigo steals in to bid his friend farewell. Carlos's incriminating documents have been found in his possession and he knows that he must die. An assassin, accompanied by an officer of the Inquisition, creeps in and shoots him. Before he dies in Carlos's arms, he tells Carlos that Elisabetta will await him at the Convent the next day. Carlos must escape to Flanders, for the sake of Spain. (Long aria, followed by friendship motive.) The King arrives and offers his son his sword back; but Carlos calls him the murderer of his friend and the King is appalled at the deed. A crowd break in calling for Carlos. Eboli is with them in disguise and assists his escape. The Inquisitor arrives and persuades the mob to kneel before the King.

ACT V

As in Act II Scene 1. Elisabetta prays sadly at the tomb of Charles V and recalls her youth in France and her frustrated love. Carlos appears and they sing a long duet in which, after dwelling on the liberal causes which Carlos must espouse for Rodrigo's sake, they take a last farewell of each other. Suddenly the King emerges with the Inquisitor who calls on guards to seize Carlos. But a monk appears clad like Charles V himself (who according to legend is still living as a monk) and carries Carlos off into the cloister.

Don Giovanni

Opera buffa in two acts. Music by W. A. Mozart. Libretto by L. da Ponte. First produced at the National Theatre, Prague, October 29th, 1787.

SCENE: Seville and neighbourhood.

TIME: Early seventeenth century.

CHARACTERS:

THE COMMENDATORE		(Bass)
DONNA ANNA	*His daughter*	(Soprano)
DON OTTAVIO	*Her betrothed*	(Tenor)
DON GIOVANNI	*A young nobleman*	(Baritone)
LEPORELLO	*His servant*	(Bass)
DONNA ELVIRA	*A lady of Burgos*	(Soprano)
MASETTO	*A peasant*	(Baritone)
ZERLINA	*His betrothed*	(Soprano)

This version of the Don Juan legend which had been treated by a number of writers, including Molière, in the seventeenth and eighteenth centuries, was one of Mozart's works to enjoy high prestige throughout the nineteenth century, attracting much literary attention. Doubtless this was because it was seen as a romantic work (with an edifying moral) and, with its many fine arias shared by five major characters, as a vehicle for the great stars of the day. But nowadays it is usually regarded as essentially the "dramma giocoso" of its title (the final sextet being no longer suppressed), with romantic and serious elements that, as usual, acquired disproportionate beauty in Mozart's hands. . The music is indeed remarkable, not only for the juxtaposition of grave and gay but for its urgent atmosphere and the speed with which it carries the action forward (apart from a few conventional arias, some added for the Vienna première in 1788). Its many ensembles (two big finales, a sextet, a quartet, and two trios) make it no less an opera for team-work than "Figaro". Its weakness, if the Vienna arias are retained, as their beauty demands, is the chain of static arias which hold up the action half-way through Act II. Their precise placing makes problems for producers and the frequent fate of "Il mio tesoro" and "Mi tradì" (and sometimes of "Dalla sua pace" as well) is to be given before the curtain to cover changes of scene.

The familiar Overture opens with an andante foreshadowing the horror of the banquet scene, which is followed by an allegro (the motives of which do not recur) leading directly into

ACT I

Scene 1. A garden before the Commendatore's palace. Night. Leporello complains, in the first section of the opening movement, of having to wait day and night for his master, but keeps out of the way when Anna emerges struggling with Don Giovanni and calling for help. Her father comes out, draws his sword, and is mortally wounded in the ensuing fight. The terzetto for the three men before he dies, concluding with four orchestral bars of great pathos, is a passage of tragic concentration. Don Giovanni is not unduly disturbed, as is shown by his exchanges with Leporello before they make off. Anna, who has rushed into the house for help, returns with Ottavio and finds her father dead. After the first shock they join in a duet in a very serious vein in which Anna, brushing aside Ottavio's attempts at consolation, makes him swear vengeance.
Scene 2. A street. Early morning. After the first of Leporello's attempts to reform his master's ways, the Don scents the approach of a woman, who is railing against the lover who has deserted her. The Don goes up to her to console her, only to find (as her aria ends) that it is Elvira with whom he had once had a short affair. He escapes from her reproaches, leaving Leporello to deal with her. Leporello takes the line that she is not the only one and sings the famous catalogue aria listing his master's many and varied conquests. Elvira vows vengeance.
Scene 3. The countryside. Zerlina and Masetto are leading a rustic celebration of their impending wedding. The Don comes upon them and, after seeing Zerlina, tells Leporello to entertain them all at his palace, while he takes care of Zerlina. The suspicious Masetto falls in with this plan reluctantly; Zerlina is flattered by the Don's attentions. Then follows the familiar duet ("Là ci darem") in which the Don entices her to go off with him. His plan is foiled by the arrival of Elvira who warns Zerlina not to trust him and carries her off. Anna enters with Ottavio and, not knowing that it was he who had killed her father, asks him for help. Elvira reappears and in an amusing quartet, rages against the Don, while he tries to calm her and the other two do not quite know what to make of it. She goes off, followed by the Don, to ensure, he says, that she comes to no harm. But Anna has suddenly recognized him as the intruder in her father's mansion. She describes to Ottavio exactly what happened that night and reminds him, in a powerful aria, of his oath of vengeance, before leaving him to muse on his devotion to her in the aria "Dalla sua pace". Leporello tells the Don (often after a change of scene) how Elvira had burst in with Zerlina on his entertainment of the peasants, raging against

him, and how he had gently thrown her out. The Don gives orders for a
gay party, with plenty of girls, in the presto aria sometimes called "The
champagne aria", though there is nothing in the text to require drinking
at this point.
Scene 4. The garden of Don Giovanni's palace. The jealous Masetto
reproaches Zerlina for her conduct. She begs his pardon in the aria
"Batti, batti" with its persistent cello solo. But her alarm at the approach
of the Don reawakens the suspicions which she has lulled. As the long
finale begins, Masetto hides so as to watch what passes between the Don
and his fiancée. The Don enters, giving orders to four servants who go
off. In a charming passage he tries to lead the nervous Zerlina into an
arbour, but is confronted by Masetto whom he chides for deserting her,
before taking them both into the house. Elvira, Ottavio, and Anna enter
masked and ready for what may prove a dangerous escapade. Leporello
opens a window and a minuet is heard. At the Don's bidding he invites
them into the palace. Before entering they utter a solemn prayer in a trio
accompanied by wind instruments alone.
Scene 5. The ballroom. The festivities are in progress though the Don and
Leporello are finding Masetto obstreperous. The masked guests enter and
exchange compliments with the host. Three stage orchestras strike up,
playing simultaneously a minuet, a contredanse, and a waltz. Leporello
forces Masetto to dance with him to get him out of the way, while the Don
leads Zerlina to another room, followed by Leporello to warn him that
Masetto is proving difficult. A scream is heard from within and Masetto
and the three masked characters break open the door. The Don comes out,
dragging Leporello and threatening to kill him. Anna, Ottavio, and Elvira
are not deceived. They unmask and tell the Don that they know all. He
stands at bay before their threats. But before they act he forces his way
through the throng and makes good his escape.

ACT II

Scene 1. A street outside Elvira's residence. Leporello tries to leave the
Don who bribes him to stay on, while brushing aside the former's
stipulation that he give up women. They exchange cloaks so that the Don
may the better pursue his fancy for Elvira's maid. Elvira appears at the
window, romantically voicing her mixed feelings for the Don. Standing
behind Leporello, the Don gradually persuades her to come down and join
him, while Leporello enjoys the situation. (This makes a fine trio.) When
she comes down Leporello, dressed as the Don, makes love to her, till the
real Don, who has been hiding, pretends to waylay them and frightens them
away. This leaves the coast clear for him to address the famous serenade
(with mandoline accompaniment) to the maid. Masetto and villagers,
armed, come upon him and, thinking him Leporello, ask the whereabouts

of the Don whom they mean to kill. In an amusing aria the Don sends the villagers in different directions but keeps Masetto back, relieves him of his weapons by a ruse and gives him a beating before making off. Zerlina finds Masetto on the ground, groaning, and consoles him, in the aria "Vedrai carino", by inviting him to listen to her beating heart. She takes him home. *Scene 2.* A courtyard before a palace. Leporello,escorting Elvira, is trying to avoid approaching lights, and moves away from her, hoping to escape in the dark, of which she is nervous. At this point a long and fine sextet begins. The lights were escorting Anna and Ottavio to the palace which is her home, and (with a wonderful change of key) they now enter, Ottavio still striving to console her.   Just as Leporello is making his get-away he runs into Masetto and Zerlina entering and when all threaten him, taking him for the Don, Elvira runs forward to intercede for him.   When, however, they are implacable, Leporello reveals his identity and pleads for mercy in a whining phrase.   There is general surprise and at the end of the sextet Anna goes inside.   Leporello continues to defend himself against all their charges, in an aria, at the end of which he manages to slip away.   Ottavio rather inexplicably decides that these events confirm that it was the Don who murdered the Commendatore and that he must inform the authorities. He sings the formal florid aria "Il mio tesoro" emphasizing his determination to console his betrothed by ensuring the Don's punishment.   It is at this point too that the beautiful Vienna aria for Elvira "Mi tradi", if retained, is usually placed.
Scene 3. A churchyard.   The Don and Leporello, each taking refuge, encounter each other.   The Don tells him in high spirits of an escapade with one of the latter's lady friends.   Suddenly the statue of the Commendatore warns him to cease his jesting.   Leporello is afraid but his master orders him with threats to invite the statue to supper.   Towards the end of their highly characterized duet the statue monosyllabically accepts the invitation.
Scene 4. A room in Anna's house.   Anna will not hear of any suggestion of marriage at such a time but assures Ottavio in an elaborate aria of her love for him.
Scene 5. A hall in Don Giovanni's palace.   The Don takes his place at table, with Leporello in attendance.   While he eats with relish a stage band plays excerpts from Martin's "Una Cosa Rara" and Sarti's "I due Litiganti", followed by "Non più andrai" from Mozart's own *Marriage of Figaro*. Suddenly Elvira breaks in with a rather incoherent plea to the Don to mend his ways.   He replies by praising women and good wine.   As she leaves she utters a shriek.   Leporello goes out to investigate and returns, panic-stricken, with an account of the approaching statue.   He hides under the table as the Don rises to admit the statue, to spine-chilling trombone chords.   The statue refuses the Don's supper but invites him to sup with him.   Despite warning mutterings from Leporello, the Don fearlessly accepts and offering his hand in token, is held in a grip of ice.   He still

refuses to repent. Flames engulf him, thunder and a chorus of devils are heard and he disappears in torment. Into the room burst the other five characters, together with police, intent on the Don's arrest. Leporello tries to explain what has happened. All seem already to have seen the spectre. Ottavio renews his request for an early wedding, but Anna tells him to wait another year. Elvira plans to enter a convent; Zerlina and Masetto to return to their own marriage celebrations; and Leporello to go to the inn to look for another master. This lively sextet ends with a presto section in which all proclaim the moral—that wrongdoers will always come to a similar sticky end.

Don Pasquale

Opera buffa in three acts. Music by G. Donizetti. Libretto by S. Cammarano. First produced at Théâtre Italien, Paris, January 3rd, 1843.

SCENE: Rome.

TIME: Early nineteenth century.

CHARACTERS:

DON PASQUALE		(Bass)
DR MALATESTA	*His friend*	(Baritone)
ERNESTO	*Don Pasquale's nephew*	(Tenor)
NORINA	*A young widow*	(Soprano)
A NOTARY		(Baritone)

"Don Pasquale" is very much the conventional opera buffa—foolish old man anxious to marry a minx, scheming doctor, and all the rest—but it is so perfect a little specimen of its kind that we happily accept the convention. Its flow of melody and its humorous ensembles carry the intrigue rapidly forward without too much recitativo secco. But what it must have is four first-class singers who can also act in this convention—a soprano and tenor who can manage all the florid line of their famous solos without losing a light touch and two buffo singers for the baritone and bass rôles equal to the difficult tasks of sustaining comic character parts with consistent style and feeling for the music.

The sprightly Overture is introduced by a phrase from Ernesto's Act III serenade but thereafter is based mainly on Norina's aria in Act I Scene 2.

ACT I

Scene 1. Room in Don Pasquale's house. The elderly Don Pasquale impatiently awaits the arrival of Malatesta who has been looking for a bride for him. He arrives with news of success and describes her innocent charms in a luscious romanza. She is his own sister. Don Pasquale expresses his eager anticipation in a lively cavatina. When Ernesto returns home and persists in his intention of marrying Norina rather than the lady of his uncle's choice, Don Pasquale announces his own impending marriage. Ernesto will have to leave his house. Ernesto's incredulity gradually turns to dismay as he realizes the effect of this on his own prospects—to his crusty uncle's unconcealed delight.

Scene 2. Room in Norina's house. She is reading from a romantic book but throws it aside to tell the audience how skilled she is in coquetry. (This is one of the most celebrated of all bel canto soprano arias.) Malatesta and a letter from Ernesto arrive together. Ernesto, in his despair, is threatening to go far away and at first Norina is inclined to disbelieve Malatesta when he says that his little plot to make Don Pasquale consent to her marriage to Ernesto is going well. But when Malatesta explains that Ernesto is not yet in the picture and that she is to be passed off as his sister from a convent and married to Don Pasquale by his cousin disguised as a notary, she enters into the spirit of the game and in a lively florid duet they plot how she is to score off the old man.

ACT II

Scene 1. Ernesto's house. Ernesto expresses his despair and fidelity to Norina in a beautiful aria.

Scene 2. Don Pasquale's house. Malatesta introduces his shy, heavily veiled sister "Sempronia" to Don Pasquale who is captivated by her maidenly modesty and domesticated tastes. (He does not hear her asides in an amusing trio.) Malatesta produces a Notary and dictates a marriage contract giving half of all Don Pasquale's worldly goods to his bride. The Notary points out that a second witness is needed. Just then Ernesto bursts in, already in a great state at being practically barred from the house. His agitation becomes even greater on discovering that his uncle's bride is Norina and she and Malatesta have some difficulty in getting him to understand the position. Eventually the contract is signed with Ernesto as second witness. Immediately Norina's disposition changes. She rides roughshod over Don Pasquale, demands vast expenditure on the household, and prefers Ernesto to Don Pasquale as escort for an outing. Don Pasquale is confused and outraged by it all. (The larger part of this scene is in the form of an extended buffo quartet.)

ACT III

Scene 1. As in Act II Scene 2. Servants are running frantically around at the orders of Norina who is preparing to go out for the evening. When Don Pasquale returns to question her about this a marital quarrel develops, in a duet which ends in Norina boxing him on the ears and telling him to go to bed. She goes out, dropping a letter proposing an assignation at the back of the garden. This is too much for Don Pasquale and he sends for Malatesta. The servants comment on these goings-on in an attractive chorus. Malatesta arrives with Ernesto, whom he dispatches to play his part in the garden. He helps the old man plan his revenge in the course of an amusing duet. Don Pasquale at first favours surprising the pair with the whole staff and handing them over to the magistrate. But Malatesta persuades him that the two of them should overhear the lovers' conversation from the bushes and that, if they are found guilty, Norina should be sent away.

Scene 2. The garden. Ernesto sings a serenade (a famous tenor piece) and the lovers are united in a brief love duet. Don Pasquale and Malatesta surprise them. Ernesto escapes and Norina tries to brazen it out with Don Pasquale. Malatesta slyly proposes that Ernesto should marry Norina and live in his uncle's house, at which "Sempronia" says she will leave. This induces Don Pasquale to give his prompt assent to the match. Ernesto is summoned and Don Pasquale is swiftly enlightened as to the true position. Relieved, he gives the young couple his blessing and a rondo finale underlines the moral—that marriage is not for old men.

Elektra

Opera in one act. Music by Richard Strauss. Libretto by H. von Hofmannsthal. First produced at Dresden, January 25th, 1909.

SCENE: Mycenae.

TIME: Antiquity.

PRINCIPAL CHARACTERS:

KLYTEMNESTRA	*Widow of Agamemnon*	(Mezzo-soprano)
ELEKTRA	} *Her daughters*	(Soprano)
CHRYSOTHEMIS		(Soprano)
ORESTES	*Her son*	(Baritone)
AEGISTHUS	*Her paramour*	(Tenor)
FIVE MAIDSERVANTS		(Contralto, two mezzo-sopranos and two sopranos)
THE OVERSEER		(Soprano)

This opera was the first of the Strauss-Hofmannsthal partnership. The librettist followed Sophocles' version of the legend and the work is in one unbroken span of nearly two hours, falling into clearly defined sections and following the pattern of Greek tragedy, though without the choral interludes. It is in the post-Wagnerian idiom with elaborate symphonic development of leading motives in a highly wrought, concentrated score for a large orchestra. Moreover, the music uninhibitedly explores extreme neurotic states of mind. The use of motives to ironical effect is a notable feature very much in the Greek spirit. When it first appeared it was thought to represent the limit of modernity, and Strauss's subsequent operas do represent a turning-back towards a more lyrical style. With powerful singers (who can also act) for the three exacting female rôles, "Elektra" is still very exciting in performance and affords subtle musical pleasure to those who can follow the way in which the motives are constantly adapted to every emotional nuance. The "recognition" scene provides a point of repose amid the many moments of strong climax. The characters of the superstitious, decayed Klytemnestra and the effeminate Aegisthus are brilliantly reflected in the music and the contrast between the overwrought, obsessed Elektra and her gentler, more feminine sister emerges strongly.

As the curtain rises the short Agamemnon motive is heard fortissimo. Five Maidservants and their Overseer exchange tales of Elektra's strange behaviour. She is "like a wild cat". (Elektra momentarily appears, like an animal from its lair.) She is condemned to the existence of a beast. The fifth Maidservant confesses her devotion to Elektra and is pushed into the house where she is heard being beaten. The others follow her in and the frenzied Elektra comes out and calls upon her father, in a great monologue. She dwells on the ghastly details of his murder and then looks forward to the day of vengeance when, with her sister and brother, there will be sacrifices on his grave and they will dance a dance of victory. She is joined by Chrysothemis for whom she displays contempt if not indeed hatred. She has come to warn Elektra that their mother and Aegisthus are planning to imprison Elektra in a dark tower. She goes on, to gentler, more conventional music, to express her inability to sit, like Elektra, peering into the darkness and her longing for fulfillment as a wife and mother, of the chance of which she feels Elektra's behaviour is depriving her. The cracking of whips announces the approach of Klytemnestra who, she says, has been dreaming of Orestes. She withdraws in terror but Elektra awaits her mother with relish.

Klytemnestra appears, with attendants, at a window. She is sallow and bloated and covered with jewels and talismans. After words of hatred for Elektra she speaks of her dreams and sleeplessness and the inability of her attendants to prescribe remedies. She decides to consult her daughter and, coming down, dismisses her attendants. She asks Elektra whether she knows of any cure for dreams. Even as she is superstitiously laden with jewels, there must surely be some ritual? She describes her sickness and her sense of oppression. Elektra replies with irony that there must be a sacrifice, by a stranger, who is yet of the House, of an unholy woman who is no virgin. When her mother presses her to expound the riddle, she speaks of her brother, Orestes. Klytemnestra comments that he is feeble-minded but that she has sent money for his keep. But Elektra replies that it was for his murder; her mother's trembling betrays her. When Klytemnestra presses her further for the secret of the necessary sacrifice, Elektra comes close to her, and in wild intoxication, speaks openly of her vision of Orestes chasing Klytemnestra through the house and striking her down. Klytemnestra is shaking with fear when her confidante comes out and whispers to her. A look of evil triumph comes over her face and she hurries into the palace, followed by the retinue she has summoned.

Chrysothemis comes running from the palace screaming that Orestes is dead. Elektra refuses at first to believe it, but after a young servant has called hurriedly for a horse to take important news to Aegisthus, she tells her sister that she must now help her to do the deed. She flatters her sister's strength (in a perverted version of the music of Chrysothemis's longing for marriage) and promises to be a sister to her as never before. When all her hysterical wheedling fails to prevent her sister tearing herself free and rushing off, she curses her and begins to dig, like an animal, for the axe with which her father was murdered. She is interrupted by a stranger in reply to whose question she says that she works in the house. He tells her that he and another have come to give the Queen an account of Orestes' death. This produces such an outburst of bitter grief that the stranger asks if she is of the Blood herself and she reveals her identity. He replies that Orestes is not dead and, when servants begin to come out and kiss his feet, she at last recognizes him. The music becomes tender in feeling as Elektra expresses her rapture and her shame at her condition. Then brother and sister exult in the deed to come, till Orestes' tutor recalls him to the need for action and he goes in (though without the axe, as Elektra exclaims). There is a moment of tension, marked by scalic passages, till Klytemnestra's shrieks are heard, followed by servants rushing back and forth. Aegisthus now arrives, to a jaunty theme, and calls for lights. Elektra holds a torch for him, circling round in a kind of dance and uttering mock-obsequious words to a background in the manner of a Viennese waltz. After another moment of tension, Aegisthus appears at the window calling for help. Chrysothemis and women of the house rush out calling excitedly that Orestes is back and there is a brief fight between the followers of Aegisthus and slaves loyal to Orestes. Chrysothemis is overjoyed but Elektra, in a trance of triumph, does not heed her and breaks into a ghastly dance to ever more frenzied music, calling on all to follow her, till suddenly she falls lifeless. Chrysothemis calls out in vain for Orestes. The orchestra repeatedly restates the Agamemnon motive.

L'Elisir d'Amore

(The Love Potion). Opera buffa in two acts. Music by G. Donizetti. Libretto by F. Romani. First produced at the Teatro della Canobbiana, Milan, May 12th, 1832.

SCENE: An Italian village.

TIME: Early nineteenth century.

CHARACTERS:

ADINA	*A wealthy farm-owner*	(Soprano)
NEMORINO	*A young peasant*	(Tenor)
BELCORE	*Sergeant of the village garrison*	(Baritone)
DULCAMARA	*A quack doctor*	(Bass)
GIANNETTA	*A peasant girl*	(Soprano)

This opera is not only almost as tuneful and effervescent as Rossini at the top of his form but its music exudes a period charm to which can best be applied the term "Biedermaier"—and after all Northern Italy was ruled from Vienna when it was written—though it is music wholly Italian in style. It demands, of course, singers who can carry off the ornate bel canto line, at least for the parts of Adina and Nemorino, and a real buffo bass for Dulcamara. The divisions of the various "numbers" are rather less clearly marked and the proportion of recitative is rather smaller than in older buffo operas. Ensembles abound. The tenor's romanza near the end is the most familiar individual item.

ACT I

Scene 1. Entrance to Adina's farm. After a brief Prelude, reapers, together with Giannetta, sing as they rest in the shade; Adina is reading and the timid Nemorino comments on her beauty. She tells them that she is reading how Tristan won the cruel Iseult with a love potion. Belcore arrives at the head of his platoon and lays siege to Adina's heart in a very direct fashion, to the dismay of Nemorino. (This works up to a lively ensemble.) When Belcore has gone and the reapers have been sent back to work Adina makes it plain to Nemorino that she finds his sighful approaches tedious.

Scene 2. The village square. The villagers excitedly await Dr Dulcamara, who arrives in a gilded waggon and offers nostrums for every imaginable complaint. Nemorino shyly asks if he has the famous love potion. Dulcamara sells him what is really a bottle of wine, saying that it will make him irresistible, but not for twenty-four hours. Nemorino drinks deeply and becomes unwontedly gay. Adina is surprised at the change in him, but is piqued at his confidence that tomorrow she will fall for him. To Belcore, who renews his suit, she promises her hand in six days' time; Nemorino is confident that all will be changed before then. But marching orders arrive for the morrow and Adina, as proof of her love, says that she will marry Belcore that very day. Nemorino, suddenly sobered, implores Adina to wait a little, but she tells Belcore to get the notary to marry them at once and invites everyone to the wedding-feast. The distraught Nemorino calls on Dulcamara for help.

ACT II

Scene 1. At Adina's farm. The feast has begun. Dulcamara and Adina sing a little barcarolle about a senator and a gondolier's daughter. All except Dulcamara withdraw with the notary to settle the marriage contract. Nemorino on entering again consults Dulcamara, who advises another bottle of the potion and gives him a quarter of an hour to find the money for it. Nemorino confides his need for money to Belcore who recommends him to enlist; the sum he needs will instantly be his.

Scene 2. A rustic courtyard. The village girls have heard that Nemorino's uncle has died and left him a fortune; he does not yet know it. He arrives, having enlisted and drunk a lot more of the potion. When he finds himself unwontedly successful with the girls, he puts this down to the love potion. But the sight kindles Adina's love for him. Dulcamara explains what Nemorino has done out of love, though he does not know the identity of the lady in question. Adina's heart is touched, but she refuses the offer of a bottle for herself and prefers to rely on her native charms. The sight of Adina's dismay moves the secretly rejoicing Nemorino to sing the charming "Una furtiva lagrima". Meanwhile she has bought him out of the army. After a little coquetry which he meets by expressing a preference for a soldier's death, the lovers are united. Belcore accepts defeat while Dulcamara claims all the credit for his love potion and takes the opportunity to sell his whole stock. To the strains of the barca—rolle he climbs into his waggon and drives off in triumph.

Die Entführung aus dem Serail

*(The Abduction from the Seraglio). Opera in three acts. Music by
W. A. Mozart. Libretto by G. Stephanie. First produced at the
Burgtheater, Vienna, July 16th, 1782.*

SCENE: Turkey.

TIME: Eighteenth century (?).

CHARACTERS:

CONSTANZE	*A Spanish lady*	(Soprano)
BLONDE	*Her maid*	(Soprano)
BELMONTE	*Constanze's lover*	(Tenor)
PASHA SELIM		(Speaking part)
OSMIN	*His overseer*	(Bass)
PEDRILLO	*Former servant of Belmonte*	(Tenor)

*This is a Singspiel, a popular form in which the action was largely
confined to spoken dialogue and the music limited to reflective arias
and duets with an occasional chorus. Mozart's music is correspondingly
simple and static, and though of great lyrical beauty, lacks the concentration
and the quality of dramatic movement which we associate with his
greatest operas. Only in the Quartet does he come near to writing
one of his kaleidoscopically shifting ensembles; even here the changes
of mood are somewhat contrived and irrelevant to the main . action.
The only character who lives in and through his music is Osmin,
one of the great comic bass rôles. The part of the Pasha requires
an actor of some stature to make its proper impact. The "Turkish"
music, and indeed the whole conception follow late eighteenth century
convention. The orchestration has all Mozart's characteristic limpidity
and the work rewards good singers. In short, while it is a piece of
modest calibre, and indifferent construction, its gaiety and musical
charm, given good production, are irresistible.*

The Overture is a kind of "Turkish" march (with bass drum, cymbals, and
triangle) with a fragment of Belmonte's opening aria as middle section.

ACT I

Outside the Pasha's palace by the sea. Belmonte sings of his joy at the prospect of seeing Constanze, who has been carried off by pirates and is held captive in the palace. Osmin appears on a ladder picking figs and singing a gravely comic song recommending a watchful eye on lady loves. It turns to a duet as Belmonte inquires whether he may have a word with Pedrillo, now a gardener in the Pasha's service. This meets with a stream of abuse of that young man and Belmonte is finally chased off by the surly overseer. Pedrillo enters. Osmin dislikes him because he sneaks about after the women. In a tremendous comic aria Osmin threatens to outwit him and have him condemned to fearful punishment. He withdraws into the house as Belmonte returns. He and Pedrillo greet each other joyfully. Belmonte speaks of a ship waiting to assist the prisoners to escape, but Pedrillo warns him that things must be handled carefully. Pedrillo goes to meet the Pasha on his return home. Belmonte expresses his anxious love, in an aria. He hides as the Pasha disembarks with Constanze from a pleasure-craft and is hailed by his janissaries in a "Turkish" chorus. The Pasha asks her why she cannot love him despite his gentle treatment of her; she answers him in a florid aria about her pain at being parted from another and her constancy to him, and goes away. Pedrillo introduces Belmonte as an architect and the Pasha welcomes him into his service before entering the palace. Belmonte and Pedrillo are joined by the suspicious Osmin who tries to drive the former away but, after an amusing trio, they manage to enter the palace together.

ACT II

Garden of the palace. Blonde, Constanze's English maid, sings of the futility of wooing a maiden by surliness. Osmin, the object of her strictures, enters and she teases him and plays on his jealousy of Pedrillo. In a witty duet she refuses obedience while he rails against the folly of Englishmen to allow their women such freedom. When he has gone Constanze discloses the weight of her sadness to Blonde in an accompanied recitative and an aria in the emotional key of G minor. The Pasha enters and warns Constanze that tomorrow she must love him or tortures await her. This provokes from her a declaration of defiance in the coloratura "Martern aller Arten", a full-length concert aria with concertante orchestral parts. When they have left Pedrillo joins Blonde with the great news of Belmonte's arrival and the plan to rescue both women that night. Blonde greets this with a rapturous little aria and rushes away to inform her mistress. Pedrillo, however, is nervous at the task before him and in his aria has some difficulty in screwing up his courage. But he persuades Osmin to overcome his Muslim scruples and taste some wine, during a sprightly duet in praise of Bacchus. By the end of the scene Osmin is quite drunk and is led off to bed. Belmonte can now safely enter and, after an aria of eager anticipation, is reunited with Constanze in the first section of the quartet. But then the two men ask in their different ways whether their women have stayed faithful; Blonde replies in soubrette fashion, by boxing Pedrillo's ears; Constanze weeps. Both men seek forgiveness, which is at first withheld, and when given leads to a final section in which all four vow never to be suspicious again.

ACT III

Outside the palace. Midnight. Belmonte has yet another soliloquizing aria about the power of love. Helped by the ship's captain Pedrillo arranges the ladders for the escape and nervously checks that all is ready. To give the signal he sings an enchanting ballad (with pizzicato accompaniment) describing just such an escape as they plan "in a Moorish land"— this touch of romance is unique in Mozart's operas. Constanze appears at the window; Belmonte enters and carries her off. But while Pedrillo climbs up to rescue Blonde the dazed Osmin arrives on the scene, summoned by a deaf-mute guard. When other guards bring in Constanze and Belmonte, whom they have intercepted, he at last takes the situation in and, refusing a bribe, breaks into a great aria in which he gloats over the prospect of his revenge. The Pasha now arrives on the scene (unless it has been moved to his apartment) and is told by Osmin what has been happening. When the prisoners are brought before him, Constanze pleads love as her justification; and Belmonte promises that his noble Spanish father will pay a handsome ransom. But the father turns out to be the Pasha's bitterest foe and he goes off with Osmin, threatening tortures. Left alone Constanze and Belmonte, in an accompanied recitative and two-part duet, resolve to die together. But the Pasha returning, announces that he scorns to behave as Belmonte's father had behaved to him and declares, to Osmin's chagrin, that all four are free to return to Spain. The finale takes the form of a vaudeville, in which a simple melody of gratitude to the Pasha for his magnanimity is sung by each of the four in turn and repeated by the chorus. It is given, in the middle, a new turn by Osmin, whose anger diverts the melody into a reprise of the last part of his big Act I aria before he makes a comic exit, and is followed by a brief "Turkish" chorus in praise of the Pasha.

Eugene Onegin

Lyric scenes in three acts. Music by P. I. Tchaikovsky. Libretto by the composer and K. S. Shilovsky after A. S. Pushkin. First produced at the Imperial College of Music, Moscow, March 29th, 1879.

SCENE: A Russian country estate and St Petersburg.

TIME: About 1825.

CHARACTERS:

LARINA	*A landed proprietress*	(Mezzo-soprano)
TATIANA	} *Her daughters*	(Soprano)
OLGA		(Contralto)
FILIPIEVNA	*An elderly retainer*	(Mezzo-soprano)
LENSKI	*Olga's fiancé*	(Tenor)
EUGENE ONEGIN	*His friend*	(Baritone)
PRINCE GREMIN		(Bass)
SARETSKI		(Bass)
MONSIEUR TRIQUET	*A Frenchman*	(Tenor)

For all its two big scenes this opera has a delicate chamber quality and the first two acts breathe the fragrant atmosphere of Russian country life of the period. The composer has successfully caught the Byronic mood of Pushkin's poem. Despite, however, the opera's slightly episodic construction the central subject here is Tatiana's heart. The interplay of the characters is handled in a sensitive naturalistic way, which makes it seem, in a number of respects, a remote ancestor of Strauss's "Arabella".

The unforced charm of the music is poles away from the rhetoric of Tchaikovsky's symphonies and concerti and it is full of tender melody and delicate orchestration. It is written in separate numbers but they are far from formal. Conversation, for instance, sometimes breaks into the solos and the use of dance music as background to the dramatic moments in the two lively, but sharply contrasted party scenes is masterly. The high points are the Letter Scene, Lenski's two arias, and the long duet in the final scene. But the romantic mood established by the introduction is held consistently.

ACT I

There is a short introduction based entirely on a theme associated with Tatiana.

Scene 1. Garden of Larina's house. She and Filipievna are making preserves and exchanging reminiscences while the voices of her two daughters are heard singing a duet in the house. Reapers approach singing. The girls come out, Tatiana dreamy and romantic and lost in a book, Olga revealing her high spirits in a little song. Larina dismisses the reapers with a glass of wine all round. Their neighbour Lenski, Olga's fiancé, arrives with his friend Onegin, whom he presents. The girls are left to entertain the visitors; Tatiana is greatly taken with the sophisticated Onegin. Lenski sings with boyish ardour of his love for Olga, interrupted at first by conversation between the other two who wander off before the end. Evening falls. Lenski is invited into the house. Tatiana and Onegin cross the stage, the latter talking about his uncle's last illness. Filipievna, who has followed them, notes Tatiana's interest in him.

Scene 2. Tatiana's bedroom. She is preparing for bed but first encourages Filipievna to talk about her youth and finally confesses that her sleeplessness is due to love. (Many repetitions of a motive associated with her romantic outlook.) Left alone she begins to write (over delicate wind and harp phrases in which the oboe leads) a naive and increasingly indiscreet letter, to music of rising passion. (The lovely Letter Scene is the core of the whole work.) When she has finished it is dawn and a shepherd's pipe is audible. Filipievna comes to call her and is persuaded to send her son to Onegin with the letter. The scene ends softly after the orchestra has recalled a phrase from the Letter Scene.

Scene 3. Another part of the garden. Girls gathering berries sing a country song. Tatiana, in agitation, hears Onegin's step. He tells her kindly but frankly that he is not a marrying man and adds the advice that she should learn to control her feelings. The chorus is heard in the distance as he leads her away.

ACT II

Scene 1. Salon in Larina's house. In the Prelude a haunting phrase from the Letter Scene, reiterated on the cello, gives way to a waltz and the curtain rises to disclose Tatiana's birthday dance in full swing. Onegin overhears some spiteful remarks about himself from some of the country ladies and is provoked into paying back Lenski for bringing him to such a party by dancing too much with Olga. After the waltz Lenski shows his jealousy to Olga, who is nettled. Everyone then gathers round M. Triquet, the French tutor, who sings a charming couplet in Tatiana's honour. The cotillon begins (a mazurka), Onegin again dancing with Olga. A quarrel breaks out between him and Lenski who insults him. Onegin is still calm. People stop dancing and gather round. A beautiful phrase of Lenski, against which Onegin voices his rancour, leads into a big ensemble, at the end of which Onegin accepts Lenski's challenge to a duel the next morning. They rush upon each other, are separated, and leave. Olga falls fainting. *Scene 2.* A mill by a wooded stream. Wintry dawn. While Lenski and his second, Saretski, await Onegin, Lenski sings a superb aria in a minor key, in which he takes leave of youth and love. Onegin arrives with only his servant as second. As the two men face each other, they sing a passage in canon, asking whether even now it would not be more sensible to resume their friendship. The parts come together in a threefold "No". Onegin fires first and Lenski falls dead.

ACT III

Scene 1. A ball in a fashionable house in St Petersburg. A polonaise is being danced. Onegin has just returned from many years of aimless foreign travel, haunted by the memory of the duel. Another dance begins. Prince Gremin and his wife, Tatiana, enter and guests comment on Tatiana's beauty. Against a slow waltz in the orchestra Tatiana inquires from those near her Onegin's identity and Onegin seeks confirmation from the Prince that it is Tatiana—his wife, the Prince adds, for the last two years. He tells Onegin what marriage to Tatiana has meant to him in a familiar if slightly pompous bass aria. The Prince presents Onegin to his wife (phrase from Letter Scene) and she manages to exchange a few conventional phrases before excusing herself. Onegin has fallen in love with her and expresses his feelings in the melody which introduced the Letter Scene. The dance is resumed.
Scene 2. Reception room in Prince Gremin's house. Tatiana has just received a letter from Onegin and awaits him with trepidation. On his arrival he falls at her feet but she makes him get up and at first reminds him coolly of the encounter in the garden and suggests that it is her high position which attracts him now. (The melody here is reminiscent of Gremin's aria.) But his ardour soon reduces her to tears and she admits that she still loves him though she is determined to be faithful to her husband. He continues to plead with her and she feels herself weakening but at last finds the courage to dismiss him. Onegin rushes out distraught.

Falstaff

Lyric comedy in three acts. Music by G. Verdi. Libretto by A. Boito after W. Shakespeare. First produced at La Scala, Milan, February 9th, 1893.

SCENE: Windsor.

TIME: Early fifteenth century.

CHARACTERS:

SIR JOHN FALSTAFF	(Bass-baritone)
FORD *A wealthy citizen*	(Baritone)
MISTRESS ALICE FORD *His wife*	(Soprano)
FENTON	(Tenor)
DR CAIUS	(Tenor)
BARDOLPH } *Followers of*	(Tenor)
PISTOL } *Falstaff*	(Bass)
MISTRESS MEG PAGE	(Mezzo-soprano)
NANETTA *Ford's daughter*	(Soprano)
MISTRESS QUICKLY	(Contralto)

"Falstaff" is one of the miracles of musical history. At the age of 80 Verdi produced for the first time a comedy opera, based on the "Merry Wives of Windsor" but with the inclusion of some of the best Falstaff passages from "King Henry IV", with music of light texture, full of wit, sparkle, subtlety, and refinement and moving at such pace as to amount to a series of melodious epigrams. The English atmosphere is caught (especially in the love music between Fenton and Nanetta with its fresh touch) and justice is done to the personality of Falstaff. In places Verdi even parodies his own style—the reading of the letter in Act I or Ford's jealousy monologue. But what especially distinguishes Verdi's last opera from all its predecessors and has made it something of a seminal work for twentieth century composers, is that while the music is all in one piece and while it reflects every nuance of the dialogue and action, the vocal line, for all the brilliance of the orchestral writing, remains Italian throughout, in the sense that it is both cantabile and readily audible. "Falstaff" demonstrated the possibility of a synthesis between the Italian nineteenth century style and the more intellectual approach of the Wagnerians to the dramatic material.

ACT I

Scene 1. Interior of the Garter Inn. Dr Caius is complaining that Bardolph and Pistol have robbed him; after Falstaff has recommended him not to get drunk in such company, he goes off. Falstaff lacks money to pay his bill; Bardolph's nose saves him money on oil for his lantern but it all goes on wine for him. He himself is losing weight as a result. He has written love-letters to Mrs Ford and Mrs Page, which Bardolph and Pistol are to deliver. When they boggle at this he sends a page instead. He asks Bardolph and Pistol, in a witty monologue, what right such scoundrels have to talk of honour and sends them packing.

Scene 2. Garden of Ford's house. Alice and Meg, with whom are Nanetta and Mistress Quickly, excitedly show each other their letters from Falstaff and find them, amid laughter, to be identical. The four plot an ambush to pay him out. Meanwhile Ford, who is walking with Dr Caius, is told by Bardolph and Pistol of Falstaff's intentions and they plan that Ford shall visit him in disguise. In the midst of all this young Fenton and Nanetta twice contrive to be alone for a little flirtation, each time ending with the same memorable phrase. Finally there is a nonet in which the two groups of scheming men and women singing in different staccato rhythms are combined with Fenton dreaming of his love. Before they disperse the two wives read the letters again amid fresh peals of laughter.

ACT II

Scene 1. As in Act I Scene 1. Bardolph and Pistol have returned, with beating of breasts, to Falstaff's service. Mistress Quickly, with many curtsies to a repeated cadence, comes in with a message—that Alice, who is deeply in love with him, can always receive him between two and three; Meg's husband is rarely away. When she has withdrawn, with a tip, Falstaff, delighted, exults, in a little march, in his attraction for women. Ford then visits him under the name of Brook, and confides in him that he is in love with Alice but can make no impression on her. He asks Falstaff to win her for him and gives him money. Falstaff, after listening sympathetically, with playful extracts from a madrigal on love, undertakes the commission and reveals that he already has a rendezvous for which he retires to adorn himself—after saying what he thinks of Alice's husband. Left alone, Ford, in a superb monologue, works himself up into a paroxism of jealousy. Then as Falstaff emerges the music suddenly relaxes into geniality. After each trying to give way to the other the two men leave arm in arm and the orchestra play again the gleeful bars which had introduced the exultant march.

Scene 2. A room in Ford's house. Mistress Quickly reports to Alice and Meg on her interview with Falstaff; he will be calling very shortly. A tearful Nanetta tells her mother that her father wants to marry her to Dr Caius; the other women promise to thwart this. They arrange the room for Falstaff's reception. All hide except Alice who begins to play her lute. Falstaff arrives and makes ardent protestations of love to her, replying to her reference to his fatness with a charming little song about his slender figure when he was the Duke of Norfolk's page. Mistress Quickly bustles in to announce the approach of Ford in high dudgeon. Falstaff is hidden behind a screen just before Ford arrives with Dr Caius, Bardolph, Pistol, and others, and conducts a thorough search, looking even in a large linen basket. They continue their search in other parts of the house and meanwhile Falstaff is bundled into the basket. Fenton and Nanetta take advantage of the general confusion to flirt again behind the screen and, when Ford and his party return and hear the sound of kissing, after elaborate preparations they throw down the screen, only to reveal the young lovers. When all the men have rushed out once again Alice tells her servants to throw the basket out of the window into the Thames. The orchestra underlines their difficulty in lifting it and there is a delicious bassoon trill as it balances on the sill before toppling over.

ACT III

Scene 1. Outside the Garter Inn. Sunset. The scene is introduced by a short Prelude based on a staccato theme which preceded Ford's arrival in the previous scene. Falstaff is seated, gloomily reflecting on the state of the world; the little march reappears in the minor. A large glass of wine restores his spirits (trills in the orchestra). Mistress Quickly arrives and persuades him (to the satisfaction of the others concealed nearby) to read a letter from Alice offering a rendezvous at midnight at Herne's Oak in the Park, when he is to appear disguised as the Black Hunter who hung himself from the oak and so left the place haunted. Falstaff withdraws with her into the inn to discuss the proposal. The others (including the men this time) arrange details of the new plot. When they have gone Ford and Dr Caius arrange for Nanetta's betrothal to the latter that night, but are overheard by Mistress Quickly. The scene ends pianissimo with the stage empty.
Scene 2. Herne's Oak in Windsor Park. Night. Fenton sings a tender invitation to love and is answered by Nanetta with the refrain from their Act I Scene 2 flirtation. They are joined by the other three women. All assume disguises and withdraw. Falstaff enters, wearing a pair of antlers on his head, just as midnight strikes. Alice comes to him for a moment but disappears when a cry is heard. Nanetta, dressed as Queen of the Fairies, summons her band and they dance round the recumbent Falstaff. The other men and women enter with followers, all in fantastic disguises. They all belabour and abuse the terrified Falstaff in a scherzoso passage. At last Falstaff recognizes Bardolph's red nose and greets Ford as Brook, only to be introduced by

Alice to her husband. All unmask and Falstaff recovers his composure somewhat. Ford announces a masked betrothal of the Queen of the Fairies and thinks that he is giving Nanetta to Dr Caius; he consents to another masked couple taking part. But it turns out that the Queen of the Fairies is now Bardolph and the second couple are Nanetta and Fenton. The laugh is now against Ford and Falstaff rubs it in with a phrase from Act II Scene 1. Ford gives his blessing to the young couple and proposes supper. But Falstaff steps forward and leads the whole cast in an enormous fugue on the words: "All the world's a jest. Man is born a jester." And so, like Mozart in *Don Giovanni* before him and Stravinsky and others after him, Verdi finds the satisfying end to a swiftly moving comedy in a formal address to the audience.

Faust

Opera in five acts. Music by C. F. Gounod. Libretto by J. Barbier and M. Carré after J. W. von Goethe. First produced at the Théâtre Lyrique, Paris, March 19th, 1859.

SCENE: Germany.

TIME: About 1500.

CHARACTERS:

FAUST *A learned doctor*	(Tenor)
MEPHISTOPHÉLÈS	(Bass)
MARGUERITE	(Soprano)
VALENTIN *Her brother*	(Baritone)
MARTHA *Her neighbour*	(Mezzo-soprano)
SIEBEL *Her lover*	(Mezzo-soprano)
WAGNER *A student*	(Baritone)

Gounod's "Faust" concentrates on the Margarethe episode but reduces Goethe to the stature of a novelette, while the music, which exudes a strong mid-Victorian atmosphere, makes little serious attempt to reflect action or character (apart from Mephistophélès, the only credible stage personality). Its continued popularity derives from an abundance of attractive melody and the great "basso cantante" rôle in which Edouard de Reszke and Plancon (and later Chaliapin) at their finest contributed to a legend which looks like continuing indefinitely. The soprano and tenor rôles also long attracted the greatest singers.

The Introduction begins in rather academic style, with a hint of a fugato, but suddenly breaks into the melody of Valentin's Act II cavatina.

ACT I

Faust's study. Dawn. He sits wearily at his desk. He thinks of his youth (oboe solo) and is ready to seek death. At the sound of passing girls he thinks vainly of spring (to the oboe melody). Before he can drain the poison before him he hears reapers greeting the new day. He curses his lot and calls on Satan. Mephistophélès promptly appears and inquires what is his pleasure. He asks for youth (to the same melody). Mephistophélès promises it to him; in return, Faust is to be his "là bas". As Faust hesitates he is shown a vision of Marguerite at her spinning-wheel and at once signs the contract. He drains a goblet and is transformed into a young man. The melody becomes a duet before they go off in eager pursuit of the young woman.

ACT II

Outside the city gates. Young and old, soldiers, and students are enjoying the fair in their several fashions, reflected in the different verses of the "Grand Chorus". Valentin, departing for the wars, commends his sister to the care of Siebel and sings the famous cavatina of farewell, composed for the singer Santley for the London première. Wagner starts the "Song of the Rat" but is interrupted by Mephistophélès who sings instead about the Golden Calf, which the company find rather odd. After prophesying ill fortune for Wagner and Siebel, at whose touch every flower will wither, he strikes the head of Bacchus on the sign of the nearby inn and wine gushes out. He drinks to the health of Marguerite to the annoyance of Valentin who draws his sword. But Mephistophélès draws a magic circle round himself and the blade breaks. When, however, they make the sign of the cross, he can only slink away. Faust is eager to be shown Marguerite and has no eyes for the girls in the crowd that begins to dance the familiar waltz. When Marguerite appears Mephistophélès contrives to keep Siebel away from her while Faust boldly offers her his arm which she declines with proper modesty. The waltz is resumed.

ACT III

The garden of Marguerite's cottage. Siebel sings of the message which flowers are to carry to her. But when he picks them they wither, until he dips his fingers into holy water, after which he is able to complete his song and leave a nosegay outside the door. Meanwhile Faust and Mephistophélès have entered (to a snatch of Faust's Act I melody). Mephistophélès goes off to get a more handsome present, leaving Faust to sing the familiar cavatina in which he praises the simple purity of the maiden living in so modest a dwelling. Mephistophélès returns with a casket of jewels which he places beside the nosegay. The two withdraw and Marguerite comes out and sings the ballad of the King of Thule at her spinning-wheel while between the verses her thoughts stray to the handsome stranger. When she enters the house she passes over the nosegay but cannot resist adorning herself in the jewels—the Jewel song. Martha, entering, encourages her to regard them as for herself. Mephistophélès, emerging with Faust, tells Martha brusquely that her husband is dead but soon suppressing his distaste for her flatters her into thinking of himself as a substitute. Meanwhile Marguerite has been confiding in Faust her grief at the death of her little sister. (The two couples in the quartet which occurs at this point must be kept well separated.) Eventually Mephistophélès takes Martha off after invoking the perfumed night to do its work. Faust and Marguerite are left alone and after she has played "he loves me; he loves me not" with a flower and received the right answer, they declare their love to each other, and arrange to meet again the next day. At the end of this love duet Mephistophélès returns and directs Faust's attention to the open window where Marguerite is seen and heard in a state of rapture. Mephistophélès mocks them.

ACT IV

Scene 1. In Marguerite's room. The voices of girls mocking the deserted Marguerite are heard. Siebel comes quietly in and offers to avenge her, but she says that she still loves Faust. Siebel consoles her and promises a brother's love. Marguerite gratefully tells him that she is going to church to pray for Faust and their child.

Scene 2. In church. The organ is heard as Marguerite enters. She tries to pray but Mephistophélès whispers in her ear of her guilt and eternal damnation. The choir is heard singing the "Dies irae". She sings with them, praying for grace but Mephistophélès calls out that she is damned and she flees in terror.

Scene 3. The street before Marguerite's house. Soldiers return singing the well-known chorus during which Siebel tells Valentin that his sister is in church. "Praying for me" comments Valentin. After the chorus Siebel hints to him that all is not well. Mephistophélès and Faust now appear. Faust wishes to enter the house. Mephistophélès sings to a guitar a mocking serenade—one of the best-known numbers—warning against kisses till the ring is on the finger. Valentin, having discovered the truth, comes out of the house, enraged by the insult to his sister. After a trio, during which he throws away the medallion given him before the war by Marguerite, he draws on Faust whose sword, guided by Mephistophélès, mortally wounds him. The two of them escape while Martha and a crowd of neighbours rush out to help. But Valentin tells them, in a descending chromatic phrase which seems to remember the Commendatore's death in *Don Giovanni* that they are too late. When Marguerite appears he tells them all that he has been killed by her lover, curses her amid general consternation, and dies. The orchestra comment softly in a phrase reminiscent of the composer's "Ave Maria".

ACT V[1]

In prison. Mephistophélès conducts Faust to visit Marguerite, condemned to death for the murder of her child. She greets him with rapture; but her mind (and the music) wander back to the waltz and the conversation that marked their first meeting and she is reluctant to escape. She shrinks from Mephistophélès who exhorts them to hurry. In a soaring phrase she calls on the angels above to take her to their bosom while the two male voices continue to urge her departure. Finally she shrinks in horror from Faust's blood-stained hands and Mephistophélès exclaims "She is condemned." But the prison wall opens and she is carried upward amid the chanting of a heavenly choir promising peace and happiness.

---

[1] For the Paris Opera Gounod wrote a suite of wildly unsuitable dances which accompany the Walpurgis Night revels from Part II of Goethe's "Faust". This scene is usually omitted.

Fidelio

Opera in two acts. Music by L. van Beethoven. Libretto by J. F. Sonnleithner after J. N. Bouilly; later revised by G. F. Treitschke. First produced at the Theater an der Wien, Vienna, November 20th, 1805. (Final version at the Theater am Kärnthnertor, Vienna, May 23rd, 1814).

SCENE: A fortress near Seville.

TIME: Eighteenth century.

PRINCIPAL CHARACTERS:

FLORESTAN *A Spanish nobleman*		(Tenor)
LEONORA *His wife, in disguise as Fidelio*		(Soprano)
ROCCO *The jailer*		(Bass)
MARCELLINA *His daughter*		(Soprano)
JACQUINO *The turnkey*		(Tenor)
DON PIZARRO *Governor of the Fortress*		(Bass-baritone)
DON FERNANDO *The Minister*		(Bass)

In this country Beethoven's only opera occupied until recently a less exalted pinnacle of public esteem than in Central Europe, perhaps because its political message, which the music underlines with passionate sincerity, was less immediately felt. A public less habituated to opera may also have been disconcerted by the changes of "gear" within it—it is not only "opéra comique" i.e., with spoken dialogue, but Act I wavers uncertainly in style. Act II however, consistently exhibits Beethoven's grandest manner.

The original version entitled "Leonora" was in three Acts and preceded by the Overture now known as "Leonora No 2". The final version is in two Acts and for it Beethoven wrote the Overture of great beauty, but lighter weight, known as "Fidelio". The Overture known as "Leonora No 3" is not infrequently played between the two final scenes—a dubious practice which helps the producer and offers the conductor an opportunity but which unbalances matters in a number of ways as well as recapitulating needlessly.

ACT I

Scene 1. A room in Rocco's quarters. As Marcellina works, Jacquino presses in vain for a definite answer to his suit, in a duet of rather conventional cut. Left alone she reveals that her heart has been captured by Fidelio, a young assistant of her father (who is really Leonora, the disguised wife of Florestan, searching for her husband). Her father comes in followed by Leonora whom she helps to relieve of her burden. Rocco notices what he takes to be their mutual affection, as does Jacquino who has returned. The action is held up while all four soliloquize in a quartet in canon in which the musical tension is suddenly raised, only to fall again when Rocco follows it with an aria about the need of married couples for money. He leads Leonora to suspect that her husband is one of the political prisoners in the fortress and this overcomes her hesitation at the dangerous part she has set herself. The scene ends with a trio between Leonora, Marcellina, and Rocco, each busy with private thoughts. *Scene 2.* On the ramparts. Pizarro learns from dispatches that the Minister will shortly be visiting the fortress. In a splendid villain's aria he therefore determines to do away with his enemy, Florestan, at once. A trumpeter on the ramparts is to blow a signal when the Minister is sighted. He gives Rocco money and bids him do away with the starving prisoner in the deepest dungeon. When Rocco protests he tells him to dig a grave and he will do the deed himself. Leonora has overheard all this. In a great scena (in which the horns figure prominently) she sings of her determination and hope, even now, to save her husband. She persuades Rocco to release the prisoners for air, in the hope of recognizing Florestan. Preceded by a shy phrase on the bassoon, the prisoners file slowly out, welcoming freedom and fresh air in a chorus which is one of the high points of the opera. Rocco tells Leonora that Pizarro has given permission for his daughter's marriage and for Rocco to have "his" help; they must go at once to the dungeons. He explains that they must dig a grave for "that poor wretch". When Leonora weeps Rocco says he will go alone; but Leonora insists on accompanying him. Marcellina enters and announces that Pizarro is in a great rage that the prisoners have been let out. Pizarro follows her and Rocco tries to calm him by saying that he has done it to celebrate the king's birthday. Pizarro orders the prisoners back to their cells and, as they slowly return, a big finale is built up over their chorus. The Act ends softly after a long diminuendo as they disappear within.

ACT II

Scene 1. Florestan's dungeon. A magnificently sombre introduction leads direct into a recitative for Florestan which begins with the cry "God, how dark 'tis here" and is followed by an aria (the opening strain of which occurs in the Leonora No 3 overture) in which he finds consolation by imagining Leonora leading him to freedom. He falls asleep as Rocco and Leonora descend. They dig, Leonora trying the while to observe the prisoner's features. (Her phrases soar above the gloomy mutterings of Rocco and the orchestra.) In the following trio Leonora extracts from Rocco permission to give bread to the prisoner who is touchingly grateful. Pizarro arrives, reveals his identity to Florestan and is about to stab him when Leonora interposes herself with the cry "First kill his wife". After a stunned moment Pizarro advances again on Florestan but Leonora threatens him with a pistol. At that moment a distant trumpet is heard (playing the fanfare in the overture Leonora No 3) and the baffled Pizarro makes off. (All this in a splendid quartet.) Husband and wife are reunited in a swiftly moving duet expressing their unutterable joy.

Scene 2. As in Act I Scene 2. Prisoners and others hail the day of liberation. In noble phrases Don Fernando, the Minister, announces his mission—to put an end to tyranny and to unite brother with brother. Rocco appears with Leonora and Florestan, still in chains, and outlines what has happened. Fernando recognizes his old friend whom he had thought dead; Marcellina is overcome to see the identity of her beloved; Pizarro is taken into captivity. The Minister entrusts Leonora with the task of undoing her husband's fetters. A moving oboe phrase ushers in a short, sostenuto passage of great beauty in which all murmur their thanks to God. The opera ends with a chorus of praise for Leonora. (We, or the producer, are left to decide whether Marcellina settles for Jacquino.)

Die Fledermaus

(The Bat). Operetta in three acts. Music by Johann Strauss II. Libretto by C. Haffner and R. Genée after H. Meilhac and L. Halévy. First produced at the Theater an der Wien, Vienna, April 5th, 1874.

SCENE: Vienna.

TIME: About 1870.

CHARACTERS:

GABRIEL VON EISENSTEIN	(Tenor)
ROSALINDE *His wife*	(Soprano)
ADELE *Their maid*	(Soprano)
ALFRED *A singer*	(Tenor)
DR FALKE *A friend of Eisenstein*	(Baritone)
DR BLIND *His lawyer*	(Tenor)
FRANK *A prison governor*	(Baritone)
PRINCE ORLOFSKY	(Contralto)
FROSCH *The gaoler*	(Speaking part)

This is by general consent the quintessential operetta of the legendary Vienna of "wine, woman, and song". It holds that position not only by virtue of a witty book and an unbroken stream of delicious melody; its music is a good deal more ambitious than most pieces in this genre. The structure of many numbers is often asymmetrical, is relatively complex, and goes far beyond the conventional verse and refrain. Indeed much of the action is carried on through and during the music with an almost Mozartian freedom. The orchestration is sparkling and the voice parts are exacting—especially for the three women—and cannot be adequately performed by other than experienced opera singers though it goes without saying that they also need a light touch and the Viennese brand of charm. The role of the wealthy young Orlofsky, however, though traditionally assigned to a leading contralto was successfully entrusted by Max Reinhardt to an actor with a light voice.

The Overture is a potpourri of melodies from the operetta, the famous waltz being heard early and again at the end.

ACT I

A room in Eisenstein's house. Alfred is outside the window serenading his old flame Rosalinde. He disappears as Adele enters with a cadenza of laughter and, against a violin melody, reads a letter from her ballerina sister Ida, suggesting that Adele come with her to the party to be given that night by Prince Orlofsky. She doubts if she will be allowed the evening off and when she asks Rosalinde, who has recognized Alfred's voice as she comes in, for leave to visit her sick aunt, she is reminded that Eisenstein begins his five-day prison sentence for assaulting a policeman that evening, and curtly refused. She goes off in tears. Alfred enters and extracts a promise to be allowed to visit Rosalinde while her husband is in gaol. He leaves hurriedly as the latter arrives quarrelling with Blind who, far from getting his sentence deferred, has only succeeded in having it increased to eight days. Blind rattles off technical terms about his further plans before, at the end of an amusing trio, being kicked out. Falke arrives and while Rosalinde is out of the room, gives Eisenstein an invitation to the Orlofsky ball and persuades him, in the course of a duet, that it will suffice if he reports at the prison after the ball, to which he is to go as the Marquis Renard—without telling his wife. When she returns she is momentarily puzzled at Eisenstein's gay manner and proposal to go to prison dressed in style. Eagerly looking forward to Alfred's visit she gives Adele leave to go out after all. She says a sad goodbye to her husband, the gay refrain of which (he and Adele joining in) belies the tearful words. Alfred at once enters through the window, makes himself at home and, while pressing Rosalinde to drink, in a charming song, does most of the drinking himself. They are interrupted by Frank, who coming to take Eisenstein to prison assumes Alfred to be he. When Alfred attempts to deny it, Rosalinde silences him and affects to resent any suggestion that she has been caught in a compromising situation. Alfred is allowed to give her a parting kiss before being bustled off to prison.

ACT II

Prince Orlofsky's mansion. The ball is in progress and the chorus testify to its delights. The blasé host is promised by Falke a "little dramatic entertainment" entitled The Bat's Revenge. The first character is Adele whom he introduces, with her sister, as Miss Olga. When she has gone he explains her real identity just as Eisenstein, masquerading as the Marquis Renard, is seen. Falke dashes off to send Rosalinde an invitation while Orlofsky explains to Eisenstein, in couplets, his eccentric ideas of hospitality. Adele reappears and is recognized by Eisenstein. She is indignant at being mistaken for his maid and reproaches him ironically, in a song full of laughter. Frank arrives, disguised as the Chevalier

Chagrin though he cannot speak French, followed by Rosalinde, masked, and posing as a Hungarian countess. She is surprised to see her husband flirting with her maid. Introduced to the "Marquis Renard" she plays up and dutifully admires his repeater watch, of the effect of which on ladies he is very confident. In a flirtatious duet he tries its effect on her but she contrives to take it from him and, amid peals of laughter, refuses to give it back. Ida and Adele try to get her to unmask, sceptical whether she is really Hungarian. This provokes her to sing an elaborate and poetical Csárdás. Orlofsky tries to get Falke to tell the story of "the Bat" but Eisenstein anticipates him, telling how three years earlier, after Falke had been to a fancy-dress ball as a bat and had too much to drink, he had left him asleep in a square from which he had to walk home in broad daylight next day. Falke has not managed to take his revenge. The Finale now begins with verses in praise of King Champagne and everyone becomes rather maudlin. Falke, in a beautiful mock-serious passage, proposes a toast to Universal Brotherhood where all are "Du" to each other and the guests echo this to the refrain "Duidu". A ballet is danced for the entertainment of the guests—usually the *Blue Danube* or another famous Strauss waltz. The guests themselves then dance to the *Fledermaus* waltz which continues almost to the end of the Act. After a further attempt by Eisenstein to get the Countess to unmask six o'clock strikes and both Eisenstein and Frank feel obliged to hurry off to the prison, going together to the corner of the street.

ACT III

The Governor's room at the prison. After a short entr'acte we see the drunken Frosch and hear Alfred singing in his cell. Frosch, after comic business, goes off to attend to him. Frank staggers in to distorted orchestral reminiscences of music from Act II, imagines that he is still at the ball and finally falls asleep, to be awakened by the returning Frosch. The bell rings. It is Ida and Adele in pursuit of the Chevalier Chagrin. Adele reveals her identity but hopes that the Chevalier can help her go on the stage. She demonstrates her dramatic talent in elaborate couplets. Frosch leads them away as Eisenstein arrives to start his prison sentence. Frank does not believe that he is Eisenstein, whom he had arrested last night after he had taken a tender farewell of his wife. Blind, summoned by Alfred, turns up. Eisenstein seizes his wig, puts it on and bundles him out just as Frosch brings in Alfred and Rosalinde arrives to try and get him out before her husband arrives. In the trio which follows, Eisenstein, pretending to be Blind and to be advising them, extorts a full confession from each and can scarcely restrain his anger. But Rosalinde baffles them by saying that her husband spent the previous night with young ladies and that she will seek a divorce. In a passage of parody

Eisenstein reveals himself and promises himself revenge, but Rosalinde says that it is she who must be avenged. She explains her meaning by producing Eisenstein's watch. Falke arrives with Frank, just in time to claim that the whole comedy is the Bat's Revenge. The remainder of the company make a timely entry for the Finale in which everything is cleared up, husband and wife are reunited, and Orlofsky, as patron of the arts, takes Adele under his wing. They decide to blame everything on the champagne and the operetta ends with a reprise of the Champagne song.

The Flying Dutchman

(Der Fliegende Holländer). Opera in three acts. Music by R. Wagner. Libretto by the composer after H. Heine. First produced at the Court Opera, Dresden, January 2nd, 1843.

SCENE: The Norwegian Coast.

TIME: Not specified.

CHARACTERS:

THE DUTCHMAN	(Bass-baritone)
DALAND *A Norwegian sea-captain*	(Bass)
SENTA *His daughter*	(Soprano)
MARY *Her nurse*	(Contralto)
ERIK *A forester*	(Tenor)
A HELMSMAN *(on Daland's ship)*	(Tenor)

Wagner's earliest opera in the repertory is based on the legend of the Dutch captain who, having defied Satan to prevent him rounding the Cape in a storm, was condemned to sail the seas for ever, unless redeemed by a woman's devotion, landing briefly every seven years. It is still romantic opera divided into the customary set-pieces linked by free recitative. But Wagner is already bursting out of this frame. The weight of his style, with the graphic representation of wild seascapes and its leading motives, albeit few and stiffly used, tends to be too great. Where the music remains conventional in shape, it is sometimes uninspired. The Overture, the Dutchman's monologue in Act I, Senta's ballad in Act II, and the choruses of Act III are its high points.

The Overture, a tone-poem of a stormy sea, introduces the more important motives, notably those of the curse, the Dutchman himself, and of redemption.

ACT I

A wild bay. A storm rages. Daland's ship has just put in seven miles from his home and waiting daughter. He leaves the Helmsman on watch; the latter (prototype of the helmsmen in *Tristan and Isolde* and *Les Troyens*) sings a ballad and falls asleep. The Dutchman's ship drops anchor alongside. The Dutchman disembarks and tells in a powerful recitative and aria that he has completed another seven years of his sentence, which can end only with a woman's love or the Last Judgment. Daland comes on deck. In a long duet, the Dutchman, after describing his wanderings, craves hospitality and offers some of his treasure. Finding that Daland has a daughter he asks for her hand. Daland, overcome by cupidity, consents. By now the storm has subsided. Daland's ship sails for home, with the Dutchman's following.

ACT II

A room in Daland's house. Girls are spinning under Mary's supervision (singing in chorus), but Senta sits aloof, gazing at a portrait of the Flying Dutchman. She sings the ballad of the Flying Dutchman but is so carried away that she ends by declaring that she will be the woman to save him, to the consternation of the girls and of Erik who has come to say that Daland has been sighted. Alone with her Erik speaks passionately of his love; but Senta declares that the portrait has captured all her sympathy. In despair Erik warns Senta, who sits in a trance, of a dream in which he had seen a dark stranger arrive in a ship with her father, and, after being greeted by her, sail away with her. This dream deeply affects Senta and Erik leaves in dismay. When Daland and the Dutchman arrive, Senta is transfixed at the sight of the latter. (Moving thirds in the orchestra.) After introducing the Dutchman as a wealthy suitor, Daland leaves them alone. In a long duet, during which leading motives underline the points, Senta rapturously pledges eternal fidelity to the Dutchman. Daland returns to learn the happy tidings.

ACT III

A bay with rocky shore and Daland's house to the side. Daland's ship brightly lit; the Dutchman's alongside, dark and silent. Sailors and girls sing a boisterous chorus; their call to the Dutch sailors to join them is met by silence. Then a storm rages round the Dutchman's ship and its crew sing a chorus mocking their captain's ill luck in love. The Norwegian crowd cross themselves in terror, taunted by the laughter of the Dutch. Senta rushes out of the house, pursued by Erik vainly trying to restrain her. The Dutchman, having overheard, thinks she has abandoned himself, reveals his identity and orders his ship to set sail. Erik summons help as Senta proclaims that she is faithful to the Dutchman. As his ship sails she breaks loose and, crying out from the summit of a rock that she is true unto death, leaps into the sea. The ship sinks but in the glow of the rising sun Senta and the Dutchman are seen ascending to heaven, clasped in an embrace.

The Force of Destiny

(La Forza del Destino). Opera in four acts. Music by G. Verdi. Libretto by F. M. Piave after the Duke of Rivas. First produced at St Petersburg, November 10th, 1862.

SCENE: Spain and near Velletri, Italy.

TIME: Mid-eighteenth century.

PRINCIPAL CHARACTERS:

DONNA LEONORA DI VARGAS		(Soprano)
DON CARLO DI VARGAS *Her brother*		(Baritone)
MARCHESE DI CALATRAVA *Her father*		(Bass)
DON ALVARO *Her lover*		(Tenor)
PADRE GUARDIANO *Father Superior* ⎱ *Franciscan*		(Bass)
FRA MELITONE ⎰ *monks*		(Baritone)
PREZIOSILLA *A gypsy*		(Mezzo-soprano)
CURRA *Leonora's maid*		(Mezzo-soprano)
THE MAYOR OF HORNACHUELOS		(Bass)
TRABUCCO *A muleteer*		(Tenor)

This opera contains some of Verdi's most beautiful "middle period" music and is rich in melodic invention. It is, however, flawed by its undue length, the largely irrelevant nature of some of its most vivid scenes (e.g., the two crowd scenes and that in which Melitone feeds the beggars), and its unconvincing and somewhat incoherent story. It is, for instance, far from clear how Leonora and Alvaro come to be separated after their elopement. But over and above the lovely arias for Leonora and other numbers of great distinction, it is noteworthy as including a full-scale duet for soprano and bass, a florid and strongly characterized part for a low female voice (Preziosilla) and, in Melitone's scene with the beggars, the only passage of comedy in Verdi prior to "Falstaff". A diffuse work containing so many disparate elements calls for particularly tactful production.

The Overture is a more elaborate piece than usual with Verdi and is sometimes heard in the concert-hall. The opening theme, associated with Leonora's fate, permeates most of it, either alone or in combination with melodies to be heard later—*viz.*, one from the tenor/baritone duet in Act IV, one from Leonora's prayer in Act II Scene 2, and one from the soprano/bass duet in the same scene.

ACT I

A room in the Marchese's castle near Seville. The stern Marchese bids good night to Leonora who, as a recitative and aria then show, is emotional at the thought of leaving the home from which she has planned to elope that night. Curra, who is privy to the plan, admits the impatient Alvaro who wishes to leave without delay. She hangs back, until he taunts her with despising his Inca blood. This duet ends with mutual protestations of love. The Marchese enters with sword drawn and threats of the gallows for Alvaro. (The "fate" theme is heard at his entry.) Alvaro gives himself up in proof of Leonora's unsullied honour, but the pistol which he throws at the Marchese's feet goes off and wounds him fatally. He dies, cursing Leonora, who escapes with Alvaro by a window.

ACT II

Scene 1. An inn in the village of Hornachuelos. Villagers dance and feast. Leonora, disguised as a boy, appears for a moment and recognizes her brother disguised as a student. Preziosilla enters and urges the villagers to join up, singing a martial song with a rousing chorus. She tells fortunes and, in an aside, informs the student that she has seen through his disguise. A chorus of pilgrims is heard and when the company joins in their prayers Leonora prays to be saved from her brother. Carlo pesters Trabucco and the Mayor with questions about the stranger, but gets nowhere. Asked in return about himself, he tells, in a ballad, how he is scouring the world for his sister who has eloped with her lover, the son of a slave-mother, after the latter had killed their father, so that he may exact vengeance and restore the family honour. Preziosilla mocks him. After a final dance all withdraw for the night, Preziosilla's mocking laughter prevailing at the end. *Scene 2.* Outside a monastery near the village. Moonlight. Leonora, still in disguise, enters, in fear because her brother has told her story at the inn and Alvaro has left her and returned to his own country. She prays to the Virgin, in an aria which introduces a melody heard in the Overture, and against which monks are heard singing. She rings the bell and the grumbling Melitone fetches the Father Superior. Alone with him, she reveals her identity and confirms that he has been forewarned of her coming. In the long and fine duet which follows she assures him of the sincerity of her penitence and he offers her sanctuary in a lonely cave, disguised as a hermit; he will bring her food himself once a week. In the final section she gives

thanks in the melody which formed the climax of the Overture. They
go into the chapel. Monks file out and the organ is heard, as well as
the melody of Leonora's prayer. Then the Father Superior and Leonora,
in a monk's habit, reappear. In a striking phrase, he pronounces a curse
on any of them who approach the cave where the "erring soul" is to live
in solitude, with a bell for summoning help in direst need. All pray to the
Virgin to watch over the penitent one, Leonora's voice floating over the
male chorus.

ACT III

Scene 1. A wood near Velletri. Dark night. The voices of men playing
cards are heard off-stage. Alvaro enters slowly, in the uniform of a
Spanish captain, and, after a long orchestral introduction, sings an
expressive recitative about his sad upbringing after the execution of his
royal Inca parents, followed by an aria in which he calls on Leonora, whom
he presumes dead, for comfort. A call for help is heard and after the
sound of fighting he returns with Carlo, in the uniform of an aide-de-camp,
whom he has rescued from the gambling gang. Without either revealing
his true identity to the other, they swear eternal friendship in a characteristic
Verdian "oath" passage, all thirds and sixths, as the call to battle is heard.
Scene 2. A small room in a military headquarters from which a surgeon
and soldiers are watching the battle. Alvaro is brought in badly wounded
with Carlo at his side. Alvaro revives a little and sharply disclaims the
suggestion of Carlo that he be given the Star of Calatrava for his bravery.
He asks to be left alone with Carlo, and, assuming the approach of death,
hands him papers which the latter promises to burn unread. A famous
duet follows, after which the surgeon carries Alvaro off. Carlo is
suspicious of the other's reaction to the name of Calatrava but resists the
temptation to read the letters. He feels free to open the case containing
a portrait, which proves to be that of Leonora, thus confirming his
suspicions, just as the surgeon returns to report that Alvaro will live.
Carlo exults at the prospect that Alvaro can yet die at his avenging hands,
and Leonora too, if he can find her.
Scene 3. A military camp near Velletri. Night. A patrol is making the
rounds. As dawn breaks Alvaro, restored to health but still troubled
in mind, is accosted by Carlo who makes it plain that he has discovered
his identity and reveals his own, challenging him to a duel. At first
Alvaro claims friendship and defends himself against Carlo's charges.
When Carlo calls him a liar for declaring Leonora dead he rejoices,
refutes the taunt of being a half-caste and proposes that they seek her
together. But Carlo is relentless and finally provokes him to a fight.
They are separated by the patrol who drag Carlo away, leaving Alvaro
resolved to seek peace in a monastery. The sun now rises and a lively

picture of camp life ensues. Carefree soldiers and vivandières sing; Preziosilla tells fortunes; Trabucco traffics in trinkets; refugees arrive from devastated areas and are comforted; Preziosilla rallies the recruits. The recruits and the vivandières dance a tarantella till Melitone interrupts them with a scolding sermon. Finally they drive him away and Preziosilla leads the whole company, with a drum, in the famous Rataplan chorus, which fills them with martial ardour.

ACT IV

Scene 1. Courtyard of the monastery near Hornachuelos. As the Father Superior paces to and fro reading his breviary, Fra Melitone runs a kind of soup kitchen for a crowd of importunate beggars. Their behaviour and their comparisons of himself with Father Raffaele finally cause him to lose patience, kick the cauldron over and chase them away. The Father Superior reproves him for being jealous of Raffaele. It emerges from discussion that Raffaele is Alvaro in disguise. The bell rings violently. Carlo enters and brusquely asks the ever grumbling Melitone for Raffaele. Alvaro appears dressed as a monk. The ensuing duet takes much the same course, though to wholly different music, as that in Act III Scene 3 and it is only after Carlo has struck Alvaro's cheek that he accepts the former's challenge to a duel, for which they rush off.

Scene 2. A valley between rocks. To the motive of her fate, Leonora emerges from her cave and sings a beautiful prayer in which she reaffirms her love for Alvaro whom she believes dead, and craves peace of mind. Sounds are heard and she hastily withdraws. Alvaro enters, sword in hand, seeking a confessor for Carlo whom he has mortally wounded. Leonora rings the bell for help. But when she appears she and Alvaro recognize each other and Alvaro tells her that the man he has killed is her brother. She rushes off to him but a moment later a cry is heard and the Father Superior reappears, supporting Leonora whom the dying Carlo has fatally wounded. Alvaro curses his fate but, in a moving trio, the Father bids him kneel before God and Leonora assures him that her death will ensure his pardon. She dies in his arms as the curtain falls.

Die Frau ohne Schatten

(The Woman without a Shadow). Opera in three acts. Music by Richard Strauss. Libretto by H. von Hofmannsthal. First produced at Vienna, October 10th, 1919.

SCENE: Legendary.

TIME: Legendary.

PRINCIPAL CHARACTERS:

THE EMPEROR	(Tenor)
THE EMPRESS	(Soprano)
THE NURSE	(Mezzo-soprano)
THE SPIRIT-MESSENGER	(Baritone)
GUARDIAN OF THE TEMPLE GATES	(Soprano or Male alto)
APPARITION OF A YOUTH	(Tenor)
THE VOICE OF THE FALCON	(Soprano)
BARAK *The dyer*	(Bass-baritone)
HIS WIFE	(Soprano)
THE ONE-EYED ⎫	(Bass-baritone)
THE ONE-ARMED ⎬ *His brothers*	(Bass)
THE HUNCHBACK ⎭	(Tenor)

This is the longest and most ambitious of the Strauss-Hofmannsthal series, though difficulties of staging and of following all its symbolism have been an obstacle to widespread popularity. Beneath its fantasy and poetry it is an allegory like "The Magic Flute". Keikobad, the divine purpose, requires us all, higher and ordinary beings alike, to undergo trials until we accept an unselfish involvement in life and especially our duty to reproduce ourselves, symbolized by the possession of a shadow. The central subject is thus the spiritual development of the Empress. The ambivalent figure of the Nurse, like the Queen of the Night, represents the Dark Forces to be overcome.

There is a wide variety in the elaborate music some of which, despite the large orchestra, has a chamber delicacy of timbre. In the scenes involving the Emperor and Empress the score is saturated with the fairy-tale atmosphere created by the imaginative libretto. To the worthy Barak Strauss allocates expressive music of a diatonic, traditional German

cast while his wife is (in the first two acts) depicted in harsh discords.
The visions shown to Barak's wife to tempt her use waltz music. The
many scene-changes are illustrated and covered by quasi-symphonic
development of the main motives in the manner of "The Ring". The
music is everywhere so responsive to the stage-action and dialogue that a
close knowledge of the libretto is particularly desirable: but it broadens
out into a number of lyrical passages of direct appeal such as those
associated with Barak in Act I Scene 2 (especially the final pages);
the whole of Act II Scene 2, with its expressive cello solo and falcon's
cries in the wood-wind; the duet between Barak and his wife early in
Act III; and the Empress's appearance before her father in its Scene 3.
The imposing finale seems to illustrate both in quantity and quality
that "too-muchness" in German music about which Hofmannsthal was to
write to Strauss at a later date.

ACT I

Scene 1. A flat roof above the Imperial Gardens. Night. A messenger from
Keikobad, king of the spirits, tells the crouching Nurse that unless his
daughter, the Empress, casts a shadow within three days, she must return
to him and her husband will be turned to stone. The Emperor emerges
for a hunting expedition but first commends his still sleeping, beloved
Empress to the·Nurse's care. We learn that he had first encountered her
when she crept from the body of a white gazelle which a red falcon had
struck in the eyes. He is looking for the falcon. When he has left, to a
powerful statement of his motive, the Empress comes out. She regrets
that in the intoxication of the first hour of love she lost her power of
transforming herself into an animal. She spies the red falcon but it sadly
proclaims that she casts no shadow (has no child in her womb, as the Nurse
explains) and the Emperor must turn to stone. The Nurse tells her that she
can only get a shadow by descending to the loathsome world of men. She
prevails on the Nurse to escort her to Earth just as the sun rises. An
orchestral Interlude depicts the journey.
Scene 2. Barak's hut. Barak's three brothers are quarrelling. His wife
wants him to throw them out, but the patient Barak has brotherly
feelings towards them still. He would like children too but his shrewish
wife has put such thoughts from her. Barak takes her bitter words calmly
and goes off to market. The Empress and the Nurse, both dressed in humble
clothing, suddenly appear. The Empress could kiss the woman's shadow.
The Nurse shows the woman a vision of herself as she would like to be
and proposes a bargain under which she is to sell her shadow after three
days and put away all thought of motherhood in return for beauty and
rich living; for these three days the Empress and the Nurse will remain
as servants in the house. As Barak is heard returning, his supper

unprepared, the Empress and the Nurse disappear till the morrow. Fish fly through the air and land in the pan. They ask with the voices of children to be allowed into the house. Barak's wife tells him that he must sleep alone where he is; she will have two cousins who are to be her maids sleeping at her feet. Barak bears this blow with resignation and as he settles down to sleep alone, the voices of watchmen are heard praising the holy purpose of wedlock. The scene ends quietly with music associated with Barak's good nature.

ACT II

Scene 1. Barak's hut. When the dyer has gone out the Nurse tempts his wife by producing the phantom of a handsome youth, representing her most secret desires. But almost at once Barak returns, with his brothers and followed by beggar-children, with a splendid meal. His wife refuses to join in the general good cheer and grumbles on.

Scene 2. The Emperor's falcon-house in the forest. His wife has written that she will be alone with the Nurse here for three days; and now his falcon has led him to this very place and she seems not to be there. He hides behind a tree and sees her enter with the Nurse, reeking of Man. In his indignation he thinks at first to kill her but cannot do so and flees.

Scene 3. Barak's hut. His wife and the Nurse impatiently await his departure to market. The Nurse puts a sleeping-draught in his drink and he falls asleep. She conjures up the Young Man; but as she and the Empress are about to leave, Barak's wife takes fright and wakens Barak who is dazed. She reviles him for falling asleep and neglecting her and goes off with the Nurse, threatening one day to leave him for good. The Empress is left alone with Barak picking up his scattered tools.

Scene 4. The Empress's bedroom in the falcon-house. She sleeps restlessly and is haunted by Barak's tormented look. She calls out that she has sinned against him. She hears the falcon's warning and has a vision of the Emperor entering a bronze door in the great cave and slowly turning to stone (minor version of his motive). She calls out in despair that it is all her fault; whatever she touches she kills.

Scene 5. Barak's hut. It is dark and a storm rages. The Empress is resolved to stay on earth and is thankful at having found such a man as Barak. But his wife still nags and tells him that she has been visited by an utter stranger while he was asleep. Moreover she has put away the unborn children from her body and sold her shadow. The flickering fire shows this to be true, and the Nurse tells the Empress that this is her chance to seize the shadow. But the Empress refuses to touch the shadow which has blood on it. And indeed Barak can hardly be restrained from killing his wife even when she denies actually having done what she confessed. But the sword which has appeared in his hand flies out again, the earth opens, and he and his wife are swallowed up while waters pour into the hut.

ACT III

Scene 1. An underground vault with a dividing wall. Barak and his wife on either side are each filled with remorse and yearn for each other. A voice tells each that the road to freedom is now open.

Scene 2. A rocky terrace with a bronze door and steps down to a river flowing beneath. A boat with the Empress and the Nurse moors at the steps. The Nurse wants them to escape but the Empress insists on entering the door and facing her father Keikobad. She dismisses the Nurse who knows too little of men's needs. Barak and his wife are still searching for each other; this only sharpens the Nurse's hatred of mankind. The Messenger comes out of the door and sends her packing.

Scene 3. A hall like a temple. The Empress enters to an expressive violin solo (a diatonic version of her original theme). She stands before a curtained niche and humbly addresses Keikobad. She has learned self-sacrifice and twice refuses to drink the waters which will give her the shadow of Barak's wife, and free the Emperor who is shown her, petrified but for the eyes (in a long crescendo on a single chord) and with whom she is ready to die. But at this supreme moment of renunciation, after her second refusal, she casts a shadow. The·Emperor rises from his throne, restored to life. Amid the singing of unborn children they greet each other ecstatically.

Scene 4. A beautiful landscape. The Emperor and Empress stand above a golden waterfall. Below, Barak and his wife find each other at last and he sees that her shadow has been restored to her. Their unborn children are heard and her shadow becomes a golden bridge on which they are reunited. The two couples, their love tempered by their trials, join with the unseen children's chorus in an elaborate finale of thanksgiving and jubilation.

Der Freischütz

(The Demon Hunter). Opera in three acts. Music by C. M. von Weber. Libretto by J. F. Kind. First produced at the Schauspielhaus, Berlin, June 18th, 1821.

SCENE: Bohemia.

TIME: Mid-eighteenth century.

CHARACTERS:

PRINCE OTTOKAR		(Baritone)
MAX	} *Rangers*	(Tenor)
KASPAR		(Bass-baritone)
KILIAN	*A peasant*	(Baritone or Tenor)
A HERMIT		(Bass)
SAMIEL		(Speaking part)
KUNO	*Head Ranger*	(Baritone)
AGATHE	*Kuno's daughter*	(Soprano)
ÄNNCHEN	*Her cousin*	(Soprano)

This piece is based on an old German tradition that seven unerring bullets may be obtained by selling one's soul to Samiel, the Demon Hunter; redemption can be achieved only by providing another victim for him within the appointed term. It has always been a popular favourite in Germanic countries; Anglo-Saxon audiences tend to find the naiveté of its sentiments and of the spoken dialogue a stumbling-block. There is, however, much charm in its fresh melodies and its feeling for nature while the sophisticated listener will enjoy the period, romantic flavour and will note the novelty of Weber's approach and orchestration. Agathe's two arias, for instance, especially that in Act III—a last-minute addition—are in a poetic vein unthinkable at an earlier date; and the famous Wolf's Glen scene explores new territory in musical description of the macabre. There are some powerful ensembles but the individual characterization remains marked throughout.

The Overture incorporates extensive melodies from the opera itself—another novel practice.

ACT I

Before a forest inn. The victory of the peasant Kilian over Max in a shooting contest is being celebrated. Max has lost his skill as a marksman. Kuno tells him that, if he fails again the next day in the Prince's tournament, he will lose both his job and the hand of Agathe. Kaspar makes Max drink; he thrusts his gun into his hand and he brings down an eagle from a great height. The bullet, Kaspar tells him, was a magic one. Max agrees to meet him at midnight in the Wolf's Glen to get more such bullets. Left alone, Kaspar sings a gloating aria.

ACT II

Scene 1. Agathe's room. Ännchen is re-hanging a portrait that has fallen and cut Agathe's forehead. Ännchen tries to cheer her anxious spirits with a song about how to capture a young man. Agathe, after alluding to a warning of great danger given her that morning by a Hermit, sings the first of her two arias, consisting of a prayer, followed (after she has sighted Max approaching) by a joyful melody already heard in the Overture. Max, in agitation, says that he must hurry away to the Wolf's Glen to bring in a stag he has shot. After a trio, in which the girls attempt to hold him back, he rushes into the night.

Scene 2. The Wolf's Glen. Kaspar calls up Samiel who is insistent that he will claim him the next day unless he brings a new victim. Kaspar promises to do so; the victim shall receive seven bullets of which six will hit the desired mark but the seventh his bride. For this Kaspar will have three years' respite. Samiel vanishes and Max arrives. Seven bullets are cast in a crucible, with magic rites, while a storm rages. Max falls senseless.

ACT III

This Act is preceded by a short entr'acte in which the well-known hunting-chorus in Scene 2 is anticipated.

Scene 1. Agathe's room. Agathe sings, in her second aria, of her faith in heaven. She tells Ännchen, who enters, of an ominous dream. Ännchen tries to dissipate her mood with a mock-heroic recitative followed by a cheerful aria. A chorus of bridesmaids bring a casket which is found to contain not the bridal, but a funeral, wreath. So she wears instead the white roses given her by the Hermit the previous day.

Scene 2. Prince Ottokar's camp in the forest. After the hunting-chorus the Prince orders Max, who has been shooting unerringly, to bring down a white dove perched on a tree before he will approve his betrothal to Kuno's daughter. Max fires but hits Agathe who appears from behind the tree and also wounds Kaspar who is hiding. After a moment of general alarm, Agathe revives. Samiel appears and claims Kaspar, whose body is thrown into the Wolf's Glen. Max confesses to the magic bullets and the Duke passes sentence of banishment. The Hermit, however, appears and urges the Prince to be merciful and let him marry Agathe after a year's good behaviour. The Prince agrees to this and the opera ends, amid general thanksgiving, with the joyful tune already heard in the Overture and in Agathe's Act II aria.

Gianni Schicchi

Opera in one act. Music by G. Puccini. Libretto by G. Forzano. First produced at the Metropolitan, New York, December 14th, 1918.

SCENE: Florence.

TIME: September 1st, 1299.

PRINCIPAL CHARACTERS:

GIANNI SCHICCHI	(Baritone)
LAURETTA *His daughter*	(Soprano)
ZITA *The "old woman"*	(Mezzo-soprano)
RINUCCIO *Her nephew*	(Tenor)
GHERARDO	(Tenor)
NELLA *His wife*	(Soprano)
BETTO	(Bass)
SIMONE	(Bass)
MARCO *His son*	(Baritone)
LA CIESCA *Marco's wife*	(Mezzo-soprano)
MAESTRO SPINELLOCCIO *A doctor*	(Bass)
AMANTIO DE NICOLAO *A lawyer*	(Bass)

Relatives of Buoso Donati (ZITA, RINUCCIO, GHERARDO, NELLA, BETTO, SIMONE, MARCO, LA CIESCA)

This, the third and best known panel of Puccini's "Trittico", is one of the few comic (as opposed to comedy) operas since the old "opera buffa", from which and the Commedia dell'Arte it is descended. It is based on a few lines in Dante's "Inferno", where Schicchi, a historical personage, is mentioned as suffering punishment in the Eighth Circle. A brilliant little piece, beautifully shaped, it is full of the spirit of Florence and Tuscany and reveals an unexpected vein of humour in the composer. Indeed it is his only successful piece in which the central subject is neither passionate love nor jealousy. A small number of motives are wittily developed but the fun derives particularly from the element of self-parody, music in his usual sentimental or melancholic manner being used to incongruous words or in farcical situations. The most familiar of such passages is Lauretta's aria in which she addresses Schicchi as "Babbino" (Daddy) and tearfully seeks his permission to buy a wedding-ring. But the music moves in too dry and rapid a manner to allow time for many expansive arias or other set-pieces.

The bed-chamber of Buoso Donati who lies dead, surrounded by mourning relatives. An ostinato motive admirably represents their crocodile tears; against it is frequently heard a gay figure associated later with Gianni Schicchi. They begin to whisper of a rumour that he has left everything to a monastery. Simone tells them that in that case the only hope is if the will is in the room. As all begin to search frantically for it, Rinuccio exclaims that the hopes of himself and Lauretta whom he loves rest on the will. He finds it and (to the motive standing for their love) exacts, before handing it over, Zita's promise that, if Buoso has left them all rich, he may marry Lauretta. He sends Gherardo's child to fetch Schicchi. The others open (to a solemn orchestral phrase) and read the will and are left speechless when they find that the rumour was true. With bitter laughter they contrast the future of the sleek monks with that of the poor Donatis. Is there no hope of changing it? Rinuccio suggests sending for Schicchi just as the child returns to say that he is on his way. They do not want him and Zita and Simone say that a Donati cannot marry a peasant's daughter. But Rinuccio vehemently praises Schicchi's resourcefulness (two more Schicchi motives, the latter a kind of fanfare) and launches into an elaborate song in which he sings the praises of Florence and the Arno (broad phrase in the orchestra) and points out that all their glories derive, like Schicchi, from the countryside.

Schicchi now arrives with Lauretta and rapidly takes it all in. When Zita rudely tells him that her nephew cannot marry a girl without a dowry he rounds upon her and, after a short ensemble, flatly refuses to help them over the will. Lauretta, in an aria based on the phrase associated with the Arno, begs his help, threatening if she cannot buy a wedding-ring, to throw herself off the Ponte Vecchio. He agrees to read the will but can at first see no way out. Then an idea strikes him and he sends Lauretta out onto the terrace "to feed the bird". Having established that no-one else knows of the death, he tells them to remove Buoso's body and make the bed. The doctor arrives. The relatives barely allow him to enter, while from the bed Schicchi, imitating Buoso's voice, tells him that he is feeling better and sends him away till the evening. The fanfare motive is heard and Schicchi gives a cry of triumph. In an aria he outlines his plan. They are to fetch the lawyer. He describes, to a funeral march based on his first motive, how he will lie under the bed-clothes in Buoso's night-cap and dictate the will. All hail the brilliant scheme. The relatives each let him know their own expectations, not without quarrelling. A tolling bell alarms them but it is for another death. Lauretta comes in to say that the bird will eat no more; Schicchi testily tells her to give it a drink. Some relatives offer Schicchi bribes. As Schicchi is dressed for his part the three women sing a trio of praise, another amusing derivation from the first Schicchi motive. Schicchi solemnly reminds them that the penalty for falsifying a will is loss of the right hand and exile. If they are caught, he goes on, in a mock aria that sounds like a Tuscan folk-song, it will be goodbye to Florence and begging like a Ghibelline. All repeat this. The lawyer arrives, with two witnesses, to the solemn phrase heard when the will was read. Amid general approval Schicchi, from the bed, begins the new will by declaring for a cheap funeral and leaving only five lire to the monastery and something to each of the relatives. But he successively leaves the main items— the valuable mule, the villa in Florence, and the sawmills at Signa—to himself, silencing the relatives' protests by quotations from the "goodbye Florence" aria. Finally he asks Zita to give handsome rewards to the witnesses and the lawyer. When these three have left there is uproar and they all set upon him. He drives them out from "his" house with a stick; they pillage what they can on the way; and he goes off in pursuit. The stage is empty for a moment and then the terrace windows open, revealing Florence bathed in sunshine and the lovers embracing happily and singing a short duet, to their love motive. Schicchi returns with what he has managed to retrieve and speaks to the audience. Could a better use have been found for Buoso's money? For this he has been consigned to the Inferno. But, with all due deference to Dante, if the audience have enjoyed themselves, perhaps they will concede a verdict of extenuating circumstances. The orchestra play the fanfare motive as he bows to the audience.

The Girl of the Golden West

(La Fanciulla del West). Opera in three acts. Music by G. Puccini. Libretto by G. Civinini and C. Zangarini after D. Belasco. First produced at the Metropolitan, New York, December 10th, 1910.

SCENE: A mining-camp in California.

TIME: 1849-50.

PRINCIPAL CHARACTERS:

MINNIE	*Owner of The Polka*	(Soprano)
NICK	*Barman at The Polka*	(Tenor)
DICK JOHNSON	(Ramerrez)	(Tenor)
ASHBY	*Agent of Wells Fargo Transport Co.*	(Bass)
JACK RANCE	*The sheriff*	(Baritone)
SONORA		(Baritone)
HARRY		(Tenor)
JOE	*Miners*	(Tenor)
LARKENS		(Bass)
SID		(Baritone)
JOSE CASTRO	*A half-caste member of Ramerrez' gang*	(Bass)
BILLY JACKRABBIT	*A Red Indian*	(Bass)
WOWKLE	*His squaw*	(Mezzo-soprano)

This opera was initially highly successful and is an accomplished work, in some ways well ahead of its predecessors. Why then does it maintain only a somewhat precarious foothold in the repertory? The main reason is perhaps a certain incompatibility between the Wild West subject, with a libretto at times reminiscent of an early film (e.g., the breathless arrival of a rescuer on horseback) and the limitations of Puccini's style and temperament—for all that he tackles the technical problems valiantly, tries hard to be hearty, and introduces some attractive American colour. A lack of really memorable melody, although there are many touching moments, perhaps stems also from the failure of the libretto, despite its resemblance to "Tosca", to fire him. A further weakness is that Minnie, the central character, is barely credible. She is at once a woman past her first youth, whom all the miners adore but who has never kissed a man, a tough, out-of-doors girl with ability to manage all the men around, and an evangelical preacher who cheats in the crucial game of poker without a pang of conscience!

ACT I

Saloon of The Polka inn. The brief Prelude announces a motive associated with Johnson's love and in effect continues after the curtain has risen and distant male voices have been heard. Miners assemble to drink and gamble. Jake Wallace enters, singing over a guitar-like accompaniment a nostalgic song—an American folk-song in Pucciniesque dress—which is taken up by all present and reduces the homesick Larkens to tears. A collection to send him home is taken. Sid is caught cheating at cards but before they can lay hands on him Rance, the sheriff, intervenes and has him sent out with the two of spades pinned on his breast. Ashby enters with the news that he is hot on the trail of Ramerrez, the leader of a gang of Mexican bandits (hint of Spanish melody). Cheers for Minnie (who has stood a round of drinks) lead to a quarrel between Rance and Sonora, each of whom thinks he is her chosen man. Just as Sonora fires his pistol Minnie strides in (to her motive *fff*), snatches away the revolver, and calms the turmoil with her rebuke. Joe, Sonora, and Harry offer small gifts and Ashby raises his glass to her. Sonora gives her a bag of gold for safe keeping. Minnie reads from the Bible to a group of the men and draws the moral that there is no sinner who cannot be redeemed. The mail arrives (to a ragtime tune) and is read. Ashby has a letter from a local siren called Nina giving him news of Ramerrez. Nick announces that a stranger is outside asking for whisky and water. While they go out to fetch him Rance makes advances to Minnie but is sharply repulsed. In an arioso he tells her of his lonely life, in which he has been attracted only by gold; but he would throw it all away for one kiss from her. She replies with a description of her childhood with poor but loving parents and her determination to find herself such love. They are interrupted by the entry of Johnson, the stranger, who is received suspiciously by the men. But Minnie and he recognize each other from a casual encounter which each has remembered. She stands up for him and he takes her off to waltz with him in the dance hall (to a primitive tune). While they are absent men come in with Castro, whom they have caught. To save his life he promises to lead them to Ramerrez. But catching sight of Johnson, he whispers to him that the gang is in the wood and will signal when ready to fall on the inn. They all go off with Castro, leaving Johnson and Minnie alone to conclude the Act with a lyrical scene of dawning love. He is surprised to find her in such a place. She assures him that she likes the life; she lives in a lonely cabin but can look after herself; she has never yet kissed a man. She is only a poor, obscure girl and good at nothing, but she is impressed by Johnson's big talk about life (and his top B natural!). He is beginning to declare his love, to music of a more expansive cast, when Nick comes in to warn them that another Mexican is hanging around and a whistle is heard. Minnie says that they will only get the hard-won gold of all those poor men over her dead body. Johnson ignores the signal and is enchanted by her defiant attitude. (The motive from the Prelude is heard in the orchestra.) Before he leaves she invites him to come and talk by the fire in her cabin. They part on the note of what each might have been with a better chance in life, Minnie sobbing violently. But Johnson consoles her by saying that she has the face of an angel and this she repeats to herself as the music dies away on an unresolved chord.

ACT II

Interior of Minnie's hut. One hour later. Wowkle sings a lullaby to her baby and converses with Billy in pidgin Italian about the wedding which her mistress, Minnie, is urging. Minnie enters, sends Billy away and tells Wowkle to prepare supper for two. She dresses up in her Sunday best, to a lyrical passage, just in time for Johnson's arrival. A further love duet follows. At first Minnie describes her life, galloping around the country, holding her "Academy" and reading love stories. Johnson tries, without success, to kiss her. But after sending Wowkle home she throws herself into his arms, as the blizzard forces the door open and the motive of the Prelude is heard "vibratissimo". They declare their love, she regarding him as perfect and he saying that it is an impossible dream and making to leave; but the snow has obliterated the track. Pistol shots are heard and Minnie persuades him to stay till the morrow. She gives him her bed and lies down on a rug by the fire. The blizzard rages outside. As they are going to sleep she asks if he ever knew Nina and he replies "Never". There is sudden knocking. She hides Johnson and admits Sonora, Rance, Ashby, and Nick who are anxious for her as they have discovered that Johnson is Ramerrez and his trail leads to her cabin. They have their information from Nina, who has given them his photograph. Nick observes the butt of Johnson's cigar but keeps quiet. Minnie laughs it all off and they withdraw. She rounds in indignation on Johnson, who admits his identity but pleads in self-defence his upbringing and the fact that his only inheritance and means of supporting his family is a gang of robbers. But since he met her he has dreamed of going far away with her and living by honest work. Unconvinced, she throws him out and a shot is heard. She opens the door and drags the wounded but resisting Johnson in, crying that he must not die. With difficulty she gets him up to the loft by a ladder, which she removes as more knocking is heard. The sheriff enters and looks for Johnson in vain. He tries to embrace her and when she resists, tells her that she may love Johnson but he shall not have her. Just as he is going, blood drips from the loft onto his hand (harp) and triumphantly he sets up the ladder and calls on Johnson to come down. Helped by Minnie

Johnson descends and faints in a chair. Minnie, desperate, proposes to Rance a game of poker. If he wins, Johnson and she herself are his; if she wins, Johnson is hers. He accepts. She wins the first hand, he the second, a throbbing double bass emphasizing the nervous excitement of the scene. When, for the decisive hand, Rance has three kings, she pretends to faint and asks for a drink. While he is getting it, she substitutes for her cards others which she had earlier concealed in her stocking and wins the hand. Rance stalks out, leaving Minnie hysterically laughing.

ACT III

A clearing in the Californian forest. Wintry dawn. Ashby and Billy are asleep. A low conversation between Rance and Nick reveals that Rance has kept his word and has not divulged Johnson's stay in Minnie's cabin. They are encamped in the snow, searching for him outside. Distant voices proclaim that they are on the trail and a man-hunt begins (offstage), with Rance exultantly anticipating his revenge over Minnie. Johnson is eventually caught and they prepare to hang him, Nick, however, bribing Billy, who is the hangman, to go slow with his preparations. Johnson is handed over to the sheriff and, though admitting to nothing but robbery, is ready to face death without flinching. However, in an aria, he asks as a last favour, that Minnie shall be left to think that he has gone away to lead a new life. The noose is placed round his neck and he is about to be executed when Minnie is heard galloping up and, despite repeated cries from Rance of "String him up!", all turn to her. She rushes to protect Johnson, flourishing a pistol, and her motive is heard. She addresses them all, pleading for the reformed bandit's life, and reproaching them for their ingratitude for all she has done for them. Gradually she wins the "rough, kindly souls" over to her doctrine that there is no sinner to whom the way of redemption is closed and, at the end of an ensemble, Sonora frees Johnson and hands him over to her in the name of them all. She leaves with him. Their voices, proclaiming "addio California", fade away, as the chorus recall the nostalgic Act I song to the words ". . . won't return no more."

The Golden Cockerel

(Le Coq d'Or). Opera in three acts. Music by N. A. Rimsky-Korsakov. Libretto by V. Bielsky after A. S. Pushkin. First produced at Moscow, October 7th, 1909.

SCENE: Southern Russia.

TIME: Legendary.

CHARACTERS:

KING DODON	(Bass)
PRINCE GUIDON } *His sons*	(Tenor)
PRINCE AFRON }	(Baritone)
GENERAL POLKAN	(Bass)
AMELFA *The Royal housekeeper*	(Contralto)
THE QUEEN OF SHEMAKHAN	(Soprano)
THE GOLDEN COCKEREL	(Soprano)
THE ASTROLOGER	(High tenor)

The precise meaning of Pushkin's fairy-tale is left obscure though its general satirical import is clear and it came for a time under the ban of the Imperial Russian censor. It is the composer's last and best opera and is familiar also from the ballet made from it. The music, like the action, is in a vein of grotesque fantasy and is nearly all based on a small number of motives which are resourcefully varied and spiced with colourful orchestration and kaleidoscopic modulations. The chromatic music given to the Queen is somewhat Caucasian in the manner of Borodin and there are passages of obvious Russian folk-song origin. Elaborate but careful staging is needed to catch the work's mixture of burlesque and imagination without unduly broadening the humour.

INTRODUCTION

The cockerel's cry is heard on a muted trumpet followed by the chromatic music associated with the Queen of Shemakhan. Then, heralded by a motive on the celesta, syncopated, the Astrologer appears before the curtain and announces that it is only a fable which he is setting before us, though with a laudable moral. He disappears and the curtain rises to a solemn measure on

ACT I

King Dodon's council chamber. The King complains to the assembly that their enemies are taking advantage of his old age to subject them to incessant attack. What should they do? (Two motives accompanying this speech recur constantly in the opera.) Guidon's advice is that they should withdraw within the walls and think up some ruse. General Polkan earns a royal reproof by pointing out the weaknesses of this plan. Afron's advice is to disband the army and then take the enemy by surprise. Polkan incurs further royal displeasure by pointing out that the enemy would be sure to take them by surprise first. The nobles cannot help and are yearning for some old-fashioned means of divination when the Astrologer presents himself and kneels before the King. He offers, from a bag, a Golden Cockerel which will give warning of any advancing enemy force and allow Dodon to relax. Dodon offers the Astrologer any reward he chooses. The latter asks only for this promise in legal form, but Dodon, astonished, replies that his every wish constitutes the law. When he has withdrawn Dodon dismisses the assembly, delighted at the prospect of pleasure and of sleep. He toys with sweetmeats brought by Amelfa and plays with his parrot, but what he most wants is his bed, to which he takes. He falls asleep, as do his guards, leaving Amelfa swatting the flies until she too succumbs. (This scene takes place to a charming lullaby accompanied by a figure based on the cockerel's cry.) The music turns towards the Queen's motive, indicating the nature of his dreams. Suddenly the Cockerel utters its warning. People crowd in terrified; Polkan reports and awakens the King who mobilizes his army and sends them forth to battle, together with his reluctant sons. The Cockerel signals that he may safely return to his bed which he at once does. Amelfa, after some false efforts, helps him pick up the thread of his dream and all fall asleep, to the lullaby as before. But again the Cockerel's cry of warning sounds. A crowd again gathers and this time, as it continues to crow, Polkan insists that the veterans, headed by the King himself, must take the field. His rusty armour is brought, he mounts a white horse and sallies out, to a march, acclaimed by the sycophantic crowd, whose last word is to bid him be careful of himself.

ACT II

A narrow pass, littered with the bodies of soldiers, including the two princes. Fog pierced by shafts of moonlight. Dodon and his retinue arrive to a mournful minor version of their march. Dodon laments over the bodies of his sons. Polkan urges the soldiers to return to the fray but no-one knows where the enemy are. Dawn breaks and a tent gradually becomes visible. Elaborate preparations are made to attack it with cannon. This frightens the troops who fire it; but from the tent steps the beautiful young Queen of Shemakhan. She sings the familiar "Hymn to the Sun" with its coloratura refrain. Dodon and Polkan timidly approach her. She tells them who she is and that she has come to conquer them by the power of her beauty. She offers hospitality and begins to speak of her beloved's approach. Polkan makes facetious remarks and she gets Dodon to send him away. She then turns all her seductive arts on to the dazed King, first describing her physical charms and then singing and dancing for him. To please her he sings a simple little song himself. Then she speaks of her wondrous realm in the East where all obey her slightest whim, tearfully telling of the suffocation she suffers and her longing to be opposed and dominated. Dodon volunteers for this service and is joyfully accepted. To celebrate, he is made to dance under the Queen's instruction, till he collapses exhausted. Quite under her thumb by now, the King offers her his hand and his throne. Both camps prepare for the journey, the Queen's slaves ridiculing her fiancé. They set off in procession amid the cheers of Dodon's soldiers and trumpet fanfares.

ACT III

A street before the council chamber. A crowd is anxiously awaiting news. Amelfa appears on the steps and to silence their inquiries, tells them that the King has had a great victory, is bringing back a young queen whom he has rescued from a dragon, and has had his sons put to death. This information puzzles the people but at that moment a motley procession comes in sight, escorting the King and Queen in a golden car. An appropriately bizarre version of the Act I march, working up to a great climax, accompanies the wedding cortège, at the sight of which the crowd is happy and acclaim the King. Suddenly, heralded by his motive, the Astrologer appears, and, invited by the King to name his reward, demands the Queen. He repeats his request, emphasizing it with a high E. The King replies that he is going too far and orders his guards to take him away. When he continues to argue the King strikes him dead with his sceptre. The sun goes in and thunder is heard. The Queen finds it all funny but Dodon is full of superstitious terror at the bad omen. When he tries to embrace her she repulses him with angry disdain. The Cockerel suddenly crows, takes wing and pecks the King's head. He falls dead. There is a moment of darkness, during which the Queen's laughter is heard. When it grows light she and the Cockerel have disappeared. The people lament the King's death.

The Astrologer appears before the curtain for the Epilogue and reassures the audience by telling them that only he and the Queen were real people.

L'Heure Espagnole

(Spanish Time). Opera in one act. Music by M. Ravel. Libretto by Franc-Nohain. First produced at the Opéra-Comique, Paris, May 19th, 1911.

SCENE: Toledo.

TIME: Eighteenth century.

CHARACTERS:

TORQUEMADA	*A clock-maker*	(Tenor)
CONCEPCION	*His wife*	(Soprano)
RAMIRO	*A muleteer*	(Baritone)
GONZALVE	*A poet*	(Tenor)
DON IÑIGO GOMEZ	*A banker*	(Bass)

This little one-act opera is one of the wittiest in the whole repertory. The voices are given a light declamatory line which admirably reflects the different characters and their emotions, fits the rise and fall of French conversation, and enables the whole of the amusing, if untranslatable "book" to be clearly heard. The orchestral part is, as usual with Ravel, fragile and graceful. It abounds in fragments of Spanish—or perhaps one should say Franco-Spanish—melody and rhythm and cleverly underlines the points in the action. The whole work is quintessentially French in its lightness of touch, but its elegance conceals much artifice.

Torquemada's shop. He sits at his bench, the sound of clocks of every kind blending with the introductory music. Ramiro enters, seeking the repair of a watch inherited from a bull-fighter uncle whose life it once saved. Concepcion reminds her husband that it is time to leave for his weekly task of regulating the municipal clocks. She chides him for not having moved two grandfather clocks up to her bedroom and displays scorn at his lack of the strength to carry them. As he hurries out saying that official time does not wait, the orchestra assumes a pompous tone. Ramiro has agreed to await his return, which irks her as she has plans for occupying her husband's weekly absence. The muleteer wonders what he can talk to her about. She timidly asks him to carry one of the clocks up for her. He is delighted to oblige, feeling more at home as a removal man than as a conversationalist. Just then Gonzalve, her lover, arrives. But he wastes the precious time with endless flowery phrases. Ramiro returns. Concepcion tells him she has changed her mind and sends him off to bring the clock down again. He is then to take the other up instead. When he is gone she pushes Gonzalve inside the second clock with the idea that Ramiro should carry him up to her bedroom inside it. But the portly and dignified Don Iñigo calls at this moment and she has difficulty in repelling his importunate advances. Ramiro returns and she is impressed by the ease with which he lifts the clock with Gonzalve inside it. She goes up with him.

Don Iñigo thinks that perhaps he has been dismissed because his stern and imposing mien has frightened her. A little practical joking may soften her and he squeezes himself into the first clock. Ramiro returns, enchanted by Concepcion's request to him to look after the shop. Concepcion soon comes down out of countenance and apologetically asks for the clock upstairs to be brought down again as it goes all wrong. Iñigo pretends to be a cuckoo clock and plays the fool. She remains unmoved, except fervently to agree when he says that a young man is often inexperienced and that poets forget the reality under their noses. Ramiro brings down the clock with Gonzalve inside and she tells him to take up the other with Iñigo inside, to the latter's delight. Its weight does not deter Ramiro. She tries to dismiss Gonzalve, who continues to coin phrases, and eventually goes upstairs in a rage leaving him in his clock. Ramiro returns more enchanted than ever with Concepcion's tact and the peace and quiet of the shop. Concepcion hurriedly returns and he at once goes off to bring the other clock down, leaving her furious that two men should have failed her—two Spaniards and only a stone's-throw from Estremadura. (A bassoon cadenza expresses her sour feelings.) Ramiro returns with the clock containing Iñigo; he is still smiling and awaiting further orders. She asks him to go up to her room—without a clock!—and follows him up.

Iñigo wishes, to sentimental music, that he was comfortably at home and that someone would help him out of the clock, but hearing Gonzalve open the door of his, he hastily draws back. Gonzalve emerges, discovers Iñigo and is caught by the returning Torquemada. Iñigo has to pretend that he had got inside his clock to inspect the mechanism and agrees to buy it. Gonzalve is obliged to buy the other. Torquemada is pleased at the business. They try, to great heaves in the orchestra, to pull Iñigo out; but it is only when Ramiro, returning with Concepcion, lends a hand, that he is extricated. Concepcion tells her husband that Ramiro, who passes the house regularly each morning, will be an excellent substitute for the clocks he has sold.

All five now move downstage and join in a formal ensemble—the old device for ending a comedy opera but this time in the shape of a habañera with an amusing cadenza at the end. The moral is "There comes a moment in the diversions of love when the muleteer has his turn."

Idomeneo

Opera in three acts. Music by W. A. Mozart. Libretto by the Abbé Varesco. First produced at Munich, January 29th, 1781.

SCENE: Crete.

TIME: Antiquity.

CHARACTERS:

IDOMENEO ·	*King of Crete*	(Tenor)
IDAMANTE	*His son*	(Soprano or Tenor)
ILIA	*Daughter of Priam, King of Troy*	(Soprano)
ELECTRA	*Daughter of Agamemnon*	(Soprano)
ARBACE	*Confidant of Idomeneo*	(Tenor)
HIGH PRIEST OF NEPTUNE		(Tenor)
VOICE OF NEPTUNE		(Bass)

It is astonishing that this great masterpiece has had to wait for the second half of the twentieth century for an assured place in the repertory. Since it shows Mozart at his best this must be attributed to the fact that this is opera seria, in all its formality. It is by way of recitative, both secco and stromentato, that the action is carried forward and this is interspersed with a chain of static arias, each deeply expressive of character and situation but each a self-contained musical whole of great beauty, and with a number of dramatic choral pieces. There are very few ensemble numbers but the quartet in Act III is justly famous and foreshadows the great ensembles of the later operas. The part of Idamante was written for a castrato, thus providing modern producers with a problem. A good deal of the part of Arbace is usually judiciously cut. No attempt is made below to enumerate each aria; almost all are characteristic Mozart, noble in manner and limpid in scoring. There is of course no place in this opera for his sense of humour.

ACT I

Scene 1. The royal palace. Ilia, a Trojan princess, is a prisoner of the Greeks. She is torn between hatred of them and love for Idamante.

Idamante enters and orders the Trojan prisoners to be set free in honour of his father's imminent return. He speaks of his love for her; but she bids him remember their situation. A chorus of Trojans and Cretans celebrates the restoration of peace. Arbace hurries in with the news that Idomeneo has been shipwrecked and lost in a storm. At this Elektra (what she is doing in Crete is not clear) breaks into a passionate outburst of jealousy. She loves Idamante and fears that with his father's death the last obstacle to his marriage with Ilia has disappeared.

Scene 2. The sea shore. A crowd of Cretans anxiously watch the home-coming fleet tossing in the storm. When they have departed Idomeneo enters with a retinue which he dismisses. His relief at being on dry land is marred by the dreadful vow which he has made to Neptune, that if he is saved he will sacrifice the first person he meets. Idamante encounters him and they do not at first recognize each other. When at length they do Idamante cannot understand why Idomeneo departs so hurriedly and forbids him to see him again. Joy and grief mingle in Idamante's breast. The Cretan warriors enter to a cheerful march and are joined by the women of Crete in a chorus in praise of Neptune.

ACT II

Scene 1. The royal palace. Idomeneo confides in Arbace who advises him to dispatch his son to Argos as escort of Electra. Ilia enters and tells him that though she may have lost her true father in Troy he has become a father to her. Something in her tone makes him realize that she and Idamante love each other and increases his distress at the disaster which his vow has caused. He is distracted by the torment within his breast. Electra, on the other hand, is overjoyed at the prospect of the journey with Idamante, away from her rival. She hears a march being played in the distance, summoning her on board.

Scene 2. The harbour. As they embark, those on board sing a barcarolle in the confident hope of a calm voyage and Idamante and Electra take leave of Idomeneo in a tender trio. (All this anticipates the farewell scene in *Cosi fan Tutte* where music of similar mood is used with ironical intent.) But a new storm suddenly breaks upon them and a terrible sea-monster appears, causing the people to disperse, while Idomeneo calls on Neptune to let his anger fall upon himself.

ACT III

Scene 1. Before the palace. Ilia meditates on her love. When Idamante joins her and tells her that he must go and fight the monster, Ilia, in her anxiety, reveals her love and a duet ensues. Idomeneo and Electra come upon them and the former orders his son to go into banishment. As he goes sadly away the meditations of each are joined in a glorious quartet which ends with the same phrase as it begins. Arbace urges the King to appear before a great throng assembling with the High Priest at its head. *Scene 2.* Before the Temple. The High Priest describes the devastation done by the monster and asks Idomeneo to render up to Neptune what is his. Idomeneo names Idamante as the victim. The people and the High Priest express their horror. After a solemn procession (which anticipates the mood of *The Magic Flute*) Idomeneo, echoed by the priests, promises his son to Neptune. At this moment a chorus of victory is heard outside and Arbace arrives to announce that Idamante has slain the monster. Idamante, who has now learned of the vow, arrives and offers himself for the fatal blow. As father and son take leave of each other Ilia interposes herself and asks to die in his place. But the voice of the god is heard proclaiming the triumph of love. Idomeneo must abdicate; Idamante, with Ilia as his bride, shall reign in his place and peace will return to Crete. The tension is resolved for all except Electra who rushes from the scene in frustrated fury. Idomeneo takes leave of his people and presents his son to them, in an aria which breathes the spirit of peaceful resignation, and the people rejoice at the nuptials of their new King.

L'Incoronazione di Poppea

(The Coronation of Poppaea). Opera in a prologue and two (three) acts. Music by C. Monteverdi. Libretto by G. F. Busenello. First produced at Teatro SS. Giovanni e Paolo, Venice, Autumn 1642.

SCENE: Rome.

TIME: A.D. 64.

PRINCIPAL CHARACTERS:

NERONE	(The Emperor Nero)	(Tenor)
OTTAVIA	*The Empress*	(Soprano)
POPPEA		(Soprano)
ARNALTA	*Her old nurse*	(Male alto or Contralto)
DRUSILLA	*Her lady-in-waiting*	(Soprano)
OTTONE	(Otho) *Her former lover*	(Male alto or Baritone)
SENECA	*The philosopher and Nero's tutor*	(Bass)
A PAGE	} *In Ottavia's household*	(Tenor)
A MAID OF HONOUR		(Soprano)
LUCANO	*Boon-companion of Nero*	(Tenor)
LIBERTO	*Captain of the Pretorian Guard*	(Baritone)
TWO SOLDIERS	*Of the Pretorian Guard*	(Tenors)
PALLADE	(Pallas Athene)	(Soprano)
MERCURIO	(Mercury)	(Tenor)
FORTUNA		(Soprano)
VIRTÙ		(Soprano)
AMORE	(Love)	(Mezzo-soprano)

Monteverdi's last opera composed at the age of 75 survives in a single manuscript in short score (in several hands) consisting for the most part of bass and vocal lines only. A number of 'realizations' have been made and there are various performing versions. Cuts in a text which is in places disproportionately long are not unusual. A given production may not therefore correspond precisely to the summary below.

The libretto abounds in almost Shakespearian contrasts of mood and displays (despite its mythological trimmings) a certain realism and directness admirably suited to Monteverdi's concept of "dramma in musica", the rôle of the music being to heighten and intensify the words and action.

The work excels in its balance between these elements; the music passes effortlessly and almost unnoticed from recitative to arioso or flexible forms of aria according to the needs of action or language, in what may strike us as an essentially twentieth century manner. The freedom of form which Verdi attained at the end of his life was in fact already exemplified 250 years earlier in this very Italian opera before the confining effect of eighteenth and early nineteenth century conventions had·been felt. The characterization is here very sharp and the musical line supple and expressive so that the work has something of that feeling of immediacy conveyed by a drawing by an Old Master. What we lose from the limitations of seventeenth century musical language (e.g., the orchestra is confined to continuo instruments and strings with occasional trumpets for more formal passages) we gain in spontaneity. And in this single work can already clearly be detected the outline of many characteristic operatic situations to come.

PROLOGUE

After a short introductory sinfonia, Love interrupts an altercation between Fortune and Virtue to claim superiority over both.

ACT I

Scene 1. Outside Poppea's house. Dawn. Ottone returning to Rome repairs to the house of his beloved and calls upon her to awake and admit him. Suddenly he sees two of Nero's guards asleep and realizes with dismay that the Emperor lies in Poppea's arms. In a vivid little passage one guard stirs, hears the laments of Ottone as he makes off and rouses his reluctant comrade who curses Love, Nerone, Rome, and the Guards at losing his rest. They speak to each other of the state of affairs in the Imperial Household but decide that it is best to keep to themselves what they know. Nerone comes out with Poppea and she begs him to stay but he replies that Rome must not know of their union till Ottavia has been set aside. She bids him farewell regretfully, her honeyed "You will return?" being insistently repeated at a higher pitch.

Scene 2. Inside Poppea's house. She sings gaily of her hope and ambition since Love and Fortune fight for her. Arnalta warns her of the folly of trusting them.

Scene 3. In the Imperial palace. Ottavia gives voice to her jealous anguish and calls on Destiny to hurl thunderbolts upon Nerone. Her Maid of Honour counsels her in vain to soothe the pangs by taking a lover. Seneca enters and offers the consolation of a Stoic philosopher which strike her ardent Page as contemptible nonsense. When she has gone to the temple to pray the Page threatens to set fire to the old man's beard and to his books. Seneca is left alone sadly musing. He has a vision of Pallas Athene warning him of his impending end. Nerone enters and speaks of his decision to divorce Ottavia and marry Poppea. He receives Seneca's remonstrations with petulant impatience that his will should be thwarted. After some argument Nerone loses his temper.

Scene 4. Poppea's bedchamber. Nerone lies in his mistress's arms enjoying her charms and her flattery. He promises to make her his Empress. She hints at the disloyalty of Seneca who claims, she says, that Nerone's sceptre depends on him alone. Nerone rises to the bait and sends a messenger to inform the "doddering old fool" that he must die that evening.

Scene 5. Outside Poppea's house. Ottone stands disconsolate in the street, while Poppea on the balcony preens herself on her good fortune. When he addresses her she haughtily bids him depart as she now belongs to Nerone. She withdraws leaving him to his own bitter reflections. Drusilla joins him and rallies him not unsympathetically. Ottone offers to make amends to her for his past disdain of her. She is at first incredulous at this sudden conversion but is soon happy to be convinced of his love for her. She withdraws to wait on her mistress, leaving Ottone somewhat consoled, with Drusilla on his lips, but Poppea still in his heart.

Scene 6. Garden of the palace. A charming scene of flirtation between the Page with beating heart, and the somewhat more knowing Maid of Honour.

Scene 7. Seneca's house. Seneca finds peace in solitary contemplation. Mercury appears to him and promises to conduct him on the journey to heaven which awaits him. Liberto arrives sadly bearing a message from the Emperor. Before he has delivered it, Seneca answers that he understands and will obey; he may tell Nerone that we will be dead before evening. His pupils come in and he tells them that he must now practise the virtue which he has long praised. In a deeply felt three-part chorus they beg him not to take leave of life which is so sweet. But he bids them prepare the bath in which he will open his veins. The scene is followed by a repetition of the sinfonia which opened the work.

ACT II

Scene 1. In the palace. Nerone and Lucano celebrate the death of Seneca in an extended drinking-song in praise of Poppea.

Scene 2. Another part of the palace. Ottone still brooding on his love for Poppea is joined by Ottavia, who commands him, with threats, to kill her that very night, disguising himself in a woman's clothes for the deed. They go out and Drusilla enters full of her new-found joy. Ottone returns, filled with conflicting emotions. He confides in her what he must do and asks her to lend him her cloak. She is happy at the opportunity to prove her loyalty to him and gladly consents.

Scene 3. Poppea's bedchamber. Poppea is rejoicing at the prospects opened for her by Seneca's death. Arnalta lulls her to sleep with a beautiful lullaby. Love appears and vows that she will come to no harm from the approaching danger. Ottone enters and prepares to kill his beloved Poppea in her sleep. But Love indignantly stays his hand. Poppea awakes and reproaches him, taking him for Drusilla. He escapes as Arnalta runs in calling on the servants to pursue Drusilla. Love is left triumphant.

Scene 4. A street. Drusilla is happy at the thought that her rival is to perish. Arnalta comes upon her with lictors who roughly arrest her. She realizes that her cloak has been her undoing. Nerone comes upon the scene and, appraised by Arnalta of the attempted deed, tries in vain to make her divulge her accomplices. In wrath he orders that she be taken away to a horrible death. But Ottone arrives. He and Drusilla vie in claiming the responsibility and the penalty for the deed. Finally Nerone pronounces banishment on Ottone but pardons Drusilla for her constancy. He proclaims his divorce from Ottavia and imperiously orders that she too be exiled from Rome.

Scene 5. Poppea's bedchamber. Poppea applauds Nerone's decision to banish Ottavia. He promises to crown her as Empress.

Scene 6. In the Imperial palace. Ottavia takes a proud and sad farewell of Rome.

Scene 7. A street. Arnalta in a humourous monologue looks forward to the deference and flattery which she, the Empress's nurse, will in future enjoy. Yet, she reflects, it is the grand persons whose death is often a painful one.

Scene 8. The palace. Nerone leads Poppea to the throne and they make ready for the ceremony. The consuls and tribunes enter to majestic strains. Poppea is crowned and they hail her in a stately two-part chorus. They withdraw and Nerone and Poppea remain alone to sing a love-duet of moving simplicity, which ends softly.

Jenufa

Opera in three acts. Music by L. Janáček. Libretto by the composer after G. Preissová. First produced at Brno, January 21st, 1904.

SCENE: A village in Moravia.

TIME: Not specified.

PRINCIPAL CHARACTERS:

GRANDMOTHER BURYJA	*Owner of the mill*	(Contralto)
LACA KLEMEŇ	} *Stepbrothers and grandsons*	(Tenor)
ŠTEVA BURYJA	} *of grandmother Buryja*	(Tenor)
KOSTELNIČKA BURYJOVKA	*The sexton's widow, daughter-in-law*	
of grandmother Buryja		(Soprano)
JENUFA	*Her stepdaughter*	(Soprano)
JANO	*A shepherd boy*	(Soprano)
BARENA	*Servant in the mill*	(Soprano)
FOREMAN	*at the mill*	(Baritone)
THE MAYOR		(Bass)
MAYOR'S WIFE		(Mezzo-soprano)
KAROLKA	*Their daughter*	(Mezzo-soprano)
A SHEPHERDESS		(Mezzo-soprano)

This is the earliest of Janáček's internationally known operas. It is a direct descendant of nineteenth century peasant opera in general and Smetana in particular. But, although the Moravian peasant atmosphere is strongly felt, Janáček's style was already mature and both book and music, in their sensitive sophistication, have moved well beyond the clichés of the earlier genre. The composer's intense feeling for the rhythms of local speech is inevitably somewhat lost in translation. The characters express themselves through flexible recitatives and arioso passages over an orchestral score full of tingling dance rhythms of obvious Moravian origin, the harmonic sequences associated with Czechoslovakian folk-song, and the short, repeated figures so characteristic of the composer. The only set pieces are the choruses. The colourful score, the strong characterization especially of the Kostelnička and Jenufa, and the poetic reflection in the music of the emotions of the characters lift a simple story of village life to a high plane of lyricism.

ACT I

A lonely mill in the mountains. Late afternoon. In the brief Prelude (and
at intervals in this Act) we hear—on the xylophone—the wheel turning.
Jenufa sits anxiously awaiting the return of her cousin Steva by whom
she is with child. If he has been drafted for military service there will be no
wedding. Grandmother Buryja chides her for being idle while Laca
complains that he is treated as a poor relation and bickers with Jenufa.
Jano comes out overjoyed that Jenufa has taught him to read. The Foreman helps Laca sharpen a stick and reveals, to the chagrin of Laca who is
jealous, that Steva was not drafted. They are joined by the Kostelnička and
then by Steva, who is drunk, and a party of recruits and musicians. They
sing and dance to a captivating rhythm. The stern Kostelnička says that
she will not consent to Jenufa's marriage till Steva has shown that he can
stay sober for a year; Jenufa must return home with her. A big ensemble is
built up on a short phrase as the others seek to console the couple. Left
alone Jenufa begs Steva, in a tender passage, to marry her quickly; but
Steva replies evasively and retires to sleep off his orgy. She is left alone
with Laca, who tries to present her with a flower thrown away by Steva
and to kiss her. When Jenufa fends him off he slashes her cheek with his
knife but immediately repents of his jealous act. Barena, the maid, has seen
what happened and the Foreman summons help and calls after Laca, who
runs away, that he did it on purpose.

ACT II

A room in the Kostelnička's house. Six months later. Night. Jenufa's child
is a week old. The Kostelnička has kept her hidden in the house giving out
that she has sent her to Vienna. The two women are restless and anxious.
Jenufa is weak but filled with maternal feelings; her stepmother is reproach-
ful and ashamed and says she should pray to be delivered from the
unwelcome burden. She gives her a sleeping draught and after a prolonged
and tender "Good night" Jenufa retires. The Kostelnička anxiously awaits
Steva who has kept away but whom she has summoned that night. He
appears. She shows him the child and pleads with him, despite her hatred
of him, to marry Jenufa. But he refuses. He has ceased to love her since
her cheek has been disfigured and is betrothed to Karolka, the mayor's
daughter. As he leaves Laca arrives and, hearing that Steva will not
marry Jenufa, asks her stepmother to let him marry her himself, but is
disconcerted when she tells him about the child. The Kostelnička,
becoming desperate, says that the child has died and sends him off to
find out the date of the hated Steva's wedding. She resolves, in a
dramatic scena, to "carry the boy to God" and rushes out with the child
in her arms to drown him in the frozen mill-stream. The music changes in

mood and Jenufa comes out a little dazed from her deep sleep and troubled by a nightmare about the baby. She looks for him but concludes that her stepmother has taken him to the mill. She says a prayer to the Virgin. The Kostelnička bursts in breathless and cold. She tells Jenufa that she has had fever for two days and that meanwhile the child has died. She also tells her about Števa's behaviour and advises her to pay more attention to Laca who at that moment returns. Laca begs her to marry him and her stepmother adds her own plea. Jenufa is sceptical at first but gives way to his ardour. Her stepmother curses Števa. A gust of wind blows the window open. The Kostelnička shrieks and breaks down, saying that it is as if Death were entering. Strong curtain.

ACT III

The same. Two months later. Wedding preparations. The Kostelnička, who looks ill, is restless; the Shepherdess who has come to help chatters on. The Mayor and his wife call. The Kostelnička pulls herself together and takes them off to see the trousseau, while Laca, who cannot forgive himself for having disfigured her, tells Jenufa that under her influence he has overcome his jealousy for Števa and invited him to their wedding. Števa arrives with his Karolka, a silly girl full of trivial conversation, and Jenufa gets the brothers to shake hands. The others rejoin them. Barena and a group of girls sing them a little folk-song and present a bouquet. Grandmother Buryja blesses the happy couple and the Kostelnička is doing likewise when Jano rushes in for the Mayor and, amid a commotion outside, announces that a dead child has been found under the ice. The Kostelnička is terrified. Jenufa claims the child as her own and the crowd which has assembled suspect her of having killed it. But her stepmother confesses to everything before them all. Karolka tells her mother she cannot marry Števa now. Jenufa forgives the Kostelnička who is led away ready to face her punishment. Jenufa and Laca, left alone, realizing that each sinned because of love, renew their pledges to each other in a duet which breathes a radiant tranquillity, especially in the final section where violins sing softly and expressively over harp arpeggios.

Katya Kabanova

Opera in three acts. Music by L. Janáček. Libretto by the composer after A. N. Ostrovsky. First produced at Brno, October 23rd, 1921.

SCENE: The little town of Kalinov on the Volga.

TIME: About 1860.

CHARACTERS:

DIKOJ *A merchant*	(Bass)
BORIS GRIGORIEVITCH *His nephew*	(Tenor)
MARFA KABANOVA (The Kabanicha) *A rich merchant's widow*	(Contralto)
TICHON KABANOV *Her son*	(Tenor)
BARBARA *A foster-child in the Kabanov household*	(Mezzo-soprano)
KATERINA KABANOVA (Katya) *Tichon's wife*	(Soprano)
VANYA KUDRJÁŠ *A teacher*	(Tenor)
KULIGIN *His friend*	(Baritone)
GLASHA *Servants of the Kabanicha*	(Mezzo-soprano)
FEKLUSHA	(Mezzo-soprano)

This setting of Ostrovsky's "The Storm" dates from late in the composer's life. The conflict between the rich, tyrannical, unfeeling upholders of the old moral code and the human and natural young people appealed to his temperament and Katya is one of the most sensitively delineated female portraits in the repertory. In this score the traits to be noted in "Jenufa" have been taken further. The voice parts now show a striking fusion of the inflections of (Czech) speech and of musical phrasing, with no set pieces apart from the folk-songs in Act II Scene 2. The beautifully orchestrated score is built on the varied expansion of a few seminal motives. Janáček's habitual short-windedness here becomes a swift-moving terseness and concentration, with a resulting intensity and feeling of sincerity. Yet he finds time not only for isolated phrases but whole scenes of great lyrical beauty—notably Act II Scene 2, which strikes a note unique among operatic love-scenes, and Katya's final scene. We are constantly aware of typically Czech harmonies and modulations and at times of a typically Czech vein of fantasy, to which, as much as to the difficulty of compressing a Russian novel, may be attributed the inconsequential impression made by certain loosely knit minor episodes.

ACT I

Scene 1. A park on the bank of the Volga, outside the Kabanovs' house. The Prelude introduces a number of the basic motives, notably the rising fourth on the timpani first heard in the fifth and sixth bars, the treble phrase which answers it, the motive (with sleigh bells) at the beginning of the allegro, the motive in sixths on clarinet and viola a little later associated with Katya, and the quiet passage just before the curtain rises. Kudrjáš is rhapsodizing on the beauty of the river to the uncomprehending Glasha, who gets out of the way as the irascible Dikoj enters, berating Boris for his laziness. When he has gone in search of the Kabanicha Boris explains to Kudrjáš that he puts up with the life here after being brought up in Moscow because his parents are dead and he and his sister can only inherit his grandmother's money when they are of age. She had disapproved of his father's aristocratic match and had stipulated that till then he must obey his uncle Dikoj. So he endures it for the sake of his sister whom their relations in Moscow do not allow to join him. But he also admits that he is in love with Katya, on whom he gazes lovingly for a moment as she enters, to characteristic music, with the Kabanicha, Tichon, and Barbara. The tyrannical Kabanicha, having ordered the meek Tichon to go to the market at Kazan, reproaches him for putting his wife before his mother. When Katya protests her respect for her she is heavily snubbed and goes proudly into the house. The Kabanicha hints, before she goes in, that so emotional a creature must be unfaithful to him. Barbara reproaches Tichon with not standing up for his young wife and caring only for drink. He leaves without a word. Alone, Barbara makes it clear that she adores Katya and would like to help her.

Scene 2. A room in the Kabanovs' house. Katya confides in Barbara, in a long monologue, her feeling of loneliness and oppression. She contrasts it with her carefree youth, filled with romantic dreams. Finally she speaks with guilty shame of her recent dreams and of her love for another man. Barbara who considers herself no innocent, does not think that so shameful. The entrance of Tichon, who is about to leave for Kazan, interrupts them. Katya falls round his neck and tearfully begs, without success (to a variant of the motive in sixths) that he either abandon his journey or take her with him rather than leave her with his mother. Hysterically she wants him to exact an oath of fidelity from her, but he cannot see any need for one. The Kabanicha now enters (to the sleigh-bell motive) and tells Tichon that it is time to leave. She forces him, according to strict convention, to order his wife, in his mother's presence, how to behave in his absence, and in particular not to look at another man. But when Katya warmly embraces him she calls her shameless for behaving as if he were her lover.

ACT II

Scene 1. A workroom in the house. In the Prelude we hear a new form of
the motive to which Katya made her first entrance. The Kabanicha
reproaches her for not weeping all day in her room, as loving wives
customarily do when their husbands go away. After she has left, Barbara,
to a hint of a new melody on the viola, gives Katya the key of the garden
which the Kabanicha thinks she removed and offers to try to find Boris.
Alone Katya feels pangs of conscience and, hearing the Kabanicha's voice,
hides the key. But when the danger is past she yields to the temptation
and goes out towards the garden. The Kabanicha comes in with Dikoj who
is drunk and wants to be soothed. He is troubled by a recent occasion when
he had harshly refused to pay a peasant his wages and had then gone down
on his knees to him for forgiveness. But her only reply is to promise to talk
to him properly when he behaves properly.

Scene 2. A lonely spot below the Kabanovs' garden.   Summer night.
Kudrjáš beguiles a long wait for Barbara by singing a folk-song. He is a
little taken aback when Boris appears, saying that he has been summoned
by a message indicating an opportunity to meet Katya. Kudrjáš vainly
points out the risks. Barbara emerges from the garden singing the folk-
melody hinted in Scene 1, to which Kudrjáš supplies the answer. She tells
Boris that Katya is coming and takes Kudrjáš off to the river. Katya now
comes out with downcast gaze and uneasy conscience for her rendezvous
with Boris. But ·when the latter summons up the courage to declare his
love, she is soon in his arms. (The hesitant form here given to her motive,
softly played, seems to underline the persisting conflict of her emotions.)
Barbara returns and encourages them to take a stroll. She and Kudrjáš
chatter happily while the rapturous voices of the other couple are
occasionally heard from the distance, over the motive in sixths from the
Act I Prelude. After a short while Barbara warns them that it is time to go
home and as she and Kudrjáš go up to the garden gate they sing a broader
and hauntingly beautiful version of her folk-song to appropriate words.
Then Katya leaves Boris and goes slowly after them, while a passionate
orchestral version of the motive in sixths speaks of her state of mind. The
scene ends with eleven quiet bars, hanging between major and minor.

ACT III

Scene 1. A half-ruined building by the Volga. A rainy afternoon two
weeks later.   Kudrjáš and Kuligin, together with others, shelter from the
rain. As, at the sight of a picture of Ivan the Terrible on the wall, the
thought strikes Kuligin that there is a tyrant in every Russian family, the
tetchy Dikoj joins them. When Kudrjáš speaks of the need for lightning-
conductors, Dikoj ridicules the thought that the wrath of God can be

deflected thus. The rain stops and he stumps off, leaving Kudrjáš and Boris alone. Barbara arrives and tells Boris that since Tichon's return today Katya has seemed ill and has behaved strangely. The two young men withdraw as Katya enters with Tichon and the Kabanicha. The storm begins again and Kudrjáš tries to calm the frightened people. Katya espies Boris and suddenly, despite Barbara's attempts to restrain her, falls on her knees and, calling to Tichon and the Kabanicha, confesses that she has slept with Boris. She falls into Tichon's arms before running out into the storm. (The motive in sixths, with a new rhythm, runs through the confession.)

Scene 2. A lonely part of the river bank. Dusk. Tichon, divided in mind, and Glasha are searching for Katya. They are followed by Barbara, who can stand the Kabanicha no more, and Kudrjáš. Over a hint of their folk-song they resolve to run away to Moscow, and disappear. Katya enters distraught. A long and moving monologue follows, largely based on variants of her motives, and broken by Kuligin who passes staring, a wordless distant chorus, and a drunk who reels by (to a vivid distortion of the motive in sixths.) She cannot face all the shame and contempt and longs to die—could she but see Boris first. She calls for him and at that moment he appears. As they silently embrace, muted strings quietly recall their meeting in Act II Scene 2. He tells her that his uncle is sending him far away. She must face her drunken husband's moods and the Kabanicha. But her mind is confused and she cannot clearly remember what she wanted to say before he takes a tender farewell. She thinks for a moment of the birds and flowers around her grave and then jumps into the river. Kuligin gives the alarm from the other bank and people go to the rescue, the Kabanicha holding Tichon back and Tichon accusing her of killing his wife. Dikoj brings in Katya's body. The Kabanicha, coldly bowing, thanks the people for their sympathy, to the sleigh-bell motive, beneath which are heard, in the final bars, the ominous timpani fourths.

Khovanshchina

(The Khovansky Affair). Opera in five acts. Music by M. Mussorgsky. Libretto by the composer and V. V. Stassov. First produced at St Petersburg, February 1st, 1886.

SCENE: Moscow and environs.

TIME: 1682-89.

CHARACTERS:

PRINCE IVAN KHOVANSKY	*Leader of the Streltsy*	(Bass)
PRINCE ANDREW KHOVANSKY	*His son*	(Tenor)
PRINCE VASSILY GOLITSIN		(Tenor)
THE BOYAR SHAKLOVITY		(Baritone)
DOSITHEUS	*Leader of the "Old Believers"*	(Bass)
MARTHA	*A young widow, an "Old Believer"*	(Contralto)
A SCRIVENER		(Tenor)
EMMA	*A girl from the German quarter*	(Soprano)
VARSONOFIEV	*A servant of Golitsin*	(Bass)
KOUZKA	*A Streltsy*	(Baritone)
SUSANNA	*An aged "Old Believer"*	(Soprano)

This chronicle piece was finished and orchestrated posthumously by Rimsky-Korsakov, who claimed that Mussorgsky was engaged in abbreviation at his death. Enthusiasts have been critical of Rimsky-Korsakov's version, which may well be displaced by that of Shostakovich which appeared in the early sixties. The opera deals with the struggle between the reformers and supporters of Peter the Great at the period of his accession and the reactionary nobles, including the Khovanskys and their militia, known as the Streltsy, who were supported by an orthodox religious sect known as the "Old Believers" and by the Regent, Peter's half-sister Sophia.

Even by Russian standards, this opera is incoherent and lacking in dramatic unity. (Had the composer fulfilled his original intention of introducing Tsar Peter it might have acquired a focal point.) Only Act I and perhaps Act III fully display the rugged intensity and the vividness of atmosphere which we associate with "Boris Godunov"; despite many individual beauties and fine passages of declamation, much of the rest

*seems excessively reflective with an unduly slow pulse and (in the
Rimsky-Korsakov version) thinly scored. The character most alive in the
music is the Scrivener; the leading rôles of Dositheus and Martha, though
grateful to sing, are not sharply etched.*

ACT I

The Red Square. The curtain rises during the Introduction, a beautiful
description of dawn on the Moscow river. Kouzka, the sentry, is half
asleep; other Streltsy have been rampaging during the night. As the
talkative Scrivener takes his place, Shaklovity dictates to him a letter to
the Tsar, denouncing the Khovanskys. (The scratchy pen is heard in the
violins.) As the Scrivener reads it back a group of Muscovites cross the
stage singing a gay folk-song. A distant chorus is heard acclaiming Ivan
Khovansky who in due course arrives with his following. His announcement
that he is resolved to protect the Tsar against rebels and traitors is
applauded and he sends out the Streltsy to patrol the city. As he departs
the crowd hail him as the White Swan. Andrew Khovansky enters,
attempting to embrace the struggling Emma. She is saved by the arrival of
Martha whom he had once loved and who now reproaches him. He attacks
her with a dagger but she successfully defends herself. His father with his
Streltsy appears and covets Emma for himself. The quarrel between father
and son is arrested by Dositheus who entrusts the girl to Martha's care and
restores peace, in a short arioso. The Khovanskys depart, leaving Dositheus
and his followers in prayer.

ACT II

The palace of Prince Golitsin. Golitsin, who is a counsellor and former lover
of the Regent Sophia but is in favour of the reforms, is reading an
affectionate letter from the Regent. He deems it prudent to keep his
distance. Martha, whom he has summoned to tell his fortune, is announced.
A bowl of water is brought and in it, in the aria called the "divination", she
descries a future of poverty and dishonour for him. Furious, he orders
that she be drowned. She overhears this and rushes out. He is meditating
on his services to Russia when Ivan Khovansky enters unannounced with
a bitter complaint about an insult to himself. Tempers are rising in an
effective passage when Dositheus arrives and tries to reconcile them on the
basis of a return to old customs. Old Believers are heard singing in chorus
outside. This only serves to widen the breach between the reformist
Golitsin and Khovansky who considers that the Old Believers will help to
save Russia. Martha rushes in with the announcement that Peter's guards
have saved her from drowning at the hands of a servant of Golitsin. She is

followed by Shaklovity with a message from the Regent that Peter has proclaimed that the Khovanskys are conspiring against the throne. There is general consternation and the orchestra recalls a phrase heard in the Introduction to Act I.

ACT III

The Streltsy quarter. Old Believers pass by, singing of their victory over the heretics. Martha, sitting on a mound near Andrew Khovansky's house, sings a ballad about their former love. Susanna overhears her and reproaches her in puritan tones. Martha replies that her love is no sin and that Susanna is incapable of understanding it. The argument is cut short by the arrival of Dositheus who reproaches Susanna and consoles Martha and takes her away. Shaklovity enters and laments the state of Russia, in a fine aria. Streltsy appear, drunk and inciting each other to fresh acts of destruction. Their womenfolk follow them and upbraid them. The Scrivener arrives, breathless and frightened, with a graphic tale of rampaging foreign mercenaries near by. The Streltsy call on Ivan Khovansky for his advice and ask him to lead them against the foreigners. Khovansky appears and advises them to submit to the will of Tsar Peter and disperse to their homes.

ACT IV

Scene 1. A hall in Ivan Khovansky's country mansion. Girls sing Khovansky a folk-song. When he demands something more cheerful they switch to a snatch of a Hungarian song, which is interrupted by the entry of Varsonofiev with a warning from Golitsin. Khovansky laughs at it and orders in his slaves who dance to music reminiscent of the Polovtsian dances in *Prince Igor*. Shaklovity arrives unceremoniously with a summons from the Regent to her council. As Khovansky prepares himself to go servant girls sing, in his honour, of the White Swan. But as he reaches the door, he is stabbed to death; Shaklovity derisively finishes the song. *Scene 2.* A square before St Basil's church. To solemn music the crowd watch the departure of Golitsin to exile, in a carriage escorted by cavalry. Martha tells Dositheus, who laments the fall of two great princes, that the Grand Council has decided that the Old Believers should pay the penalty. He tells her to save Andrew Khovansky who now appears demanding Emma. When Martha replies that she is far away and perhaps married to her lover he curses her as a witch. But when he calls on the Streltsy so that they can seize her, they appear carrying blocks for their own execution, followed by their womenfolk demanding their death. He begs Martha to save him and she takes him to a place of safety. The Tsar's guards appear and a herald announces that the Streltsy are pardoned but must return to their homes.

ACT V

A pine wood by a hermitage. Moonlight. Dositheus sings a fine prayer in which he looks forward to the glory of martyrdom. The Old Believers come out from the hermitage and he tells them that their cause is lost and that they must all die together. After a chorus of self-dedication they withdraw. Martha is left alone with the now desperate Andrew who still calls for Emma. Martha reminds him of their love and tells him they must die side by side. The Old Believers reappear in white, carrying tapers and prepare a pyre. Then, as the Tsar's guards are heard approaching, they set fire to it and all mount into the flames, Andrew fearful and calling on Emma to the last, Martha reminding him of their former love, and the Old Believers singing a hymn. The guards arrive and recoil in horror at the sight.

Lohengrin

Opera in three acts. Music by R. Wagner. Libretto by the composer. First produced at Weimar, August 28th, 1850.

SCENE: Antwerp.

TIME: First half of the tenth century.

CHARACTERS:

HENRY THE FOWLER	*King of Germany*	(Bass)
LOHENGRIN		(Tenor)
ELSA OF BRABANT		(Soprano)
FRIEDRICH OF TELRAMUND		(Baritone)
ORTRUD	*His wife*	(Mezzo-soprano)
THE KING'S HERALD		(Bass)

Completed when he was 34, this is the last of Wagner's youthful works before he had worked out the characteristic style of his maturity. The fabric still falls into recognizable sections and the musical motives, though imaginatively used, are still labels rather than symphonic themes. There is much four-square declamatory recitative in predictable paragraphs in common time and much orthodox choral comment. But at times, notably in the Act III love-duet, the music almost attains the fluency and the metric freedom of "unending melody". The great glory of "Lohengrin" is the lyrical and eminently singable music given to, and associated with, the hero and heroine, which strikes a highly original note of poetry. On the other hand, Friedrich and Ortrud are stage villains none too clearly motivated, given the musical clichés appropriate to such in German romantic opera of the period and failing therefore to become wholly credible. But, for all its weaknesses and undue length, the total effect of the work is one of absorption in a romantic legend and with well cast singers of the highest calibre in the roles of Elsa and Lohengrin, it can offer beauty of a kind unparalleled in the German repertory.

The Prelude, familiar in the concert hall, is an ethereal piece, founded solely on a motive associated with the Knights of the Grail, opening out to a big climax and ending as softly as it began. The motive will be constantly heard.

ACT I

A meadow on the banks of the Scheldt. King Henry is presiding under the Oak of Judgment at an assembly of nobles. He has come to Brabant to raise an army against the invading Hungarians but has found the local nobles rent by faction. Friedrich explains that the late Duke left him guardian of his children, Gottfried and Elsa. Elsa had returned from the forest one day without her brother and is suspected of having murdered him, so as to become heir to Brabant and thus have the right to repudiate his own claim to her hand—a claim which he had in disgust renounced. He had married Ortrud who is of royal descent and now, as next-of-kin, claims the kingdom for himself. The dreamy Elsa was planning, after succeeding to the Kingdom herself, to indulge a secret passion. The King orders Elsa to appear and all are struck by her shy and innocent mien. Her only answer to the charge is to tell of a dream in which she saw a knight in shining armour who will be her champion. (This is the familiar "Elsa's dream".) Friedrich tells the baffled King that he is willing to have the issue decided in combat. The heralds sound the challenge and Elsa prays for her champion to appear. A swan is descried drawing a boat, in which stands a knight, by a golden chain. Lohengrin steps ashore, amid general awe and bids a tender farewell to his swan. He offers Elsa his protection and is accepted. Elsa agrees, if he is victorious, to become his wife and accepts the condition that she will never ask his name or origin (motive of warning). They embrace and he formally accepts the challenge. The lists are prepared. The King solemnly prays to heaven to ensure that the just cause prevails and the prayer is echoed by all present in a brief ensemble. The fight begins and Lohengrin triumphs, but spares Friedrich's life. There is a big finale of jubilation on the part of all except Friedrich and Ortrud whose plans have been foiled.

ACT II

The citadel, with the palace of the knights and ladies and the cathedral. Night. Friedrich and Ortrud, humbly clad, sit brooding, a motive of temptation in the basses and a hint of the warning motive indicating the trend of their thoughts. Revelry is heard in the knights' palace. The thought of his dishonour induces an outburst of passion and Friedrich reviles Ortrud as responsible for his sorry state. She meets his onslaught with scorn. She tells him that Lohengrin's power will be broken if he is forced to reveal his name and station and that Elsa must be tempted to question him by a public accusation of sorcery. Moreover, his power is vulnerable to the slightest wound. All this she has learned from her own study of the black arts. They take an oath of vengeance in a brief unison passage. Elsa emerges in white onto the balcony, addressing the breezes in rapture on her wedding morning. While Friedrich draws aside, Ortrud speaks to her and by dwelling on her own wretched state, prevails on the guileless Elsa to admit her. As Elsa is descending, Ortrud calls on Odin and Freia to speed her vengeance. Elsa now appears below and promises to intercede with her knight to save Friedrich. Ortrud cunningly plants in Elsa's mind the thought that her knight might desert her as swiftly as he came and in simulated gratitude offers her own supernatural powers. Innocent and schemer enter the palace together after a brief duet, while Friedrich utters some (musically) conventional villainies.

Dawn now breaks, with trumpets on the ramparts sounding réveillé (no elaborate tone painting) and people assemble for the festive day (chorus). The herald proclaims Friedrich's banishment and the conferment on Elsa's bridegroom of the title "Guardian of Brabant". He also announces that the latter proposes on the morrow to lead forth the King's army. All these announcements are dutifully hailed by the chorus and Friedrich, muttering that the knight is a sorcerer, is hustled away. The bridal procession now appears and Elsa is greeted in an elaborate chorus.On the cathedral steps she is suddenly confronted by Ortrud claiming precedence. When Elsa replies with spirit Ortrud taunts her with her ignorance of her bridegroom's very name, let alone when and whither he may depart, and with her fear of questioning him. The King and Lohengrin now advance in procession. Elsa, weeping, falls on her bridegroom's breast while Ortrud cowers away. The procession is moving off when Friedrich interrupts it and, accusing Lohengrin of sorcery, demands that he make his name and station publicly known. Lohengrin flatly refuses to answer and is upheld by the King and nobles but is dismayed at the effect which the accusation is having on Elsa. Friedrich creeps up to her and whispers (to the temptation motive) that if she will let him cut off the merest tip of Lohengrin's finger, he will tell her all and never leave her. Lohengrin drives Friedrich and Ortrud away and comforts his bride in her confusion. The procession at last enters the cathedral, Elsa averting her gaze from the threatening Ortrud.

ACT III

Scene 1. The bridal chamber. The exuberant introduction (with a quiet middle-section) is a familiar passage. It leads into the even more familiar Bridal-March, as processions of ladies and knights escort Elsa and Lohengrin to each other and then retire. The love-duet which follows, introduced by a tender phrase first heard on the clarinet, is highly poetical, especially in its opening sections. Lohengrin seeks to divert the insistent curiosity of Elsa as to his name, but when he assures her that he comes from a place of light and joy, her fear that he may one day return there is too much for her (temptation motive) and she fancies she hears the sound of his swan come to fetch him. Finally she asks outright the forbidden question (warning motive). At the same moment Friedrich and four companions break in with drawn swords and Lohengrin kills him with his sword. Elsa sinks fainting to the ground. Lohengrin slowly lifts her up (while the clarinet theme is heard) and orders the four men to carry the body to the King's judgment seat. He tells Elsa that he will answer her question in the King's presence. The warning motive sounds again. Dawn is breaking and trumpet calls lead direct into

Scene 2. As in Act I. The nobles and King assemble, ready to march out to war. The covered body of Friedrich is borne in. The sorrowing Elsa soon follows (temptation motive); and then Lohengrin in full armour. He tells them that he cannot lead them forth. He uncovers the body and his deed is pronounced justified. Then he arraigns Elsa for breaking her promise and proceeds to proclaim his secret to them all in the lightly accompanied passage generally known as his "Narration". He is Lohengrin, a Knight from the Temple of the Grail at Montsalvat and the son of Parzival, its sovereign. The mission of its knights to protect the innocent can only be accomplished so long as they remain unknown; recognized, they must withdraw. He catches the swooning Elsa and again reproaches her, but is unmoved by her and the assembly's plea to him to stay and lead them to victory (big ensemble). The swan and the boat approach. He sadly tells Elsa that, had they lived together for one year, the Grail would have returned her brother Gottfried to her. He leaves her his horn, his sword, and his ring to give to Gottfried should he ever return. As he goes to the bank Ortrud steps forward and triumphantly proclaims that the swan is Gottfried who will now be denied liberation from her spell. Lohengrin sinks in prayer. A white dove hovers over the boat. Lohengrin undoes the swan's golden chain. The swan sinks and Gottfried steps forth and embraces his sister. Lohengrin steps into the boat and the dove draws it off. As it disappears, Elsa, with a cry of woe, sinks lifeless in her brother's arms. The curtain falls to the motive heard in the Prelude.

Lucia di Lammermoor

Opera in three acts. Music by G. Donizetti. Libretto by S. Cammarano after Sir Walter Scott. First produced at Teatro San Carlo, Naples, September 26th, 1835.

SCENE: Scotland.

TIME: End of the seventeenth century.

CHARACTERS:

LORD ENRICO ASTHON (sic)	(Baritone)
LUCIA *His sister*	(Soprano)
SIR EDGARDO DI RAVENSWOOD	(Tenor)
LORD ARTURO BUKLAW (sic)	(Tenor)
RAIMONDO BIDEBENT *Lucia's chaplain and tutor*	(Bass)
ALISA *Lucia's duenna*	(Mezzo-soprano)
NORMANNO *Captain of the guard at Ravenswood*	(Tenor)

This is the best known of Donizetti's operas, apart from the "buffo" pair. Doubtless it owes its continued popularity to the scope which the name-part gives to a soprano, nowadays a rarity, who is mistress of the bel canto' style and can convey through her voice the emotions and inflections which often seem so lacking in the music itself. Apart from the Mad Scene the best number is the sextet in Act II Scene 2. But there are some fine arias and duets, and at times the composer writes melodies with a pathos almost worthy of his contemporary, Bellini. The motivation of the action is only just intelligible to those ignorant of their Walter Scott and the naive romanticism is difficult for a modern audience to take seriously if not handled with the greatest tact.

ACT I

Scene 1. The grounds of Ravenswood Castle. Normanno dispatches Enrico's retainers to search for an intruder. Enrico speaks of his sister's reluctance to make the match which will retrieve the family fortunes. Raimondo defends her but Normanno speaks of her association with a man whom Enrico at once takes to be his enemy, Edgardo. He expresses

his horror in a cavatina. The retainers return to repeat that they have seen
the intruder and ascertained his name to be Edgardo. Enrico vows
vengeance on them both and cannot be restrained.
Scene 2. The park, by a fountain. After a harp introduction, Alisa speaks
to Lucia of the imprudence of meeting Edgardo, whom she awaits, now
that her brother has wind of the affair. Lucia tells, in a cavatina, how
once she saw a ghost at this fountain. Alisa regards this as a bad omen.
But Lucia goes on, in a famous florid aria, to speak of her love for Edgardo
and pays no heed to Alisa, who retires to keep watch as Edgardo arrives.
Edgardo tells her that he must leave for France but will seek reconciliation
with her brother and ask for her hand. She begs him, in terror, to keep their
love secret, whereat he rages vehemently about their feud and his vow to
pursue it, from which only the sight of herself had caused him to relent.
When she has calmed him they exchange rings as a sign that they are
husband and wife in the sight of God. Then he takes a long and romantic
farewell. All this takes place to an elaborate duet in which passages in
thirds and sixths abound.

ACT II

Scene 1. Enrico's apartment in the Castle. Enrico fears that Lucia will
oppose the planned marriage with Arturo, but Normanno is confident
that the interception of Edgardo's letters and the forged letter which they
have prepared will suffice to quench her passion. He leaves and Lucia
enters. At first Enrico addresses her coaxingly but when Lucia obstinately
says that she has plighted her troth to another he thrusts into her hand a
letter suggesting that Edgardo has been unfaithful. In a duet Lucia sings of
her distress, while her brother rubs it in. Sounds of festivity are heard.
Enrico tells her that her bridal bed is being prepared, but she fears that it
is her grave. In the second part of the duet he speaks of the fate awaiting
him if she deserts him; but she wishes only to die. Enrico leaves her and
Raimondo comes in with the further blow that he himself has written to
Edgardo in France on her behalf, but has had no reply. He advises her
to submit to fate. In an aria he appeals to her to give way for her mother's
sake and to have pity on her brother. She capitulates and he expresses his
satisfaction and his conviction that her sacrifice will be recorded in heaven.
Scene 2. The Great Hall of the Castle. Guests sing a chorus of good wishes
to Arturo who replies that he looks forward to restoring Enrico's fortunes.
Enrico excuses Lucia's late arrival by her mourning for her mother and
Arturo elicits from him that Edgardo has made advances to her. Lucia
joins them, downcast and sad, and the contract has just been signed when
Edgardo suddenly appears. There follows a famous sextet in which the
characters soliloquize, Enrico even showing some remorse. When it is over
a fight is only averted by the intervention of Raimondo. When Edgardo is

shown Lucia's signature on the contract, he returns Lucia's ring and demands his own, cursing her. There is a grand, but not very subtle, finale for the whole company in which all but Lucia urge Edgardo to leave or be killed. Edgardo bitterly suggests that his death would be a pleasant accompaniment to the wedding, while Lucia prays for Edgardo's protection.

ACT III

Scene 1. A room in the tower of Edgardo's castle. Stormy night. Enrico visits the brooding Edgardo while the wedding feast is still in progress, to arouse his jealousy and deliver a challenge to a duel at dawn in the Ravenswood burial ground, which Edgardo eagerly accepts. Both express their hatred and anxiety to settle scores, in a rumbustious duet.

Scene 2. As in Act II Scene 2. The wedding guests are still celebrating when Raimondo enters with the horrifying tale that, hearing a cry from the bridal chamber, he had entered and found Arturo stabbed and Lucia out of her mind. There is general consternation. Lucia enters, dishevelled in white. The Mad Scene begins by Lucia imagining herself being married to Edgardo. There are disjointed fragments of melody (including a reminiscence of the Act I Scene 2 duet) and some highly ornate recitative followed by a florid melody; but otherwise for us at least there is little madness in the music itself. Enrico arrives and his first thought, before he has taken in her condition is to punish his sister. Soon, however, he is filled with remorse and, like everyone else, with pity. Lucia now goes on to beg Edgardo's forgiveness for what her brother made her do; she still loves him. Finally, in a pathetic aria in waltz rhythm, she begs him to weep on her grave. At the end of her scene she falls in a faint and Enrico commends her to Alisa and Raimondo, who turns upon Normanno as the cause of it all. (This final recitative is usually omitted.)

Scene 3. The burial ground of the Ravenswoods. Night. Edgardo laments (recitative) and looks forward to death but hopes that Lucia will not pass by his grave with her husband at her side (aria). People come from the castle and he learns that Lucia is at death's door. Then Raimondo arrives with the news of her death. Edgardo sings a beautiful aria in which he anticipates reunion with her and stabs himself before them all. Before he dies he manages a final stanza, accompanied by horrified comments from the bystanders.

Lulu

Opera in three acts. Music by A. Berg. Libretto adapted by the composer from F. Wedekind. First produced at the Stadttheater, Zürich, June 2nd, 1937.

SCENE: A German city (Berlin?), Paris, and London.

TIME: About 1890.

PRINCIPAL CHARACTERS:

LULU	(Soprano)
COUNTESS GESCHWITZ	(Mezzo-soprano)
A SCHOOLBOY	(Contralto)
THE PAINTER	(Tenor)
DR SCHÖN *A newspaper editor*	(Baritone)
ALWA *His son, a writer and composer*	(Tenor)
SCHIGOLCH *An old man*	(Bass)
AN ANIMAL TRAINER	(Bass)
RODRIGO *An athlete*	(Bass)
A DRESSER	(Mezzo-soprano)
THE THEATRE DIRECTOR	(Bass)
THE PRINCE *A traveller in Africa*	(Tenor)

Berg's second opera is a reduction of Wedekind's once sensational plays "Earth-Spirit" and "Pandora's Box". As such, the action is not always wholly clear and there is an awkward gap between the two scenes of Act II. Berg envisaged filling this by a film sequence during the connecting music, which has in practice proved too short for the purpose. Berg completed the work in short score but lived to orchestrate only 268 bars of Act III Scene 1, together with the Interlude between the two scenes and a condensation of Scene 2 (including the final section with the vocal part for Geschwitz), which formed part of the Lulu symphony finished in 1934. Until such time as someone can orchestrate the rest of Act III, it is usual to substitute for it the two movements from the symphony.

Wedekind's erotic tragedy was not taken by Berg as showing simply the rise and fall of the destructive female serpent (known to every man by another name). He saw it, with the eye of his period, as a social protest.

This female Don Juan comes to her horrible end because (in Karl Kraus's words) she is made "to serve the egoism of her proprietors"; she "became the destroyer of all because everyone destroyed her." The words of her song in Act II Scene 1 are thus crucial and she emerges as deserving of the profound pity with which Berg depicts her end. The devoted self-sacrifice of the Lesbian is another ambivalent feature of a work open to more than one interpretation.

The music is dodecaphonic, being almost all derived from a single tone-row heard just before the death of Dr Schön. Each character is given his own motives (or timbre). The work can be broken down into conventional forms, influenced by the participating characters—much of the music associated with Dr Schön being, for instance, in sonata form. There is much structural ingenuity (correspondence, retrogression, inversion, etc.), which is not expected to be consciously grasped by the listener. The vocal parts are sung, half-sung, in "Sprechstimme", or spoken (alone or against accompaniment). The part of Lulu is often cruelly high and florid, giving it a stylized quality. The orchestration is relatively light; piano, alto saxophone, and vibraphone figure prominently. Technically it is at times almost too clever, but the beauty of many passages is readily apparent, especially the music between scenes.

PROLOGUE

An animal trainer comes out and addresses the audience, as at a circus, on the wonderful wild beasts which they are about to see—notably the tiger (Schön motive) and the bear (Rodrigo motive). He makes an assistant carry out in his arms the dangerous serpent—Lulu dressed for the first scene (first Lulu motive)—and then put back on the stage the "sweet innocent thing" (second Lulu motive). Three bars lead into

ACT I

Scene 1. The Painter's studio. He is painting Lulu as Pierrot. Dr Schön is there and Alwa drops in for a moment. They are surprised not to find Lulu's husband there. Lulu makes a sly allusion to Dr Schön's fiancée. When Schön and Alwa have gone, the sitting rapidly becomes a flirtation, with the Painter chasing Lulu all round the studio (canon on second Lulu motive). Just when he has caught her, the voice of her husband is heard. He breaks open the door, but has a heart attack on catching them in so compromising a position and falls dead. The Painter in dismay goes to call a doctor, while Lulu takes an unconcerned farewell of the dead man in a canzonetta with a prominent saxophone part. The Painter, on his return, is shaken by her heartless manner and, in a duet, questions her on her beliefs; but to all his questions she replies "I don't know." While she is changing her clothes, the Painter, addressing the body in an arioso, says that he would gladly change places with him. Lulu returns asking the Painter to do up her dress as her hand is unsteady. The orchestral Interlude treats material from the previous scene symphonically and leads direct into

Scene 2. Salon in the Painter's apartment, on the wall of which hangs Lulu's portrait as Pierrot. Lulu and the Painter, now married, go through their letters, one of which formally announces the engagement of Dr Schön. The Painter speaks of his happy life with Lulu in a cheerful duettino. The doorbell rings and the Painter, thinking it a beggar, goes off to work. It is Schigolch, a disreputable old man with asthma, who has indeed come to ask for money. He is happy to find Lulu living in such luxury. When the bell rings again he leaves, passing Dr Schön on his way out. The latter has come to ask Lulu that they should stop seeing each other now that he is engaged (the music of this scene is in the form of the exposition of a sonata movement). This is the second time he has married Lulu off—the Painter is a healthy young man, whose position he helped to build up and with whom she should settle down. Lulu brushes this aside, saying that her husband is blind and does not treat her as a real woman. In the coda of the exposition of the sonata, she tells him dramatically (to her first motive) that she owes everything to him and belongs to him alone. When the Painter comes in she leaves, and in a scene marked "Monoritmica", with an accelerating tempo, Schön warns him to watch his wife more carefully and reveals that he has known her since she was twelve, when she sold flowers outside a café, and has looked after her. She never knew her mother, and her father was the beggar who called. She had tried hard to marry himself after the death of his first wife. All this, which Lulu had kept from him, upsets the Painter, who goes out saying that he wants to speak to her. But a groan is heard from a locked room. As Schön calls to Lulu to fetch a meat-chopper, the bell rings and Alwa comes in, excited at the news that a revolution has broken out in Paris. They break down the door and find that the Painter has cut his throat. (From this point the tempo slows down.) Lulu rushes off to her room. Schön fears that the scandal will be the ruin of his engagement. He telephones for the police but regains his composure at the thought that the news from Paris will dominate the late edition. Lulu reappears, in outdoor clothes, saying that she cannot stay for the arrival of the police. She washes a drop of her husband's blood from Schön's coat with the remark that it leaves no trace and goes out telling Schön that he will marry her alright. The music of the Interlude resumes the sonata and dwells gravely on Lulu's first motive.

Scene 3. Lulu's dressing-room in a theatre. A rag-time is heard off-stage. Alwa converses with Lulu, reminding her sentimentally, how, on his mother's death, he had wanted his father to marry her. She replies that the latter has now made her go on the stage so that some rich admirer should take her off his hands (English waltz). She goes off to do her act and Alwa muses that an interesting opera could be made about her. The Prince comes in and speaks of his admiration for her (chorale with variations). Suddenly there is confusion and Lulu is brought in, having fainted on the stage because, she says, she saw Schön in the audience with his future bride. Schön rushes in, furious at her behaviour. There is a brief sextet, in which the Director and her Dresser join, at the end of which she agrees to resume her dance a little later. She is left alone with Schön and the sonata is resumed (with occasional sounds from the jazz band added). She threatens to marry the Prince and go off to Africa and taunts him with his delay in marrying his fiancée and with his inability to give her up. Finally he surrenders and she dictates to him a letter to his fiancée, phrase by phrase, breaking off the engagement. After writing what seems to him his death-warrant, he exclaims "Now comes the execution", and the first Lulu motive is heard in the orchestra before the Act closes on a questioning chord.

ACT II

Scene 1. A luxurious hall in Schön's residence, with a gallery and staircase. Countess Geschwitz, dressed in masculine clothes, is concluding a social call and is evidently much taken with Lulu. Left alone for a moment, Schön reveals his madly jealous state in an arioso, toying with a revolver and looking behind the curtains. When Lulu returns she presses him, with apparent affection, to stay at home, but he says he has business to attend to. (This scene is set, ironically, to music resembling her duet with the Painter early in Act I Scene 2.) When they have left the stage first Geschwitz creeps in and hides, and then there arrive Schigolch with a lovesick schoolboy who has bribed him to bring him, and Rodrigo. They make themselves very much at home. In a brief conversation with Lulu, who comes to say that a visitor is expected, it emerges that Schigolch is not her father and (in an amusing canon) that all three would be happy to marry her. When Alwa is announced they all hide in different places. Lulu encourages him passionately to declare, after some reluctance, his love for her (rondo), at which she says that she poisoned his mother. Schön, who is also hiding, overhears the last part of their scene together and also observes Rodrigo. He takes Alwa away, returns revolver in hand, discovers Geschwitz and in jealous fury at Lulu's behaviour, hands her the revolver, with which to shoot herself. She suggests that he might get a divorce and answers him back in a florid song (dedicated to Webern) in which she claims that she never wanted to seem other than what she was taken for and that no-one ever took her for other than what she is. When Schön continues to behave melodramatically she shoots him. He calls for water and she brings him champagne; and before he dies he warns Alwa, as the next victim, not to let her escape. (Just before his death the bare tone-row is heard in wood-wind and harp). In a passionate arietta Lulu pleads with Alwa to save her from justice but he does not intervene when the police arrive. The Interlude (during which Berg planned the showing of a film of the main incidents of Lulu's arrest, trial, imprisonment, cholera attack, and escape) brings some of the principal motives to a climax and then falls away, backwards and muted. (This is clearly symbolical of Lulu's career.) It has a strikingly fugitive quality as has much of the music of the following scene.

Scene 2. As in Scene 1, but now disordered and dirty. One year later. Geschwitz lies on a sofa, convalescent from cholera. Rodrigo is dressed as a footman and conversation between them and Alwa reveals that they have planned to rescue Lulu from prison and marry her to Rodrigo in Paris. Rodrigo however is wavering. Schigolch comes in and takes Geschwitz off for the rescue. Alwa and Rodrigo are disconcerted when, at this moment of tension, the schoolboy appears, having broken out of Borstal, with a plan for Lulu's escape. They persuade him that she is already dead of cholera and he departs disconsolate. Lulu now enters, in Geschwitz' clothes and supported by Schigolch. Rodrigo is so appalled by her appearance that he walks out, threatening to inform the police. They are glad to be rid of him and Schigolch goes off to collect the sleeping-car tickets. (All this to dreamy reminiscent chords.) Alone with Alwa she hails her freedom in three ecstatic bars (which call to mind Beethoven's *Leonora*) and then, casting off her wan manner assumed to get rid of Rodrigo, becomes almost her old self. The music of the love scene with Alwa in Scene 1 is continued. It is broken off when she tells him how Geschwitz, after training as a nurse, had been looking after victims of a cholera epidemic and had found a way of infecting herself and, during a prison-visit, Lulu also. Both had been placed in the same hospital isolation ward, Geschwitz being released two days ago. Now she had returned for her watch and had changed clothes with Lulu and taken her place in prison. The love scene with Alwa is resumed. They resolve to go to Paris together. Alwa sings a passionate hymn of praise as she reclines on the sofa. At its close Lulu asks if it was the sofa on which his father had bled to death and the Act closes with another questioning chord.

ACT III

[*Scene 1.* Paris. Lulu lives in style with Alwa but is now a demi-mondaine, blackmailed by Rodrigo, Schigolch, and a procurer called Casti-Piani, who is one of her lovers. She is destitute and Casti-Piani threatens to expose her unless she agrees to be sold to an Egyptian brothel. She escapes in disguise to London.]

The Interlude is a fine set of variations on a ballad tune by Wedekind himself, given to Casti-Piani in the previous scene. The concluding statement of the tune is set in a barrel-organ timbre, hinting at a London slum.
[*Scene 2.* Attic in a London slum. Lulu is now a prostitute, keeping Alwa and Schigolch. The devoted Geschwitz has followed her from Paris, with the Pierrot portrait. Lulu receives three clients—a professor, a negro who kills Alwa, and Jack the Ripper.]The scene with Jack the Ripper takes place, with dreadful irony, to a beautiful adagio, in Berg's most compassionate vein, reminiscent of love scenes heard earlier. Lulu's shriek is heard when she is murdered. Geschwitz, who hastens to save her, is killed too, but before expiring her voice floats over the sad orchestral nocturne, calling on Lulu to show herself once more and promising to stay with her for eternity. The work ends with an unresolved chord of the "added sixth".

Macbeth

Opera in four acts. Music by G. Verdi. Libretto by F. M. Piave after W. Shakespeare. First produced at Florence, March 14th, 1847 (revised version at Paris, April 21st, 1865).

SCENE: Scotland and the Border country.

TIME: Eleventh century.

PRINCIPAL CHARACTERS:

MACBETH	} *Generals in King Duncan's army*	(Baritone)
BANQUO		(Bass)
LADY MACBETH		(Soprano)
MACDUFF	*A Scottish nobleman*	(Tenor)
MALCOLM	*Duncan's son*	(Tenor)

It is strange that it is only in recent years that this opera has won a firm foothold in the repertory. Though an early work, Verdi revised and added to it at the height of his powers and he and Piave successfully reduced the tragedy to a coherent outline, faithful to Shakespeare, except that Lady Macbeth, a tremendous rôle for a dramatic soprano, is here even more the dominant partner. For an English-speaking listener, however, the trappings of Italian opera can never sit quite comfortably on this play. The music is a little uneven. That for the witches' chorus does not quite come off, and there are banal passages such as the off-stage music to which Duncan arrives at the castle and the assassins' chorus. But for the most part it is music of great power, even when conventional, and in some parts—Lady Macbeth's three great scenas and the Act I Scene 2 duet, for instance—it rises to the level of the mature Verdi, combining his exquisitely sinuous cantilena with reflection of the dramatic atmosphere and the psychology of the characters.

ACT I

Scene 1. The heath. The witches' incantation is interrupted by the arrival of Macbeth and Banquo. They hail Macbeth as Thane, not only of Glamis but of Cawdor and as King of Scotland. Banquo is hailed not as king but as ancestor of a royal line. Messengers from the King announce that Macbeth has been made Thane of Cawdor. He and Banquo brood sotto voce on what they have heard, before leaving. The witches, after a short chorus, melt away.

Scene 2. Courtyard of Macbeth's castle. Lady Macbeth reads a letter from her husband about these events and gives vent to her ambitions for her husband, in the first half of a tremendous scena. News that King Duncan is arriving that evening precedes a second half in which her intentions become clear. When Macbeth arrives the decision is quickly made before the advent of the royal party (Duncan is a mute figure). There follows a long duet for Macbeth and his wife, covering Macbeth's sight of the imaginary dagger, the murder of Duncan, his terrified description of the scene to his wife and her return with the dagger to the King's chamber—almost all this is sung in muffled tones. Banquo and Macduff arrive. The former is left alone for a moment before Macduff rushes out with news of the murder. The whole household assemble and appeal for divine aid in a grandiose finale.

ACT II

Scene 1. A room in the castle. Macbeth and his wife determine on the death of Banquo and his son. She gives voice to her resolve in a fine aria (one of the numbers added in 1865).

Scene 2. The castle park. A band of assassins assemble, sing a chorus and hide. Banquo enters with his son and expresses gloomy forebodings. The assassins set upon him but his son escapes.

Scene 3. Banqueting hall. To music of hectic gaiety a banquet is in progress. Lady Macbeth begins a brindisi. An assassin appears at the door and tells Macbeth that Banquo is dead but that his son escaped. Macbeth tells the company that Banquo is needed to complete the occasion and sits in the latter's chair. He sees his ghost and addresses him in terror. Macbeth pulls himself together and the drinking-song is resumed. But the ghost reappears and Macbeth is beside himself. This time Lady Macbeth cannot rally him or conceal his condition from the guests. Another big finale is built up.

ACT III

A dark cave. Another witches' chorus (with ballet). They summon up Hecate. Macbeth visits them and receives their prophecies about Macduff "none of woman born" and Birnam Wood, but also sees the line of crowned descendants of Banquo stretching till "crack of doom". He faints and after further song and dance the witches disappear. Lady

Macbeth finds him and is told what he has learned. She refuses to believe the final prophecy and they renew their resolution in a vigorous duet.

ACT IV

Scene 1. A lonely place in the Border country. A chorus of Scottish exiles lament their oppressed country and Macduff grieves over the murder of his wife and children in a bel canto aria. Malcolm and an English army arrive. He bids them cut the branches from the nearby Birnam Wood to camouflage themselves and advance. The scene ends with a stirring call to liberation.

Scene 2. A room in Macbeth's castle. Night. The sleep-walking scene— a long scena for Lady Macbeth (with comments from a gentlewoman and doctor) which is deservedly the best-known "number" in the opera.

Scene 3. A hall in the castle. Macbeth feels that life is losing its meaning but is still buoyed up by the witches' prophecies. He has a final aria before learning in quick succession that his wife is dead and Birnam Wood is on the move. But he leads his men bravely forth.

Scene 4. A wide plain. The change of scene and following battle are accompanied by a strenuous fugato. Macbeth encounters Macduff and learns that he was "untimely ripp'd" from his mother's womb. They go off fighting. The battle dies down. Macduff has killed Macbeth. Malcolm is hailed as King and the opera ends with a martial chorus.

Madame Butterfly

(Madama Butterfly). Opera in two acts. Music by G. Puccini. Libretto by L. Illica and G. Giacosa after J. L. Long and D. Belasco. First produced at La Scala, Milan, February 17th, 1904.

SCENE: Nagasaki.

TIME: Early years of the twentieth century.

CHARACTERS:

MADAME BUTTERFLY *(Cio-Cio-San)*	(Soprano)
SUZUKI *Her servant*	(Mezzo-soprano)
LIEUTENANT B. F. PINKERTON, U.S.N.	(Tenor)
KATE PINKERTON *His wife*	(Mezzo-soprano)
SHARPLESS *U.S. Consul*	(Baritone)
GORO *A marriage broker*	(Tenor)
PRINCE YAMADORI	(Baritone)
THE BONZE *Cio-Cio-San's uncle*	(Bass)

This, the last of the three popular early operas of Puccini, is in many ways the best. This judgment is not based merely on the succession of delightful and familiar melodies, the use of vaguely oriental tunes to give atmosphere, or the effective, if somewhat sentimental, libretto. One notes a greater refinement, delicacy, and purely musical interest throughout the score, extending beyond the famous passages, and something of a chamber music quality. The orchestral writing has a new independence and subtlety. The rôle of Butterfly, which is composed with a touching simplicity matching the character, offers a lyrical soprano scope almost unmatched in the whole repertory and a challenge which the greatest singers of the century have been anxious to meet, while, with its single set and single ensemble, the opera is not difficult to stage effectively.

ACT I

A Japanese villa. After a Prelude based on a running theme which frequently recurs we see Goro showing Lt Pinkerton over the house in which he is to live with Cio-Cio-San, with whom he is about to contract a Japanese marriage. Suzuki and other obsequious servants are produced. The consul, Sharpless, arrives and to a hint of the "Star-spangled Banner" Pinkerton proclaims his belief in the Yankee creed of getting the best out of local conditions. Sharpless disapprovingly calls it a facile gospel. While Goro goes to fetch the girl Pinkerton sings her praises and Sharpless vainly tries to point out that she may be more serious than he. The famous duet ends with Pinkerton toasting his real marriage to an American wife one day. Madame Butterfly, as she is known, and her friends are heard approaching, her voice soaring above them in a phrase which breathes her happiness. There are introductions and some artless conversation in which she reveals that her age is fifteen and her family is in reduced circumstances. Numerous relations now arrive with two officials. While the guests chatter and enjoy themselves Butterfly shows Pinkerton her modest possessions which include the sword with which, on Imperial orders, her father killed himself (staccato theme in the bass), and confides that the day before she had become a Christian. The ceremony takes place. Sharpless and the Japanese officials leave, the former warning Pinkerton once more. Butterfly's family toast them in a colourful little chorus. But the party is interrupted by the arrival of the Bonze who has discovered her conversion of faith, curses her, and compels the whole family to disown her, before they leave, scandalized. Butterfly is now in tears. Pinkerton consoles her and she changes into a garment of pure white. The music then glides imperceptibly into a long love duet, characterized at first by its restrained mood, though in the end the soaring phrase of Butterfly's first entry takes charge and the vocal parts end in unison on top C.

ACT II

As in Act I. *Part 1*. Three years later. Suzuki is praying, but without hope, for the return of Pinkerton who has had to leave the Japan station. The household is almost penniless. Butterfly remains confident and recalls his promise to return when the robins nest. She looks forward to the great day in the familiar aria "Un bel di vedremo". Sharpless and Goro call and are made welcome. Sharpless draws a letter from Pinkerton from his pocket, but Butterfly will not hear more than that he is well and asks when the robins nest in America. They are interrupted by Prince Yamadori, a wealthy suitor for her hand. Goro is trying to promote the match. But she receives his advances with raillery on his previous marriages, so lightly dissolved; her marriage is under American law and is lasting. Sharpless whispers to Yamadori that Pinkerton's ship is approaching but that Pinkerton does not want to see Butterfly. The lovesick Yamadori sadly withdraws. Sharpless tries again and manages to read most of the letter (to a delicate arpeggio figure in the orchestra). Butterfly does not at first seem to take in its import and, when Sharpless advises her to accept

Yamadori, nearly turns him out. Then she fetches the son she has borne Pinkerton and tells Sharpless that if he writes to Pinkerton to tell him of his son, he will surely come. The boy is called Trouble, but on Pinkerton's return his name will be changed to Joy. She could never become a geisha again and would prefer to die (more elaborate version of the theme first associated with her father's sword). Sharpless, much moved, departs. Suzuki drags in Goro who has been spreading· word that the paternity of the child is unknown and who points out that the child would not be accepted in America. Butterfly threatens to kill Goro who makes his escape. Just then a cannon is heard and, through a telescope, Butterfly makes out that the ship arriving is Pinkerton's. Wild with joy, ("Un bel di", "Star-spangled Banner", and Butterfly's happiness motives in quick succession) she and Suzuki ransack the garden to decorate the house with every flower they can find. The charming melody of their scherzo-like duet modulates with delightful freedom. Butterfly then puts on her wedding-robe and piercing three holes in the paper wall of the house—for herself, Suzuki, and Trouble—she settles down, as night falls, to watch and wait. The orchestra softly plays the arpeggio figure which accompanied the reading of the letter while the women hum the bass. First Trouble and then Suzuki fall asleep but Butterfly is still rigid and motionless as the curtain falls.

Part 2. An Interlude, of a fragile beauty almost worthy of Debussy, in which at one point the song of distant sailors is heard, denotes the passage of time and continues when the rising curtain discloses dawn breaking to an eloquent crescendo, and Butterfly still watching. Suzuki wakes and persuades Butterfly to go to rest. Pinkerton and Sharpless steal in and break the news to Suzuki that he is married. They hope that she will help them tell Butterfly. The thick-skinned Pinkerton at last begins to comprehend and a trio follows; Suzuki is sent to fetch Pinkerton's American wife from the garden. Pinkerton now takes an emotional farewell from the house in a fine phrase but leaves the luckless consul to handle the situation. Kate Pinkerton and Suzuki enter, Suzuki promising to tell Butterfly that she and her husband will look after the child with loving care. Butterfly appears, expecting to find Pinkerton. Suzuki's tears and the presence of the strange woman soon make all plain to her. With outward composure she congratulates Kate and agrees to hand over the child to Pinkerton in half an hour. Alone with Suzuki she darkens the room and tells her to send the child to her. She takes down her father's sword on which is inscribed: "Death with honour is better than life with dishonour." She takes leave of the child in a famous passage, makes the child play with a doll and the American flag, bandages his eyes and kills herself behind a screen, tottering forward at her last gasp just as Pinkerton and Sharpless burst into the room. The sword motive is heard fortissimo in the orchestra.

The Magic Flute

(Die Zauberflöte). Opera in two acts. Music by W. A. Mozart. Libretto by E. Schikaneder (? with or after C. L. Giesecke). First produced at the Theater auf der Wieden, Vienna, September 30th, 1791.

SCENE: Egypt.

TIME: Legendary.

CHARACTERS:

THE QUEEN OF NIGHT		(Soprano)
THREE LADIES *Her attendants*	(Two sopranos and one mezzo-soprano)	
PAMINA *Her daughter*		(Soprano)
TAMINO *A prince*		(Tenor)
PAPAGENO *A bird-catcher*		(Baritone)
PAPAGENA		(Soprano)
SARASTRO *High Priest*		(Bass)
MONOSTATOS *A Moor in his service*		(Tenor)
THE SPEAKER *(of the Temple)*		(Bass)
TWO PRIESTS		(Tenor and bass)
THREE GENII	(Soprano, mezzo-soprano, and contralto)	
TWO ARMED MEN		(Tenor and bass)

This work was originally planned by Schikaneder, an actor-manager, as a popular fairy-tale, with spoken dialogue and comic opportunities for himself. The Queen was to be the heroine and Sarastro the villain. But while it was being written, the plot was probably changed in view of a rival production. From Act I Scene 3 onwards their rôles were reversed. Moreover Masonic symbolism was introduced and the piece became a glorification of the Freemasons, to which Mozart belonged, under a thin Egyptian veneer. Since the Freemasons had returned to disfavour after the death of the liberal Josef II in 1790, the piece thus became risqué, if indeed it was not a sincere protest. What was performed a few weeks before Mozart's death is at once a crude and ill-constructed popular entertainment and an operatic allegory about the need for purification and light before entering on earthly trials. It has inspired many such allegories and has deeply impressed non-musicians, from Goethe onwards. The music, which is more "vertical" than in Mozart's Italian operas, is renowned for its crystal clarity and lyrical purity matching the subject. But there are many ensembles and Mozart shows a heightened ability to mould accompanied recitative, and indeed phrases of more formal numbers, to the inflections of speech. Many numbers are thus distinctly "free" in style and achieve a fusion of words and sound rare at any period.

The Overture begins with a short adagio introduced by the three chords to be heard in the temple scene, followed by an allegro combining elements of fugal and sonata form and interrupted by a repetition of the three chords. The main subject has affinities with the Queen of Night's second aria.

ACT I

Scene 1. A rocky place. Tamino, pursued by a serpent, calls for help and falls senseless. Three Ladies emerge from a temple and slay the serpent. They are struck by Tamino's good looks. They feel that his presence should be reported to their Queen but quarrel as to which should stay with him, till finally they all decide to go. (All this in a trio.) When Tamino revives, he is approached by Papageno, who sings a simple song about his interest in catching birds and in the opposite sex. This is punctuated by calls on his pipe. He tells Tamino that he is in the realm of the Queen of Night, whom he serves, and boasts that it was he who strangled the serpent. At this the Three Ladies reappear, padlock Papageno's mouth as a punishment for his lie and give Tamino a portrait of the Queen's daughter, which at once evokes from him a beautiful aria about his love for her. When the Ladies tell him that she is the prisoner of an evil magician he resolves to free her. The Queen herself briefly appears; in the first of her two brilliant arias, she speaks of her sorrow and promises her daughter's hand. A quintet follows, in the course of which Papageno's mouth is freed, Tamino is presented with a flute with the magic power of changing men's passions, and Papageno with a protective chime of bells. Three Genii will guide them to the place. They take leave of the Ladies.
Scene 2. A room in Sarastro's palace. Monostatos is maltreating Pamina, who falls senseless. Papageno enters, but he and Monostatos are terrified at the sight of each other and run off in opposite directions. Papageno returns, recognizes Pamina and tells her that he and Tamino have come to rescue her. The Prince loves her, but alas, for himself there is no Papagena. Before they leave they describe, in a little duet, what love means to every man and woman.
Scene 3. A grove, encircled by temples of Wisdom, Reason, and Nature. The finale begins. The Three Genii conduct Tamino to the spot and give him sage counsel. He tries to enter the temples to left and right, but a

voice each time calls out "Back!" When he knocks at the third temple, a
priest (the Speaker) comes out, who tells him that he has been deceived
by woman's talk. Sarastro did indeed carry off Pamina but his purposes
are not as Tamino supposes, though they cannot be revealed till he is
initiated. Unseen voices echo his solemn final phrase (accompanied by
trombones) with the tidings that that will be soon and that Pamina still
lives. Tamino plays his flute and wild animals come out to listen.
Suddenly he hears Papageno's pipe and hurries away to find him.
Papageno and Pamina arrive, in search of Tamino, singing a charming
duettino, but are overtaken by Monostatos who orders his slaves to fetter
them. But when Papageno plays his bells they all go off singing and
dancing, leaving Papageno and Pamina rejoicing, in another duettino. A
chorus of Sarastro's followers is now heard, hailing his arrival in state.
Papageno is terrified, but Pamina declares that they must tell him the
truth. She kneels before Sarastro. In a superb accompanied recitative she
tells him that she was trying to escape Monostatos's amorous attentions.
Sarastro replies understandingly and adds that he has rescued her from her
mother because she would have wrought her destruction; without a man's
guiding hand woman is apt to overstep her sphere. Monostatos now brings
in Tamino whom he has captured, but to his surprise is sentenced to
seventy-seven bastinado strokes. Sarastro orders Pamina and Tamino to
be veiled and led into the temple to face the ordeals of initiation. A
brief chorus rounds off the Act.

ACT II

Scene 1. A grove of palms. Priests assemble to a solemn march and accept
Sarastro's proposal that Tamino should be a candidate for initiation. They
blow three chords on their horns. Sarastro invokes divine protection for
him and Pamina in the familiar prayer "O Isis and Osiris".
Scene 2. Porch of the temple. Priests explain to Tamino and the timid
Papageno that they must undergo ordeals, beginning with that of silence,
before admission to the temple. A maiden's hand awaits Papageno also.
Two Priests warn them, in a short duet, against woman's wiles. In darkness
the Three Ladies try to turn them, with threats, from their purpose. They
stand firm and silent (apart from asides to each other, so that we get a
quintet) and the Ladies are driven away by the Priests who take the
candidates off separately.
Scene 3. A garden. Monostatos steals up on the sleeping Pamina, declaring
in a somewhat "Turkish", though lightly accompanied, aria that even a black
man feels the pangs of love. The Queen of Night appears amid thunder
and foils him. She gives the waking Pamina a dagger with which to slay
Sarastro and recover the power-bestowing seven-fold shield of the sun,
emphasizing her injunctions with a formidable aria. Monostatos, who has

overheard, proposes to Pamina in her distress that the way out of her dilemma is to entrust herself to him. When she refuses, he is prevented from killing her with the dagger by the arrival of Sarastro, who assures her, in a noble aria, that within the temple vengeance is unknown. He has other plans for foiling her mother's designs.

Scene 4. A hall.   Papageno has difficulty in maintaining the silence enjoined and is disconcerted by an old woman who claims him as her lover. The Three Genii return with food and drink, of which Papageno partakes, and restore to them the flute and bells.   When Pamina enters, Tamino refuses to speak to her and she expresses her despair in a wonderful G minor aria.   The candidates are summoned to further trials.

Scene 5. A vault.   After a chorus of Priests Tamino is confronted by Pamina, of whom he is told by Sarastro to take farewell. This generates a trio notable for its flexible treatment.   Papageno, left behind, is told that he has failed his test but is consoled with wine and proclaims his longing for a wife, in an aria accompanied by the chime of bells.   The old woman reappears and, on his promising to be true to her, is turned into a young girl but at once separated by the Speaker from the still unworthy Papageno.

Scene 6.   The scene for the finale which now begins is largely a matter for the producer's imagination and ingenuity.   The Three Genii greet the rising sun and resolve to aid the distraught Pamina, whom they restrain from stabbing herself with her mother's dagger and promise to take to Tamino. The Ordeal of Fire and Water is now introduced by a confrontation between Tamino and Two Men in Armour who sing a Protestant chorale over a fugal accompaniment—a remarkable passage.   Pamina is allowed to join him for these ordeals and they embrace.   She tells him that they must rely on his flute, which her father endowed with magic qualities.   After a short quartet they pass successively through fire and water, Tamino playing his flute, to a mysterious and disembodied slow march.   A chorus of priests welcomes them, in triumph, into the temple.

Papageno is now seen in despair at the loss of Papagena, and making a comically hesitant attempt to hang himself.   But the Genii appear and tell him to play his bells, whereupon Papagena is brought to him.   The pair look forward to domestic bliss, in a duet with a comic patter on their names.

The Queen of Night and her Ladies, joined by Monostatos, in return for a promise of Pamina's hand, now steal on in darkness in a final attempt on the temple.   But they are foiled by a thunderstorm and sink below.   The scene is flooded with light.   Sarastro, with Pamina and Tamino at his side, proclaims their defeat in a fine phrase.   The priests hail the initiates and give thanks to Isis and Osiris in a splendid chorus.

Manon

Opera in five acts. Music by J. Massenet. Libretto by H. Meilhac and P. Gille after the Abbé Prévost. First produced at the Opéra Comique, Paris, January 19th, 1884.

SCENE: France.

TIME: 1721.

PRINCIPAL CHARACTERS:

LE CHEVALIER DES GRIEUX		(Tenor)
LE COMTE DES GRIEUX *His father*		(Bass)
LESCAUT *Of the Royal Guard, Manon's cousin*		(Baritone)
GUILLOT DE MORFONTAINE *Minister of Finance*		(Tenor)
DE BRÉTIGNY *A nobleman*		(Baritone)
MANON LESCAUT		(Soprano)
POUSETTE		
JAVOTTE	*Actresses*	(Sopranos)
ROSETTE		

Generally ranked first among Massenet's works, this is "opéra comique"— i.e., with spoken dialogue, though here often against an orchestral background (which nowadays is apt to suggest the more romantic kind of film). Though the work, which is longer than that of Puccini on the same subject, finds time to indicate the hero's dilemma, it concentrates on Manon and her ambivalent character and, in so doing, provides a difficult and many-sided rôle which has appealed to famous sopranos. The music is conventional and unambitious but is highly accomplished and displays a mellifluous, if sometimes sentimental charm. The composer has been at pains to create a credible period background to the tale and the whole piece is theatrically effective, in the tradition of French good taste.

ACT I

Courtyard of an inn at Amiens. The brief Prelude foreshadows melodies to be heard later—notably des Grieux's aria in Act IV. Guillot and de Brétigny, who are dining with three actresses in a pavilion, are clamouring for food and drink to be brought. There is a brief quintet. Their meal is served to a little march. Townspeople assemble for the arrival of the Arras mailcoach. Lescaut and two guardsmen arrive. The latter repair to another inn. Lescaut, however, must first meet his cousin, Manon, who alights from the coach, confused by all the bustle. They introduce themselves. Manon's character is established, in an aria, as a high-spirited but simple girl of sixteen who has never left home before but is now on her way to a convent because she is thought too fond of pleasure. While Lescaut goes to look for her luggage Guillot comes out and, catching sight of her, is much struck by her beauty, as is de Brétigny who follows him. The three actresses, in a gay little trio, call on Guillot not to make a fool of himself, but he tells Manon that his coachman will shortly present himself and that his carriage is at her disposal. Lescaut reappears and, after a little homily to Manon to behave well, goes off to gamble with the guardsmen. Manon, full of good resolutions, sings of her determination to put behind her the thoughts of a life of pleasure awakened by a glimpse of the actresses' finery. Des Grieux comes in, to a passionate cello phrase, musing on his reluctance to return to his father. Seeing Manon, he cannot resist speaking to her (a violin accompanies with a tender melody). He falls in love at once and, to the cello phrase, calls her an enchantress. A love duet, based on the cello phrase and the violin melody, develops with great rapidity and when the coachman appears Manon suggests, and des Grieux agrees, that they take the carriage. Des Grieux proposes that they go to Paris and live together, and Manon's scruples are soon overcome. As they drive off the actresses' trio and the drunken Lescaut's voice are heard.

ACT II

Their apartment, rue Vivienne, Paris. A short Prelude, made up of the cello phrase answered by a lighter phrase on the violins, which evidently stands for Manon, leads into a tender scene in which Manon is seen, trying to read, over her lover's shoulder, a letter which he is writing to his father about her. They read it aloud together in the Letter Song (notice the horn counter-melody in the second part). Before he can dispatch it they are interrupted by two guardsmen, Lescaut and (as the maid whispers to Manon) de Brétigny in disguise. Lescaut is so aggressive that, after a quartet, de Brétigny has to restrain him. He then bluntly asks des Grieux, in a trio, whether or not he intends to marry Manon. Des Grieux draws him aside and reads the letter to him, while de Brétigny tells Manon of a plan, arranged by des Grieux's father, to carry him off that night. He advises her not to warn him, hinting that if she refrains, he will provide for her in luxury. During another spirited quartet she protests her love for des Grieux but is plainly tempted. Lescaut affects to be satisfied by the letter and congratulates the pair. He and de Brétigny withdraw and des Grieux goes out with the letter. While he is away Manon makes her decision and sings the familiar "Adieu, notre petite table." When des Grieux returns he sings, over an exquisite string accompaniment, his dream of life with Manon. There is a knock on the door. She makes an effort to dissuade him from opening it, without telling him why. He insists. There is the sound of a struggle and he is carried off.

An entr'acte, in the form of a minuet of the period, precedes (and is heard from time to time during)

ACT III

Scene 1. The promenade of Cours-la-Reine on a fête day. Amid the noisy crowd of hucksters and their customers there is a momentary glimpse of the three actresses who have escaped from the jealous eye of their protector. Lescaut buys wildly for one Rosalinde, whose praises he sings. Guillot encounters the three girls with young men and is chaffed by de Brétigny, who expresses the hope that he will not try and steal Manon from him. Guillot ascertains from him that the rumour is correct that the latter had refused her request to bring the Opéra ballet to perform in her house. This evokes from Guillot a little rhyme of triumph. Townspeople admire the fashionable ladies and especially Manon who is with de Brétigny and other young noblemen. She sings a florid song about the pleasures of exciting universal admiration (rather like Musetta in *La Bohème*), followed by a gavotte on the theme of enjoying youth before it is too late. While she has left him to make some purchases de Brétigny encounters Comte des Grieux, up from the country, and learns from him that his son is becoming an abbé and is to preach at St Sulpice that evening. Manon overhears this and, sending de Brétigny on an errand, asks the Comte whether his son remembers her, but is told that he has forgotten. Guillot now returns and proudly announces that the Opéra ballet are on their way to perform for Manon in the Cours-la-Reine. The ballet are greeted by the crowd and perform several dances. Manon informs the crestfallen Guillot that she has seen nothing and tells the puzzled Lescaut to send for her chair and have her taken to St Sulpice. *Scene 2.* Ante-chapel of the St Sulpice seminary. Ladies come out of the chapel full of praise for des Grieux's sermon, which has gently warmed their hearts with fervour. The Comte tries to dissuade his son from taking orders, urging him in a paternal aria to marry some nice girl and finally giving him his share of his mother's estate before saying "adieu". Alone, des Grieux tries, in a big aria, to banish the sweet vision and dedicate himself to a life of tranquillity. When he has gone out Manon enters and sends the porter to fetch him, praying (against an unseen choir) for his heart to be restored to her. It takes a long and fine duet before Manon's pleading to be taken back at last overcomes his resistance and Love (in the form of the Act I violin melody) emerges triumphant.

ACT IV

The gaming room at the Hotel de Transylvanie. We see gamblers, sharpers, the three actresses (who think a pretty face a surer road to fortune), Lescaut who sings in praise of the Queen of Spades, and Guillot who sings a lampoon on the Regent with all the dangerous words left out. Manon and des Grieux enter. He is reluctant to gamble; she wants him to restore his fortunes. In a passionate outburst he rails against her power over him. Manon and Lescaut join in and urge him to the tables where Guillot challenges him. While they play Manon, excited at the prospect of his winning, sings another aria in praise of the pleasures of the moment. Des Grieux consistently wins and is accused by Guillot of cheating. There is a scene. Guillot leaves, to return soon after with the police to whom, in revenge for Manon's treatment of him, he denounces des Grieux and "his accomplice". The Count steps forward and his son begs his pardon. The Count promises to get him released. Manon is to be taken "where such women are taken". Des Grieux throws himself in front of her but is overpowered. They are led away to a future of separation.

ACT V

The road to Le Havre towards evening. The sound of marching soldiers is heard as des Grieux awaits the group of women of easy virtue who are to be deported and their military escort. Lescaut meets him with the news that a plan to rescue her has miscarried. When soldiers approach, singing a marching song with a period flavour, Lescaut, restraining des Grieux from behaving rashly, bribes the sergeant to release her for a few hours. Manon, ill, totters down a path and, after embracing des Grieux, collapses in tears. The ensuing duet is in two sections. In the first she begs, and receives, his forgiveness; in the second they look forward to renewed happiness. They go on to recall the past (against the violin melody of Act I, now on the oboe). Manon feels herself growing weaker and, after wryly comparing the evening star with a beautiful diamond and joining with her lover in some repetition of their Act III Scene 2 duet, dies in his arms.

Manon Lescaut

Opera in four acts. Music by G. Puccini. Libretto after the Abbé Prevost. First produced at the Teatro Reggio, Turin, February 1st, 1893.

SCENE: France and Louisiana.

TIME: Second half of the eighteenth century.[1]

PRINCIPAL CHARACTERS:

LESCAUT *Sergeant of the King's Guards*	(Baritone)
MANON LESCAUT *His sister*	(Soprano)
THE CHEVALIER DES GRIEUX *A student*	(Tenor)
GERONTE DI RAVOIR *Treasurer-General*	(Bass)
EDMONDO *A student*	(Tenor)
THE INNKEEPER	(Bass)
A DANCING MASTER	(Tenor)
A MUSICIAN	(Mezzo-soprano)
A LAMPLIGHTER	(Tenor)

This is the earliest of Puccini's works with a place in the repertory and already displays many characteristic features of his style. It was a deliberate challenge to Massenet's recent opera on the same subject and, though an instant success, modern assessments tend to be luke-warm and certainly place the Massenet version higher. This is largely due to the libretto which remains anonymous because of the number of participating hands and in the outcome enabled (or permitted) the young composer to concentrate on "despairing passion" to an extent which can easily become monotonous. And even if it is acceptable that des Grieux should be no more than a loyally protesting tenor the ambivalent Manon demands a higher degree of dramatic and musical characterization to become credible. By jumping straight from the ingénue's elopement with des Grieux to the courtesan's establishment chez Geronte, Puccini passes over all that evolution of her character and career which is central to the action. Also, its climax comes too early, with two tragic acts to follow. Act IV is dramatically superfluous though the occasion for further emotionally charged song. Act III with its contrasting song for the lamplighter and its big ensemble reflecting elaborate stage action looks most obviously forward to Puccini's later work.

[1] But Prévost's novel appeared in 1731.

ACT I

Amiens. A square in front of an inn. A crowd of students and townspeople are enjoying the evening. After a short scherzo-like passage
(which recurs during the act), Edmondo, a would-be poet sings a half-
serious madrigal and the gay crowd join in. Des Grieux arrives and is
taunted for his lack of success in love, replying with a mocking serenade.
The coach from Arras arrives and as Geronte hands the young Manon
down the crowd notes her beauty—as does des Grieux. While Lescaut
and Geronte go inside the inn to arrange for lodging he approaches
Manon (while the orchestra play a melody standing for his tender feelings)
and addresses her gallantly. He elicits that at her father's wish she is on
her reluctant way to a convent. He asks her to return so that they can
find a way of escape. When she has gone in he muses ecstatically on his
feelings for her, to the previously hinted melody. The students laugh at
him, with fragments of his serenade, and settle down to gamble. A short
conversation between Lescaut and Geronte against the background of a
gay chorus emphasizes the wealthy Geronte's interest in Manon and
Lescaut's lack of enthusiasm for his family's plan for her. Lescaut now
joins the gamblers while Geronte arranges with the innkeeper for a
carriage to be ready in an hour. His plan to abduct Manon is overheard
by Edmondo who promptly tells des Grieux. Manon returns to him and
after a short love duet he persuades her to elope with him in the waiting
carriage. When Geronte reappears and discovers what has happened
Lescaut calms his anger and, against a mocking chorus by the students,
points out that a student's purse will not long suffice for Manon's tastes
and that this will give Geronte an opportunity to take charge.

ACT II

An elegant room in Geronte's house in Paris. To a melody of an affected
refinement, first heard on the flute, Manon is having her hair dressed.
Lescaut enters and after praising her appearance expresses his satisfaction
at her exchange of her life of poverty with des Grieux for such luxury.
But in a beautiful paragraph Manon replies that she finds in it an icy silence
and looks back with regret on her life with des Grieux of whom she seeks
news and is told that in his distraction he has taken to gambling. Musicians
enter and sing her a madrigal composed for her by Geronte (actually from
an early Mass of Puccini). But Manon is bored and Lescaut goes off to tell
des Grieux where he can find her. Geronte and his friends enter and a
dancing master teaches her a minuet amid much flattery from the others.
Manon expresses her delight in a florid gavotte and the company then
withdraw. Des Grieux enters quietly and Manon overjoyed begs his forgiveness, which he cannot long withhold, and another love duet follows. But

Geronte surprises them and Manon adds fuel to the flames by holding a mirror to his face. He goes out threateningly promising to see her again soon. Des Grieux wants her to depart at once and reproaches her when she is reluctant to leave so much luxury. Lescaut now rushes in, to a fugato passage, with the news that Geronte has denounced her to the police. He urges them to flee quickly, but Manon delays to gather up her jewels. The door opens and reveals Geronte laughing ironically as Manon drops the jewellery in fright and the police come to arrest her for immorality. Lescaut restrains des Grieux who has drawn his sword with the thought that if he too is arrested no-one will save Manon.

ACT III

A square near the harbour at Le Havre. Before dawn. (The Act is preceded by a sad intermezzo entitled "The Journey to Le Havre".) Over a dirge-like ostinato which persists for much of the Act, Lescaut speaks to des Grieux of his plan to free Manon who is in the barracks with other fallen women who are to be deported to Louisiana by man-of-war. Manon appears at the window. Des Grieux rushes to it and takes her hand. It is dawn. Their brief conversation is interrupted by the lamplighter putting out the lights and singing to himself a delightful fragment of some song. But when he has gone, just at the moment of hope (marked by the orchestra's playing of a phrase which crowned the Act 2 duet) a gun fires the alarm and Lescaut comes to tell the lovers that the plan of escape has failed. Des Grieux refuses to flee. A crowd assembles and the captain of the ship tells the sergeant that he is ready to sail. In a fine ensemble the sergeant calls the roll of the women to be embarked, the crowd comments on each as she appears, while Manon and des Grieux sadly prepare to take leave of each other. Des Grieux cleaves to her. He calls out to the captain that he is mad and begs to be allowed to sail too. The captain gruffly assents and des Grieux rushes on board as the orchestra thunders out the phrase from the love duet.

ACT IV

A vast waterless plain on the borders of New Orleans. Manon and des Grieux are struggling on.[1] She sinks down exhausted and asks him to go in search of help. When she is alone we hear the love motive softly in the orchestra. This is followed by a section for Manon alone over striking wood-wind parts. When des Grieux returns unsuccessful, she is near to death. She recalls her faults (hint of the Act II minuet) but her last words are that her love will never die. Des Grieux falls senseless over her body. The orchestra repeats the minor chords with which the Act had begun.

[1]To seek asylum in an English colony, though we are not told this in the opera.

The Marriage of Figaro

(Le Nozze di Figaro). Opera buffa in four acts. Music by W. A. Mozart. Libretto by L. da Ponte after P. A. C. de Beaumarchais. First produced at the Burgtheater, Vienna, May 1st, 1786.

SCENE: Count Almaviva's château near Seville.

TIME: Eighteenth century.

CHARACTERS:

COUNT ALMAVIVA	(Baritone)
FIGARO *His valet*	(Baritone)
CHERUBINO *His page*	(Soprano)
ANTONIO *His gardener*	(Bass)
COUNTESS (ROSINA) ALMAVIVA	(Soprano)
DOCTOR BARTOLO	(Bass)
DON BASILIO *A music master*	(Tenor)
DON CURZIO *'A lawyer*	(Tenor)
SUSANNA *The Countess's maid*	(Soprano)
MARCELLINA *The housekeeper*	(Contralto)
BARBARINA *Antonio's daughter*	(Soprano)

Da Ponte has kept most of the complicated action of Beaumarchais' satirical comedy and Mozart, though working within the formal limits of the old opera buffa, has managed to reflect every turn of the intrigue, every mood of the characters, in music as fluent as it is enchanting. He did not confine the action to recitatives, interspersed with static arias and duets of lyrical beauty (though there are a number of such) or reflective ensembles, but was able to carry it forward during formal ensembles of some complexity without holding up their flow or requiring the voices to sing out of character. The great finale of Act II plays for 20 minutes and is packed with dramatic incident and the shorter finale of Act IV is similar, not to mention the two trios and the sextet. That is why fairly close acquaintance with the story is essential to full enjoyment of the music, which in this respect is at least 70 years ahead of its time. The music is also full of small touches which admirably underline psychological moments and since Mozart is the composer, for all that he was setting an artificial comedy, genuine emotions keep breaking through. The Countess and Susanna are women deeply in love with their men, despite their high-spirited enjoyment of intrigue; the Count is not just a conventional philanderer but both a proud aristocrat and a passionate sensualist; and Cherubino feels the emotional confusion of an adolescent in a lax moral milieu.

The familiar and sparkling Overture foreshadows the pace at which the opera moves but has no thematic connection with it.

ACT I

A half-furnished room. In the opening little duet Figaro is measuring the room and Susanna trying on a hat. This is to be their room when they are married and Figaro thinks its situation, between the rooms of the Count and Countess, convenient. But in a further duettino Susanna points out the risks in having the Count so close to herself. Indeed, from what Don Basilio has told her, he intends to revive on her his "droit de Seigneur" which he has renounced. She answers the Countess's bell, leaving Figaro to warn the Count, in an aria, that if he wishes to dance he himself will call the tune. He goes off as Bartolo and Marcellina enter. The latter (formerly in Bartolo's service) plans that Susanna shall refuse the Count's attentions and that the Count, in his rage, will insist on Figaro marrying herself. Figaro's debts to her will be a useful lever. Bartolo sees this plot as his revenge on Figaro for helping the Count steal Rosina, now the Countess, from himself (cf. *The Barber of Seville*). In the Revenge aria Bartolo promises to use all his legal wiles to further it. As he leaves Susanna returns and, in another duettino, the two rivals for Figaro's hand exchange bitchy civilities, until Marcellina, worsted, flounces out. Cherubino now enters, disconsolate at having been found alone with Barbarina by the Count and dismissed. He wants Susanna to intercede for him with the Countess. He pays her for this service with a song, addressed to all women, in which he expresses his adolescent ardour. The Count is heard approaching and he hides behind a chair. The Count seeks a rendezvous with Susanna in the garden but before she can reply Basilio enters and the Count hides behind the chair, Cherubino managing to creep into it, unseen, where Susanna covers him with a dress. Basilio presses the Count's suit on her. Surely he is preferable to Cherubino who has been hanging around this very room? His tittle-tattle about Cherubino provokes the Count into emerging, at which point a trio, the first of the opera's great action ensembles, begins. The Count, in a rage, wants Basilio to go and have Cherubino sent away; Basilio excuses himself for his tactlessness, while thoroughly enjoying the situation; Susanna, to gain time, pretends to faint, but recovers quickly when Basilio leads her to the chair where Cherubino is concealed, and tries to defend Cherubino against Basilio's "suspicions".

But the Count describes how he had found him with Barbarina by gently removing a tablecloth. He illustrates this by picking up the dress and revealing Cherubino to Susanna's discomfiture and Basilio's glee. After the trio the Count sends for Figaro, but suddenly realizes how awkward it is for him that Cherubino has overheard all he said to Susanna. A chorus of peasants enters, singing the Count's praises. Figaro seeks to get the Count publicly to confirm his abnegation of his "droit de Seigneur" by placing a bridal veil on Susanna's head, but the Count puts this off for a more formal occasion. When the peasants have left the Count agrees to pardon Cherubino but makes him an ensign in his regiment which he must join at once. The Act ends with the well-known aria "Non più andrai" in which Figaro tells Cherubino that he must exchange his soft and amorous life for military hardships.

ACT II

The Countess's boudoir. The Countess sighs in the aria "Porgi amor" for her husband's love to be restored to her. After she has had a few words with Susanna on modern husbands Figaro enters in high spirits, with a plan. He has sent the Count a letter warning him that the Countess has an assignation that evening. Susanna is to agree to meet him in the garden but they will send Cherubino in disguise in her place and the Countess shall surprise them. He goes off, singing a fragment of his first aria, to fetch Cherubino who, when he arrives, is very happy to sing to the Countess his latest composition, the famous "Voi che sapete" in which he asks the ladies if his symptoms are those of love. Susanna locks the door, dresses, and rehearses the page as a girl (aria) and goes out for a moment. But the Count's knock is heard. Cherubino runs into the Countess's bed-chamber. The Countess locks the door to that room and takes the key before she admits the Count. He is becoming jealously suspicious, having received Figaro's letter and hearing a noise from his wife's room which she attributes to Susanna, who in fact enters and hides in an alcove. Then follows a fine trio in which the suspicious Count calls on Susanna to come out of his wife's room, the Countess tries to restrain him, and Susanna comments in asides from the alcove. The Count goes off to fetch tools to force the door, taking his wife with him and locking the outer door. In a breathless little duet Susanna calls out Cherubino and he makes his escape by jumping out of the window. Susanna takes his place in the bedroom. The Count and Countess return, he with tools in his hand, and she confesses that Cherubino is in her room. Now begins the finale. In the first part the Count, in a jealous rage, demands the key and the Countess, after vainly trying to deflect him by telling him something of the truth, eventually hands it over. He draws his sword and opens the door. Susanna comes demurely out, to the amazement of both the others (andante) while the

Count goes into the bedroom to see whether Cherubino is there. Susanna quickly indicates to the Countess what has happened. The tables are now turned. The Count can only apologize while the women make the most of their advantage before the Countess forgives him. They explain that the offending letter was written by Figaro. (An allegro over sprightly orchestral motives.) In the next section Figaro comes in to announce that all is ready for the wedding but the Count confronts him with the letter. There is an awkward moment when Figaro, despite hints from the women, tries to deny knowledge of it. Just when this hurdle is surmounted, in comes the drunken Antonio, carrying a broken pot of carnations and bitterly complaining that an unknown man has jumped from the balcony upon them. Figaro says that it was he who jumped but Antonio maintains it looked more like the page. He produces a paper which had been dropped and the Count snatches it from him, and asks Figaro what it is. The three gain a little time by dismissing Antonio. Just in time the Countess remembers that the page had his commission with him and that it lacked a seal and the women prompt Figaro accordingly. The dangerous corner has almost been turned when Marcellina sails in together with Basilio and Bartolo. She claims that Figaro has contracted to marry her and should honour his bond. The Count prepares to give judgment between the two groups. As the tempo reaches a final prestissimo, the calm phrases of Marcellina's camp contrast with the agitation of Figaro, Susanna, and the Countess and the Act ends with the position unresolved.

ACT III

A large hall decorated for the wedding. As the Count ponders the situation, Susanna comes nervously to him, on a pretext, and hints that if she is rewarded for the assignation she might change her mind. This leads to a duet in which she agrees to meet him in the garden. But as she leaves he overhears her telling Figaro that the suit is decided in their favour. He gives vent to his anger that his servants should thus be playing with his affections in an accompanied recitative and dramatic aria which shows him in a more dignified light than hitherto. When Marcellina, Don Curzio, and Bartolo enter with Figaro the Count insists that Figaro must marry Marcellina or pay her. Figaro protests that he cannot marry without consent of his parents from whom he was stolen. This leads, via a strawberry mark on his arm, to the discovery that he is the long-lost (illegitimate) son of Marcellina and Bartolo and foils the Count's plan. During a formal sextet in which the humour of the situation is exploited, Susanna enters with money to pay Marcellina off and is at first so disconcerted to find her embracing Figaro that she slaps his face. When the facts are explained to her she is overjoyed. All leave and there is a short encounter between Barbarina and Cherubino, thought by the Count to be already in Seville. The Countess enters and justifies to herself the ruses to which her husband's conduct has reduced her. In the beautiful aria "Dove sono" she dwells on her deep love for him and her hopes of winning him back. Antonio tells the Count that he has found evidence of Cherubino's presence in his own cottage. To confirm Susanna's assignation with the Count the Countess dictates, and Susanna takes down, in a charming duet, a note which the latter is to send him. It is sealed with a pin which is to be returned to acknowledge receipt. Barbarina and peasant girls now arrive to present flowers to the Countess as the ceremony begins. Cherubino is discovered masquerading among them but Barbarina foils the Count by reminding him that when he kissed her he always promised her whatever she wanted. Now she wants to marry Cherubino. Figaro now proposes that the double wedding begin, and after an anxious moment when he is confronted with Cherubino, he gets his way. A march begins and all take their places. The praises of the Count for abolishing his "droit de Seigneur" are sung. While a fandango is being danced, Susanna kneels before the Count and slips him the note. The Count pricks his finger on the pin which amuses the unsuspecting Figaro. The Count dismisses the company and invites them to return at nightfall for the wedding celebrations.

ACT IV

The garden, with two small arbours. Night. Barbarina is looking, in a half-serious cavatina in a minor key, for the pin for Susanna which she has lost. Figaro and Marcellina find her and elicit from the naive girl the nature of her errand and the accompanying message. They send her off with another pin. Figaro is now furiously jealous of Susanna, and, while Marcellina goes off to warn Susanna, sings an aria—with an apposite pair of horns entering in its coda—railing against women. He hides in an arbour as the Countess and Susanna arrive disguised in each other's clothes. Left alone, the latter addresses her "dear one" for whom she waits, in the exquisite "Deh vieni, non tardar". Figaro assumes, as she intended, that she is thinking of the Count. Cherubino enters looking for Barbarina, finds the Countess and, thinking her Susanna, tries to flirt with her. The finale begins at this point, with the Count, Figaro, and Susanna all watching. When Cherubino attempts to kiss the Countess, the Count intervenes and sends him packing. In the next section the Count makes ardent love to his own wife (in disguise) and gives her a diamond ring. He persuades her to enter an arbour with him. After a beautiful modulation Figaro has a moment of self-pity before Susanna calls to him. He soon recognizes her, but he makes love to her as if he still thought her the Countess and is boxed on the ears. Then, to a more natural strain, he lets her know that she is recognized and they swiftly make their peace. But when the Count is heard looking for Susanna, they decide to play the comedy out. Susanna withdraws into an arbour, but not before the Count sees them, is taken in and summons everyone. He enters the arbour and pulls out successively Cherubino, Barbarina, Marcellina and what he takes for his contrite wife. He refuses all forgiveness until the real Countess suddenly appears, saying that she at least will secure their pardon. There is a pause, and then, in a lovely andante passage the Count seeks, and is accorded, his wife's forgiveness and all the principals applaud the reunion. In a final allegro they propose that so harrowing a day should end in festivity.

Die Meistersinger von Nürnberg

(The Mastersingers of Nuremberg). Music drama in three acts. Music by R. Wagner. Libretto by the composer. First produced at Munich, June 21st, 1868.

SCENE: Nuremberg.

TIME: Middle of the sixteenth century.

PRINCIPAL CHARACTERS:

HANS SACHS	*A cobbler*	⎫	(Bass-baritone)
VEIT POGNER	*A goldsmith*	⎬ *Mastersingers*	(Bass)
SIXTUS BECKMESSER	*The Town Clerk*		(Baritone)
FRITZ KOTHNER	*A baker*	⎭	(Bass)
WALTHER VON STOLZING	*A Knight from Franconia*		(Tenor)
DAVID	*Sachs's apprentice*		(Tenor)
EVA	*Pogner's daughter*		(Soprano)
MAGDALENE	*Eva's companion*		(Mezzo-soprano)

This opera is Wagner's only work dealing with real people and involving comedy situations. Its humane, genial, and tender spirit is in the finest German tradition. It is essentially a protest against the hide-bound in art. It has been a seminal work for operatic composers working in realistic vein, not least because of its amazingly resourceful score, in the "infinite melody" of which "leading motives" undergo every kind of development, permutation, and combination to match the stage action. Yet, although the music dates from Wagner's maturity, it contains a number of set pieces—the chorales in the first and last scenes, Walther's two songs in Act I, the versions of his Prize Song, and the glorious quintet at the end of Act III Scene 1 when the action is held up while the five singers soliloquize.

The well-known Overture, which introduces some of the main "leading motives", beginning with the pompous Mastersingers' theme, leads into

ACT I

Inside St Katherine's Church. The congregation is singing a chorale. Eva and Walther exchange glances (to motives associated with their love) and after the service Walther manages to speak to her of his feelings. He learns from Magdalene that her hand is to be the prize offered by her father (a keen member of the Mastersingers' Guild) in a contest of song to be held next day (Midsummer Day). When they have gone David tells him about the Guild, which Walther has come to join, and the qualifying rules, while the other apprentices arrange the vestry for a meeting. The Mastersingers slowly assemble and Kothner calls the roll (long crescendo and climax). Pogner then formally announces the morrow's contest and they discuss its conditions. The radical Sachs's proposal that the people have a say in the choice of victor is turned down as a threat to the purity of their art. Walther is introduced and, after a lyrical passage describing how he learnt his art from Walther von der Vogelweide and the music of the woods, and some further indoctrination on the rules, begins his Trial Song. Beckmesser, having explained that only seven breaches of the rules are allowed, takes his place in the Marker's box. Walther sings passionately of spring and young love but is interrupted by the emergence of Beckmesser with his board covered with marks. Amid the ensuing hubbub Sachs alone is for hearing the singer out. He finds the song new but not confused and tells Beckmesser that his judgment would be sounder if he listened more carefully. But the Masters declare that Walther has failed and the meeting breaks up in confusion leaving Sachs pondering a fragment of the Trial Song. The bassoon quizzically alludes to the Mastersingers' theme.

ACT II

A street, with Pogner's house on one side and Sachs's shop opposite. Evening. David tells Magdalene of Walther's failure and withdraws with Sachs into his house. As Pogner and Eva sit for a moment Pogner insists that only a Master can win tomorrow's contest. Sachs then sits in his doorway and tries to work; but fragments of the Trial Song go through his head and he cannot reconcile its spontaneous poetry with the rules of the craft. Eva joins him and coyly hints that rather than let Beckmesser win her tomorrow he himself, a widower, might compete. She extracts from him details of Walther's failure but her angry departure gives away her feelings for the latter. Sachs closes his door but leaves a gleam of light. Magdalene is trying to get Eva home when Walther arrives. He speaks with bitterness of the Masters and urges her to elope with him. She reappears in Magdalene's dress; but Sachs who has overheard, opens his door and frustrates their scheme. Just then Beckmesser arrives to serenade her and they withdraw into hiding and watch. Magdalene appears at the window in Eva's clothes. Sachs works noisily at Beckmesser's shoes and sings lustily a song about Eva in Paradise. When Beckmesser can at last begin Sachs infuriatingly hammers at the shoes. The row brings out David and the neighbours. A brawl ensues. Sachs hurries Walther into his house and Pogner takes Eva home, just as the Night-watchman's quaint horn is heard. Everyone quickly disperses. The watchman, alone on the stage, sings his ritual cry. Finally the stage is empty; the full moon comes out; and as muted strings, flute, and bassoon dwell softly on some of the preceding music, we reach perhaps the most exquisite "quiet curtain" in the whole range of opera.

ACT III

A reflective Prelude, based on two themes from Act II and the chorale to be heard in the final scene, leads into
Scene 1. Sachs's workshop. Early morning. Sachs sits reading. David, after alluding to the affection between Magdalene and himself, urges Sachs to marry again. Left alone, Sachs broods on human folly, in a famous monologue. Walther enters and speaks of a beautiful dream he has had. As Walther describes it (first version of Prize Song) Sachs writes it down and gives him some wise counsel. They go off to dress for the festival. Beckmesser limps in pain from last night's beating-up (distorted fragments of his serenade). His eyes fall on the manuscript which he assumes that Sachs intends to sing in the contest and he quickly pockets it. Sachs enters, assures the envious Beckmesser that he is not competing and presents him with the text for his own use. Beckmesser leaves in high spirits. Eva then visits him on the pretext that her shoes do not fit. Walther reappears, dressed as a Knight and Sachs intercepts their spellbound glances. While he works at Eva's shoe Walther sings the third verse of his dream-song. Eva falls sobbing on Sachs's breast, exclaiming that once she would not have hesitated to award him the prize; but Sachs gruffly replies that he does not want the fate of King Marke in *Tristan and Isolde* (quotation therefrom in the orchestra). David and Magdalene enter in their festal dress and the Mastersong is solemnly christened. David is admitted to the Shoemakers' Guild by Sachs; he and Magdalene can now think of marriage. The thoughts of all five blend in an ecstatic ensemble. Between the scenes festive music is heard.
Scene 2. A meadow outside the city with a holiday crowd of townspeople. Processions of various guilds assemble and the apprentices perform a bucolic dance. Finally the Mastersingers arrive and take their places, Pogner leading Eva by the hand. All join in a chorale in honour of Sachs. He announces the contest. Beckmesser makes a comical mess of the stolen song and is laughed down, blaming Sachs as the author. Sachs disclaims authorship but to the general surprise calls it a beautiful song and says that whoever can render it properly will proclaim himself the author. Walther comes forward, sings the Prize Song and is acclaimed by all. He is crowned by Eva with a wreath. The Guild offers to make him a Mastersinger but he declines the honour. Sachs takes him by the hand and admonishes him to hold the Masters in proper respect. The crowd acclaims Sachs. (In the final pages much of the Overture is repeated by the orchestra.)

The Midsummer Marriage

Opera in three acts. Music by Michael Tippett. Libretto by the composer. First produced at the Royal Opera House, Covent Garden, January 27th, 1955.

SCENE: Not specified.

TIME: The present.

CHARACTERS:

MARK *A young man of unknown parentage*	(Tenor)
JENIFER *His betrothed, a young girl*	(Soprano)
KING FISHER *Her father, a businessman*	(Baritone)
BELLA *His secretary*	(Soprano)
JACK *Her boy-friend, a mechanic*	(Tenor)
SOSOSTRIS *A clairvoyante*	(Contralto)
THE ANCIENTS *Priest and priestess of the temple*	
	(Bass and mezzo-soprano)
STREPHON *Dancer*	

This is an allegorical opera on the theme of the need for illumination and purification before love can be consummated. It is thus a lineal descendant of "The Magic Flute" (and to some extent "Die Frau ohne Schatten"). There are two contrasting couples and their trial is effected by participation in a fertility rite loaded with anthropological and symbolic allusions. The mystic poetical heart of the work is given a contemporary setting and the action takes place at varying levels of experience. The composer has thus set himself a heavy task. The musical core of a beautifully shaped, if uneven work is the Four Ritual Dances, charged with atmosphere and now fairly familiar in the concert-hall, and the fine choruses. The long final scene of withdrawal, as the chorus descend the hill, is deeply impressive, but some of the earlier effects need careful handling by the producer if the impact of a serious and highly-wrought score, full of the composer's busy counterpoint and rhythmic freedom deriving from Elizabethan madrigal technique, is not to be muffled by the occasional obscurity or banality of the action and of the imagery by which it is illustrated. Perhaps this is why it was at first slow to win acclamation.

ACT I   MORNING

A clearing on a wooded hill with a sanctuary on a lofty platform at the
back.   Dawn.   After an introductory passage the curtain rises on an
empty stage and the chorus are heard directing each other to "the place".
They enter and greet the rising midsummer sun, but, when the mist
clears, finding the site eerie, hide among the trees. Dancers led by Strephon
and followed by the Ancients come out of the temple and perform a rite.
Mark, running on, breaks the dance up and demands a new dance for this his
wedding-day.   The Ancients protest but when he persists the He-Ancient
promises him one. It is the old one but the He-Ancient trips Strephon who
falls, to drive home the dangers of change. He warns Mark that he will
learn a new dance today. The dancers and Ancients retire into the temple.
Mark explains to their friends, who have made the ascent for the celebration
of his runaway marriage to Jenifer and now come out of hiding, that he has
sometimes seen these unchanging beings since boyhood; he thinks they know
the secret of his birth. He sings of his happiness at his love for Jenifer. She
appears dressed for a journey and tells the protesting Mark that there will
be no wedding today. She wants truth, not love. For her the light, for
him the shadow; and she slowly climbs the steps "up to Paradise", her voice
soaring over a choral commentary, until she disappears from view. The
girls laugh while the boys attempt to console Mark who disappears through
the gates of a cave, below the temple—into the shadow. King Fisher now
hurries in, followed by Bella, in pursuit of his daughter. He pompously
makes Bella knock on the temple gates and inquire of the Ancients, who
appear, if they know where his daughter is. But they give him no help.
The masterful King Fisher says that the gates of the cave must then be
forced and Bella goes off to fetch her friend, the handyman Jack, to do it.
Meanwhile King Fisher sends Mark's friends, well paid, to spy behind the
wall and see what dangers lurk. He tries to do the same with Jenifer's
friends but the girls refuse to be bribed and he drives them away. Bella
returns with Jack, who as an honest working-man gets out his tools and
prepares to do as he is asked; but the warning voice of Sosostris is heard
from behind the gates. The chorus return and there is an ensemble in
which Bella and the girls urge him to stop and King Fisher and the young
men to go on. He is continuing with the task when Jenifer appears,
partially transfigured, at the top of the steps. Jack and Bella slip away.
Jenifer slowly descends in a mystic trance. The gates of the cave open and
Mark is seen, also half transfigured. The Ancients appear and call on them
both to justify their earlier strife. Jenifer tells of her compulsive urge to
leave Mark and seek the light and of the joy of her experience. King
Fisher's attempt to bring her down to earth is silenced by the Ancients.
Mark's experience in the dark places has been the opposite and it is an
animal intoxication of the senses which he has undergone. Jenifer shows
Mark his image in a golden mirror which he strikes from her hands with a

golden wand. "There is no union but in full communion" and she enters the gates of the cave to share his experience while he slowly climbs the steps. The Ancients withdraw. King Fisher rails against this "midsummer madness" and hints that if Mark will rescue Jenifer then perhaps he may be allowed to marry her. He departs, leaving the chorus mocking him. The Act ends with music similar to that of the introduction.

ACT II   AFTERNOON

The same scene as in Act I but viewed from another angle. Strephon is discovered motionless on the temple steps, to brooding chords which will dominate the Act. The chorus is heard off-stage enjoying the midsummer day. The uncomplicated couple, Bella and Jack, enter. She proposes that they marry and he accepts. They dwell, in a duet, on the domestic bliss before them before withdrawing, as in a dream, into the wood. Strephon and the brooding chords now return and three of the ritual dances are performed. In each a female dancer pursues a male (Strephon) and a sacrifice is averted by an ever narrower margin. In the first (The Earth in autumn) a hound pursues a hare; in the second (The Waters in winter) an otter pursues a fish; and in the third (The Air in spring) a hawk pursues a small bird. (A fanfare-like progression of chords precedes the first and second dances). Bella has been terrified by what she has seen, not "being born for all these mysteries". Pulling herself together, she makes Jack hold her mirror while she restores her appearance, in a lyrical passage, and wins his admiration. They go off to rejoin King Fisher. The chorus is again heard off-stage and just before the curtain falls the brooding chords return.

ACT III   EVENING AND NIGHT

As in Act I. The chorus are carousing at dusk. Does the night hold Love or Death? King Fisher, entering with Bella, exclaims that he has summoned them for Victory. He has called his private clairvoyante to unravel the Ancients' mysteries. He sends them to conduct Madame Sosostris up with honour. The Ancients are summoned by Bella and he challenges them to a contest for which his daughter is the prize. The four of them join in a soliloquizing quartet before the He-Ancient, his warning spurned, accepts the challenge. The chorus return, ceremonially bearing, to a march, a cloaked figure with a crystal bowl, which they set down. Bella recognizes it as Jack and the chorus mock him. But a large contraption of black veils becomes visible. This conceals Sosostris and the crystal bowl is placed beside her by Jack as acolyte. King Fisher calls on her to say where Jenifer is and how she may be rescued.

Sosostris, after some show of conventional oracular reluctance ("Oh bitterness of a Pythia's fate") sees a girl approached by the glorious lion of love. King Fisher interrupts and snatching the bowl from Jack orders him to unveil her. Jack is restrained by Bella, in the name of their unborn child. After a big ensemble he "chooses his destiny" to strip the veil "not from Sosostris but myself" and runs off with Bella as the Act II chorus is heard again. King Fisher himself begins to unveil Sosostris and reveals Jenifer and Mark, radiantly transfigured, in mutual contemplation. He draws a pistol but, before he can fire at Mark, falls dead, clutching at his heart. He is carried into the temple. The way is now cleared by this human sacrifice for the final ritual dance (Fire in summer) on which voices are superimposed. Strephon and the dancers emerge to perform it as the chorus sing the fanfare-like chords to the words "Fire! Fire! St John's Fire!" The chorus sing of "carnal love through which the race of men is everlastingly renewed" as Jenifer and Mark gradually disappear. The fanfare-like chords are repeated, the brooding music of Act II returns, the fire dies down and only the chorus remain on the dark stage, invoking the sun to make haste to return. Dawn comes and the sanctuary is veiled in mist. Jenifer and Mark, dressed for their wedding, advance to meet each other, purified by the visionary night and happy in their love. As it grows light the chorus go slowly down the hill rejoicing, their unaccompanied voices growing ever more distant. But the orchestra has the final word, with the empty stage bathed in bright sunlight.

Norma

Opera in two acts. Music by V. Bellini. Libretto by F. Romani after L. A. Soumet. First produced at La Scala, Milan, December 26th, 1831.

SCENE: Gaul.

TIME: About 50 B.C.

CHARACTERS:

NORMA	*The High Priestess*	(Soprano)
OROVESO	*The Archdruid, her father*	(Bass)
ADALGISA	*A temple virgin*	(Soprano)
CLOTILDA	*Norma's confidante*	(Soprano)
POLLIONE	*Roman pro-consul in Gaul*	(Tenor)
FLAVIO	*A centurion*	(Tenor)

"Norma" is as "old-fashioned" as any opera remaining in the repertory, with long recitatives and with arias and duets strictly conventional in form and bland in harmony. Yet it is a great deal more than a vehicle for a soprano with personality and ability to sing its florid line with ease. Bellini's languid melodies, with their many turns and drooping cadences, are charged with surprising emotional power and if ever the bel canto style can acquire a dramatic life of its own in the hands of a great singer—or rather singers, since the part of Adalgisa is also most exacting—it is here. Moreover, the action moves inexorably forward to the final scene which offers a fitting musical climax.

ACT I

Scene 1. Sacred grove of the Druids. After a Prelude, Druids, High Priests, and Oroveso assemble for their rites. Oroveso prays, as their introductory andante turns to a march, that Norma, when she comes to cut the sacred mistletoe, will be inspired with hate and anger against the Romans and will give the signal for revolt. They depart. Pollione and Flavio enter cautiously. Pollione confides that he no longer loves Norma, who has borne him children, but loves Adalgisa. He tells Flavio, in a cavatina, how Adalgisa was snatched from his side at the altar of Venus in Rome and a voice was heard

saying: "This is the vengeance of Norma upon her faithless lover." Hearing
the Druids returning Pollione and Flavio go off, Pollione vowing to destroy
the temple and forest of the Druid god. Druids and Druidesses assemble to
the music of their march, over which they announce the arrival of Norma.
Norma informs Oroveso and the others that the time for the sword has
not yet come. Rome will die consumed by her own vices; let them await
that hour. She then cuts the mistletoe and prays to the moon to temper
her people's ardour in the justly famous "Casta diva". The assembly assures
her that they are ready to fall upon Pollione and the Romans when God,
through her, gives the word. The ornate cabaletta of Norma's aria is an
aside in which she tells herself that her heart can never give that word and
prays for the return of Pollione's love. All depart (to the march) except
Adalgisa who meditates on the fatal Roman who has made her traitor to
her vows. Pollione joins her and in a long duet overcomes her scruples and
persuades her to meet him the next day to flee with him to Rome.

Scene 2. Outside Norma's dwelling. Norma bids Clotilda take her children
away. She is filled with foreboding as Pollione has been recalled to Rome
and will, she fears, desert her. Adalgisa visits her and confesses that she is
in love. Norma, reminded of her own experience, releases her from her
sacred vows. (This to a fine duet). But, just as she inquires who Adalgisa's
lover is, Pollione appears and Adalgisa tells her it is he. She cannot at first
understand Norma's outburst of anger directed at Pollione. A big trio
follows in which Norma denounces Pollione, Pollione seeks to defend
himself and Adalgisa, becoming aware, dismisses him and, heartbroken,
declares that she will restore him to Norma. At the close the sacred gong
and the voices of the Druids calling Norma to the rites are heard, as she
drives Pollione out.

ACT II

Scene 1. Interior of Norma's dwelling. In a recitative and arioso passage
(the sad melody of which has been heard before the curtain rises) Norma
resolves to kill her sleeping children but cannot bring herself to do it. She
sends Clotilda for Adalgisa. She tells her that she is going to take her own
life and makes her promise to take her children to Pollione and marry
him. In another splendid duet Adalgisa replies that she will go to Pollione,
but to plead with him to return to Norma. She begs Norma to relent for
her children's sake and eventually prevails on her. They swear lifelong
friendship.

Scene 2. In the Druid's forest. The Druids are hoping to hear that Pollione
has left and that the moment for revolt has come. Oroveso points out that
another, even crueller Roman will succeed him and counsels further
patience. The Druids leave. Norma enters, awaiting the outcome of
Adalgisa's mission. When Clotilda arrives with the news that Adalgisa has

failed and has returned to the temple to renew her vows, and that Pollione has sworn to abduct her, Norma strikes the gong with fury. She orders the slightly dazed Druids, who duly appear, to wage war against the Romans. They respond, in a fierce chorus. Clotilda arrives with the news that a Roman has been captured desecrating the temple of the virgins and Pollione is led in by armed Gauls. Norma is about to strike him with her sacred dagger but her hand fails and she says she must question him in private. In the ensuing duet, with Pollione in her power, she offers to save his life if he will promise never to see Adalgisa again. When he refuses she threatens to kill their children. Adalgisa too shall die so that she may strike at him through her. This brings him pleading to her feet. (The second part of the duet is based on a melody heard in the Prelude to the opera.) Norma, now calls the Druids and announces that a priestess has broken her vows and betrayed the country and must die on the pyre—it is herself. There is general horror and incredulity. Norma turns upon Pollione and declares that they are to die together on the pyre. Pollione at last shows remorse and recognition of her worth and craves forgiveness before they die. While Norma reaffirms her guilt her father rejects her and refuses her plea to save her children. Then, against ejaculations from the chorus and with support from Pollione, she presses her plea in a wonderful phrase which soars over the ensemble, until Oroveso at last relents. She is covered with a black veil and is led with Pollione, who now protests his love for her, into the flames.

Oedipus Rex

Opera-oratorio in two acts. Music by I. Stravinsky. Libretto by J. Cocteau after Sophocles (Latin translation by J. Daniélou). First produced (as oratorio) at the Théâtre Sarah Bernhardt, Paris, May 30th, 1927 and (as opera) at Vienna, 1928.

SCENE: Thebes.

TIME: Antiquity.

CHARACTERS:

OEDIPUS	*King of Thebes*	(Tenor)
JOCASTA	*His wife*	(Mezzo-soprano)
CREON	*Her brother*	(Bass-baritone)
TIRESIAS	*A blind soothsayer*	(Bass)
A SHEPHERD		(Tenor)
A MESSENGER		(Bass-baritone)

Stravinsky intended this imaginative reworking of Sophocles' drama to have a stylized quality. There is to be a minimum of movement on the stage and the words are Latin—a language "not dead but turned to stone . . . and monumentalized." The action is explained in the vernacular by a Speaker.

The music itself has something remote and monumental about it—especially in its great choral passages—but at the same time responds with sensitivity to every nuance of the action, so that the overall effect has something of the same emotional dignity and restraint as Sophocles' tragedy itself. Yet the characters emerge with extraordinary clarity—Oedipus for instance with a self-confident coloratura until his humiliation, Jocasta with her rapid repetitions "protesting too much", the straightforward Creon, and the minor parts no less vivid. The orchestration is subtle, with many striking effects.

ACT I

The people of Thebes, afflicted by the plague, call on Oedipus to save them. (Note the rising minor third usually in triple rhythm on timpani or basses—it will appear constantly.) Oedipus promises confidently to do so; Creon has been sent to consult the oracle. (The florid line of Oedipus' aria perhaps suggests his pride.) Creon is saluted by the crowd and reports, in 4/4 time and the key of C major, that the murderer of Laius is still living in Thebes and must be driven out. In another aria Oedipus boasts of his skill at solving riddles and promises to save Thebes. After a prayer to the gods the people hail Tiresias and press him to speak. The aged Tiresias tries to evade this duty (wandering bassoon and other wood-wind) but when accused by Oedipus of being himself the murderer, speaks out: the murderer is among them and is a king. Oedipus replies with an appeal to the people against the envious: Creon wants to be king and Tiresias is in his pay. (A superb phrase to the words "Invidia fortunam odit" occurs three times.) Jocasta appears and is greeted by the people.

ACT II

Jocasta reproves Oedipus and Creon for quarrelling in public. She goes on rather hectically, in an aria the middle section of which has a rapid clarinet accompaniment, to declare that oracles always lie. Was her son not to kill Laius? But Laius is dead, killed at the crossroads. She becomes almost hysterical. The chorus underline the word "crossroads" (trivium). Oedipus, who joins her in a duet, confesses with sudden fear that he once killed an old man at a crossroads on his way from Corinth. He wishes to question the shepherd who was a witness. A messenger arrives with news of Polybus' death; but, he adds, Polybus was not Oedipus' father since he himself had brought him as an infant to the King, having with the shepherd found him exposed on the mountain with his feet pierced by a thong. The chorus comment that Oedipus must be the son of a god and of a nymph. Jocasta, guessing the truth, disappears; but the shepherd, to a pastoral strain, corroborates the story. Oedipus does not yet understand and thinks Jocasta is ashamed of his origin. He floridly exclaims that he is resolved to know his ancestry. But the shepherd and messenger, speaking in close canon, go on to say that he is the son of Laius and Jocasta. Now Oedipus understands and his utterance becomes direct in style to mask his agony. His final words before he leaves—"lux facta est"—are set to a phrase of moving simplicity.

The messenger returns to announce the suicide of Jocasta, which the chorus describe in a kind of march, leading to a fugato passage as the doors are opened and they describe the sight of Oedipus who has put out his own eyes. They resume the opening chorus as they comment on his wretched state and take a tender farewell of their once-loved King.

L'Orfeo

(Orpheus). Legend set to music in a prologue and five acts. Music by C. Monteverdi. Libretto by A. Striggio. First produced at the Accademia degl'Invaghiti, Mantua, February 22nd, 1607.

SCENE: Thrace and Hades.

TIME: Antiquity.

PRINCIPAL CHARACTERS:

LA MUSICA (Prologue)	(Soprano)
ORFEO	(Tenor)
EURIDICE	(Soprano)
A NYMPH	(Soprano)
TWO SHEPHERDS	(Male alto or Tenor; Tenor)
THE MESSENGER (Silvia)	(Soprano)
SPERANZA (Hope)	(Mezzo-soprano)
CARONTE (Charon)	(Bass)
PROSERPINA	(Mezzo-soprano)
PLUTONE	(Bass)
APOLLO	(Tenor)

This work, the earliest in the repertory, was written for private performance at the Ducal Court and printed two years later. It combines pre-existing styles—e.g., madrigals, orchestral "sinfonie", and monodies in which the words had heavily dominated the music. Earlier forms of stage music are left behind and opera begins to emerge. The orchestral passages contain the germ of leading motives while changes of instrumental colour underline changes of scene and mood. Monody becomes an expressive recitative constantly spilling over into arioso. But, though the work admirably balances words and music, it is weak, especially in Acts I and V, in action. It is not until "L'Incoronazione di Poppea" 35 years later that Monteverdi attained a wholly satisfying fusion of all three elements. Here, despite beautiful choruses and arias and much subtle musical construction, it is perhaps only in the second part of Act II and in Act III that a modern audience will instantly feel the pull of strong dramatic tension. The convention of a Prologue in which gods or supernatural beings take part here seems entirely natural.

PROLOGUE

After an orchestral toccata, marked to be played three times, and a short ritornello Music introduces herself to the princely audience. She speaks of her powers and calls for silence while she sings of Orfeo. Her recitative is broken up and concluded by five repetitions of the ritornello.

ACT I

The glades of Thrace. This is a static scene of rejoicing over the wedding of Orfeo and Euridice. It is introduced by a Shepherd. Nymphs and shepherds sing (in five part chorus) a chorale followed by a madrigal and a dance-like ritornello. Called upon by another Shepherd, Orfeo then sings of his happiness to which Euridice briefly replies. The madrigal and its ritornello and the chorale are then repeated in reverse order. A more serious note is struck by a solo, a duet, and a trio, each followed by a further ritornello. Finally a further chorus underlines Orfeo's happiness.

ACT II

As in Act I. Another pastoral scene of rejoicing in which gay songs are successively sung by Orfeo, a Shepherd, and two Shepherds in thirds. In response to a request by the chorus Orfeo then sings a more formal aria with four strophes in which duple and triple rhythms alternate attractively. The atmosphere is suddenly transformed by the arrival of the Messenger Silvia, a friend of Euridice—with tidings the bitter import of which the Shepherd is the first to apprehend. She tells Orfeo that his bride is dead and goes on, in a justly famous recitative underpinned by modulations which increase the tension, to describe how Euridice had been bitten by a serpent when picking flowers and had died in her arms calling upon Orfeo. After a moment of stunned silence Orfeo cries out to his bride, in another moving passage, that if she is dead, so is he. He will go down into the abyss and either soften the heart of the King of the Shades and bring her back or else remian with her. He ends with a touching farewell to earth, sky, and sun. The alternate mourning of the chorus and the two Shepherds is broken by a passage for the Messenger in which she laments her own fate as the bringer of the bad news, an outcast hateful to them all. The act ends with a repetition of the ritornello from the Prologue.

ACT III

Shores of the River Styx. A sinfonia given to brass instruments sets the scene. Orfeo has been accompanied thus far by Speranza, but the latter tells him, in an expressive recitative, that she must now leave him because it is decreed "Abandon hope, all ye who enter here." The suspicious Caronte forbids him passage, and a second sinfonia is heard on the trombones. Orfeo pleads with Caronte in the highly ornate aria "Possente spirto" with concertante parts successively for two violins, two cornetti, a double harp, and string trio. Caronte replies that he has enjoyed this· exhibition of Orfeo's skill but that he is unmoved from the path of duty. Orfeo renews his plea in a simple recitative culminating in the thrice repeated "give me back my love" on rising semitones. Caronte has been lulled to sleep and seizing his opportunity Orfeo enters his bark and crosses to the further shore, singing again the rising phrase. Preceded and followed by repetitions of the first sinfonia, a chorus of spirits comment in a beautiful madrigal.

ACT IV

Hades. Proserpina begs Pluto, by the love which he bears her, to heed Orfeo's piteous cries of "Euridice" and restore the latter to the world. Pluto consents on condition that Orfeo does not turn and look upon his bride so long as they are in his kingdom. Two solo spirits, Proserpina, and the chorus of spirits receive his commands with deferential satisfaction. Orfeo's initial strains of joy turn to longing to set eyes on Euridice and to suspicion of a trick. Exclaiming that what Pluto forbids Love commands, he turns. Euridice sadly tells him that through excess of love he has lost her. Orfeo attempts to follow her as she recedes but an unseen power draws him back to the hateful light of day. The chorus comment in another madrigal and the Act ends with the return of the Prologue ritornello.

ACT V

As in Act I. Orfeo wanders lamenting and calls on Nature to join in sympathy. (An echo is three times heard.) He sings the praises of Euridice and forswears all other women. The second Act III sinfonia is repeated. Apollo descends in a cloud and reproaches him for his excesses of joy and sorrow. He offers him immortality in heaven to which Orfeo, once he has been assured that he will see the semblance of Euridice in the stars, assents. Together, to a florid duet, they ascend, and a cheerful chorus is sung below. The work ends with a moresca, a country dance.

Orfeo ed Euridice

(Orpheus and Eurydice). Opera in three acts. Music by C. W. von Gluck. Libretto by R. da Calzabigi. First produced at Vienna, October 5th, 1762.

SCENE: Greece and Hades.

TIME: Antiquity.

CHARACTERS:

ORFEO	(Contralto)
EURIDICE	(Soprano)
AMOR *God of Love*	(Soprano)

"Orfeo" is Gluck's best-known work. It displays at their best both his classical simplicity and his power of combining dramatic expression with the purest bel canto. The name-part was written for a male alto but has usually been allotted in recent times to a contralto of the highest quality. A full corps de ballet and imaginative choreography are desirable for the two scenes in Act II, while sensitive production is more than usually important.

ACT I

The tomb of Euridice. After a brief Overture we see Orfeo, the famous singer, and his friends lamenting the death of his bride, Euridice. He sends them away and continues the lamentation in an aria. Amor appears and bids him descend with his lyre, and prevail with his sweet song on the rulers of Hades to let her depart. But if he looks back at her until they have returned to earth, he will lose her for ever. He does not shrink from the trial and Amor bids him obey the commands of the gods. (A florid aria, added for the Paris production of 1774, when the part was sung by a tenor, is usually omitted.)

ACT II

Scene 1. Entrance to Hades. As Orfeo approaches the Furies rage against his intrusion and call up Cerberus (whose bark is heard in the orchestra). But Orfeo's plea for pity, which at first meets with emphatic cries of "No", finally softens them and they let him pass.

Scene 2. The Elysian Fields where abide the pure spirits. The utter tranquillity of the scene is expressed by the silvery tones of the flute to which the spirits slowly dance. Orfeo acknowledges the place's peace in a lovely aria with oboe obbligato, but yet yearns for Euridice. He is conducted to her but averts his gaze and leads her from the valley.

ACT III

A forest. Orfeo urges Euridice on; but she tarries, chiding him for his failure to cast her even a single glance. She prefers the calm of Hades to life on these terms. At last Orfeo can bear the ordeal no longer and turns to embrace her. At once she falls dead. In distraction Orfeo sings the celebrated aria "Che farò", asking how he can live without her. But Amor reappears and says that his constancy has been tried enough. He restores Euridice to life and the opera ends with thanks and praise to Amor and with dancing.

Orphée aux Enfers

(Orpheus in the Underworld). Opéra-Féerie in four acts. Music by J. Offenbach. Libretto by H. Crémieux and L. Halévy. First produced at Les Bouffes Parisiens, Paris, October 21st, 1858.

SCENE: Thebes, Mount Olympus, and the Underworld.

TIME: Antiquity.

PRINCIPAL CHARACTERS:

PUBLIC OPINION	(Mezzo-soprano)
ORPHEUS *A violinist*	(Tenor)
EURYDICE *His wife*	(Soprano)
PLUTO *God of the Underworld, disguised as Aristée*	(Tenor)
JOHN STYX	(Baritone)
JUPITER	(Baritone)
DIANA	(Soprano)
VENUS	(Contralto)
CUPID	(Soprano)
MARS	(Bass)
MINERVA	(Soprano)
JUNO	(Mezzo-soprano)

This operetta is an early and justly celebrated example of Offenbach's formula of simultaneously satirizing Third Empire Society and debunking mythological personages. It contains some of his most charming and witty numbers including the dig at Gluck. Offenbach tends to be thought unsuitable for Anglo-Saxon taste without heavy adaptation (as well as, understandably, some cutting) and it cannot be precisely predicted what will be the action which the reader will encounter, nor how many choral or balletic episodes will remain. Elaborate description of so light-weight a piece of nonsense is in any case superfluous. But the following summary covers what is likely to be the hard core of any production.

ACT I

The countryside near Thebes. After a short Overture nymphs and shepherds return from the fields and the municipal council assembles, together with Public Opinion who announces that she is keeping an eye on the goings-on from the wings. Eurydice confides in the audience, in couplets with a charming flute accompaniment, that she has lost her heart to a beautiful shepherd, to whom she is bringing flowers. Her husband, Orpheus, catches her, and in the ensuing marital altercation it emerges that she cannot bear his violin. In indignation he threatens to punish her by playing his new concerto—an hour and a quarter long—and a solo violin plays one of Offenbach's best loved melodies to Orpheus's great self-satisfaction and her irritation. He goes off saying that in his position he cannot afford to offend Public Opinion and threatening to set snakes to catch her lover, Aristée. The latter enters and sings a pastoral song about the simple pleasures of the life of a shepherd and bee-keeper. He is not afraid of snakes but Eurydice gets bitten. When Aristée reveals himself as Pluto she gladly consents to die, leaving a note for Orpheus behind her. Finding this he is overjoyed, but Public Opinion appears and, yielding to her insistence that honour requires it and taking a touching farewell of his young pupils, he sets off in pursuit of his wife.

ACT II

Mount Olympus. The gods, bored, are all asleep. Venus, Cupid, and Mars successively steal home from "a little journey to Cythera". Jupiter is awakened by Diana's horns. She explains, in couplets with a touch of a hunting song, that she is upset because Actaeon was not at his usual trysting-place. Jupiter tells her that he has changed him into a stag as she seemed to be compromising herself with him. Mercury, having been sent at Juno's insistence to inquire, brings news of Pluto's escapade with Eurydice and Jupiter sends him to fetch Pluto. Jupiter rebukes him. This, coming on top of the Actaeon episode, is too much for the other deities who break into a chorus of revolt, which is followed by couplets to a witty tune, in which in turn they remind him mockingly of some of his own amorous adventures. Orpheus and Public Opinion are announced, and they group themselves round Jupiter on his throne, expressing their eager anticipation in a Rossini-like ensemble. Egged on by Public Opinion, Orpheus formally complains that Eurydice has been stolen from him, to the opening phrase of "Che farò" from Gluck's *Orpheus,* which being already familiar with it, the deities take up. To his dismay Jupiter at once rules that Eurydice must be returned to Orpheus and announces that he will himself descend to the underworld to see that Pluto complies. The bored deities beg Jupiter to be taken with him and he assents. They sing his praises in a solemn chorale which suddenly breaks into the gay and familiar quick march with which the finale ends.

ACT III

A room in Pluto's palace. After an entr'acte we see Eurydice disenchanted
with Pluto and beginning to miss her husband. John Styx, who is keeping
an eye on her, tells her, in couplets as simple as himself, that if only he
still were king of Boeotia he could have offered her his own love. He
locks her in the next room. Jupiter arrives with Cupid who summons the
Policemen of Love. Together they discover where Eurydice is by making
kissing noises to which she replies. Having taken a look at her through
the keyhole, Jupiter joins her by that route, disguised as a fly which
settles on her shoulder. In the ensuing duet Jupiter buzzes like an insect
and finally Eurydice, quite enchanted, follows suit. Jupiter reveals his
identity and Eurydice begs him to carry her off, which he promises to do
that evening. Pluto comes in search of Eurydice, but John Styx has
forgotten where he left her and Cupid distracts him with a ballet of flies.

ACT IV

A hall in Pluto's palace. Pluto is entertaining his divine guests. His subjects
sing a chorus in praise of him. Cupid calls on Eurydice, who has now been
turned by Jupiter into a Bacchante, to sing a hymn in praise of Bacchus in
which all join. Jupiter leads them all in a minuet and this is followed by the
celebrated "Galop Infernal" or cancan. Pluto is incensed at Jupiter's
attempt to elope with Eurydice, which he foils. But just then Orpheus's
fiddle is heard playing "Che farò" and, accompanied still by Public
Opinion, he enters to claim, somewhat hesitantly, his wife. Jupiter does
not fail to return her to him but imposes the condition that he must walk
in front of her and that a single backward glance will lose her forever.
They set out—to the joy of Public Opinion. But Jupiter looses a
thunderbolt behind Orpheus and he involuntarily looks back. Jupiter
claims Eurydice from Pluto. She is delighted to remain as a Bacchante
and leads the reprise of the cancan with which the operetta ends.

Otello

(Othello). Opera in four acts. Music by G. Verdi. Libretto by A. Boito after W. Shakespeare. First produced at La Scala, Milan, February 5th, 1887.

SCENE: Cyprus.

TIME: End of fifteenth century.

CHARACTERS:

OTELLO	*A Moor, general in the Venetian army*	(Tenor)
IAGO	*His ensign*	(Baritone)
CASSIO	*His lieutenant*	(Tenor)
DESDEMONA	*His wife*	(Soprano)
RODERIGO	*A Venetian gentleman*	(Tenor)
MONTANO	*The previous Governor of Cyprus*	(Bass)
LODOVICO	*Envoy of the Venetian Republic*	(Bass)
A HERALD		(Bass)
EMILIA	*Iago's wife*	(Mezzo-soprano)

"Otello" appeared sixteen years after "Aida" when Verdi was 74. It is the greatest of all his tragic and melodramatic operas. In part this is due to Boito's splendid libretto which, beginning with Shakespeare's Act II, manages to reproduce most of the action and much of the dialogue of the prototype within the requirements of an Italian opera. But over and above the sheer dramatic force of the music the work's strength is that in it Verdi had burst right through the conventional framework of nineteenth century opera and gives its characters an arioso line which, while it deploys the glory of Italian voices and is full of memorable paragraphs and phrases, allows the action to be carried continuously forward without being constantly held up for the verbal and musical repetitions of formal "numbers". With the solitary exception of the mandoline chorus (the one weak passage) these are only admitted where they are an intrinsic part of the action—e.g., the Act I drinking-song, the duet finale of Act II and the Willow Song. While remaining Italianate it is psychological music, moving with the shifting nuances of the words—a trait best exemplified in Otello's wonderful Act III monologue "Dio! mi potevi scagliar". Needless to say, the orchestra plays a fuller part than in Verdi's earlier scores and the title-rôle is vocally and histrionically exacting.

ACT I

A quay by the sea outside the castle. Evening. A violent storm is raging and the people are anxiously watching while a ship bearing Otello, the new Governor, makes for harbour. Their random comments cohere in a great cry of supplication. The ship makes harbour to a shout of "È salvo!" and Otello is welcomed ashore. In a single mighty phrase, with a cruelly high tessitura, he proudly announces victory over the Turks and enters the castle. The storm subsides. In a short exchange between Iago and Roderigo two striking phrases given to Iago underline the main points—that Roderigo loves Desdemona and that Iago hates Otello for letting Cassio usurp his place. The crowd now dance and sing in celebration round a fire which they have been kindling. Iago makes Cassio drink. Cassio proposes a toast to Desdemona, which Iago bids Roderigo note. He then starts a drinking-song in which others join until finally Cassio is too drunk to repeat the words. Roderigo provokes him to a fight. Montano, trying to separate them, is attacked and wounded by Cassio. Roderigo is dispatched by Iago to proclaim a riot and finally Otello comes out to calm the tumult. On hearing Iago's account he relieves Cassio of his post and, as Desdemona appears, awakened by the noise, sends everyone to rest. Otello and Desdemona now sing a long and beautiful love-duet—not one of passion but of serenity. "You loved me for the dangers I had passed, And I loved you that you did pity them." The dark colouring and harmonies of the opening phrases recur in the orchestra at the very end, after an exquisite change of key. The phrase which accompanies their embrace assumes importance later.

ACT II

A hall in the castle. A triplet figure in the short Prelude, continued into the first scene between Iago and Cassio, somehow suggests that it is after a long conference that Iago now advises him to approach Desdemona to intercede with Otello for his reinstatement. Alone, Iago sings his "credo", an arioso in which the brass is conspicuous and the climax is in a sense the soft brass cadence which answers the question "What is there after death?" Cassio now engages Desdemona in conversation in the garden. Iago invites the attention of Otello, who enters, to the scene and in the ensuing conversation cunningly sows the seeds of suspicion. Among the many suggestive phrases in this scene is one in which Iago warns Otello against jealousy. Before they part a deputation of townspeople appear in the garden and in a chorus with mandoline accompaniment make Desdemona a presentation. After their departure Desdemona comes in and asks Otello to pardon Cassio in phrases of touching simplicity. When Otello waves her aside and refers to an aching forehead she makes to tie her handkerchief round it but he throws it down and roughly repulses her. She begs his pardon for any unwitting offence in another touching phrase; but it is clear from the ensuing quartet that the poison is working in Otello's mind. Iago meanwhile wrenches the handkerchief from the hand of the troubled Emilia who has picked it up. After the quartet Otello dismisses the women. He is beside himself with angry self-pity and bids farewell to arms, in a famous passage over a strongly rhythmic accompaniment. He turns upon Iago and throws him to the ground. For further proof of his suspicions Iago tells him in a graphic paragraph how he had heard Cassio murmur in his sleep of his love for Desdemona. He has also seen Desdemona's handkerchief, Otello's first gift to her, in Cassio's hands. This works Otello up still further and, falling to his knees, he vows vengeance. Iago kneels with him and the Act closes with the last and most powerful of Verdi's oath duets.

ACT III

The great hall of the castle. The Prelude recalls the jealousy motive heard in Act II. The approach of a delegation from Venice is announced to Otello and Iago briefly reminds him of the handkerchief. Desdemona enters and greets him to a phrase of such transparent honesty that his suspicions are momentarily lulled. But when she reverts to the subject of Cassio the music becomes confused and he seeks to borrow the handkerchief which has, he says, special qualities. Her inability to produce it provokes him to call her unchaste and Desdemona, now alarmed, protests her innocence in a lovely cantabile passage. But Otello continues to rage, calls her a strumpet and finally conducts her to the door with calm irony, to the phrase with which she had entered. Alone, Otello sadly soliloquizes in a famous passage over a modulating accompaniment. Iago enters to announce the approach of Cassio and makes Otello hide behind a pillar. In a swiftly moving trio Iago leads Cassio to say things which Otello, half-hearing, misunderstands, and gets him to produce Desdemona's handkerchief which he himself has hidden in Cassio's lodging. As trumpets resounding round the walls announce the arrival of the delegation from Venice, Otello resolves that his wife shall die that night and promotes Iago to be his lieutenant. The whole court assemble to welcome the Venetian dignitaries and Lodovico hands Otello a dispatch. While he is reading it he overhears Desdemona speaking about Cassio to Lodovico and almost strikes her. He sends for Cassio and asks Iago to mark her demeanour. He then announces his own recall and the appointment of Cassio as his successor. When Desdemona comes near him in an imploring attitude he hurls her, before all, to her knees. What is perhaps Verdi's finest big ensemble is now built up, all voicing their thoughts except for Otello who sits silent. Suddenly he rises and abruptly dismisses them all, cursing Desdemona. Overcome by emotion he then falls in a faint. As the crowd is heard hailing him from a distance, amid triumphal calls, Iago places his foot on the prostrate Otello, exclaiming "Behold the Lion!"

ACT IV

Desdemona's bedchamber. After a muted introduction, foreshadowing the Willow Song, Desdemona bids Emilia lay her wedding-night sheets on her bed. She then sings the Willow Song, occasionally interrupting it to address Emilia. Then she dismisses her, after a passionate phrase of farewell. Alone she kneels in prayer, says a moving "Ave Maria" and goes to bed. Otello comes quietly in, to a passage of double-bass recitativo. He gazes on her and kisses her three times (to the phrase from the end of the Act I love-duet). She wakes. She denies his accusations of giving the handkerchief to Cassio who, he says, is dead. He smothers her. There is a furious knocking at the door. He opens it and Emilia rushes in with the news that Cassio, who lives, has killed Roderigo. Desdemona feebly protests her innocence from the bed and dies. Otello tells Emilia that he had it from Iago that she was Cassio's mistress. She calls for help. Lodovico, Cassio, Montano, and Iago enter. The facts about the handkerchief are established and Montano confirms them from Roderigo's dying confession. Iago rushes out and is pursued. Otello stands at bay, refusing to surrender his sword and, in noble tones, tells them not to be afraid of him. He gazes at the dead Desdemona and addresses her in touching tones. Then he draws a dagger furtively and stabs himself. He drags himself to her corpse and dies with the words "a kiss" on his lips, as the phrase from the love-duet is softly repeated in the orchestra.

I Pagliacci

(The Strolling Players). Opera in two acts. Music by R. Leoncavallo. Libretto by the composer. First produced at the Teatro dal Verme, Milan, May 21st, 1892.

SCENE: Near Montalto, Calabria.

TIME: Feast of the Assumption, 1865-70.

CHARACTERS:

CANIO (Punchinello) *Leader of the troupe*		(Tenor)
NEDDA (Columbine) *His wife*		(Soprano)
TONIO (Taddeo) *A player*		(Baritone)
BEPPE (Harlequin) *A player*		(Tenor)
SILVIO *A villager*		(Baritone)

This is the only familiar opera of its composer. It is based on events encountered in' his childhood and he constructed an admirable libretto. Taken on its own undemanding terms it is a highly effective piece. The Prologue was in its day a coup de théâtre and the transitions between the slightly archaic music for the play and that of "real life" in Act II are skilfully managed. We must not look for much poetry or elaborate beauty of form in the music; but there are some melodious phrases (which everyone remembers) repeated with ironic effect and the voices are given some grateful rhetoric to sing.

PROLOGUE

After some theatrical flourishes, broken by a hint (on the horns) of Canio's lament and of the love-scene between Nedda and Silvio, Tonio appears through the curtain and sings the familiar passage explaining that actors too are creatures of flesh and blood. This leads to

ACT I

Entrance to a village, with travelling theatre erected. The people excitedly greet the arrival of Canio's troupe. Tonio tries to help Nedda down from the cart but is boxed on the ears by Canio amid the jeers of the crowd. Canio and Beppe are invited to the inn but Tonio says he must look after the donkey. A villager's suggestion that he is waiting behind to court Nedda provokes quite an outburst from Canio who says that Stage and Life are quite different and that, if Nedda deceived him in real life, there would be a much less meek finish to the story than "up there." The general embarrassment is dissipated by the arrival of bagpipers and the summons of church bells to Vespers. After a "ding dong" chorus the high-spirited Nedda is left alone, a little anxious at her husband's brutal ways. But the summer sun and the birds move her to flights of song which bring Tonio to her side, passionately declaring his love. She mocks him, bidding him keep his grimaces till they are on the stage together, and strikes him with a whip. He slinks off, vowing vengrance, just as Silvio appears urging her to elope with him that very night. After an attractive duet she surrenders and agrees to his plan. But Tonio has overheard and fetched Canio from the inn. Canio rushes at Silvio but Nedda bars the way and he escapes. She refuses to tell him her lover's name and he is about to stab her when Beppe appears and restrains him. Tonio whispers to him to dissemble; the man will return for the play and give himself away. All now get ready. Canio sings his famous self-pitying lament "On with the motley...laugh Punchinello, laugh!"

ACT II

The same. After a short intermezzo, which repeats the climax of the Prologue, we see the audience assembling for the play. (There is some repetition of the opening ensemble of Act I.) Silvio and Nedda only exchange a word or two. The play begins. To a minuet Columbine (Nedda) impatiently awaits her lover. Punchinello is away and Taddeo has gone to market. Harlequin (Beppe) serenades her. They are interrupted by the return of Taddeo (Tonio) with a chicken in his basket. He makes love to her in mock-tragic style. Harlequin jumps in through the window, clutching a bottle, and kicks him out. The lovers sup (to a gavotte) and Harlequin gives Columbine a philtre to pour into her husband's wine, so that they may elope. She agrees, to the phrase (words and music) which Canio had heard her use to Silvio in the afternoon. Canio, now appearing as Punchinello, hears it again and can barely keep to his part. Soon he breaks out of it and fiercely demands to know her lover's name. He declares that he is a man again and seeks vengeance, passionately denouncing her. The crowd (other than Silvio) applaud such acting and Nedda resumes the gavotte in a vain attempt to get back to the play. But he still fiercely demands her lover's name, and now she answers him back. She tries to escape but he stabs her to death. Silvio rushes to her help and Canio stabs him too. Amid general confusion Canio says to the audience "the comedy is finished" and the "laugh Punchinello" phrase is heard fortissimo in the orchestra.

Parsifal

Sacred festival drama in three acts. Music by R. Wagner. Libretto by the composer. First produced at Bayreuth, July 26th, 1882.

SCENE: Montsalvat, Spain.

TIME: Middle Ages.

CHARACTERS:

AMFORTAS *Guardian of the Grail*	(Baritone)
TITUREL *His father*	(Bass)
GURNEMANZ *An aged Knight of the Grail*	(Bass)
PARSIFAL	(Tenor)
KLINGSOR *A magician*	(Bass-baritone)
KUNDRY	(Soprano or Mezzo-soprano)
TWO KNIGHTS	(Tenor and bass)
FOUR ESQUIRES	(Two sopranos and two tenors)
SIX FLOWER MAIDENS	(Sopranos)

This last of Wagner's operas, in which he returned to the legend of the Holy Grail already drawn on for "Lohengrin", is less well loved than others of his maturity, due in part, no doubt, to the difficulty of adequate staging (for many years it was not given outside Bayreuth). But other factors are the weakly constructed libretto (much of the story lies in the past), the consistently slow tempo, stretches where the musical tension sags somewhat, and the fact that its religiosity and theme of redemption from the sins of the flesh do not appeal to contemporary taste. Nevertheless, though the scoring is in relatively subdued colours, it contains passages that equal anything that Wagner did—the Prelude for instance, the two Grail scenes with their carefully calculated choral effects and the music of Amfortas's agony, and the fine piece of nature-painting known as the Good Friday Music. The Flower Maidens' scene, for all its naiveté, is a complicated ensemble of much charm. Kundry's is a highly original and psychologically interesting character, which offers much scope to a singer who can also act; Amfortas's part is grateful to the true baritone; and though Gurnemanz is long-winded and his vocal line is not always musically very interesting, he offers a great opportunity to a bass who knows how to phrase and colour Wagner's declamatory style.

The Prelude is a meditation in slow time based mainly on four motives to be heard all through the work. It sets the devotional mood.

ACT I

Scene 1. A forest clearing near the shrine, with a lake in the background. Dawn. Gurnemanz and two Esquires offer prayer. They learn from two Knights that Amfortas is coming to take the bath that will give some relief from his ceaseless pain which no herbs can assuage. Kundry arrives exhausted on her wild steed, a strange uncouth being, bringing a vial of balsam for Amfortas, who is now carried in groaning on a litter. Release, he says, can come to him only through a "guileless fool". He is borne away, to a lovely orchestral passage. Gurnemanz rebukes the Esquires for abusing Kundry who lies on the ground; she seeks atonement, through serving the Grail, for her terrible sin. Gurnemanz tells them how Titurel had founded the shrine to preserve the Holy Grail—the cup used at the Last Supper—and the spear which pierced the Saviour's side. Klingsor had been too impious to be admitted as a Knight and had turned to magic arts, dwelling amid a magic garden full of beautiful maidens waiting to seduce the Knights. Amfortas had strayed there once and succumbed to Kundry, a woman who had laughed at Christ and was doomed to wander until delivered by him who can resist her charms. Amfortas having fallen under Klingsor's sway, Klingsor had taken the spear and with it given him the wound from which he is in physical and spiritual torment. Only a guileless fool can recover the spear and heal him with its touch. There is a commotion and a wounded swan flutters down, shot by the simple youth Parsifal who is brought in. Gurnemanz bitterly reproves him and he breaks his bow. The dead swan is carried reverently away. Parsifal cannot answer the questions put to him. He knows only that he had a mother from whom he had run away. Kundry tells them that she had reared Parsifal in loneliness to escape the fate of his father, killed in battle. Now his mother too is dead. Parsifal springs angrily at Kundry and is restrained by Gurnemanz. Kundry brings him water to calm him and then quietly disappears into a thicket to sleep. Amfortas's procession is seen returning. Gurnemanz, struck by the bearing of the ignorant boy, leads him to the holy Sacrament. As they walk the scene gradually changes and bells and a marching motive are heard. *Scene 2.* A pillared hall. Gurnemanz and Parsifal watch as the Knights and Esquires assemble. Amfortas is carried in and placed before the veiled shrine of the Grail. The voices of boys are heard floating down from the dome. The voice of Titurel is heard urging Amfortas to perform the sacred ritual and unveil the Grail. Amfortas is in wild despair; the agony of his wound reminds him of his unworthiness. He prays for release through death in a superb monologue. But at last he consents. A ray of light falls on the Grail and all make their communion. Amfortas, who has been in spiritual ecstasy, sinks down on his couch. His wound is bleeding again and he is borne away. All depart. Gurnemanz asks Parsifal if he knows the meaning of the ceremony. When he cannot answer, Gurnemanz pushes him impatiently outside.

ACT II

Klingsor's castle. On the keep of a tower, Klingsor sits before a magic mirror in which he descries the approach of Parsifal. At his summons, Kundry ascends in a blue light, seemingly roused from sleep. He mocks her desire to serve the Knights of the Grail and orders her, against her will, to seduce Parsifal, as once she did Amfortas. This will ensure that Amfortas cannot be healed and that one day he himself will guard the Grail. As Kundry disappears with a shriek, Klingsor sees Parsifal overcoming the castle guards and advancing to his own undoing. He and the tower disappear. A magic garden rises up. The Flower Maidens are in commotion at the struggle but, when Parsifal springs from the wall to join them and pays them a compliment or two, they crowd around him, quarrelling among themselves and in a charming ensemble, to a slow waltz tune, try vainly to seduce him. He is about to escape when Kundry, in young and beautiful guise, calls his name and dismisses the Maidens. She speaks to him of his mother and how, after he had left her, she died of grief. He sinks at her feet overcome with 'remorse and longing for his mother. Kundry bends over him and gives him, as his mother's last greeting, his first kiss of love. Parsifal starts up in horror, crying that Amfortas's wound now burns in his own heart; he feels Amfortas's anguished yearning for redemption after the temptations of the flesh. Kundry now tells him of her own sin in mocking Christ and of the curse upon her; she hopes to find redemption on Parsifal's breast. Parsifal repels this approach also. She will find redemption if she will abjure sin and show him the way to Amfortas. This she refuses and, repulsed once more, curses him and summons help. Klingsor appears on the rampart and hurls the spear. It remains suspended over the head of Parsifal who makes the sign of the Cross with it. Castle and garden disappear. Kundry sinks down and Parsifal hurries off, with the spear, on his mission.

ACT III

Scene 1. A pleasant landscape near the shrine with a hermit's hut. Early morning. Some years later. Gurnemanz, now very old, hearing groans, finds Kundry seemingly lifeless and rouses her. She has come to serve the brotherhood. Parsifal steps out of the forest in black armour with helmet closed. He does not return Gurnemanz' greeting, even when the latter reminds him that it is Good Friday, but thrusts his spear into the ground and, opening his helmet, kneels silently before it. They recognize each other. Parsifal speaks of his long wanderings, driven by Kundry's curse. Gurnemanz tells of Titurel's death and of the neglect of the holy office by Amfortas who longs only to die. The sorrowing Parsifal is led to the holy spring to prepare for the day's ceremony. Kundry washes his feet from the contents of a golden vial, drying them with her hair; with the remainder, Gurnemanz anoints him as King. His first act is to baptize Kundry who weeps passionately. Then, as the orchestra plays the Good Friday Music, Gurnemanz explains that the magic of Good Friday is that nature, on this spring day, does not mourn for the Saviour but expresses its gratitude. Gurnemanz then leads Parsifal, bearing the spear, and Kundry to the shrine, to transformation music similar to that in Act I.

Scene 2. The pillared hall. Titurel's coffin is carried in, as is Amfortas, while the Knights assemble, singing a solemn dirge. When they call on Amfortas to unveil the Grail he prays for death and, in mad despair, uncovers his wound and bids the Knights slay him. Parsifal now steps forward and touches his side with the point of the spear. He takes out the Grail, which glows, while a dove hovers over Parsifal's head. Amfortas and Gurnemanz kneel before him as he waves the Grail in the blessing of Redemption. Kundry, her gaze fixed upon him, sinks lifeless to the ground. Soft arpeggios bring the music to an ethereal close.

Pelléas et Mélisande

(Pelléas and Mélisande). Opera in five acts by C. Debussy. Libretto after M. Maeterlinck. First produced at the Opéra Comique, Paris, April 30th, 1902.

SCENE: "Allemonde".

TIME: Mediaeval.

CHARACTERS:

ARKEL *King of Allemonde*		(Bass)
PELLÉAS		(Tenor)
GOLAUD	} *Stepbrothers and grandsons of King Arkel*	(Baritone)
GENEVIÈVE *Mother of Pelléas and Golaud*		(Contralto)
YNIOLD *Golaud's son*		(Soprano)
MÉLISANDE		(Soprano)
A DOCTOR		(Bass)

This is a direct setting (almost complete) of Maeterlinck's now anaemic-seeming play. It is an extreme case of "words before music" since Debussy gives the voices virtually no expansive moments, still less set pieces which might hold up or vary the speaking tempo of this poetic prose, and confines them to a gently rising and falling recitative faithfully following the inflections of French speech. Ironically, however, the play, with its heavy symbolism, would by now have been forgotten but for the music— i.e., the mood or atmosphere which Debussy creates for each of the thirteen short scenes by his exquisite orchestral cushion and the eight important linking interludes. Oboes, horns, and harp are prominent in his palette for this poetic and impressionistic score which contains few motives, other than those of Mélisande and Golaud, the use or development of which extends beyond individual scenes. It is music of the utmost reticence, with no operatic "heart-on-sleeve" manner. But this enables those moments, when deep feeling is expressed or implied by the words or where some poetic image is to be underlined, to stand out the more effectively with only a slight increase of tension or closer harmonic involvement of the vocal line. The work indeed requires from the singers, on the scale of a theatre, the subtle inflections appropriate to lieder or Debussy's own songs. Moreover, all except the more down-to-earth Golaud must convey the dreamy and fatalistic quality of Maeterlinck's beings. Mélisande must seem childlike and ingenuous in addition. Satisfactory performances of so exacting a work are necessarily rare.

ACT I

Scene 1. A forest. In the brief Prelude is heard almost at once on the oboe a motive on two adjacent notes, barely more than a rhythm, associated with Golaud and soon after, also on the oboe, the plaintive wisp of melody associated with Mélisande's unhappiness, which will constantly recur in many forms. Golaud, lost while pursuing a wild boar, comes upon Mélisande weeping by a spring. She is frightened, though of what she will not say; nor will she say where she belongs, except that it is far away. Her crown has fallen in the water but she will not let Golaud retrieve it. They tell each other their names and, with difficulty, he persuades her to come with him.

Scene 2. A room in the castle. Geneviève reads a letter to Pelléas from Golaud describing his encounter with Mélisande. He has been married to her for six months—his first wife had died leaving a young son, Yniold—but still knows no more about her. He fears what Arkel will think; but if he will receive Mélisande, Pelléas is to light a lamp on the tower on the third day after receiving the letter, so that he may disembark. The aged, half-blind Arkel feels that destiny must take its course. Pelléas enters with another letter—from a dying friend to whose side he wishes to go. But Arkel persuades him to delay a little to await his brother and be close to his sick father.

Scene 3. Before the castle. Geneviève conducts Mélisande through the dark woods. Pelléas encounters them. A ship, the one which brought Mélisande, is seen sailing away through the mist past a lighthouse and sailors' voices are heard. Geneviéve leaves Pelléas to conduct Mélisande back. She is distressed when he says that he may be going away the next day.

ACT II

Scene 1. A well in the park. (The music for this scene is brighter in tone.) Pelléas has brought Mélisande to this cool "Blind Man's Well" which used to open the eyes of the blind till King Arkel himself became almost blind. Mélisande leans over the water, entranced. She plays with her wedding-ring and, after a small climax, it falls into the water to a downward harp glissando, just as twelve o'clock strikes.

Scene 2. A room in the castle. Evening. Golaud, with Mélisande beside him, is on his bed, having been thrown from his horse which had galloped blindly against a tree just as twelve was striking. But he is not seriously hurt. Mélisande weeps and explains that she feels oppressed here. Golaud asks if it is due to Pelléas, who does not talk to her very much. She says that it is not that, though she does not think that he likes her. She agrees with Golaud that it must be the sunlessness of the castle. Suddenly he sees that she is not wearing her ring and becomes strangely excited. She says that it must have been lost in a cave by the sea from which she had been driven out by the incoming tide. He tells her to go and look for it at once and take Pelléas as escort.

Scene 3. Outside a cave on the shore. The music here is full of the sound of the sea. Pelléas conducts Mélisande in the dark. As they are about to enter the cave the moon comes out and frightens her by revealing three white-haired beggars asleep. Pelléas explains that there is a famine in the land. They leave.

ACT III

Scene 1. A tower of the castle. Mélisande sits at the window combing her long hair and singing an unaccompanied song. Pelléas approaches on the path below. He is going away the next day but is readily persuaded to stay. She leans out so that he may kiss her hand and her hair falls down over him and fills him with ecstasy, the music growing ever more ardent. He kisses her hair (in a passage with a tender viola solo) and will not let it go. Golaud approaches and tells them they are like a pair of children.

Scene 2. The dungeons of the castle. To sombre music, in which bassoons are prominent, Golaud conducts Pelléas to a stagnant pool. Pelléas feels stifled and they go out in silence.

Scene 3. A terrace at the entrance to the dungeons. The preceding Interlude depicts the light. Pelléas welcomes the return to fresh air and midday radiance. Golaud tells him that he had heard what was going on the previous evening and warns him not to see much of Mélisande who will soon be a mother.

Scene 4. Before the castle. Golaud tries to extract from Yniold information about something improper in the relations between Pelléas and Mélisande, but the child maddens him by replying inconsequentially and in his jealous impatience Golaud frightens him and hurts his arm. The window of Mélisande's room lights up (and the music broadens). Golaud lifts Yniold up and asks what he sees. Yniold replies that Pelléas is with her and that they are looking at the light in silence. He grows frightened and has to be allowed down.

ACT IV

Scene 1. A room in the castle. Pelléas tells Mélisande that his father is recovering and that he will be setting out the next day. She agrees to meet him by the well. He goes out and Arkel enters, happy that joy and sunlight will at last return to the house to cheer Mélisande's sad heart. She will create young, fair, and happy events, as young people always do. He embraces her tenderly, saying that old men close to death need beauty to remind them of the freshness of life. Golaud enters in an emotional state and uttering innuendoes. The innocence of Mélisande's eyes exasperates him. He forces her to her knees and drags her in anger by her long hair. He tells her that he will not play the spy but will wait on chance. Arkel comments that if he were God he would have pity on the hearts of men and this sentiment seems to be carried forward into a big Interlude heavy with foreboding.

Scene 2. The well. Yniold can see his ball wedged behind stones too heavy for him to move. A shepherd passes with a herd of sheep. Yniold runs off as Pelléas enters and in a monologue with a touch of the conventional recitative affirms his determination to leave, now that he realizes that he is in love, but his anxiety for a final meeting before doing so. Mélisande enters breathless. Precipitately Pelléas declares—in a simple unaccompanied phrase—that he loves her and she replies similarly. The music of the love scene which follows is mainly in a low key but with isolated phrases of great intensity; the lovers rejoice at the symbolic sound of the castle gates being shut, and there is a passionate moment as they embrace. Mélisande thinks she hears Golaud but they are past greatly caring and are still embracing when Golaud descends upon them and strikes Pelléas dead. Mélisande flies in terror.

ACT V

A room in the castle. Mélisande lies ill in bed. (Her motive is now transformed into a kind of dirge.) The Doctor seeks to assure Arkel and the contrite Golaud that she will not die. Mélisande, still slightly delirious, awakens and asks for the window to be opened. She does not understand Golaud's embarrassment. Golaud asks the others to withdraw. He begs for and receives her forgiveness. With mounting excitement he presses her to say whether her love for Pelléas had been a guilty one. She denies it but so innocently that he is not sure that she has understood. The Doctor and Arkel return and she is now too weak for further questions. She cannot even hold her baby daughter whom Arkel brings her. Serving-women file silently in, to the annoyance of Golaud, and soon they fall on their knees and bells toll at the moment of her death. Arkel leads Golaud away and has her child taken out "to live in her place and have its turn."

Peter Grimes

Opera in three acts and a prologue. Music by Benjamin Britten. Libretto by M. Slater after G. Crabbe. First produced at Sadler's Wells, London, June 7th, 1945.

SCENE: The Borough, a small fishing-town on the East Coast.

TIME: Towards 1830.

CHARACTERS:

PETER GRIMES *A fisherman*	(Tenor)
ELLEN ORFORD *A widow, schoolmistress of the Borough*	(Soprano)
CAPTAIN BALSTRODE *Retired merchant skipper*	(Baritone)
AUNTIE *Landlady of The Boar*	(Contralto)
HER TWO NIECES *Main attractions of The Boar*	(Sopranos)
BOB BOLES *Fisherman and Methodist*	(Tenor)
SWALLOW *A lawyer*	(Bass)
MRS (NABOB) SEDLEY *A rentier widow of an East India Company's factor*	(Mezzo-soprano)
REV. HORACE ADAMS *The rector*	(Tenor)
NED KEENE *Apothecary and quack*	(Baritone)
HOBSON *Carrier*	(Bass)

This opera, Britten's first, won instant and wide success. Much of its music makes a ready appeal and it is recognizably descended from nineteenth century peasant opera (cf. the opening chorus of Act I) yet vividly illustrating a realistic and moving story constructed with a strong sense of the stage. The atmosphere of a Suffolk fishing village is faithfully presented and all the characters are firmly drawn, both in the music and libretto, even though some of the detail is not fully integrated into the story. The choral writing is lively and at times (e.g., in Act I Scene 2 and the opening of Act III) a note of taking gaiety is struck. At the same time this tale of a social misfit has aroused Britten's characteristic quality of compassion and the profoundest music, that given to Peter Grimes and to Ellen Orford, is by no means simple to grasp. But the opera's special glory is the four Interludes (two really Preludes), which (with much else in the score) describe the sea in its varying moods in a way rare since Debussy's "La Mer", and a magnificent passacaglia.

PROLOGUE

A room inside the Moot Hall. Swallow, as coroner (his motive is in the first bar) is presiding at the inquest, attended by hostile townspeople, on Grimes's apprentice who died at sea. When the facts have been established Swallow gives a verdict of accidental death, adding "But that's the kind of thing people are apt to remember" and advising Grimes to get a fisherman "big enough to stand up for himself" to help him. Grimes excitedly seeks an opportunity to refute the hostile gossip but the Court is cleared and he and Ellen are left alone. In an unaccompanied passage, in which they sing in different keys, she tries to soothe him, with some success as they end in unison.

The first Interlude reflects the swell (brass) and luminosity (harp and clarinet arpeggios) of the sea and continues during the opening of

ACT I

Scene 1. The beach and street on a grey morning. Fishermen and their womenfolk sing at work, interrupted by small episodes of daily life. Peter calls for help in hauling his boat but no-one is willing till Balstrode and Keene give a hand at the capstan (graphically pictured in the orchestra). Keene tells Peter that he has found him a new apprentice but Hobson refuses to go and fetch him from the workhouse. Ellen volunteers to look after the boy despite the opposition of the crowd and eventually, after an arioso passage of gentle rebuke, wins Hobson over. Balstrode observes that the storm out at sea is approaching. There is a big ensemble of apprehension, ending in a prayer to the tide "to spare our coasts." In a short conversation against the rising storm, Balstrode advises Peter to get away to sea, but Peter replies that he is "native, rooted here." He is moved, however, to tell Balstrode the story of how the apprentice died of exposure. He is determined to silence the gossip by fishing till he is wealthy. Then he will marry Ellen. He refuses Balstrode's advice to marry her now. Alone, he asks himself (to a rising ninth) "what harbour shelters peace" and finds the answer in "her breast." The second Interlude gives us the full force of the storm with a middle section in which Peter's phrase, played broadly, is answered by dancing quavers. This leads to

Scene 2. Inside The Boar that night. Whenever anyone comes in, as most of the townspeople gradually do, the storm is heard outside the door. A fight is averted by Balstrode leading a chorus "We live and let live". News is brought that the cliff is down by Grimes's hut. Then Peter himself comes in and everyone shrinks from him. He sings a reflective passage "Now the Great Bear and Pleiades", which they cannot understand, and the peace is only preserved by Keene starting a complex round, with three tunes in 7/4 time, in which all join. Finally Hobson, Ellen, and the new apprentice arrive, all wet through. Peter wants to be off home with the boy at once. The crowd comment derisively "Home! Do you call that home?"

ACT II

Scene 1. As in Act I Scene 1. A fine Sunday morning. The introductory Interlude seems to express the sparkle of the waves with a persistent, staccato figure for upper strings and wind over sforzando horn chords, the middle section being a broad melody for violas and cellos, which is taken up by Ellen when she begins talking to the silent apprentice as villagers enter the church. (The remainder of her scenes with the boy and with Peter are set against passages of Morning Service, intermittently heard.) She speaks of her fondness for children and her hopes that Peter has made a new start, but these are dashed when she finds that the boy's coat is torn and his neck bruised. Peter comes in and wants to take the boy off after a shoal. Ellen tries to persuade Peter that he is overworking the boy, but Peter still harps on what money will do for himself. Finally she asks whether they were mistaken to scheme to "solve your life by lonely toil" and whether they have failed. At this Peter angrily strikes her just as the congregation sing "Amen". He goes off with the boy and she departs in tears. Auntie, Boles, and Keene, who have been watching, appear and sing a short trio based on Peter's last phrase, with the refrain "Grimes is at his exercise." People come out of church and join in indignantly, though they do not understand what is up. The ensemble ends by Ellen, who has returned, being called on by Boles to explain. She tries to do so, but is overwhelmed by the weight of hostile comment which ends by openly crying "Murder". The rector and Swallow lead a threatening procession of men, with Hobson beating the drum, to Grimes's hut. A little reflective trio for Ellen, the two Nieces (in unison), and Auntie on women's relationship with men prepares the way for the next Interlude, a long and intensely serious passacaglia on a bass which is close to that of "Grimes is at his exercise." It leads to

Scene 2. Peter's hut, an upturned boat. He comes in bullying the boy who weeps. Then follows an arioso passage in which he dreams on life with Ellen when the gossips have been silenced. This is interrupted by the memory of the vigil with his dead apprentice. The sound of the approaching procession is heard. Grimes hustles the boy down to the boat and, just as there is knocking on the door, the boy falls down the cliff with a scream. Grimes climbs quickly after him and to nothing but an uncanny celesta chord the rector, Swallow, Keene, and Balstrode enter. Taken aback to find all in order Swallow (to a version of his motive) says that this will quieten Borough talk. Balstrode stays behind and (to a viola solo over the celesta, which tails away to nothing) looks over the cliff's edge and discovers what has happened.

ACT III

As in Act I Scene 1. Some nights later. There is an introductory
"Interlude" depicting calm moonlight. Slow chords of great beauty are
dappled by a triplet figure for flute and harp. When the curtain rises the
sound of a dance can be heard in the Moot Hall. To a barn dance Swallow
flirts with the Nieces in pseudo-legal language (singing a new version of his
motive). Against a sugary Ländler Mrs Smedley tries in vain to persuade
Keene that Grimes has murdered the missing apprentice. As a hornpipe is
heard some of the older folk say good night. Mrs Smedley goes on
muttering suspiciously over a chromatic subject in the bass. Balstrode tells
Ellen that Peter's boat is in and that he has found the boy's jersey, which
she had embroidered. She is moved to sing a florid aria of sad resignation—
"Now my embroidery affords the clue whose meaning we avoid." They
go off, resolved to stand by him. To a gallop from the off-stage band
Mrs Smedley has the unwilling Swallow brought out from Auntie's pub and
tells him that Grimes's boat is back, whereupon he calls on Hobson (who is
constable as well as carter) to search for him. A crowd assembles and
work up to a big ensemble of hatred, ending with fortissimo cries of
"Peter Grimes." A mysterious passage marks the transition to early
morning; horns sustain a chord of the dominant seventh softly throughout
it. When the curtain rises Peter struggles in, now quite demented, and has
a monologue which quotes fragments of previous music, unaccompanied
except by distant cries of "Peter Grimes" and a remote fog-horn. Ellen
and Balstrode come up to him but, absorbed in a reminiscence of the
middle section of the second Interlude of Act I, he does not recognize
them. The thin music fades completely away and Balstrode tells him in
ordinary speech to take his boat out and sink her. He helps him to launch
his boat and leads Ellen away.

As the day dawns the orchestra softly resumes the music of the first
Interlude leading to a resumption of the chorus of Act I Scene 1 as
Peter's boat is descried sinking far out at sea. People begin their daily
round and they and the music sing, finally, of the sea, "in ebb yet
terrible and deep."

Prince Igor

Opera in a prologue and four acts. Music by A. P. Borodin, posthumously completed by N. A. Rimsky-Korsakov and A. K. Glazounov. Libretto by the composer after V. V. Stassov. First produced at the Maryinsky Theatre, St Petersburg, November 4th, 1890.

SCENE: The town of Poutivl and the Polovtsian Camp.

TIME: 1185.

CHARACTERS:

IGOR SVIATOSLAVITCH	*Prince of Seversk*	(Baritone)
JAROSLAVNA	*His wife*	(Soprano)
JAROSLAVNA'S NURSE		(Soprano)
VLADIMIR IGOREVITCH	*His son*	(Tenor)
VLADIMIR GALITZKY	*Brother of Jaroslavna*	(Bass-baritone)
KONTCHAK	*Polovtsian Khan*	(Bass)
KONTCHAKOVNA	*His daughter*	(Mezzo-soprano)
OVLUR	*A Polovtsian*	(Tenor)
SKULA	} *Gudok players*	(Bass)
EROCHKA		(Tenor)

This is everybody's idea of a Russian opera—colourful scenes, loose construction (Act III can be, and often is, omitted), exotic music, and a pair of "comics" are all there, as well, of course, as the celebrated Polovtsian dances which are done, without choir and out of context, by almost every ballet company equal to the exacting choreography of Fokine. There is, however, more to it than that. The separate numbers, of which it is composed, are on a large scale, though their structure is not elaborate; there are magnificent choruses and grateful melodies for the soloists; the barbaric, semi-oriental music given to the Tartars is quite different in feeling from that for the Russians. The part of Kontchak is linked for older opera-goers with memories of Chaliapin.

The Overture works up material to be heard later, particularly that associated with Igor himself (especially in his Act II aria) and with Kontchakovna.

PROLOGUE

A square in Poutivl. Igor and the boyars come out of the cathedral and are hailed by the people in a great chorus, prior to leaving with his son Vladimir for battle against the Polovtsi, a Tartar tribe. After a sudden eclipse the people urge him to cancel his expedition, but Igor is undismayed. He bids Jaroslavna, his wife, a tender farewell and entrusts her to her brother, Galitzky.

ACT I

Scene 1. Courtyard of Galitzky's house. A carousal is taking place, led by the dissolute Galitzky. A chorus of young girls appeal to him to order the release of one of them, whom his retinue have abducted, but he mockingly refuses. Skula and Erochka, two rustic musicians who have deserted from Igor's army, sing in praise of the profligate life in Galitzky's establishment and hint that he rather than Igor should be their prince. This thought is taken up by the crowd of revellers.

Scene 2. Jaroslavna's apartment. In an arioso, which offers a moment of tranquillity, Jaroslavna gives voice to her anxiety for her husband. The young girls enter with their complaint, followed shortly by her brother. After an argument, in which he taunts her with her unnatural fidelity, she prevails upon him to give up the abducted maiden. Boyars arrive and break the news (in a two-part chorus over a striking ostinato bass) that Igor has been beaten in battle and captured together with Vladimir; ravaging hordes of Polovtsi are approaching the city. They declare their loyalty to her. The sound of the tocsin, the sight of distant flames, and the prayers of those present mingle in a powerful finale.

ACT II

The camp of the Polovtsi. Kontchakovna's handmaidens sing and then dance for her. She herself then sings a florid cavatina in which she yearns for love. They give food and water to a passing group of Russian prisoners who thank them. Their guards follow them. Vladimir now sings a beautiful cavatina in which he expresses his love for Kontchakovna, who comes to him. They sing a love duet and go off into the night. Igor appears, brooding over his captivity and dreaming of freedom and his wife (in a justly famous aria). As dawn appears he is joined by the Polovtsian traitor Ovlur, who offers ingratiatingly to help him escape, but Igor refuses to break his parole. The Khan Kontchak enters and in an aria offers him hospitality and anything he likes to reduce the tedium of captivity. He even offers freedom and an alliance, but Igor refuses to promise not to make war on him again.

Pleased by this spirited reply, Kontchak calls for entertainment for his guest and the Act ends with the familiar suite of wild dances, with choral accompaniment.

ACT III

The Polovtsian camp. A barbaric march precedes the rise of the curtain and continues as Gsak, another Khan, and his warriors return, with Russian prisoners, from fresh victories and are acclaimed by the Polovtsians in the camp and by Kontchak himself. Igor, Vladimir, and the Russian prisoners have been spectators of it all, and the prisoners press Igor to put duty before honour and escape. After the arrival of more booty the stage is left to the guards, who after a further chorus and dancing relapse into drunken slumber. Ovlur approaches Igor's tent and this time obtains his consent to escape. But Kontchakovna has learned of the plan and reproaches Vladimir for leaving her. A strong trio ensues, Igor pressing his hesitating son to escape with him, as themes associated with both Kontchakovna and Igor are heard. In desperation she gives the alarm; Igor escapes but Vladimir is caught. Kontchak forbids his warriors to harm him. He forbids them also to pursue Igor for whom he continues to express admiration. He gives his daughter's hand to Vladimir and bids his followers prepare for further conquests.

ACT IV

Poutivl. Jaroslavna sits by the city wall, lamenting her lot. After her scena a group of peasants passes by, likewise lamenting the state of their land. She descries two horsemen in the distance approaching. Soon she recognizes one as Igor and a moment later husband and wife are reunited (over reminiscences of Igor's Act II aria) in a long duet, towards the close of which Igor vows to do battle against the Tartars once more. They go slowly towards the citadel. Skula and Erochka, slightly drunk, appear and are reviling Igor, when they suddenly catch sight of him. After a moment of consternation they hit on the idea of sounding the alarm-bell and being the first to announce Igor's return. They are rewarded for their pains. One of those chorales over an ostinato bass, with which Russian operas often end, now marks the joyful assembly of the people, who hail the ceremonial appearance of Igor and Jaroslavna.

The Queen of Spades

(Pique Dame). Opera in three acts by P. I. Tchaikovsky. Libretto by M. Tchaikovsky after A. S. Pushkin. First produced at St Petersburg, December 19th, 1890.

SCENE: St Petersburg.

TIME: Late eighteenth century.

PRINCIPAL CHARACTERS:

HERMAN	} *Officers*	(Tenor)
TCHEKALINSKY		(Tenor)
SOURIN		(Bass)
COUNT TOMSKY		(Baritone)
PRINCE YELETSKY		(Baritone)
THE COUNTESS		(Contralto)
LISA *Her granddaughter*		(Soprano)
PAULINE *Lisa's companion*		(Contralto)
MASTER OF CEREMONIES		(Tenor)
CHLOË *(in the Interlude)*		(Soprano)
LISA'S GOVERNESS		(Mezzo-soprano)

This may be regarded as a companion piece to "Eugene Onegin", to which there are similarities, but it falls considerably below the level of the latter. One reason for this may be excess of local colour and background, often insufficiently integrated. The first Act is generally successful and Act II Scene 2 is outstanding and highly dramatic, capturing and sustaining the weird mood; but elsewhere there are longueurs and the final climax is musically not strong enough. So highly romantic a subject requires greater atmospheric saturation of the entire score than, apart from Act II Scene 2, the composer managed, for all its incidental beauties, to give it.

ACT I

Scene 1. The Summer Garden, St Petersburg. After a short Prelude in which is heard the three-note figure associated with the Countess, followed by a motive from the climax of Act I Scene 2, the curtain rises on a spring day and a charming chorus of children, nurses, and governesses enjoying it. Tchekalinsky and Sourin briefly discuss the strange habit of the penniless, gloomy Herman who ceaselessly watches the gambling of others but takes no part. Herman enters with Tomsky to whom he confides (in an attractive arioso in two parts) that his gloom is due to his love for a girl whose name he does not know and whom he has not dared to approach. Promenaders interrupt them, making the most of the weather which, like everything else, is not what it once was. Yeletsky tells his brother officers of his engagement, which only increases the gloom of Herman (in canon). Yeletsky's fiancée, Lisa, and the old Countess arrive and Herman recognizes Lisa as his beloved, while they recognize him as a pale, mysterious stranger constantly pursuing them. (Brief quintet.) When they have left, Tomsky sings a ballad to the officers about the Queen of Spades (as the Countess is known). Once she had been the belle of Paris but preferred cards to love. One evening, when she had lost everything, an admirer, in return for a rendezvous, had given her the secret of "three cards" with which she had then had fantastic success. She had told her secret to her husband and another, but a ghost had warned her that if she revealed it to a third man, she would die. The others laugh and depart, but Herman is left, in a sudden thunderstorm, brooding over the tale and determined to win Lisa.

Scene 2. Lisa's room. Lisa and Pauline, surrounded by girl friends, sing a formal duet. Pauline is persuaded to follow it by a sad song, succeeded by a gay folk tune to which all dance. This brings in the Governess who reproves them for their unladylike behaviour and sends the girls home. After commenting on Lisa's glum demeanour, Pauline withdraws, leaving Lisa to express a sad foreboding which does not, she knows, accord with her betrothal to so worthy a man. Suddenly Herman appears from the balcony. He meets her protest by drawing a pistol, and by a passionate declaration of love which greatly moves her. He hides when the Countess, who has heard a noise, comes in to ask why Lisa is not in bed (many repetitions of the three-note figure). This reminds Herman of the three cards. When the Countess has gone Lisa surrenders to him and they embrace passionately.

ACT II

Scene 1. A masked ball in a rich house. There is an introduction and chorus of guests in a vaguely eighteenth century style. The guests go out into the garden to see fireworks and the officers resolve to play a trick on Herman, obsessed by the three cards. Yeletsky, alone with Lisa, sings a touching aria expressing his devotion and anxiety to make her less sad. Herman, encouraged by a note and whispers from the unseen officers, thinks how the cards could make him rich enough to win Lisa. The guests return to witness a pastoral interlude, again with eighteenth century music, in which Chlöe resists the advances of Plutus, played by Tomsky, and remains faithful to Daphnis, played by Pauline. (The duet of Daphnis and Chlöe seems to echo *The Magic Flute*.) After it Herman is further worked up by the sight of the Countess and more whispers from Sourin. Lisa gives him the key by which he can reach her room through that of the Countess. The unexpected arrival of the Empress Catherine is announced and, drilled by the Master of Ceremonies, the guests greet her with a hymn of praise. *Scene 2.* The Countess's bedroom. Night. To a mysterious figure with repeated notes on the violas and later the cellos, alternating with a smooth phrase which recurs throughout the scene, Herman enters, meditates a moment on his rash adventure and hides. The Countess enters, followed by a chorus of endlessly flattering servants. While she retires to undress Lisa confides the reason for her agitation to her maid. The Countess returns in night attire. She broods for a while on her past triumphs at the French Court and the decline of society and softly sings to herself a snatch of a song by Grétry before dismissing her servants and dozing off on a couch. (Throughout the scene the bassoon is brilliantly used to suggest old age.) Herman appears and, as she mumbles speechlessly, begs and bullies her to reveal the secret of the three cards. Finally he draws his pistol at which she falls dead, taking her secret with her. Lisa comes in, blames Herman and, when he says that he only wanted to learn about the cards, reproaches him with caring nothing for herself. She sends him away.

ACT III

Scene 1. Herman's quarters in the barracks. He has a letter from Lisa, forgiving him and begging him to meet her at midnight. But, amid the howling of the wind, he is haunted by conscience and memories of the Countess's funeral. Her ghost appears and tells him to marry Lisa. The three lucky cards are three, seven, and Ace.
Scene 2. The canal opposite the Neva Palace. Lisa anxiously awaits Herman, with a sad and weary aria. At last he appears and there is a moment of rapture. But when he says that he must go to the gaming-house, tells her about the Countess's appearance and raves on about the three cards, she regards him as a murderer and throws herself into the canal.
Scene 3. The gaming house. There is a chorus of revellers. Yeletsky is paying his first visit to take his revenge. "Unlucky in love, lucky at cards," he says. Tomsky sings to the company and others follow him with a gay song and dance. As the gambling begins, Herman, pale and distraught, surprises all by seeking to take a hand himself. He names huge stakes and wins with the three and the seven, singing exultantly that luck must be taken in the game of life. Only Yeletsky is willing to accept his further challenge. Herman calls the Ace; but it is the Queen of Spades and Herman sees the ghost of the Countess. He stabs himself and with his last breath begs forgiveness of Yeletsky and the dead Lisa. The others sing a short prayer for his spirit and, as the curtain falls, the motive from the end of Act I is heard again in the orchestra.

The Rake's Progress

Opera in three acts and an epilogue. Music by I. Stravinsky. Libretto by W. H. Auden and C. Kallman. First produced at the Teatro La Fenice, Venice, September 11th, 1951.

SCENE: England.

TIME: Eighteenth century.

CHARACTERS:

TRULOVE	(Bass)
ANNE *His daughter*	(Soprano)
TOM RAKEWELL	(Tenor)
NICK SHADOW	(Baritone)
MOTHER GOOSE	(Mezzo-soprano)
BABA THE TURK	(Mezzo-soprano)
SELLEM *An auctioneer*	(Tenor)

For this opera, based on Hogarth's pictures, with a touch of "Faust" in the person of Nick Shadow, the composer went back to eighteenth century conventions. There are formal recitative (with continuo), accompanied recitative, and a clear division of the remainder into "numbers". Nevertheless, although in places the feeling is Mozartian, the style is Stravinsky's own—reedy orchestral colours, "motor" accompaniments, infinite rhythmic variety, and harmonic progressions with a dash of the Russian romantic in them. The vocal lines are elaborate but the small orchestra plays a full part. Sections of the score are light-hearted, or breathe a light sentiment, as befits the comedy, or even farcical, nature of some of the action. Anne, the "nice girl", is treated seriously throughout, and some of Tom's music, (e.g., his cavatina) and the last two scenes have led the composer far beyond any question of pastiche to create music, which, though fully appropriate to the action is "serious" in every sense of the term, with a characteristic grave beauty and an unwonted compassion.

ACT I

Scene 1. Garden of Trulove's house in the country.   Spring afternoon.

Anne and Tom rejoice, as lovers, in the season, to pastoral music, while Trulove voices a touch of scepticism. When Anne has left them he tells Tom that he has secured him a post in the City. Trulove is disconcerted when Tom refuses it. Tom sings an aria on the theme "Since it is not by merit we rise and we fall but the favour of fortune . . ." but adds "I wish I had money." Nick Shadow at once appears at the garden gate with a tale of a fortune left Tom by a forgotten uncle. Tom takes him into his service. The family rejoicing is interrupted by Nick's pointing out that Tom must go to London to settle his estate. Tom and Anne exchange a tender farewell; he arranges with Nick to pay him for his services after a year and a day. They depart.

Scene 2. London. Mother Goose's brothel. Roaring boys and whores sing a whirling chorus. Tom and Nick enter. Tom has been taught "One aim in all things to pursue: My duty to myself to do." But he breaks down in his catechism at the word "love" and as his initiation song sings a sad cavatina (with clarinet arpeggios) to "love too frequently betrayed." The whores grow maudlin but Mother Goose claims Tom for the night and they slowly retire through the lines of inward-facing men and women as the chorus sing a nursery rhyme with the refrain "Lanterloo".

Scene 3. As Scene 1. A full-length scena for Anne. She resolves to join Tom who needs her more than does her father.

ACT II

Scene 1. Morning room of Tom's town house. In a long scena (the slow section of which has a haunting tune) Tom sings of the gap in his heart despite London's distractions which begin to bore him. Nick arrives, full of a bearded circus lady called Baba the Turk whom he advises Tom to marry; for "he alone is free whom neither Passion may compel nor Reason can restrain." Tom is amused by the prospect of notoriety and they go off to get the marriage arranged.

Scene 2. Street before Tom's house. Autumn dusk. Anne is waiting nervously. (There is a pathetic trumpet solo.) She is puzzled by a procession of servants who enter the house carrying strange parcels. A sedan chair is set down and Tom steps out. He pleads with Anne to go home; in London "virtue is a day coquette" and he is unworthy of her. Baba, heavily veiled, puts her head impatiently out of the sedan and Tom tells Anne she is his wife. A trio follows in which Baba expresses her dislike of being kept waiting against the vain regrets of Tom and Anne. When Anne has gone Baba descends, removes her veils and makes a theatrical entry into the house amid the applause of a gathering crowd.

Scene 3. As in Scene 1. The room is now cluttered with objects collected by Baba who is chattering about them as she and Tom breakfast. When at last she puts her arms lovingly round him he repulses her and she rages jealously against Anne till, finally, Tom plumps his wig, back to front, on her head. Suddenly silenced, she remains motionless. Tom goes to sleep and Nick enters with a fantastic machine which appears to turn stones into bread. Tom wakes up, saying that he had dreamed that he had invented just such a machine which would restore Paradise on earth. When Nick demonstrates his machine Tom reaches a pitch of exaltation and readily agrees to Nick's proposals for putting it on the market. When Nick suggests that he tell the good news to his wife he says that he has buried her.

ACT III

Scene 1. The same but cobwebs and dust everywhere. Spring afternoon. Baba still sits motionless in the same place. Respectable citizens gather for an auction and refer to the widespread ruin caused by the collapse of Tom's project. Anne enters looking for Tom; but no-one knows or cares about him. Sellem begins the auction, alternating highflown patter (with rapidly repeated trumpet notes) with a naive little waltz. But when he tries to sell Baba and takes the wig off her head she resumes the phrase cut off in the previous scene and turns upon the crowd. The voices of Tom and Nick are heard from below in a street-cry offering old wives for sale. Anne rushes in. Baba magnanimously offers her Tom to "set right" and announces her own intention to return to the stage. Tom and Nick are heard singing snatches of a nonsense ballad. Baba makes a grand exit, leaving the crowd dazed by their hectic day.

Scene 2. A churchyard. Night. A grim little Prelude introduces music of greater intensity in which Tom's fear is mirrored by his expressively florid vocal line. Nick tells him that the time is up (to the ballad tune), and claims Tom's soul as reward for his services. He finally concedes Tom the chance to name three cards which he will cut from a pack. Tom's luck holds and, as the tension mounts, he succeeds and sinks down senseless. Furious, Nick (to villain's music of some earlier school) deprives him of his reason and then sinks into the grave dug for Tom. At dawn Tom is found sitting on a green mound, putting grass on his head and singing (to the ballad again but alternating with orchestral distortions of his earlier phrases of fear) that his name is Adonis.

Scene 3. Bedlam. After a short introduction which subtly varies the ballad we see Tom calling on a sceptical band of lunatics to prepare for the visit of Venus to her Adonis. At the sound of a key they scatter to their cells and a keeper brings Anne in. She greets Tom as Adonis. He is overjoyed and (to modulating chords) bids Venus mount her throne. As Venus she forgives Adonis in a duet in which the "mad" phrase is given a new turn. Tom sinks down exhausted and she sings him to sleep (to another variation of the ballad) before the keeper and Truelove take her away. Tom wakes, calls out for Venus, and after a final florid phrase dies. The other madmen sing a brief dirge for Adonis.

EPILOGUE

The house lights go up and the five principal characters, before the curtain, point the moral briefly, to cheerful music. Stravinsky successfully follows *Don Giovanni*, though in his own way, in returning, after a daemonic ending, to a lighter mood to round things off.

The Rape of Lucretia

Chamber opera in two acts. Music by Benjamin Britten. Libretto by R. Duncan after A. Obey. First produced at Glyndebourne, July 12th, 1946.

SCENE: Rome and neighbourhood.

TIME: 500 B.C.

CHARACTERS:

MALE CHORUS	(Tenor)
FEMALE CHORUS	(Soprano)
PRINCE TARQUINIUS *Son of Tarquinius Superbus*	(Baritone)
JUNIUS *A Roman general*	(Baritone)
COLLATINUS *A Roman general*	(Bass)
LUCRETIA *His wife*	(Contralto)
BIANCA *Her nurse*	(Mezzo-soprano)
LUCIA *Her maid*	(Soprano)

A feature of Obey's "Le Viol de Lucrèce", produced with great effect by the Compagnie des Quinze in Paris and London around 1930, was the stationing of a Male and Female Chorus on either side of the stage, on which some of the action was mimed. Britten has retained this scheme. They read from history, fill in and comment on the action, relating it to the message of Christianity, and sometimes join in the ensembles. To them thus falls some of the reflective rôle usually given in a modern opera to the orchestra (who have here relatively few passages on their own) and some of the material appropriate to recitative, while the persons in the play are freer to concentrate on the moments of tension suitable for lyrical treatment. The musical texture is light and the scoring is for a chamber orchestra (with a conspicuous harp part). The experiment, which, historically, can be traced back to the mimed recitative of the early seventeenth century exemplified in Monteverdi's "Il Combattimento di Tancredi e Clorinda" and in which something of Britten's later church parables can be foreseen, is highly successful and despite the brevity of the scenes a rising curve of emotional intensity is maintained in each part though the work takes a little time to get off the ground. In the second Act there are passages of outstanding beauty; all the music has a quality of "gravitas" which matches its subject.

ACT I

Male Chorus reads how the Etruscan upstart, Tarquinius Superbus, came
to rule Rome by force and (adds Female Chorus) to involve the Romans
in war against the Greeks. In a striking phrase they declare in unison that,
as observers, "they'll view these human passions and these years through
eyes which once have wept with Christ's own tears."
Scene 1. The inner curtain now rises on a camp outside Rome. Male
Chorus and the orchestra describe the sights and sounds of a warm,
thundery dusk. Collatinus, Junius, and Tarquinius are singing the
praises of wine in the generals' tent. They discuss how last night
all their wives in Rome were discovered in compromising situations
save only Lucretia; Collatinus had therefore won their wager. The
profligate Tarquinius taunts Junius with his cuckoldry and they drink
a toast to Lucretia (who has a six-note turning figure). Junius rushes
from the tent, full of jealousy at Lucretia's name and of self-pity.
Collatinus comes out and attempts to assuage his feelings. He tries
to reconcile Tarquinius, who joins them still singing the drinking-
song, with Junius and goes off to bed. After a short duet Tarquinius who
makes no secret of his sensuality, confesses that he is tired of willing
women and Junius remarks that virtue in women is lack of opportunity.
This plants in Tarquinius's mind the thought of testing Lucretia's chastity.
Left alone, he turns the idea over in his mind, against the sounds of the
night and the comments of Male Chorus, and suddenly calls for his horse.
In an exciting Interlude Male Chorus and the orchestra graphically
describe Tarquinius's furious ride and how he makes his Arab stallion swim
across the Tiber.
Scene 2. The hall of the home of Lucretia, who is sewing while Bianca and
Lucia spin. Female Chorus, to a flute and harp accompaniment, sings a
spinning-song in which she describes how the lives of women are woven.
Each woman in turn breaks in with her thoughts and finally all four
together speak of death, "woman's final lover." Lucretia imagines that
she hears a knock at the door and, disappointed, sings a short arioso "How
cruel men are to teach us love." They prepare for bed, Bianca and Lucia
folding the linen and wordlessly embroidering, in a lovely trio, Female
Chorus's musings on the theme "Whatever their hearts hold, they must fold
clean linen." Then, as Female Chorus speaks of the peace of the night,
Male Chorus, to the ride music crescendo, describes Tarquinius's approach
through the streets of Rome, until a loud knocking is heard. Male and
Female Chrous describe, as the characters mime, his entrance and
request for hospitality and his courteous reception; for "etiquette
compels what discretion would refuse." All four exchange a formal
"good night" in a beautiful passage as the Prince of Rome is conducted
to his chamber. The inner curtain falls. Male and Female Chorus
continue reading.

ACT II

Female Chorus reads of the establishment of the supremacy over the Romans of the Etruscans, with their "passion for creation and lust to kill." Voices within chant of the Roman hatred of the Etruscan tyranny. Male Chorus comments that "violence is the fear within us all" and they repeat the unison phrase which ended the introduction to Act I.

Scene 1. The inner curtain rises on Lucretia asleep in bed while Female Chorus sings a lullaby over the unusual combination of bass flute, muted horn, and bass clarinet. Male Chorus, half speaking, describes Tarquinius's approach over Indian-sounding drums. Standing over her, Tarquinius has an unexpectedly tender aria, but when in the middle section he bids her wake, Female Chorus urges her (to the lullaby) to sleep on. He kisses her as she dreams of Collatinus and she wakes to the sound of the "whip" in the orchestra. For a time he seeks in vain to win her, while the music grows in intensity. Male and Female Chorus try to dissuade him (in a quartet); but eventually he pulls the coverlet from the bed and threatens her with his sword. As he mounts her bed there is a short unaccompanied quartet in which the motive of Lucretia can be heard (among others). The inner curtain falls and during the Interlude Male and Female Chorus sing a unison chorale (against a complex accompaniment).

Scene 2. As in Act I Scene 2. Early morning. Bianca and Lucia revel in the coming fine day and arrange the flowers brought in by their "spendthrift" gardener. They leave the orchids, Collatinus' favourite flower, for Lucretia to do. But when she has appeared and been greeted she calls them hideous and hysterically tells Lucia to send an urgent message to Collatinus to come home. She makes a wreath of the orchids, singing an arioso about flowers over a lovely accompaniment figure for oboe and bassoon, later inverted. (It was hinted at the first mention of orchids.) She goes out. Bianca tries to stop the messenger but almost at once Collatinus and Junius are there, the latter revealing knowledge of Tarquinius's visit. Lucretia now enters in purple mourning while the cor anglais plays an infinitely sad version of her motive over strings and despite comforting words from the half-aware Collatinus tells him starkly what happened the previous night (suggestions of music from the previous scene). Collatinus forgives her at once but she stabs herself and falls dead at his feet. There follows a wonderful chaconne in slow march time, before the close of which Male and Female Chorus join with the four characters of the drama who kneel round Lucretia's body. "How is it possible that she, being so pure, should die.... Is this it all?" Female Chorus takes up the question, as the little three-note figure which has punctuated the chaconne continues to be heard. Male Chorus replies confidently "It is not all.... In his passion is our hope, Jesus Christ, Saviour, He is all." The lights fade on the mourning group. Male and Female Chorus sing once more the striking passage which ended the introduction, this time to the words "Now with worn words and these brief notes we try to harness song to human tragedy".

Rigoletto

Opera in three acts. Music by G. Verdi. Libretto by F. M. Piave after Victor Hugo. First produced at the Teatro la Fenice, Venice, March 11th, 1851.

SCENE: Mantua.

TIME: Sixteenth century.

PRINCIPAL CHARACTERS:

THE DUKE OF MANTUA		(Tenor)
RIGOLETTO	*His hunchback jester*	(Baritone)
GILDA	*Rigoletto's daughter*	(Soprano)
SPARAFUCILE	*An assassin*	(Bass)
MADDALENA	*His sister*	(Contralto)
COUNT CEPRANO		(Bass)
COUNT MONTERONE	*Courtiers*	(Baritone)
BORSA		(Tenor)
MARULLO		(Baritone)
GIOVANNA	*Gilda's duenna*	(Mezzo-soprano)

This is the earliest of the small group of Verdi's operas which have consistently and universally held their place in the repertory and, though composed in great haste, he never found any need to revise it. The admirable libretto must have played its part in this success-story; it has no pretensions to tragedy or literary merit but is a melodrama with its climactic points ideally placed for "strong" music. Though some of the music is conventional, it is all bursting with vitality and striking melodies abound. It is in the music for Rigoletto and Sparafucile that Verdi's latent power of characterization is most apparent, though that for the Duke manages to be at the same time an expression of his reckless character and just the material for an Italian tenor of the period. (Later Caruso was to make it especially his own.) While "Caro nome" and "La donna è mobile" are the most familiar numbers, the musical high point is the Act IV quartet, in which four parts, wholly differentiated, both musically and dramatically, are successfully combined. The Storm and terzetto which follow have a strength far in advance of Verdi's "first period" and the irony of the final reprise of "La donna è mobile" is a brilliant coup de théâtre.

ACT I

Scene 1. The Duke's palace. After a few introductory bars, to be associated with Monterone's curse, a brilliant party is seen to be in progress. Festive music is sometimes heard from inner rooms and forms a background to much of the action. The amorous Duke tells Borsa of an unknown girl living in a remote street and visited nightly by a mysterious man. He has seen her in church. For the moment he is engaged in flirting with Contessa Ceprano and is not afraid of the Count's displeasure. His ruthlessly pleasure-loving character is underlined in the dashing aria "Questa o quella". While he dances with the Countess, Rigoletto mocks the Count. Marullo announces to a group of guests that the hunchback has a mistress. At this news Ceprano bids them meet him on the following evening so that they can wreak their vengeance on the hated jester who aids and abets the Duke's adventures. The ensemble is broken by the arrival of the aged Count Monterone who denounces the Duke for dishonouring his daughter and curses both him and Rigoletto, to the latter's dismay. The Duke has him arrested.

Scene 2. A street and courtyard outside Rigoletto's house. As the hunchback returns, brooding on the curse, he is accosted by an assassin who offers his services to rid him of a rival whom, with a woman in the house, he must surely have. The assassin uses his sister as a decoy. He tells Rigoletto, who has no immediate need for his services, that he is Sparafucile, a Burgundian. (This sinister little duet takes place over a mysterious melody on a muted solo cello.) Alone, Rigoletto meditates on his lot, deformed and forced to jest but hating them all. He is still troubled by the curse. He is greeted by Gilda, his daughter, and in the long duet which ensues we learn that she is kept jealously guarded in the house and in ignorance of the identity of her father and her dead mother and that her natural high spirits are repressed by her too loving father. The Duke in disguise as a student has meanwhile bribed Giovanna and hidden in the courtyard, unseen by Rigoletto, who departs. She and Gilda have not told Rigoletto of the handsome young man who has followed Gilda to church and of whom she dreams. It was the Duke, who now steps forth, gets rid of Giovanna, and protests his love in a paragraph of such melting beauty that her scruples are swiftly overcome. Their love duet is interrupted by footsteps outside and he departs, after telling her that he is a poor student called Gualtier Maldé. She muses on the dear name, in the famous florid aria. The footsteps were those of Ceprano, Marullo, Borsa, and other courtiers come to abduct Rigoletto's mistress, as they assume Gilda to be. Rigoletto appears. They tell him that their scheme is to abduct the Countess Ceprano who lives nearby and when they give him a key with the Ceprano crest on it he agrees to assist them. He must be masked as they are. They manage to obstruct his vision and in the darkness and confusion he assists them, by holding the ladder, to carry off Gilda in the belief that she is the

Countess. He is vastly amused by the episode and it is only when they have gone that, tearing off the mask, he discovers, from the scarf which she has dropped, that it was Gilda. "The old man's curse!" he cries.

ACT II

A room in the palace. The Duke has returned to Rigoletto's house and found it empty. He is disconsolate at the loss of the first woman to have wakened in him, he says, feelings of devotion and the thought of Gilda's sufferings moves him to a beautiful aria. The courtiers enter and describe the attraction of Rigoletto's mistress in a jaunty chorus. They have brought her to the palace. The Duke feels, in another aria, that he must exploit this stroke of luck, though the courtiers are disconcerted at his unexpected seriousness. As he goes off Rigoletto appears, looking for his daughter but keeping up his jesting before the courtiers who chaff him. He is given grounds for suspecting that Gilda is with the Duke and reveals, to the general surprise, that Gilda is his daughter and not his mistress. He abuses the courtiers but is finally reduced to humble pleas for her return to him. (This famous scena is the baritone's great moment.) Gilda, distraught, now comes running to him and he orders the courtiers so firmly to leave them alone that they do so. Gilda then recounts the story of her first meeting with the Duke and the night's events. A duet follows, in the first part of which father and daughter lament and console each other. After Monterone has been led through the room on his way to prison, Rigoletto in hgih emotion vows vengeance on the Duke while Gilda vainly pleads with him, as the duet reaches its climax, to spare him.

ACT III

A lonely spot outside the city. Night. Sparafucile is seen sharpening his sword in an inn which he keeps. Outside, Rigoletto promises Gilda revenge; but she still loves the Duke. He tells her to watch. The Duke, in disguise, arrives and orders a room and wine. Then, in high spirits, he sings "La donna è mobile", an aria about the fickleness of woman. Sparafucile then produces his sister, a gypsy wanton. There follows the quartet in which, after an introductory passage, the Duke has the lead throughout, making love to Maddalena with a ravishing melòdy while the others comment in character—Maddalena sceptical of his advances, Gilda disillusioned and shocked, Rigoletto muttering vengeance. Rigoletto tells Gilda to go home and leave for Verona disguised as a boy. He then bargains with Sparafucile to kill the young man, whose name he conceals, but says that he will return to throw the body in a sack into the river himself. A storm approaches. Maddalena is reluctant for the Duke to go in as she knows what is afoot and has found him a charming young man. But he goes to his room for a rest and is heard singing his song while her brother sends her to fetch his sword. Gilda returns dressed as a boy and overhears Maddalena pleading with her brother to spare the young man. Her proposal is to kill the hunchback and take the balance of the money from him but her brother is outraged at such treatment of a customer. He is willing, however, if any other traveller comes on such a night to kill him and substitute his body for that of the Duke. Gilda resolves to die for the Duke. She knocks and is admitted. (This takes place to a terzetto based on a strikingly dramatic fragment of melody.) The storm now breaks and it is darker than ever. When it is over Rigoletto returns, pays the money and receives the sack. But just as he is leaving, gloating, to drop it in the river, the Duke emerges from the house, still singing "La donna è mobile" and strides into the distance. Rigoletto in dismay opens the sack and finds Gilda, just able to join him in a final duet before she dies. "The old man's curse!" cries Rigoletto once more.

Der Ring des Nibelungen

(The Nibelung's Ring). Stage-festival play for three days and a preliminary evening. Music by R. Wagner. Libretto by the composer. First produced in its entirety at Bayreuth on August 13th, 14th, 16th, and 17th, 1876.

The "Ring" is on a vast scale. It is a single work (though the two middle operas which have been compared to the slow movement and scherzo of a symphony are sometimes given separately) requiring four evenings and 14-15 hours playing time. But the passages in which the musical interest flags are few, as are those which are dramatically superfluous; some at least of the latter can be regarded as the kind of repetition commonly found in epic poems—from Homer onwards—though some may derive from the fact that Wagner wrote the four books in reverse order. The overall time of composition was 21 years, but this included an interruption after Act II of "Siegfried" for the composition of "Tristan" and of the "Meistersinger".

Innumerable attempts have been made to interpret the allegorical meaning of the "Ring". On a first approach, at least, it is wisest to regard it simply as an epic tale compiled from old German mythology as a vehicle for Wagner's new ideas about Music Drama, though at the same time underlying themes, such as the curse attaching to the gold, and individual episodes provide fertile ground for the kind of didactic symbolism to which he was much addicted.

It is in the "Ring" that Wagner's pictorial powers are most apparent. It is full of felicitous examples of the painting of natural phenomena. What, for instance, could more vividly illustrate in music the kindling and steady burning of flames round a rocky crag than the closing pages of "Die Walkure"? But although the orchestra, large in numbers, especially of brass, and with a characteristic dark and glowing sound (heard to best advantage from a sunken pit as at Bayreuth), dominates and is continuously used for depicting the background to the action as well as for a running commentary upon it, it would be wrong to regard the singers' parts as of secondary musical interest (save in a few passages) or as hopelessly unvocal. They have always been recognized as demanding big voices and a high level of operatic acting, but certain modern performances have underlined that even in the more intense and fully scored scenes there remains scope for lyrical and dramatically inflected singing. The latter quality is of course especially needed in the passages of declamatory recitative, most of it apt to the cadences of German speech, into which Wagner sometimes drops. For, at least in the first three operas, the musical writing is less close-knit and consistently symphonic than in "Tristan".

Wagner uses "leading motives" far more extensively in this work than in his others. The many motives function, to some extent, as labels or indicators and constantly underline points in the dialogue, illumine thoughts, or comment ironically, being used separately or in combination, in the original or a modified form. While early German musicologists may have overdone the business of naming the motives, which like the conventional epithets in Homer can be appreciated without always being precisely understood, some prior acquaintance with the more important ones is desirable. An attempt has been made in the descriptions of the individual operas to indicate the first, or an early, appearance of crucial motives as an aid to recognition of their subsequent treatment.

New ground is broken in the "Ring" by the elaborate orchestral interludes used to cover changes of scene (with the main curtain up) without any break in musical continuity. There are three in "Das Rheingold", one in "Siegfried" and three in "Götterdämmerung". These brilliant symphonic poems not only illustrate the scenic transformation but review the leading motives in a kind of commentary on the action. "Siegfried's Journey to the Rhine" is a familiar example of the former and his "Funeral March" of the latter.

Wagner was aiming at a "Gesamtkunstwerk" and doubtless regarded his elaborate and demanding scenic directions as no less integral a part of his overall conception than his text and his music. But they are conceived in terms of naturalistic theatre which to the present generation is apt to seem not only old-fashioned but also, with so much described in the music, superfluous. Recent productions have tended to follow the example of his grandsons and have aimed at a simpler style leaving more to the imagination. What is the ideal balance is a difficult matter of artistic judgment.

Das Rheingold

(The Rhinegold). Prologue of Der Ring des Nibelungen in four scenes. Music by R. Wagner. Libretto by the composer. First performed at Munich, September 22nd, 1869.

SCENE: The Rhine and neighbourhood.

TIME: Legendary.

CHARACTERS:

WOTAN			(Bass-baritone)
DONNER	Gods		(Bass-baritone)
FROH			(Tenor)
LOGE			(Tenor)
FRICKA	Wotan's wife		(Mezzo-soprano)
FREIA		Goddesses	(Soprano)
ERDA			(Contralto)
FASOLT	Giants		(Bass-baritone)
FAFNER			(Bass)
ALBERICH	Nibelungs		(Baritone)
MIME			(Tenor)
WOGLINDE			(Soprano)
WELLGUNDE	Daughters of the Rhine		(Soprano)
FLOSSHILDE			(Mezzo-soprano)

The Prelude, suggesting primeval peace as well as the flowing river, is an expressive crescendo on the simple triad of E flat lasting for 136 bars, at the 17th of which is first introduced the arpeggio-like motive of the Rhine.

Scene 1. The bed of the river with rocky crags. The three Rhinemaidens are swimming around, guarding the gold. The dwarf Alberich clambers slipping up a rock and eyes them lasciviously. In turn each approaches and tempts him, only to dart mockingly away from his reach. Suddenly the sun rises and lights up the gold, as a horn announces the motive of the gold (a rising arpeggio staccato). The three maidens greet it with joy. They explain to Alberich that he who fashions a ring from it can enjoy unlimited power (ring motive on wood-wind), but must first forswear love (renunciation motive) which no-one would wish to do. But Alberich's desire has instantly turned towards the gold and, taking advantage of the sisters' over-confidence, he manages to reach and make off with the gold, cursing love. The motives are reviewed during the ensuing change of scene.

Scene 2. An open space on a height by the river valley, across which is seen a castle on a cliff. Dawn. The sumptuous Valhalla motive is heard on the brass. Fricka, awakening, rouses Wotan, who is filled with pride at the completion of the building. But Fricka reminds him that the price to be paid to the giants who built it is her sister, the lovely Freia. (The descending scalic motive stands for Wotan's spear, or the compact engraved thereon.)

From Fricka's strictures it also emerges that she has been hoping that their new stately home will keep Wotan from his faithless ranging. Wotan indicates that he never had any intention of giving up Freia, who now enters, calling on Froh and Donner for help against the pursuing giants. He is anxiously awaiting Loge, the Fire-god who has promised to find a way of saving Freia. Fasolt and Fafner arrive, to their ponderous motive, and claim Freia as their fee, incredulous and menacing that Wotan should seek release from his contract. How can they give up Freia who grows golden apples which will give her kin eternal youth? (Motive on the horns.) Froh and Donner are barely restrained from coming to blows with the giants when Loge (with his chromatic semi-quaver motive) at last arrives. He reluctantly admits his promise but has no immediate solution to justify Wotan's confidence in him. In his travels he has found nothing more desirable to men than the beauty of woman. Only Alberich had forsworn love for gold; and the grieving Rhinemaidens had appealed to Wotan to bring the thief to justice and restore them the gold. The giants are in fear that Alberich should have the gold, especially when Loge speaks of the power which it would confer when fashioned into a ring by one who renounced love. Fricka shows a woman's interest. Loge cunningly suggests that Wotan must steal the gold from the thief and return it to the Rhinemaidens. Fafner thereupon declares that the gold is worth more to them than Freia. They drag Freia away, saying that they will give her up if they can have the gold as ransom that evening. The gods visibly languish and Loge explains that the loss of Freia and her apples is causing them to age. Wotan's mind is made up. They must have the gold—and not so as to return it to the Rhinemaidens. He and Loge set out for Nibelheim. In the latter part of the music which accompanies the change of scene, the Nibelung motive—a pulsing rhythm—is strongly heard on anvils.

Scene 3. Nibelheim, a subterranean cavern. Alberich is berating the dwarf Mime for not having delivered the Tarnhelm—a helmet which he was to make from the gold. Mime produces it and the mysterious chords of the Tarnhelm motive are heard. Alberich puts it on and is turned into a column of vapour. He is exultant at the power which it gives him but continues unseen to beat Mime. Loge and Wotan now appear and when the former asks Mime what is afflicting him, Mime tells him how Alberich, fortified by the power of the ring which he has made, now forces the Nibelungs to toil ceaselessly to amass gold for him. He himself, having made the Tarnhelm, had hoped to keep it for himself, but had been outwitted. Alberich approaches with the Tarnhelm on his girdle, driving a crowd of heavily laden Nibelungs fearful of the ring's master. He is suspicious of Wotan's flattery and Loge's attempt, as God of Fire, to establish a bond between them. He boasts of the power which the hoarded gold will give him over the gods themselves. He will protect it by the ability to transform himself, which the Tarnhelm confers on its wearer. By expressing disbelief in its power Loge gets him to become a serpent (writhing motive on tubas) and then a toad. Wotan puts his foot on the toad; Loge seizes the Tarnhelm; they tie up Alberich, now in his real shape again, and carry him off. The change of scene music paints their return journey from the principal motives so far heard.

Scene 4. As in Scene 2. Wotan and Loge drag up Alberich still bound and raging and inform him that the price of his liberty is his hoard of gold. Alberich agrees to pay it, hoping to keep the ring and with it win new wealth. They loosen his right hand and, with the ring to his lips, he summons the Nibelungs and orders them to fetch the hoard of gold. There is a fine climax as the Nibelungs pile up the gold and then turn in terror. But Loge claims that the Tarnhelm too is part of the ransom and Alberich gives it up, with the thought that Mime can make him another. When, however, Wotan claims the ring also he rages against him till, finally, Wotan tears it from his finger and has him set free. Syncopated, repeated chords on the low register of the clarinets mark the motive of the Nibelung's hate and before he leaves Alberich pronounces, to another leading motive, a curse on all who shall possess the ring. The giants are now espied returning with Freia. It grows lighter and the gods enjoy a feeling of renewed well-being. The giants demand sufficient gold to cover Freia. When she is no longer visible and all the gold has been used—to the anger of Froh and Donner at the indignity—they claim that her hair can still be seen and the Tarnhelm is added to the pile. But the giants say that there is still a crevice and that the ring must stop it up. This Wotan stubbornly refuses and they are preparing to carry Freia off when the mysterious figure of Erda, the primal goddess who has borne Wotan the three Norns, appears in a blue light, to a rising motive somewhat similar to that of the Rhine, and warns him to give up the ring. She disappears. Wotan gives the giants the ring and, to the general joy, Freia is released. The giants at once quarrel over the ring. Fafner kills Fasolt with a single blow and wrenches it from him, as three trombones twice sound the curse. Wotan, brooding, at first ignores Fricka's proposal that they enter Valhalla, which is still veiled in mist. Donner ascends a rock and swings his hammer till all the mists gather about him. He strikes the rock and, after thunder and lightning, Valhalla is seen radiantly lit, with a rainbow forming a bridge across the Rhine valley. Froh points the way, as Wotan greets the gleaming castle. Then, picking up a sword which Fafner, departing with his hoard, has left behind (sword motive, a leaping trumpet arpeggio) he takes Fricka by the hand and leads the gods into Valhalla, while the orchestra play the majestic "Entry of the Gods". Loge comments that they are hastening to their end and hesitates to join them. The Rhinemaidens are heard from the valley lamenting the gold. Wotan bids Loge silence them and Loge adds to the message the advice that they should bask in the gods' new radiance. But they continue to lament, calling those who rejoice above false and cowardly and adding a note of irony to the triumphant close.

Die Walküre

(The Valkyrie). Music drama in three acts. Music by R. Wagner. Libretto by the composer. First produced at Munich, June 26th, 1870.

SCENE: Neighbourhood of the Rhine.

TIME: Legendary (A generation after *Das Rheingold*).

CHARACTERS:

WOTAN		(Bass-baritone)
FRICKA *His wife*		(Mezzo-soprano)
SIEGMUND ⎱ *Brother and sister,*		(Tenor)
SIEGLINDE ⎰ *Wälsungs*		(Soprano)
HUNDING *Sieglinde's husband*		(Bass)
BRÜNNHILDE *A Valkyrie*		(Soprano)
8 SISTER VALKYRIES *daughters of Wotan and Erda*		
	(Four sopranos and four contraltos)	

ACT I

Interior of Hunding's forest hut with a great ash in the centre. The Prelude depicts a raging storm (in the course of which Donner, the God of Thunder, is heard), which gradually subsides till the curtain rises. Siegmund staggers in exhausted and throws himself on the hearth. Sieglinde enters, thinking it to be Hunding. She bends over the stranger and a motive in thirds tells of her solicitude. She brings him water and, as their eyes meet, the love motive is first heard on a solo cello. He revives and tells her how, without spear and shield, harried by foes and the elements, he has been driven to take shelter though his wounds are slight. A draught of mead kindles his feelings towards her still further. But ill-fated as he is, he feels he must leave. Sieglinde presses him to stay as there is already misfortune in the house. (The Wälsung motive is heard.) Hunding's motive (heavy, rhythmic, on the brass) now heralds his entrance. He bids his wife fetch food for the stranger, whose resemblance to her strikes him. He questions him as to who he is. Siegmund does not reply directly. He tells, as they sit at table, how when young he returned one day from hunting with his father, "Wolf", to find their dwelling razed and his mother and twin sister gone. Years of hiding in the forest from their enemies had followed. After a foray he had lost his father. (The softly sounding Valhalla motive informs us that, though known to Siegmund as Wälse, the father of the Wälsungs was Wotan himself.) Since then ill fortune had continued to dog him. Now he has lost his arms, defending from a horde of oppressors a girl being pushed unwillingly into wedlock. As his narrative concludes we hear the Wälsung motive, followed by another Wälsung motive of great sadness, as Sieglinde gazes, deeply moved, upon him. But his foes were of Hunding's race and Hunding now challenges him to combat next morning, before retiring to bed. Sieglinde lingers and puts a sleeping potion in her husband's drink, gazing earnestly at the trunk of the ash-tree (sword motive) before joining him. Siegmund is left alone, brooding, longing for the sword his father had promised he would find in his hour of need. The falling embers suddenly illumine the ash-trunk, in which a sword is embedded. As darkness returns Sieglinde slips back to his side. She tells how at her wedding-feast a stranger had appeared and given her, an unwilling bride, a look of comfort, thrusting a sword into the tree-trunk. None had the strength to pull it out. She would embrace the man destined to retrieve it. Siegmund declares that he is the man who will win both sword and woman. As they embrace the door flies open and reveals a moonlit spring night. Siegmund, in a beautiful paragraph, describes how spring has come in search of his sister, Love. Sieglinde hails him as spring and as their rapture mounts each seems to recognize something in the other. When at length Sieglinde elicits from him that his father was Wälse, beside herself with excitement she exclaims that the sword is then for him and greets him as Siegmund. He grasps the sword, names it "Nothung" ("Needy") and pulls it from the tree. Sieglinde reveals herself as his sister and they passionately embrace.

ACT II

A rocky pass. The strenuous Prelude gradually turns to the rhythm of galloping hooves and the motive of the Valkyries' Ride is heard as the curtain rises. Wotan instructs Brünnhilde to ensure that Siegmund wins the combat with Hunding. She springs from rock to rock, uttering the Valkyries' yodelling cry and warns Wotan before she leaves of the approach of Fricka, furiously driving her ram-drawn chariot and spoiling for a quarrel. Fricka, imperiously, as guardian of wedlock, demands vengeance for Hunding on the adulterous pair and brushes aside Wotan's suggestion that it is love which sanctifies a union, pointing out that this union is incestuous. Further, she rubs in forcefully that the Wälsungs are the fruit of his own adulterous union with a mortal woman. Wotan replies that she is, as ever, bound by convention, whereas the situation requires a hero, to do the deed (*i.e.*, to recover the ring) which the gods may not do for themselves. Fricka is unimpressed, regarding the Wälsungs as Wotan's creatures, though Wotan retorts that Siegmund had grown up by himself and won the sword in adversity. (The descending string phrase, preceded by a mordant, stands for Wotan's disillusion.) She insists that he, and Brünnhilde too, withdraw all protection from Siegmund. In a final regal paragraph she makes Wotan swear, as Brünnhilde reappears, that the latter will uphold "his wife's sacred honour." Alone with Brünnhilde, Wotan gives vent to an outburst of despair. She settles at his feet and coaxes him to explain it. This he does in a long narrative which begins by recapitulating the main events of *Das Rheingold*. He goes on, however, to tell how subsequently he had visited Erda to learn more of her secret wisdom. She had borne him, during this time, Brünnhilde and her eight sisters, whose task it is to carry slain heroes to Valhalla to form a protective force. Erda had warned him of the danger to the gods if Alberich should succeed in recovering the ring from Fafner. He himself is precluded from seizing the ring from Fafner by his covenant to give it him as his reward for building Valhalla. It must be done spontaneously by a hero whom he has not helped. He had planned that it shall be Siegmund. But in giving him the sword he had been guilty of self-deception; Fricka had seen through it and he must yield to her. Now he can only await the end. Erda had said that it would be at hand when Alberich begot a son and he has heard that a woman is with child by him. (The two strong chords later associated with Hagen are heard). He bitterly bequeaths the child the "empty glory of divinity." Meanwhile, Brünnhilde's task is to secure Hunding's victory and Siegmund's death and when she hesitates, he warns her, before storming out, of the terrible wrath which awaits her if she is disobedient. Brünnhilde, in a beautiful passage, sadly takes up her arms and prepares for her hateful task. She withdraws into a cave. Siegmund and Sieglinde appear. He urges her to rest, but she is distraught—with exhaustion, guilt, and fear of Hunding's kinsmen and dogs now in hot pursuit. Siegmund, armed with the sword, is not afraid of combat, but sobbing and full of foreboding she sinks senseless in his arms. He sits down, with her head in his lap, as Brünnhilde advances slowly towards him from the cave (to the motives of fate and of death). She tells him that she appears only to those doomed to die in battle, to conduct them to Valhalla. In a dialogue of poetical sadness, Siegmund, on learning that Sieglinde may not follow him there, defiantly refuses to accompany her and prefers, if die he must, that the sword should make an end both of Sieglinde and himself. Brünnhilde, touched by his devotion, promises him victory and life after all, before rushing away. In gathering darkness Siegmund takes leave of the sleeping Sieglinde, who is dreaming of the sack of her father's house. Hunding and Siegmund fight, in a storm, on a hill-top, Brünnhilde protecting the latter. But Wotan appears, the sword is shattered on his spear and Siegmund falls dead. Brünnhilde carries Sieglinde away on her horse. Wotan strikes the victorious Hunding dead with a gesture of contempt and disappears, raging against the disobedient Brünnhilde.

ACT III

The summit of a rocky mountain. Storm clouds. The Valkyries are seen galloping to their place of tryst. The Prelude and first scene are the piece of wild nature-painting known in the concert-room as "The Ride of the Valkyries". They call to each other of the day's exploits. Brünnhilde is espied, riding furiously, with Sieglinde across her saddle. She arrives breathless, leading Sieglinde and seeking protection from the pursuing Wotan for them both. None dares to lend her her horse. Sieglinde does not wish to live without Siegmund, until Brünnhilde tells her that she will have a child by him. Brünnhilde decides that the East is the safest direction to escape the approaching Wotan, even though it is where Fafner, who has changed himself into a dragon, keeps watch over the ring. She tells Sieglinde, to the majestic motive standing for Siegfried, to be ever mindful that she carries in her womb the noblest hero in the world, who shall be named Siegfried. Sieglinde expresses her gratitude in a glorious phrase and hastens away to her destiny. Brünnhilde hides among the Valkyries. Wotan storms in in furious anger. He will have none of their pleas for mercy; Brünnhilde, his most trusted daughter, has defied his will and must meet her punishment. She comes forward. He tells her that she has ceased to be a Valkyrie and is banished from Valhalla. She is to be locked in sleep here on the mountain, a mere woman to be captured by the first man to find and waken her. Her sisters attempt to intercede but are told to keep their distance from her, and are dismissed. Brünnhilde sinks to the ground at Wotan's feet. In a pathetic orchestral passage a motive with an upward leap of a seventh, standing for her pleading, is heard, alternating with Wotan's disillusion. She argues that what she has done in defending Siegmund in his piteous plight was his real will. But he pours scorn on her surrender to the luxury of emotion, when he had steeled himself to contemplate the ruin of his world. (The curse is heard.) In reply she asks that if he is inexorably resolved, he should grant that only a worthy hero should win her and speaks of the Wälsung child in Sieglinde's womb and of the shattered sword which the latter is preserving. Let her sleep be guarded by flames which only a fearless hero will dare to penetrate. Now follow the familiar "Farewell and Fire Music" in which two motives representing sleep—a series of descending chromatic chords and a gently lulling strain—and a fire motive in semi-quavers akin to that of Loge are constantly heard, together with those of Siegfried and of fate. Wotan takes a long and tender farewell of his beloved daughter. He grants her wish and promises that only he shall win the bride who is freer than himself, the god. After a last embrace she sinks unconscious in his arms and he lays her on a mound, covered with her helmet and shield. He summons Loge to ring the rock with fire. Flames shoot up. Saying that whoever fears the tip of his spear shall never pass through the fire, Wotan takes a last sorrowing look at the sleeping Brünnhilde and disappears through the now

steadily burning flames which are mirrored to the end in music of equal
brilliance and pathos.

Siegfried

*Music drama in three acts. Music by R. Wagner. Libretto by the
composer. First produced at Bayreuth, August 16th, 1876.*

SCENE: Neighbourhood of the Rhine.

TIME: Legendary (About 20 years after *Die Walküre*).

CHARACTERS:

SIEGFRIED	*Son of Siegmund and Sieglinde*	(Tenor)
MIME	} *Nibelungs*	(Tenor)
ALBERICH		(Baritone)
WOTAN	*Disguised as the Wanderer*	(Bass-baritone)
FAFNER	*A giant, now a dragon*	(Bass)
VOICE OF A FOREST BIRD		(Soprano)
ERDA		(Contralto)
BRÜNNHILDE		(Soprano)

ACT I

A rocky cave. The dark and mysterious Prelude recalls motives from
Das Rheingold, especially the rhythms of the Nibelung anvils, with,
towards the end, the writhing theme in the bass which now stands for the
dragon Fafner. Its general import becomes apparent when Mime is seen
brooding on his inability to forge a sword which the young Siegfried
does not at once shatter. His ambition is to forge one with which the
young man can slay Fafner and win him the ring. Only "Nothung" will,
it seems, suffice and he lacks the strength to weld the fragments. The
carefree young man enters, leading a bear (to a characteristic horn call)
and at once begins to revile Mime for the inadequacy of the sword he has
just made. Mime whiningly complains of such ingratitude for all the care
with which he has brought him up. But Siegfried breezily replies that he
has not taught him to tolerate himself. He goes on, to a motive which
seems to tell of nature and its wonders, to describe how he has studied the

habits of the beasts. He cannot understand how he has no mother and, having seen his own image in a stream, how the ugly Mime can be his father. Mime tells him how he had given shelter to his mother who had died giving birth to him. She had said that he must be named Siegfried. She herself had been called Sieglinde but had not told him the name of his dead father. The only proof of this tale he can offer is the fragments of a sword which Siegfried at once says must be forged for him. He wishes to go forth with it into the world, never to return. He runs out into the forest, leaving Mime fretting over this new anxiety.

Wotan enters, disguised as the Wanderer, to solemn chòrds, and craves hospitality which Mime is most reluctant to accord. But Wotan sits down and wagers his head if he cannot answer any three questions Mime chooses to put; the latter agrees to this battle of wits. His three questions are: "Which race dwells in the earth's depths?", "Which dwells on the face of the earth?", and "Which race lives in the cloudy heights?"—to which Wotan respectively replies, in some detail and with some musical repetition, "the Nibelungs", "the giants", and "the gods". He now presses Mime to agree to a return match. To Wotan's first two questions—"What is the race which Wotan used so harshly, yet loved so dear?" and "With what sword shall Siegfried slay Fafner?" he correctly replies "The Wälsungs" and "Nothung". But to the third question "Who shall forge this sword from its splinters?" he cannot find the answer. Wotan answers for him "Only he who has never known fear." To such a one, Wotan adds, he will leave Mime's head, which he has just won, forfeit, and disappears quickly into the forest. Mime is left in terror at what these last words may mean, and at the play of the sunlight on the forest which seems like fire to him, suggesting the approach of Fafner. But it is Siegfried who bursts in, inquiring for his sword. Mime, mindful of Wotan's words, tells Siegfried that he has omitted to teach him the meaning of fear; but Siegfried has no idea what he can mean. When Mime tries to explain, Siegfried remarks that it must be a pleasurable experience (and the orchestra, by softly playing Brünnhilde's slumber motives hints how he is to learn it). Mime replies that Fafner, to whom he will conduct him, will teach him fear, at which Siegfried again demands his sword and declares that he will forge it himself. As he stokes up the fire and breaks down the fragments of the sword, Mime broods on his dilemma. If Fafner does not teach Siegfried fear, he will lose his own head; if he does, Siegfried will fail to slay the dragon and gain him the ring. As Siegfried works the bellows and melts down the steel, to a familiar passage of immense vitality, Mime decides that Siegfried will slay Fafner but that he must then be given a sleeping-draught and killed with the sword. As Siegfried proceeds to beat out the molten metal, to another animated song, Mime anticipates the success of his cunning plan and exults at the prospect of lording it, as possessor of the ring, over Alberich and the whole world. The Act works up to a stirring climax as Siegfried finally brandishes the finished sword and cleaves the anvil with a mighty blow.

ACT II

Deep forest with the entrance to a cave. Night. After a sinister Prelude
in which the motives of Fafner (both as giant and dragon), the curse, and
the Nibelung's hate stand out, Alberich is discovered keeping watch over
Fafner's lair. The Wanderer approaches in a blue light. Alberich taunts
him with his inability to recover the ring himself and emphasizes his own
determination to get it and exploit its power. Wotan replies darkly of the
lad who, guided by Mime, will slay Fafner and, unaided, seize the ring. He
jestingly proposes that Alberich should wake Fafner and suggest that, in
return for his warning that his life is in danger, he should give him the
treasure. This he does; but Fafner sleepily replies that he is holding on.
The Wanderer departs, after giving him the advice (to the motive of Erda)
that everything goes its own way and nothing can be altered. Day now
breaks and, as Mime and Siegfried enter, Alberich hides in a crevice. Mime
describes the terrible dragon, but Siegfried shows no fear, only defiance.
Mime leaves him to await the hour when Fafner emerges, hoping that each
will kill the other. Siegfried, glad to be rid of him, lies down and muses on
what his parents could have been like, while the orchestra paints the scene,
in the passage known in the concert-room as "Forest murmurs". Siegfried's
attention is drawn to the song of a bird. He hopes that if he imitates it he
will understand it. He cuts a reed with his sword but does not have much
success in playing it. So he plays his horn instead and this brings Fafner
from his lair. Fafner's threats provoke a fight, which ends by Siegfried
plunging his sword into the beast's heart. With his last breath Fafner warns
him against the one who prompted him to this exploit. Siegfried sucks the
dragon's blood from his fingers. He hears the bird again and now can
understand it. The bird tells him of the gold, the Tarnhelm, and the ring in
the cave which are now his and he enters it to fetch them. Alberich and
Mime reappear quarrelling violently over the spoils. The former makes off
as Siegfried emerges with the ring and the Tarnhelm but ignorant of their
virtues, to a beautiful paragraph recalling the first scene of Das Rheingold.
The forest bird warns him against Mime whose thoughts he can now, having
tasted blood, understand. In the following passage the music represents
the cajoling words which Mime thinks he is uttering. His actual words are
his inner thoughts—that he will kill Siegfried when he has taken the
drugged drink which he is offering and then seize the spoils for himself.
These are what Siegfried hears and in sudden exasperation he kills the
dwarf. As he dies, Alberich's mocking laughter is heard. Siegfried throws
the body on to the gold in the cave and drags the dead dragon across the
entrance. Then he sits down under a tree to rest, tells the bird of his
loneliness, and asks for a companion. The bird fires his senses by speaking
of Brünnhilde asleep on her rock. Only he who knows no fear can win her.
Siegfried replies that he has still failed to learn fear and burns to learn it
from Brünnhilde. He urges the bird to lead him to her rock. The bird

circles for a moment and then flies off, with Siegfried in pursuit.

ACT III

Scene 1. A wild region at the foot of a rocky mountain. The strenuous Prelude has highlighted motives connected with Wotan and Erda. Wotan, still disguised as the Wanderer and in search of the key to his besetting problem, strides resolutely through a storm and calls on Erda, who awakens from her long sleep (to the descending chromatic slumber motive). But she is confused in mind and has no helpful counsel to give. Before dismissing her Wotan tells her that he now freely renounces his heritage (important new motive) in favour of Siegfried who is to awaken Brünnhilde to the deed that will redeem the world. Siegfried approaches, the bird having just flown away. In reply to Wotan's questions he recounts his earlier exploits until his patience is exhausted by the old man blocking his way. Wotan in a final attempt to stave off the loss of his power which will follow Brünnhilde's awakening, tries to deter him from penetrating the flames and to bar the way with his spear. Siegfried, recognizing his father's foe and the opportunity for revenge, cuts the spear in half with his sword. Wotan exclaims "Forward! I cannot hold you" and disappears. Siegfried presses forward into the flames. The transformation music that follows, picturing his progress through them to the mountain top, is particularly fine.

Scene 2. As in *Die Walküre*, Act III. Siegfried approaches the sleeping Brünnhilde, to a passage for violins alone (a variant of the Freia motive) followed by the Fricka motive, standing for conjugal love. He gazes tenderly at what he takes to be a warrior but as he gradually removes the armour, he starts back with the cry "this is no man." In great unease he calls on his mother. For he realizes that it is a woman and that he has learnt fear. He rouses Brünnhilde with a kiss. She slowly awakens and greets the sun (in a sequence of chords that will recur), the radiant earth, and the hero Siegfried, her awakener, whom she has always loved, even before he was born. Siegfried cannot quite follow her reference to Wotan's thought (which she identifies with her love for himself) but is increasingly filled with longing for her. She thinks of Valhalla when she was a warrior virgin and is overcome by shame at the thought of being a defenceless woman. In a passage beginning with the flowing motive which opens the Siegfried Idyll and continuing as she greets him as the treasure of the world with a motive in contrary motion also familiar therefrom, she pleads that their relationship be calm and undisturbed, but finally she is infected by his ardour. When he says that he has already forgotten the fear which she so recently taught him, she surrenders to the laughter of womanly love, reckless of the fate of the gods, and a joyous new motive (first heard on the horns) surges through the final section of this huge love duet.

Götterdämmerung

(Twilight of the Gods). Music drama in a prologue and three acts. Music by R. Wagner. Libretto by the composer. First produced at Bayreuth, August 17th, 1876.

SCENE: Neighbourhood of the Rhine.

TIME: Legendary (Shortly after *Siegfried*).

CHARACTERS:

SIEGFRIED	(Tenor)
BRÜNNHILDE	(Soprano)
ALBERICH	(Baritone)
HAGEN *His son, half-brother of Gunther*	(Bass)
GUNTHER *King of the Gibichungs*	(Baritone)
GUTRUNE *His sister*	(Soprano)
WALTRAUTE *A Valkyrie*	(Mezzo-soprano)
THREE NORNS	(Contralto, mezzo-soprano, and soprano)
WOGLINDE ⎫	(Soprano)
WELLGUNDE ⎬ *Daughters of the Rhine*	(Soprano)
FLOSSHILDE ⎭	(Mezzo-soprano)

PROLOGUE

Brünnhilde's rock, with fire gleaming from the valley below. Night. The orchestra begins with the chords to which Brünnhilde awoke and continues by weaving together allusively strands of motives previously heard, but all in dark colours, while the Norns spin the rope of life. They recount to each other cryptically the main events of the previous dramas, adding that Wotan, after the shattering of his spear, had had the branches of the world-ash (from which it had been made) piled into a mighty wall round Valhalla. When this is consumed by fire the final downfall of the gods will ensue. The rope snaps and the Norns, their wisdom gone, disappear, as the curse and fate motives are heard. Day dawns, as we hear a new Siegfried motive on the horns followed by a motive with a turn, standing for Brünnhilde's love. Siegfried emerges in full armour from the cave, followed by Brünnhilde who, having lovingly taught him all her wisdom, is now sending him forth to glorious deeds. Before they part, vowing remembrance of each other, he gives her the ring and she gives him her steed. She gazes after him as he disappears down the rock and his horn-call is heard from below. The music during the change of scene is that known as "Siegfried's Journey to the Rhine", during which his passage through the fire down to the river is graphically described, with reminders of the Rhinedaughters and the gold. It leads straight into

ACT I

Scene 1. Hall of the Gibichungs on the Rhine. A ponderous motive for the sinister Hagen is heard, followed by the Gibichung motive with a dotted rhythm. Gunther looks to him, the son of a mother in common, for advice and Hagen points out that both he and his sister are unmarried. He proposes Brünnhilde as a bride for Gunther, to be won for him by Siegfried who alone can pass through the flames. (He conceals that Brünnhilde is already Siegfried's.) The mysterious potion motive shows that he has worked out how this is to be done. Siegfried is to be given a potion and will then forget all other women. Siegfried's horn is heard from the river. Siegfried is hailed, invited in and disembarks with his horse, which Hagen leads away. Gutrune withdraws. An exchange of courtesies follows during which Hagen elicits the whereabouts of the gold and the ring and explains to the guileless Siegfried the virtues of the Tarnhelm hanging from his belt. Gutrune returns (to a motive that will follow her) with a drinking horn. Siegfried accepts it and drinks to Brünnhilde, but as soon as he has drunk he is struck by Gutrune's beauty and asks her hand. She bows her head and leaves the hall. Gunther then tells him of his own ambition to win Brünnhilde on her rock. Siegfried has no memory of her and at once offers to woo her for Gunther, assuming the latter's form by means of the Tarnhelm. They swear blood-brotherhood in an elaborate oathing ceremony (preceded by the curse in the orchestra) in which Hagen takes no part. Then they hasten away in Siegfried's boat. After Gutrune has reappeared for a moment, Hagen sits down, over a heavily descending bass tritone, to guard the hall and to brood over the prospect of gaining the ring for himself and the Nibelungs—his purpose all along—and with it supreme power. The transformation music continues for a time in similar vein but later turns, via the potion motive, back to Brünnhilde's love and motives from the scene of her awakening by Siegfried.

Scene 2. As in the Prologue. Brünnhilde sits in contemplation of the ring and of Siegfried. She hears distant thunder and Valkyrie music becomes audible. With a loud thunder-clap Waltraute alights on the rock in some trepidation since she has ignored Wotan's prohibition. She has not come with news that Brünnhilde is forgiven or to share her new-found bliss, as Brünnhilde at first supposes. In a wonderful monologue, the music of which is shot with reminiscences painted in new and sombre colours, she tells, as have briefly the Norns in the Prologue, of the sad state of Valhalla behind the ring of logs from the world-ash, where Wotan, who partakes no more of Freia's apples, sits in perpetual silent council. Once he had said to her that if only Brünnhilde would give back the ring to the Rhinedaughters the gods would be freed from the curse. It is to beg her to do this that she has stolen secretly to Brünnhilde. But the latter, now a woman, cannot understand this appeal to former loyalties. To ask her to give up the ring is to ask her to renounce love itself and this she will not do, even though Valhalla fall in ruins. Waltraute departs in dismay. The fires shoot up and Siegfried's horn is heard. But to the expectant Brünnhilde there appears Siegfried wearing the Tarnhelm and in the guise of Gunther. "Betrayed" she shrieks. In a voice of feigned roughness he tells her that he is Gunther come to claim her in marriage. She calls out against Wotan whose punishment (as she thinks) she now understands and tries to ward "Gunther" off with the ring. But is is impotent against him and after a struggle he tears it from her finger. She sinks, broken, into his arms, and at his bidding, leads the way into the cave. He draws his sword and in his own voice calls upon it to testify to the chastity of his wooing by separating him and the bride. As he follows her in this huge Act ends with a loud sinister version of the Tarnhelm motive.

ACT II

An open space on the river bank before the Gibichung's hall. After a menacing Prelude in which the motive of the Nibelung's hate is prominent, Hagen is seen asleep, leaning against a pillar. Alberich crouches before him, urging him to be ruthless. He fears Wotan no more, but Siegfried who has the ring does not know its power and Brünnhilde might counsel him to return it to the Rhinedaughters. Hagen swears to gain the ring for the Nibelungs and Alberich disappears. There follows perhaps the most beautiful of all Wagner's dawns. Siegfried arrives exultantly, in advance of Gunther and Brünnhilde who are following by boat. Hagen summons Gutrune and Siegfried recounts to them how he won Brünnhilde. Then he and Gutrune go within as Hagen, standing on a rock, blows a cow-horn and summons the vassals to the wedding-feast by sounding the call to arms. A barbaric scene follows as the chorus of vassals assemble from all sides to meet the call to danger and relax with laughter on being told by Hagen that they are to sacrifice and feast to celebrate Gunther's wedding. Gunther and Brünnhilde arrive and disembark. Gunther presents his bride with downcast gaze to the vassals. But when Siegfried and Gutrune come out and the former's name is heard, Brünnhilde looks at him in astonishment and almost faints. Then, seeing the ring on his finger, she asks in indignation how he got it from Gunther. Neither Gunther nor Siegfried, who remembers only that he got it from Fafner, can follow her. Then, partly understanding, she realizes that it was Siegfried in disguise who had come to her on the rock and stolen the ring from her. She cries out that she has been betrayed and, calling on the gods for vengeance, proclaims that it is to Siegfried that she is wed. Siegfried, remembering only the previous night, denies that he has betrayed Gunther who feels, however, that the slight to his own honour must be cleared. Siegfried solemnly swears on Hagen's spear that he did not break faith. But Brünnhilde equally solemnly swears that he is a perjurer and deserves to die by the spear. Siegfried, grasping merely that the Tarnhelm had only half concealed him, leaves her complacently to Gunther and cheerfully leads Gutrune and the wedding-guests inside to the feast. Brünnhilde, Gunther, and Hagen are left alone, each for a time busy with his own reflections (as a fine orchestral passage emphasizes). To Brünnhilde, baffled and miserable, Hagen (to a motive with a falling semitone in the upper part) promises vengeance. He elicits from her that Siegfried's back alone does not enjoy the protection of her magic spells. They turn on Gunther, sunk in dejection at having been both deceiver and deceived, and propose that only Siegfried's death can expiate his shame, Hagen adding that thus they can gain the ring and limitless power. Gunther's scruples about breaking his oath of brotherhood are overcome and those about Gutrune evoke Brünnhilde's scorn and the suggestion from Hagen that if his death is contrived on the morrow's hunting expedition it can be represented to her as an accident. Gunther agrees and in a brief trio, while the other two vow vengeance, Hagen promises his father the ring. Siegfried and Gutrune emerge with the bridal procession. Hagen forces Brünnhilde to Gunther's side. They join the procession, leaving Hagen gloating, in the final bars, over the vengeance motive.

ACT III

Scene 1. A wild valley by the Rhine. In the Prelude, hunting horns playing Siegfried's call are heard first, followed by music of the Rhine and its daughters, who are swimming around on its surface still lamenting the loss of the gold and yearning for the hero who will return it to them. Siegfried appears in pursuit of his quarry. They ask for the ring as a reward for helping him find it and, when he refuses, chide him banteringly for being miserly. Nettled, he offers them the ring after all but they refuse to accept it till he has found out about the curse upon it. They solemnly warn him of his impending death. But Siegfried treats this as a threat, for which, unlike the favour of love, he will not give up the ring. So they swim slowly away, foretelling that the proud woman who will inherit it this day will pay better heed, leaving Siegfried railing against the flattery and threats of women. Hagen, Gunther, and the vassals now join Siegfried after an exchange of horn calls. They refresh themselves and Hagen leads

Siegfried on to tell the story of his youth. This he does, summarizing what took place in Acts I and II of *Siegfried*. At this point Hagen puts a herb in his drink to refresh his memory and he describes how he won Brünnhilde. Gunther springs up in horror. But two ravens circle over and, as Siegfried turns to look at them, Hagen thrusts his spear into his back. Siegfried falls, and Hagen quietly makes off from the desolate scene. With Gunther bending at his side, the hero's dying words are of Brünnhilde's awakening. Gunther orders the vassals to carry his body in solemn procession. It is now night, broken by moonlight, and mist fills the scene. They move off to the Funeral March, which forms the Interlude, during which motives of the Wälsungs and Siegfried are reviewed with mournful solemnity. *Scene 2.* As in Act I Scene 1. Moonlit night. Gutrune is anxious and cannot sleep. She peers into Brünnhilde's chamber, but the latter has gone down to the river. The procession arrives, heralded by Hagen's mocking tones. Gutrune, learning that Siegfried is dead, falls on his body, reviling Gunther, who blames Hagen. Hagen claims the ring. Gunther resists him and in the ensuing fight, is killed. But as Hagen goes to take the ring the dead man's hand raises itself threateningly and all remain motionless with terror. Brünnhilde enters and advances firmly upon them. She silences the charges of Gutrune, on whom the truth at last dawns and who crouches in shame over Gunther's body. Brünnhilde calls on the men to build a lofty pyre. She apostrophizes Siegfried and denounces Wotan for condemning him to be a victim of the curse. Now she understands it all and Wotan, redeemed by her, may go to his rest. As Siegfried's body is carried to the pyre, she takes the ring from his finger and promises the Rhinedaughters to follow the counsel she has had from them and to return it to them. She casts a brand on the pyre, bidding the two ravens fly home to Valhalla and tell the gods that their end is dawning. In growing exaltation she mounts her steed and makes him leap onto the pyre. The flames rise up and engulf the whole hall. At the same time the Rhine, with the Rhinedaughters on its waves, surges forwards. Hagen plunges in in an effort to save the ring. Woglinde and Wellgunde draw him down while Flosshilde joyously holds up the ring and the river returns to its bed. The fire grows in the heavens and is seen to devour Valhalla and the gods and heroes assembled therein, as the final orchestral passage, in which many motives, and especially those of Valhalla and the Rhinedaughters, are simultaneously heard, swells to a huge climax.

Der Rosenkavalier

(The Rose Cavalier). Comedy for music in three acts. Music by Richard Strauss. Libretto by H. von Hofmannsthal. First produced at Dresden, January 26th, 1911.

SCENE: Vienna.

TIME: About 1750.

PRINCIPAL CHARACTERS:

THE FELDMARSCHALLIN FÜRSTIN VON WERDENBERG (The Marschallin), *Aged about 32*	(Soprano)
BARON OCHS AUF LERCHENAU *Aged about 35-40*	(Bass)
OCTAVIAN *A young gentleman of noble family, aged 17*	(Mezzo-soprano)
HERR VON FANINAL *A rich merchant newly ennobled*	(Baritone)
SOPHIE *His daughter, aged 14*	(Soprano)
MARIANNE LEITMETZERIN *Her duenna*	(Soprano)
VALZACCHI ⎱ *Two Italian intriguers*	(Tenor)
ANNINA ⎰	(Mezzo-soprano)
A COMMISSIONER OF POLICE	(Bass)
A LANDLORD	(Tenor)
A NOTARY	(Bass)
A SINGER	(Tenor)

The ready appeal of this work lies in the vitality and melodic charm of its music (with its anachronistic use of waltzes to express high spirits or a mood of resignation), its effectiveness as theatre, its contrast of real people drawn in depth and evoking a sympathetic response with the central Falstaffian figure of Ochs, its blend of high comedy and farce in the action, and its attractive picture of Vienna "high life" under Maria Theresa. Hofmannsthal's book is a work of literature in its own right, though much of its detail and of the period flavour of its language is inevitably lost in performance. The score is no less subtle with its variety, its flexible use of broadly applied motives to underline dramatic and psychological points, and its wealth of graphic detail (e.g., the hairdresser in Act I and the candle-lighting early in Act III). Much of it also displays a more refined texture and a more grateful vocal line than in Strauss's previous operas and marks the evolution of his conversational style, though at times (e.g. during the comedy of errors in Act III) it is heavy and noisy and the inspiration flags. The Marschallin's monologue in Act I, the Rose music in Act II, and the great trio and final scene of Act III (leading to an imaginative curtain) are the most famous passages—all affording happy examples of Strauss's skill in exploiting female voices.

ACT I

The Marschallin's bedroom. The Introduction depicts passionate love-making falling away after a climax into a mood of tranquillity. It introduces a number of motives of which that in the first bars plainly stands for the impetuous Octavian and the luscious bitter-sweet melody just before the curtain rises on Octavian kneeling beside the recumbent Marschallin reflects the love between them. He resents the sound of the morning birds which spells the end of their ardent night together. A tinkling bell announces (to graceful music) the arrival of her negro page with her chocolate, Octavian meanwhile hiding. They have a tender breakfast together to a charming dance-measure. She upsets him by saying that she dreamt of the sudden return of her husband from his hunting expedition and is alarmed at a noise outside the room. But it is only a visit from her cousin Ochs whose recent letter she has been too occupied with Octavian to read properly, and the music relaxes into a waltz, as she tells him to get dressed and stay hidden. But he returns dressed as her maid (his motive now transmuted into a waltz) just as Ochs, a seedy but noble cousin from the country, forces his way in. (His motive with a turn and a heavy bass tread is heard.) He immediately shows interest in the maid and will not allow her to be sent away while he explains the object of his call. He is to marry the daughter of the only recently ennobled Faninal; but the latter is rich and in poor health. He has come to seek the Marschallin's advice as to which member of the family to send formally to present the Silver Rose of betrothal on his behalf and also as to a notary to draw up the marriage settlement. All the time he continues to flirt with Mariandel, the maid, to whom he vainly proposes a rendezvous. When the Marschallin feels obliged to refer to this behaviour he launches into a long monologue in a very fast tempo about the number and variety of his amatory escapades with the peasant girls on his estate. This culminates in a swift trio after which he asks for Mariandel to serve his future wife and cheerfully imparts that his own lackey is a natural son. The Marschallin has Mariandel bring a locket of Octavian and gets Ochs's agreement to the latter's acting as Bridegroom's Envoy. He is struck by the likeness to Mariandel. Octavian at last makes his escape as the Marschallin's morning levée begins. The stage rapidly fills with a concourse of people seeking audience with her while she submits to the attentions of her hairdresser. Musically the most conspicuous of these is a Tenor who sings an amorous song in the Italian manner of which the second verse is heard in counterpoint with a motive associated with Ochs's marriage. It is interrupted as the latter, in conference with the Notary, vainly seeks to have the law bent to his advantage in the marriage contract. Valzacchi and Annina offer their services as private detectives and intriguers and undertake to help with Mariandel. Ochs's lackey hands over to the Marschallin the case with the Silver Rose and, the levée being over, Ochs at last withdraws and leaves the Marschallin alone at her dressing-table. The prospect of the young bride being ordered into marriage, as she once was, with so conceited a fellow, has thrown her into a mood of reminiscent melancholy. She looks into the mirror and expresses her feelings at the passage of time in a beautiful, lightly accompanied monologue. Octavian's return in riding-clothes only serves to deepen her feeling of the transitory nature of things, even of the love of men who protest as much as Octavian now does (over the bitter-sweet motive and others heard early in the Act). He weeps and she has to console him for his future infidelity, speaking again of the pervasive effects of time. She sees clearly that today or tomorrow he will leave her for someone younger and prettier and that she must see that their parting is light. Exquisitely though her sentiments are expressed in both words and music Octavian cannot follow them. She dismisses him with the promise that if she drives in the Prater that afternoon he may ride near her carriage. No sooner has he gone than she realizes that she has omitted to kiss him and she sends four footmen to bring him back. They return breathless to report (in a graphic little passage) that he had already gone like the wind; so she contents herself with dispatching her negro page (over the bitter-sweet melody) with the case containing the Silver Rose—he will understand. She remains in thought as violins play a sentimental extension in thirds of an earlier motive, which winds towards a pianissimo cadence and a slow curtain.

ACT II

The Hall in Faninal's palace. The ceremonial call of the Rose Cavalier is eagerly awaited by the household. Faninal is about to leave to fetch Ochs, taking care not to meet the Rose Cavalier; Marianne is watching the scene out of the window; Sophie (whose shy motive has been heard as she kisses her father's hand) is vowing to herself, in stilted phrases learnt at her convent, to remain humble despite her splendid match. Marianne signals the arrival of the Cavalier and Octavian's motive is heard. He makes a splendid entry, dressed in silver and followed by his retinue, presents the Rose—to an oboe motive answered by celesta chords in a conflicting key— and shyly delivers his formal message. She speaks in embarrassment of the Rose's beauty. But their two voices, soaring in a rapturous duet, make it

plain that each is inwardly asking the cause of such sudden bliss. All
now withdraw except Marianne and the young pair sit down together,
Sophie's ingenuous chatter charming Octavian. (A graceful waltz
accompanies this episode.) Soon Faninal arrives with Ochs and his
retinue (a staccato theme standing for his courtship) and presents his
daughter to the latter, who appraises her, as Sophie whispers, like a
horse-coper. Ochs's coarse conversation and crude manners repel Sophie
and enrage Octavian, though Faninal is in an ecstasy of snobbish
satisfaction. Ochs tries to mollify Sophie by singing her a popular song
(the best known of all the opera's waltzes) with salacious words. He now
withdraws with Faninal and the Notary to complete the legal business,
leaving Sophie to Octavian who bluntly asks if she is going to marry such
a fellow. There is a commotion caused by Ochs's retainers in pursuit
of Faninal's maids. Marianne runs off to put things right. Sophie, now
alone with Octavian, asks for advice and he tells her to stand up for
them both and remain "as she is". They kiss and a tender love duet
follows, in rapt half-voice, the music being founded on their two
motives. But Annina and Valzacchi pounce upon them and summon
Ochs who takes the situation with such composure that Octavian has
difficulty in making him grasp that Sophie refuses to marry him.
Octavian's temper rises; he challenges Ochs to a duel and wounds him
in the arm. Ochs makes a tremendous fuss. The whole household
rushes in together with Faninal wringing his hands at such a catastrophe
in his house and furiously threatening Sophie, who persists in her refusal
to marry Ochs. Marianne takes her away and Octavian leaves. A doctor
has bandaged Ochs's wound. Ochs's composure returns sufficiently to
forgive Faninal who retires deferentially. Wine restores his usual good
humour and he begins to sing the salacious waltz again. Annina steals
in with a letter which he makes her read to him. It is from Mariandel
(the waltz version of Octavian's motive) offering to meet him for supper
the following evening. Ochs is overjoyed at his Lerchenauisch good
fortune but omits to give the outraged Annina the expected tip. He is
left finishing the wine and singing the waltz so exuberantly that he holds
on to a bottom E for six bars before going out.

ACT III

A private room in an inn. The Act is prefaced by a rapid but furtive
introductory fugato which continues after the rise of the curtain, as
accompaniment to a "pantomime", in the course of which preparations
are completed for the supper between Ochs and Mariandel. Valzacchi is
disguising Annina as a lady in mourning; dubious characters are hidden
behind trap-doors and false windows; candles are lit; a stage band is heard
playing a waltz from an ante-room; and Octavian is briefly seen, in girl's

clothes over his breeches. Ochs arrives, escorting Mariandel, has candles put out (partly for economy), sends the waiters away and sits down to supper alone with her, to a languid waltz (to be heard again later). But she will not drink wine and pretends to be shocked at discovering an alcove with a bed. When he attempts to kiss her (to another waltz which will recur) he is again troubled by her resemblance to Octavian. The salacious waltz is heard from next door but Mariandel spoils the party by growing maudlin. When Ochs takes off his wig faces begin to pop up in the windows and from the trap-door and finally, in fright, he rings the bell—only to be greeted by the lady in mourning, who claims him as her husband, and a flock of children. During the hubbub Octavian makes sure that someone has gone for Faninal. Ochs now summons the police and a Commissioner of the Morality Police presents himself. He is not impressed by the wigless Ochs's patronizing approach, especially when Valzacchi fails to identify him, and is determined to get to the bottom of the goings-on. Ochs tries to account for Mariandel by saying that she is his fiancée, Herr von Faninal's daughter; but at this moment Faninal arrives, annoyed to be summoned but addressing Ochs as son-in-law (which Ochs makes a feeble attempt to deny). Faninal of course denies that Mariandel is his daughter and sends for Sophie who is waiting downstairs. He is scandalized by Ochs's behaviour and by the widow and children and when Sophie enters and joyfully adds fuel to the flames by saying that she does not consider Ochs her bridegroom any more, he is taken ill and has to be escorted by her to another room. The Commissioner is about to question Ochs further when Mariandel whispers to him. He watches with amusement as Mariandel goes behind the curtain and her clothes are flung out, piece by piece. Just as the surprised Ochs is trying to save her from the wicked Commissioner the Marschallin makes a dignified entrance (presumably summoned to help by Ochs's lackey), her thoughts evidently on Octavian. She recognizes the Commissioner as her husband's former orderly. Sophie enters with a message from her father to Ochs, delivered with relish, never to darken his doors again. The Marschallin fails to get Ochs to leave with dignity. She dismisses the now obsequious Commissioner and Octavian emerges in his own clothes. The truth slowly dawns on Ochs, including of course the affair between her and Octavian, but he takes her hint to keep quiet about that. He is made to see at last that he must renounce his marriage and prepares to leave. Immediately the salacious waltz bursts out as Valzacchi, Annina, and the inn staff all press round with bills and open palms and he can barely get away, pursued by them all. The Marschallin, Sophie, and Octavian who hovers between them in embarrassment remain alone. The Marschallin, who has guessed the situation, haughtily tells him to go to Sophie. She receives him rather coolly, sensing that she has hurt the Marschallin who is steeling herself to face the situation which she had foreseen at the end of Act I (the bitter-sweet motive is heard for the last time). She comes to Sophie and asks whether she has learnt to love so soon. The embarrassed girl breaks into a flood of excuses for her pallor which the Marschallin cuts short, promising to drive her father, as well as the two young people, home in her carriage. But before she leaves the three soliloquize in a soaring trio, which is based primarily on the languid waltz from the supper scene, but with motives from Octavian's earlier scenes with both women worked in. Left alone, the young lovers embrace and sing a tranquil duet of rapture founded on a simple tune used by Mozart (in *The Magic Flute*) and Schubert. They are interrupted by the passage of Faninal and the Marschallin to the door of the inn (to motives from Act I). The second stanza of the resumed duet is interspersed with the celesta chords from the Rose music and concludes with a phrase from their first duet which followed it. She falls into his arms, letting her handkerchief drop and they go out. The stage is empty for a moment and then a tinkling sound is heard; the negro page, sent by the Marschallin to pay her rival a small attention, enters to music resembling that which accompanied his appearance in Act I, looks round, retrieves the handkerchief and trips out to a final gay orchestral flourish.

Sadko

Opera in seven scenes. Music by N. Rimsky-Korsakov. Libretto by the composer. First produced at Moscow, January 7th, 1898.

SCENE: Novgorod.

TIME: Dawn of history.

PRINCIPAL CHARACTERS:

SADKO	*A minstrel and gusli player of Novgorod*	(Tenor)
LIUBAVA	*His wife*	(Mezzo-soprano)
NIEJATA	*A minstrel from Kiev*	(Contralto)
TWO ELDERS	*of Novgorod*	(Tenor and bass)
DUDA } *Buffoons*		(Bass)
SOPIEL }		(Tenor)
A VIKING MERCHANT		(Bass)
AN INDIAN MERCHANT		(Tenor)
A VENETIAN MERCHANT		(Baritone)
THE KING OF THE OCEAN		(Bass)
VOLKHOVA	*His daughter*	(Soprano)
A LEGENDARY HERO		(Baritone)

Spectacle is an intrinsic part of this fairy-tale which is one of those picture-book Russian operas best thought of as vocalized ballets. Though the composer is at pains in his preface to emphasize that verbal rhythm must in opera give way to musical rhythm, some of the music itself is hardly more than incidental to the stage picture. It is a "number" opera, the individual items tending to be based on a short phrase of folk-song type which is then repeated in different keys and with constantly varying orchestration. Some of these phrases become labels and are recalled, or combined with others, to dramatic effect. The "real life" characters are distinguished in the music from those of Sadko's fantasy, whose music is more chromatic and more highly coloured. The chorus play a prominent part. The two buffoons are conventional figures.

The short Prelude is headed in the score "The blue ocean" and its motive recurs, especially in Scenes 5 and 6.

Scene 1. Palace of the merchants guild. The merchants are feasting and celebrating the renown of Novgorod. Niejata sings them a song about a hero of Kiev. They want someone to extol their own city and Sadko enters. His song which describes what he would do if he had money and friends displeases them with its reminder that they have no access to the sea and he leaves them amid obloquy. Duda and Sopiel mock him as a dance begins and the feast becomes increasingly lively.

Scene 2. Shores of Lake Ilmen. On a summer night Sadko laments that no one on earth wishes to hear his songs. Swans swim up, turn into a Princess and accompanying maidens and dispose themselves on land. (To judge by their harmonies they are Slavonic relations of Wagner's Rhinemaidens.) The maidens sing a charming chorus which the Princess decorates with a florid passage. She tells Sadko that thanks to his singing she has fallen in love with him, that she is Volkhova daughter of the King of the Ocean and that one day they will be married. Sadko returns her love. Before leaving she promises that he will catch three golden fish in his net and will travel afar but that she will wait faithfully for him. The King of the Ocean briefly appears to fetch his daughter and her suite and, as dawn breaks, they all turn back into swans and swim away. (The duet between the lovers with female chorus, partly offstage, is delightful.)

Scene 3. In Sadko's house. Liubava anxiously awaits her husband early next morning. She cannot understand his absence and is much relieved when he appears. But he is cold, broods over the happenings of the night (reminiscences of Scene 2), and finally rushes off to the harbour after abusing his puzzled and unhappy wife, who falls in prayer.

Scene 4. The port. A great crowd surround merchants from many lands, proud to receive them in Novgorod. Pilgrims, soothsayers, Niejata, Duda and Sopiel, and others briefly emerge in the course of a long ensemble in which the figure heard in the first bar is almost constantly present. Soon after a merchant has jestingly said that all this merchandise would suit Sadko, Sadko appears amid ribald laughter and bets his head against all their goods that golden fish can be caught in the lake. He goes off in a boat and the voice of the Princess is heard renewing her promise. When the nets are hauled in there are three golden fish in them and, when he comes ashore, he is acclaimed by the crowd. After another intervention by the Princess all the fish in the net are found to be changed into gold which Sadko distributes to all adventurous enough to follow him on his travels. Niejata hails Sadko as a nightingale but Sadko, heedless of the general flattery, gives the merchants back all their goods. He asks the foreign traders to sing about their own countries so that he may know which is the most beautiful to visit. A Viking, an Indian, and a Venetian sing in turn. There is general agreement that Venice (with its barcarolle refrain) is the place to visit, but it is the Indian's song with its chromatic scale and its hesitation between major and minor which has become universally familiar. As Sadko is about to embark in the *Falcon* Liubava runs distractedly in; Sadko refuses to be delayed but commends her to the elders' safe keeping. The final chorus as Sadko embarks and sets sail for the ocean is based on an old Russian folk-song.

Scene 5. On board the *Falcon* in mid-ocean. The *Falcon* and the rest of the fleet is becalmed, to music similar to the Prelude. Sadko tells his men (who sing a nautical chorus) that he has failed to pay tribute to the King of the Ocean in twelve years at sea. They throw treasure overboard but in vain. They draw lots by throwing tablets of wood overboard and Sadko's sink. Sadko takes a sad farewell of his companions and of life and with his gusli climbs down a ladder onto a plank thrown in the sea. Immediately a breeze gets up, the ship sails away and Sadko is alone on the sea. He hears the voice of the Princess who has been faithful to him all the time. He sinks into the sea and mist covers the transformation to

Scene 6. The bottom of the sea. The King and Queen are seated in state with Volkhova spinning seaweed. At Volkhova's suggestion Sadko sings in honour of the royal family and the King agrees to give him his daughter in marriage. He summons all the denizens of his kingdom to the wedding-feast. They arrive in procession. After a nuptial hymn there are dances of brooks and of gold and silver fish and finally of the whole company, whose abandon agitates the waves and causes shipwrecks. Suddenly a Legendary Hero (clad as an elderly pilgrim) appears and announces the end of the Kingdom of the Ocean; Sadko and his bride are to return to Novgorod. They take their places in a shell drawn by sea-gulls while the court slowly disappears. An intermezzo in which the voices of the lovers are heard behind the curtain, marks their journey and the transition to

Scene 7. A meadow by Lake Ilmen. Early morning. The Princess sings a lullaby to the sleeping Sadko and then vanishes into the mist to become the river Volkhova. The lamenting Liubava finds Sadko and they are reunited in a duet, at the close of which the mists disperse and the new river is seen. The *Falcon* appears upon it and Sadko's companions singing the chorus from Scene 5 greet him. All the townspeople together with the three foreign merchants now appear, delighted at the new outlet to the sea, and there is a big ensemble in praise of Sadko, the Legendary Hero, and of God, culminating, as Russian operas are apt to do, in a formal chorale.

Salome

Opera in one act. Music by Richard Strauss. Libretto after Oscar Wilde, translated and abridged by H. Lachmann. First produced at Dresden, December 9th, 1905.

SCENE: Herod's Palace at Tiberias.

TIME: About 30 A.D.

PRINCIPAL CHARACTERS:

HEROD *Tetrarch of Judea*		(Tenor)
HERODIAS *His wife*		(Mezzo-soprano)
SALOME *Her daughter*		(Soprano)
JOCHANAAN (John the Baptist)		(Baritone)
NARRABOTH *Captain of the Guard*		(Tenor)
PAGE OF HERODIAS		(Contralto)
FIVE JEWS		(Four tenors, one bass)
TWO SOLDIERS		(Basses)
TWO NAZARENES		(Tenor and bass)

This, Strauss's earliest opera in the repertory, is in some ways even more extreme than "Elektra" in its musical exploration of psychopathic states, the essentially orchestral and symphonic conception, and the size and sheer volume of sound engendered by the orchestra. It was only later that he began to strike a more lyrical vein, with a better balance between orchestra and voices. "Salome" is very exciting theatre, which does not aspire to tragic stature but successfully captures the lurid atmosphere of Wilde's once sensational play, set, unusually, straight, and not in an adaptation. The perversity of Salome (a rôle which makes great vocal and histrionic demands) is reflected in many imaginative musical touches (some of which are apt to be lost in performance) and as a neurotic study Herod anticipates Klytemnestra. The relative normality of the Baptist—by contrast with Herod and his family—is given music of a more diatonic cast. The famous Dance of the Seven Veils, when well performed, can still make a theatrical impact even in an era of commonplace striptease. But musically it must be ranked below the general level of the piece, soon resolving itself into the inevitable Viennese waltz, tricked out with tawdry and conventional pseudo-oriental trimmings.

A great terrace adjacent to the banquet hall. Moonlight. Narraboth and two soldiers guard a cistern in which Jochanaan is imprisoned. Narraboth is looking enraptured at Salome, who is at Herod's table in the hall. The Page, devoted to him, tries in vain to warn him of the danger of constantly gazing at her. The voice of Jochanaan is heard prophesying. (The cellos first announce, at the seventh bar of his entry, the solemn motive associated with him throughout, often in the horns.) The comments of the soldiers reveal that his utterances are found unintelligible but that Herod has forbidden all access to him. Salome comes out disturbed at the way in which Herod has been eyeing her. She ignores a message from Herod to return to table and shows interest in the still audible prophet who has, she knows, been denouncing her mother's conduct. She does not heed Narraboth's attempts to distract her. Ascertaining from the soldiers that the prophet is quite young she tries to get them, against orders, to bring him to her. Foiled, she ruthlessly exploits her attraction for Narraboth and persuades him to give the order. After an orchestral passage based on Jochanaan's theme with others perhaps representing Salome's awakening excitement, the prophet is brought out, inveighing against Herodias. When Salome says "he is terrible" we hear on the clarinet the four-note motive beginning with two demi semiquavers, which seems to stand thereafter for her lust for him. She now expresses her admiration for his bodily beauty and makes advances to him which Jochanaan repels with disgust. She thereupon praises the beauty of his hair only to be repulsed again. Finally her desire is focussed on his mouth which she tries (to a passionate motive with a rising third) to kiss. The now desperate Narraboth can bear it no longer and kills himself, falling unnoticed between them. Jochanaan only replies that she must turn and seek forgiveness from the One who alone can save her. Finally her repeated cries to be allowed to kiss his mouth elicit a curse from him and he returns to the cistern. The frenzied orchestral outburst which follows depicts Salome's frustrated desire and subsides into a quieter passage at the end of which (after a double bassoon solo) the brass adumbrate the motive to which she will later demand Jochanaan's head.

The sensual, conscience-stricken, half-drunk Herod and the icy Herodias now join her. She chides him for constantly looking at Salome. He slips in Narraboth's blood and, remembering the languorous looks the latter had cast at Salome, orders the body to be removed. He seeks in vain to get her to drink wine and eat fruit, for the pleasure of putting his mouth where hers has been. When Jochanaan's voice is heard Herodias wants him silenced and when Herod replies that he is a great prophet, taunts him with fear of him. Herod refuses to give him up to the Jews. This starts a theological dispute among the Jews and Nazarenes—a strident passage reminiscent of "the Critics" in *Ein Heldenleben*. Jochanaan's voice is again heard inveighing by implication against Herodias. Herod puts an end to the altercation with his wife by calling on Salome to dance. At first she refuses and her mother applauds her decision. But after he has sworn to give her whatever she asks she ignores her mother's protests and agrees to dance for her stepfather. She performs the Dance of the Seven Veils during which she casts off one veil after another. At the end, Herod, quite beside himself, asks her to name her reward. When she asks, with her mother's strong approval, for the head of Jochanaan on a silver charger, Herod does his utmost to dissuade her and tempt her with other gifts. He reminds her that perhaps the man is holy and "touched by the finger of God". But Salome continues to demand the head of Jochanaan. Finally he gives way and Herodias draws from his hand the ring of death. It is passed to the negro executioner who goes down into the cistern. Salome looks down into the cistern and there are some moments of acute tension marked by a repeated strangled high note on a solo double-bass over a bass drum roll. Salome fears that the negro is afraid and calls for soldiers to go down and do the deed. But a huge black arm appears holding a silver shield with the head of Jochanaan on it. Salome seizes it and kisses his mouth. In ecstasy she addresses the head in mingled sensuality, triumph, and revenge in that he chose to look upon his God rather than upon herself and love her. The horror of the scene is underlined by its being set to soaring expansive music, based on earlier motives, appropriate to a great closing scene of love. Herod cannot stand it and calls her a monster. In fear he calls for the torches to be put out and begins to withdraw. The moon goes in and on the darkened stage, against an eerie accompaniment in which is heard a minor version of the motive of her lust, Salome murmurs that the mouth had a bitter taste—perhaps it was the taste of love. "But what of that? Jochanaan, I have kissed thy mouth." The moon re-emerges and illumines her. Herod calls for her death and soldiers crush her beneath their shields.

Simon Boccanegra

Opera in a prologue and three acts. Music by G. Verdi. Libretto by F. M. Piave, later revised by A. Boito. First produced at the Teatro La Fenice, Venice, March 12th, 1857.

SCENE: In and near Genoa.

TIME: End of fifteenth century.

PRINCIPAL CHARACTERS:

SIMON BOCCANEGRA	*Corsair in service, and later Doge, of Genoa*	(Baritone)
AMELIA GRIMALDI	*(in reality his daughter)*	(Soprano)
JACOPO FIESCO	*A patrician*	(Bass)
PAOLO ALBIANI	*A plebeian*	(Baritone)
PIETRO	*A plebeian*	(Bass)
GABRIELE ADORNO	*A nobleman*	(Tenor)

This opera, dating from Verdi's middle period, was extensively revised by Boito 20 years later and Verdi, then at the height of his powers, made a number of additions including the whole of Act I Scene 2. Even so the action and motivation often remain somewhat obscure since so many vital events take place offstage and are mentioned rather casually. And why is Amelia unable to reveal in Act II that she is Simon's daughter, though he is ready to do so himself? It is only during the last 40 years that performances have been frequent and then often with further changes. Nevertheless, while the music is naturally uneven in style, some of it shows the composer at his best; and the name-part is one of the great Italian baritone roles. There are affinities with "Don Carlos" and "Otello" as is to be expected of an opera with a political background; in more than one passage we sense the Mediterranean Sea. Much of the writing is for dark male voices; and numbers in minor keys abound. The outstanding music is in Act I Scene 2 and Act III each with massive ensembles resembling that in Act III of "Otello". But of Verdi's earlier manner there are such fine examples as Fiesco's well-known aria in the Prologue, the duet between Amelia and the Doge in Act I Scene 1, and the duet between Amelia and Gabriele in Act II. The musical characterization especially of Simon himself and the aristocratic Fiesco is sharp.

PROLOGUE

A street before the palace of the Fieschi. Night. After a short prelude, the plebeians Paolo and Pietro, as a gambit against the hated patricians, offer to have Simon, a successful corsair, whom they have summoned, chosen by the people as Doge. This will enable him to marry the patrician Fiesco's closely guarded daughter by whom he has had a child. Simon agrees and departs. Paolo and Pietro work up popular feeling. Fiesco comes out of his dark palace lamenting the death of his daughter which has just taken place. Simon returns and tries to allay Fiesco's hatred of him; but Fiesco will only end their feud if Simon will return his grandchild to him. This Simon cannot do as the child has been kidnapped by pirates and lost. Simon enters the palace and discovers that his mistress is dead, as the populace arrive proclaiming him Doge.

ACT I

Scene 1. Garden of the Grimaldi palace by the sea outside Genoa. Twenty-five years later. Dawn. Amelia, who has been brought up by Count Grimaldi, awaits her lover Gabriele who joins her. She is nervous about a patrician conspiracy in which he and Andrea (as Fiesco, now in disguise, her guardian during Grimaldi's banishment, is known to her) are partaking. She fears too that Simon, the Doge, whose approach is announced, intends to betroth her to Paolo, now a favourite courtier, and begs Gabriele to arrange at once for their marriage. After she has gone into the palace Gabriele asks her hand of Fiesco who tells him that she is not a Grimaldi but a foundling. Gabriele continues to express his love for her and receives Fiesco's blessing. The Doge arrives and she tells him that she is in love, but that Paolo wishes to marry her for the Grimaldi fortune. She tells the Doge what she knows of her origin, producing a locket of her mother, and he realizes that she is his long-lost daughter. They are reunited in an ecstatic duet. After her departure the Doge tells Paolo that he must give up any hope of marrying her. Paolo and Pietro plot to abduct her. *Scene 2.* The Council Chamber in the Doge's Palace. The Doge is conducting business in council when a commotion is heard outside. A crowd bursts in dragging Gabriele and Fiesco. Gabriele, in searching for the abducted Amelia, has killed a plebeian and accuses the Doge of responsibility for the abduction. Before he can strike him Amelia herself arrives on the scene having made her escape. There is uproar between patricians and plebeians which the Doge calms in a moving arioso, while Amelia adds her plea for peace, in a superb ensemble. The Doge orders Gabriele to be detained but refuses his sword. Suspecting Paolo of the abduction he orders him publicly to lay his curse on the guilty man.

ACT II

The Doge's apartment. Paolo puts slow poison in the Doge's cup. Pietro brings Fiesco and Gabriele secretly from prison. Fiesco refuses a proposition that he should kill the Doge but Paolo detains Gabriele and by mentioning that Amelia is in the palace lets him think she is the Doge's mistress; but after an emotional outburst he is joined by Amelia herself who reassures him by promising to die with him if he is condemned, but is not free to tell him that the Doge is her father. She hides Gabriele on the balcony as the Doge enters. She reveals that it is he whom she loves and pleads with the Doge for his life. Left alone and torn by conflicting emotions the Doge drinks the poisoned cup and falls asleep. (A phrase from his duet with Amelia in Act I tells us of what he is dreaming.) Gabriele enters but Amelia prevents him from stabbing the Doge, who wakes. The Doge chances to reveal that he is Amelia's father. After a brief trio exploiting the situation the sounds of the patricians in revolt are heard. The Doge promises to pardon the now repentant Gabriele if he will calm the revolt.

ACT III

Interior of the palace with a view over Genoa and the sea. The revolt has ended. Fiesco is set free. Paolo is led off to execution for his part in the revolt. The Doge enters dying and greets the sea, in a lovely phrase. Fiesco comes forward. The Doge recognizes him, though he thought he was dead, and tells him that Amelia is his dead daughter's child. They are reconciled at last. Amelia and Gabriele receive the Doge's blessing. Another fine ensemble is built up and, before he dies, the Doge names Gabriele as his successor. Fiesco announces his death from the balcony.

The Snow Maiden

(Snegurochka). Opera in a prologue and four acts. Music by N. A. Rimsky-Korsakov. Libretto by the composer after A. N. Ostrovsky. First produced at St Petersburg, February 10th, 1882.

SCENE: Legendary.

TIME: Legendary.

CHARACTERS:

SNEGUROCHKA	(Soprano)
LEL *A shepherd*	(Contralto)
KUPAVA	(Soprano)
MIZGIR	(Baritone)
FAIRY SPRING	(Mezzo-soprano)
WOOD-SPRITE	(Tenor)
KING FROST	(Bass)
BOBIL	(Tenor)
BOBILIKHA	(Mezzo-soprano)
CARNIVAL	(Bass)
TSAR BERENDEI	(Tenor)
BERMYATA *A courtier*	(Bass)

This is an early work, combining fairy-tale and peasant ingredients. As Russian operas go, it is relatively well constructed with some coherence of theme, despite picturesque episodes, and fair dramatic tension. But the work is too long for its weight and there is some loss of musical interest in Acts III and IV, with a certain failure to rise to the climax of the action at the end. At its best in the earlier acts, it abounds in charming melody, often of folk-song origin, nature-painting and pleasing fantasy. The characters of the three demi-mortals—the cold-hearted Snegurochka, the wayward artist Lel, and the benign old Tsar—are very well drawn in the music. The orchestration is always colourful and there are delightful numbers for both soloists and chorus. The long declamatory passages for the soloists are often apt to the situation and admirably matched to the Russian language, but at times become mechanical or lapse into stretches of conventional recitative which are saved only by the interest of the orchestral support beneath them. The name part requires a singer who

*combines small stature with a child-like but accomplished voice, and for
the Tsar acting ability and a high tenor voice are essential.*

PROLOGUE

Snow-covered slopes of the Red Hill. Early spring. Midnight. After a short
passage of orchestral tone-painting the Wood-sprite announces that his
winter vigil is over and withdraws into a tree-stump to sleep. Spring (whose
motive is like a bird-cry) arrives, drawn by a train of birds and announces
herself in a recitative and aria (the melody of which passes at times to the
clarinet). She then addresses the birds, explaining her late arrival by her
flirtation with old Frost which has produced their daughter, Snegurochka.
The birds then dance for warmth, to music full of their various cries, but
hide at the arrival of Frost who sings a blustering aria. He then explains
his anxiety for their daughter, whose child-like heart the sun is planning
to kindle with the fire of love. Snegurochka joins them and in a charming
aria, followed by an arioso, sings of her longing for freedom, and
especially freedom to learn songs from Lel, whose voice far excels that of
the birds. They leave her behind but first Frost orders the Wood-sprite to
keep an eye on her. A crowd of Berendeians now approach with a dummy
of Carnival. They sing an elaborate chorus of folk-song inspiration,
bidding Carnival farewell for another year. The drunken peasant, Bobil,
and his wife discover Snegurochka hiding and agree to her request to be
allowed to live with them.

ACT I

In the village between Bobil's hovel and Kupava's home. Lel comes,
piping, to sing to Snegurochka. He sings for kisses but, when she says that
his songs are worth more than that, he agrees to accept a flower before
singing her two songs, the first grave with only a light wood-wind
accompaniment, the second lively with a fuller accompaniment. Other
girls call to him, and to Snegurochka's chagrin he casts away her flower and
goes to join them. In vexation she sings an aria admirably illustrating the
dawn of feeling. Kupava comes out of her house and tells her, to a figure
which expresses her excitement, that she is engaged to marry a young
merchant called Mizgir, who appears together with young villagers. A
delightful betrothal ceremony follows in which Mizgir has to bribe the girls
to give up Kupava to him. But as soon as the ceremony is over he sees
Snegurochka and promptly switches his affection to her. Despite
encouragement from Bobil and Bobilikha, she shows little interest in his
warm advances. The villagers are shocked and Kupava has a bitter outburst
before rushing desperate to the river. But Lel restrains her by proposing that
she should petition the Tsar.

ACT II

Tsar Berendei's Palace. Musicians sing the Tsar's praises in a male chorus to which Bermyata adds the further flattery that all is bliss in the kingdom. The kindly old Tsar does not believe it. He has observed that for fifteen years summers have grown shorter and springs colder, with coldness in his people's hearts. Yarilo, the Sun-god, must be propitiated, upon his day, by the solemn marriage of all the young men and maidens at dawn. Bermatya has just begun to speak of the devastating effects of Snegurochka on the young men of her village when Kupava demands audience and is admitted. She begins a long and breathless account of her troubles, which the Tsar interrupts from time to time with the phrase: "Go on, go on" always repeated a little higher. In the end he is quite touched and orders Mizgir to be brought before his court of justice which all are to attend. Two heralds summon people of every kind in a fantastic proclamation, ending in canon. Courtiers bring in Lel and Mizgir and people assemble to a miniature march. The Tsar asks Mizgir if he will atone and marry Kupava but he replies that his only bride is Snegurochka and Kupava says that henceforth she loathes him. The Tsar therefore declares him banished. Just then Snegurochka, with Bobil and Bobilikha, enters. The Tsar, struck by her beauty, sings a cavatina in praise of nature's wonders and resolves that she too must marry. But when he presses her to name her sweetheart she replies that she has none. He promises a great reward to the man who can win her love before dawn. The court-ladies advise that Lel is the man and Lel accepts the task. Mizgir asks for his sentence to be cancelled and to be allowed to attempt the task also. The Tsar is delighted to have two such strong candidates and is confident that the Sun-god will be propitiated in the morning rite. All hail the Tsar's wisdom.

ACT III

A forest clearing. Sunset. The population is celebrating. There is a chorus with occasional interjections from the soloists. The Tsar sings a cavatina urging further marry-making and a Tumbler's Dance follows (a familiar number) and then a song of ballad type by Lel (with a charming refrain for clarinet and tambourine). The Tsar tells him, as a reward, to kiss any girl he chooses. He passes over the eager Snegurochka, who runs into the bushes, and ceremoniously kisses Kupava. The Tsar retires for the night, delighted by the revels. Mizgir appears and presses his suit upon Snegurochka who shows no interest, and finally, after an intervention by the Wood-sprite, escapes, leaving Mizgir in pursuit of phantom visions of her. Kupava and Lel return to sing a love-duet. Snegurochka runs out and, when she reproaches Kupava for stealing Lel, is bluntly told by him that she should learn to replace child-like affection by love. In the trio which ends the Act she begs Spring to give her a maiden's loving heart.

ACT IV

Yarilo's valley. Dawn. After a Prelude which sets the scene Snegurochka calls on her mother for help and Spring, with attendant flowers, rises slowly from a lake in the distance. Snegurochka begs for the gift of a young girl's love. Spring consents and she and the flower-chorus teach her love, in an ensemble for women's voices that weaves a spell over her till her eyes are opened to the beauties of nature. Before returning to the lake Spring warns her to hide from the eyes of Yarilo. When Mizgir comes again this time Snegurochka joyfully returns his love; but he does not heed her plan to hide from the sun. The Tsar, the betrothed couples, and all his subjects now enter, as the first rays of the sun appear. The chorus sing a folk-song extolling the joys of summer; the Tsar blesses the couples; and Mizgir assumes that he has won Snegurochka. She acknowledges her love for him but the rays of the sun fall upon her and, warmed by the sweet sunshine of love, she melts away. Mizgir throws himself into the lake. But the Tsar recognizes that with her wondrous end the fifteen cold years are over and Lel leads off the final ensemble in praise of the sun, over one of those ostinato basses which often mark the final choruses of Russian operas.

La Sonnambula

(The Sleepwalking Girl). Opera in two acts by V. Bellini. Libretto by F. Romani. First produced at the Teatro Carcano, Milan, March 6th, 1831.

SCENE: A village in Switzerland.

TIME: Early nineteenth century.

CHARACTERS:

COUNT RODOLFO	*Lord of the castle*	(Bass)
TERESA	*Proprietress of the mill*	(Mezzo-soprano)
AMINA	*Her foster-daughter*	(Soprano)
ELVINO	*A young farmer*	(Tenor)
LISA	*Keeper of the village inn*	(Soprano)
ALESSIO	*A villager*	(Bass)
A NOTARY		(Tenor)

This opera, though generally ranked after "Norma", is in some ways more characteristic of Bellini. The story is artless and even clumsy, in that Amina's physical danger in the last scene adds nothing to the dénouement. The composer makes only a minimal attempt to reflect situation or character—e.g., the chorus about the ghost is quite bland, and the big quartet and ensemble at the end of Act I Scene 2 is simply concerted vocal music. The work lives in its vocal line and the long, uncoiling melodies— not the sort that the audience comes out humming, but a lyrical vehicle of great refinement for accomplished singers, who can not only manage with ease all the coloratura of recitative and aria, but can convey subtle inflections of mood by voice alone. It is fine singing, especially in the great rôle of Amina, which maintains this work in the repertory, though it cannot be denied an engaging, period charm.

ACT I

Scene 1. The village street with the mill in the background. Villagers sing a chorus in praise of Amina whose civil wedding to Elvino is to be celebrated. Between its two parts a cavatina for Lisa reveals her jealousy that her lover should have turned from her to Amina; and she shows disinterest in the attentions of Alessio. Amina, an orphan, comes out of the mill with Teresa, and in an elaborate recitative and two-part aria expresses her gratitude and joy. The Notary arrives, followed by Elvino, who has been praying at his mother's tomb. The ceremony takes place to a long duet, Elvino giving Amina a ring and receiving protestations of love from her. The sound of horses' hooves is heard and Rodolfo arrives, inquiring for the castle. In the first part of a familiar aria he recognizes the village from his young days, and, in the second part, expresses his admiration for the bride. He explains that he used to live in the castle and is told that the old Count is dead and his son has gone away. Rodolfo brings news that the son is living. As the sun sets Teresa warns everyone that the village ghost is liable to appear. The villagers elaborate the story in a chorus; Rodolfo remains incredulous. It is too late for him to travel further and he retires for the night to the inn. His civilities to Amina upset the possessive Elvino. Amina, left alone with Elvino, reproaches him for his jealousy in a recitative; but in the ensuing tender duet they are reconciled and part lovingly.

Scene 2. Rodolfo's room in the inn. Lisa comes to see if Rodolfo is comfortable and reveals that he has been recognized as the new Count and that the village is preparing a welcome. They begin to flirt but are interrupted by the entrance of Amina, sleepwalking, through the window. Lisa hides in a cupboard, dropping her handkerchief. Amina's thoughts are on the scene with Elvino (reminiscence of their duet). Lisa slips out. In a duet with Rodolfo, introduced by flutes in thirds, Amina, still asleep, dwells on the morrow's church ceremony, while Rodolfo declines to take advantage of the situation. He leaves by the window as Amina sinks down on the bed. Villagers enter by the door in timid chorus, fearing to disturb the Count. They are amused to find a woman asleep on his bed. Elvino, summoned by Lisa, arrives and Amina wakes up in confusion, to be denounced by him. She protests her innocence to her incredulous lover in a duet, which turns into a quartet with chorus, the most ambitious number in the work. Only Teresa, who picks up Lisa's handkerchief, believes that Amina's confusion does not spring from guilt. In the final stretto Elvino breaks off the engagement, while Amina continues to protest.

ACT II

Scene 1. A valley outside the village. Villagers are making their weary way to the castle. In the second section of their chorus they naively rehearse their plea to the Count to intercede for Amina, and in the final section they imagine their joyful return from a successful mission. Amina appears with Teresa, who seeks to comfort her. They go aside as Elvino approaches, singing (against a horn solo) of his inconsolable grief. This prompts Amina to approach him again, but without success. Their duet is followed by villagers running in with the glad tidings that the Count has declared her innocent. But Elvino will not listen and snatches the ring from her finger. In a brief cavatina the insufferable young man declares, however, that he does not hate her and wishes for her nothing but another lover like himself!

Scene 2. As in Act I Scene 1. Elvino has gone back to Lisa and they are going to church, when Rodolfo arrives and testifies to Amina's virtue. He tries to explain that she was sleepwalking but neither Elvino nor the villagers have ever heard of somnambulism. Teresa comes out of the mill and asks for quiet so that Amina can rest undisturbed. But seeing Lisa on her way to marry Elvino and goaded by spiteful remarks from her, she produces Lisa's handkerchief. All turn to the Count for an explanation. He is spared it by the appearance of Amina who walks in her sleep along a plank across the mill-stream. The plank partly gives way, but she reaches the street in safety. The rest of the scene is largely a scena for her. Still asleep, she speaks sadly in a recitative of Elvino's wedding with Lisa and wishes him happiness. Then taking out a withered posy given to her by Elvino, she addresses it in a mournful aria. Elvino, convinced at last, places the ring on her finger and Amina, still asleep, expresses her happiness. Then the villagers awaken her and she sees Elvino waiting to lead her to church. She gives vent to her joy in a florid cabaletta of great brilliance.

The Tales of Hoffmann

(Les Contes d'Hoffmann). Fantastic opera in a prologue, three acts, and an epilogue. Music by J. Offenbach. Libretto by J. Barbier after E. T. A. Hoffmann. First produced at the Opéra Comique, Paris, February 10th, 1881.

SCENE: Nuremberg.

TIME: Early nineteenth century.

PRINCIPAL CHARACTERS:

HOFFMANN *A poet*		(Tenor)
NICKLAUS *His companion*		(Tenor or Mezzo-soprano)
LINDORF *A councillor*		
COPPELIUS *A scientist*	*His evil genius*	(Bass-baritone)
DAPERTUTTO *A sorcerer*		
DR MIRACLE		
OLYMPIA		
GIULIETTA *A courtesan*	*His beloved*	(Soprano)
ANTONIA		
STELLA		
LUTHER *An innkeeper*		(Bass)
SPALANZANI *An inventor*		(Tenor)
SCHLEMIL *Giulietta's lover*		(Bass)
PITTICHINACCIO *Her admirer*		(Tenor)
CRESPEL *Antonia's father*		(Baritone)
FRANZ *His servant*		(Tenor)
VOICE OF ANTONIA'S MOTHER		(Mezzo-soprano)

In this, his last and most ambitious work, Offenbach left the world of operetta for that of romantic opera. He left out his characteristic wit and sparkle and brought in a new note of pathos; his pert tunes broaden out into melodies charged with tender sentiment, almost in the vein of Donizetti, of which the familiar barcarolle is only one. The arias and a few big ensembles are linked by recitative and only occasional dialogue. The linking idea of the ardent lover seeing the object of his desire everywhere and always thwarted by his evil genius, is in a vein of self-mockery that appeals to Offenbach. But the total effect of the libretto is contrived. We get three one-act operas, which the prologue and epilogue fail to combine into a single whole. The former is not tautly enough constructed and the latter is musically very weak. There is little attempt to use the music itself as a unifying medium. This makes it the more desirable that the heroines and villains should each be played by a single singer, as is usual.

PROLOGUE

Luther's tavern. Moonlight. After a few introductory bars a distant drinking-chorus is heard. Lindorf bribes Stella's servant to give him a love-letter from his mistress to Hoffmann. He sings a sardonic little song about his own electric effect on women and his determination to get the better of his rival. Students arrive and sing in praise of Luther and his wine. All·drink to Stella who is singing at the nearby opera-house. Hoffmann and Nicklaus enter, the former depressed by seeing Stella, the latter singing a snatch of *Don Giovanni*. Hoffmann starts drinking and is persuaded to sing a song, with a grotesque refrain, about the dwarf Kleinzack at the court of Eisenach, but the middle section is a romantic passage about a lady. Hoffmann is displeased to see Lindorf whom he regards as bringing him bad luck and a quarrel is only averted by Nicklaus's intervention. The talk turns to their loves. Hoffmann says that Stella is three mistresses in one and offers to tell them the story of his three passionate affairs. They prefer this to returning to *Don Giovanni*.

ACT I

Spalanzani's house. After a short intermezzo (a minuet) we see Spalanzani hoping to make a pile of money from his latest invention— Olympia, a performing doll—despite his rival, Coppelius. Hoffmann presents himself as a pupil and Spalanzani promises to show him his beautiful daughter. Left alone, Hoffmann espies her asleep behind a curtain and immediately falls in love, addressing a tender aria to her. Nicklaus arrives and chaffs him for being in love again. He tells him of Spalanzani's skill in making mechanical dolls but Hoffmann still gazes rapturously at Olympia. Coppelius enters and persuades him to buy a pair of his magic spectacles which increase his rapture. Coppelius reminds Spalanzani that it was he who made Olympia's eyes, and extracts from him a cheque on a bankrupt banker. When he has gone guests arrive, to the minuet, to see Spalanzani's "daughter". Spalanzani leads in Olympia, amid general admiration. A harp is fetched and Olympia entertains them with a doll-like coloratura song. After Spalanzani has surreptitiously wound Olympia up the guests depart to supper leaving Hoffmann alone with her.

He resumes his tender aria but Olympia suddenly rises and leaves the room. Hoffmann follows, ignoring Nicklaus's warning that she is only a doll. Coppelius returns, furious that the cheque is worthless, and enters Olympia's room intent on revenge. A dance begins—the famous waltz—and Hoffmann dances with Olympia. She dances faster and faster until, when at last she is stopped, Hoffmann falls dazed on a couch. Olympia now adds a coloratura line over the waltz and then goes to her room. The breaking of machinery is heard and Coppelius emerges in triumph. He and Spalanzani quarrel while the guests mock Hoffmann's discomfiture.

ACT II (The order of Acts II and III is sometimes reversed.)

Venice. A loggia of Giulietta's palace overlooking the Grand Canal. Evening. Giulietta and Nicklaus sing the barcarolle "Belle nuit, o nuit d'amour." Hoffmann calls for something gayer and sings in praise of wine. Giulietta introduces him to her lover, Schlemil, and all go off to play cards, except Nicklaus and Hoffmann. Hoffmann promises the former that not even the devil could make him fall in love with her. Dapertutto, when they have gone, produces a great diamond which, in a villain's aria, he confidently predicts will win over Giulietta who is to cast a spell on Hoffmann. He tells her to procure him Hoffmann's reflection (*i.e.,* his soul). With the diamond on her finger she agrees and soon has Hoffmann declaring his love in a passionate aria. During an amorous duet she persuades him, before he leaves, to humour her by leaving his reflection in her mirror. Schlemil discovers them and angrily shows them to the other guests. Hoffmann perceives with dismay the loss of his reflection but refuses to leave. A sextet with chorus in the grand manner follows, in which each soliloquizes and which works round to the barcarolle. To its strains Giulietta proposes a gondola trip. But Hoffmann and Schlemil fight for the key of Giulietta's room. Hoffmann kills his rival with Dapertutto's sword and takes the key from his neck, only to find that Giulietta has gone off with Pittichinaccio. Nicklaus drags him away.

ACT III

Crespel's house. Munich. Antonia sits thinking of her mother, a famous singer dead of consumption. She sings a sad romance "Elle a fui, la tourterelle", and collapses into a chair. Crespel, entering, reproves her for singing in her state of health. She says that it was the thought of her mother (hint of a melody to come) but promises not to sing again. Crespel, who fears that she too will die of the disease, blames her love for Hoffmann. His deaf servant, Franz, ordered to admit no-one, sings a comic little song about his penchant for singing and dancing. Hoffmann enters and, while Franz is fetching Antonia, tries the love song lying open on the harpsichord.   When she comes in they sing a love duet and then, urged by Hoffmann to defy her father's prohibition, the song on the harpsichord. When Crespel surprises them she leaves quickly and Hoffmann hides.   Dr Miracle is announced.   Crespel thinks that he killed his wife and wants to kill his daughter.   He tries to prevent him from treating Antonia. Undeterred, Miracle opens the door of her room by magnetic passes and examines her from a distance, making her sing a cadenza.   While Hoffmann watches Crespel manages with difficulty, after a trio, to get rid of Miracle and his medicine flasks.   Hoffmann, alone with Antonia, gets her to promise him too that she will renounce her singing.   But Miracle returns and tempts her to sing.   He causes her to hear her mother's voice, singing the melody earlier hinted, and urges her to cultivate her inherited talent. At the climax of a fine trio her voice soars to top C and she falls dying. Crespel, entering, blames Hoffmann for her death.   Hoffmann calls for a doctor but Miracle reappears.

There is a tender intermezzo recapitulating the barcarolle.

EPILOGUE

As in the Prologue.   As Hoffmann finishes his tales cheers for Stella are heard and Nicklaus remarks that she is Hoffmann's three loves in one person.   But Hoffmann refuses to drink to her and wants only to drown his memories in yet more wine.   The students go off singing their chorus and Hoffmann is left alone in a stupor.   The Muse appears and calls on him to devote himself to Poetry.   He starts up and for a moment addresses her passionately with phrases from his duet with the courtesan, Giulietta. When Stella enters he is too drunk to notice and she goes off with Lindorf, while the students outside keep up their chorus.

Tannhäuser

Opera in three acts. Music by R. Wagner. Libretto by the composer. First produced at Dresden, October 19th, 1845.

SCENE: Thuringia.

TIME: Thirteenth century.

CHARACTERS:

HERMANN *Landgrave of Thuringia*		(Bass)
ELISABETH *His niece*		(Soprano)
HEINRICH TANNHÄUSER		(Tenor)
WOLFRAM VON ESCHENBACH		(Baritone)
WALTER VON DER VOGELWEIDE	*Knights and*	(Tenor)
BITEROLF	*Minstrels*	(Bass)
HEINRICH DER SCHREIBER		(Tenor)
REINMAR VON ZWETER		(Bass)
VENUS		(Soprano)
A SHEPHERD BOY		(Soprano)

This, the work of a young man, is still very much in the German romantic tradition and, for the most part, cast in the conventional mould of recitative and aria, ensemble and chorus. Some of the lyrical passages for solo voice are beautiful specimens of their kind—Tannhäuser's Act I song, Elisabeth's two arias, Wolfram's Act III song, and, of course, the Pilgrim's Chorus. But the Venusberg music, added for the Paris production in 1861, underlines the distance between all this and Wagner's maturity, though Tannhäuser's fine narration in Act III is already pointing the way with its more flexible style to his future development. For the rest there is much pedestrian declamation and much of the overlong Act II is either banal (as in the March) or dull. The central idea of Redemption is typically Wagnerian and there is doubtless something autobiographical in the preoccupation with the contrast between chaste and sensual love.

The familiar Overture is made up of three main elements. First the Pilgrim's Chorus introduced in the wind and continued by the cellos; secondly the Venusberg music; and thirdly Tannhäuser's song in praise of Venus.

ACT I

Scene 1. A grotto by the Horselberg. The knight Tannhäuser sleeps with his head in Venus's lap, while nymphs, fauns, bacchantes, and satyrs dance voluptuously and the distant voices of sirens are occasionally heard. Tannhäuser wakes with a start and cries out of surfeit and desire to see the spring. Venus bids him sing of love. He seizes his harp and sings in praise of love but each verse ends with a prayer to the goddess to let him depart. She tries seductively to recall him to pleasure but he sings a third verse in the same strain. Thereupon she angrily bids him go and foretells misery and humiliation for him. He replies that his salvation is in Mary whereupon she disappears and there is a quick transformation to

Scene 2. A beautiful sun-lit valley with the Wartburg in the background. Sheep bells and gay piping on the cor anglais are heard and a shepherd sings a poetic song in praise of May. A band of pilgrims passes singing their hymn. The shepherd wishes them God-speed to Rome and his piping blends charmingly with their song in the distance. Tannhäuser, who has watched the scene, kneels in contrite prayer before a shrine. Hunting-horns are heard and the Landgrave, with his knights, approaches. Wolfram recognizes Tannhäuser. All greet him warmly and, in a spirited septet, press him in vain to rejoin them till Wolfram mentions the name of Elisabeth. With the Landgrave's permission he tells Tannhäuser how his singing had captivated the girl's heart. The septet is resumed and this time Tannhäuser expresses a desire to return to the Wartburg. The Act ends in an ensemble of general rejoicing, in which the huntsmen's horns are again heard.

ACT II

The Hall of Song in the Wartburg. After a joyful Prelude Elisabeth, radiantly happy, greets once again the hall which is associated for her with Tannhäuser (Elisabeth's address). Wolfram brings Tannhäuser in. After a show of modesty and somewhat perfunctory inquiries about his long absence she uninhibitedly tells him of the feelings aroused in her heart by his singing. Tannhäuser replies that it is the God of Love who has led him back to her and a love duet (though not a very interesting one) follows. Tannhäuser and Wolfram depart and the Landgrave enters. After a tender exchange he tells her that the nobles are assembling for a Tournament of Song over which she is to preside. The assembly now take their places to the well-known march, which is repeated while they greet the Landgrave and the Hall of Song. The Landgrave then announces the contest. The theme is to be the nature of love and Elisabeth is to present the prize. Lots are drawn and four pages call on Wolfram to begin. After some introductory phrases to harp accompaniment he paints a chivalresque picture of ideal love and is applauded. But Tannhäuser, who claims to know love better, sings of a more passionate emotion (Elisabeth restrains her approval when the others stay silent). Walter replies that true love involves chastity and the company approve. This provokes Tannhäuser into saying that to him love implies pleasure and, amid rising excitement, Biterolf challenges him to combat. Tannhäuser answers him with withering scorn. Wolfram returns to his ideal of love. Tannhäuser, now beside himself, breaks out into his Act I song in praise of Venus and calls on all who know not true love to go to the Venusberg. At this there is confusion. The women leave and the men, realizing the cause of his long absence, rush upon him. But Elisabeth, who has more cause for indignation than they, shields him and calls on them to allow him to work out his salvation through repentance. In a septet Tannhäuser, the Landgrave, and the Knights accept her as an angel sent from heaven and Tannhäuser stands contrite. The Landgrave solemnly banishes him. Let him go to Rome with a second band of pilgrims shortly to depart and return not if the Holy Father's blessing be withheld. There is a big ensemble on the theme of expiation, at the climax of which the pilgrims are heard and Tannhäuser hurries away crying "To Rome!"

ACT III

As in Act I Scene 2. Autumn. There is a long Prelude in grave tones, based on the motive of Elisabeth's intercession, the second phrase of the pilgrim's chorus, and a moaning phrase representing Tannhäuser's weary progress. The climax anticipates Tannhäuser's account of his rejection by the Pope. When the curtain rises Elisabeth is kneeling at the shrine. Wolfram enters and observes her. He comments that she constantly prays there for "his" salvation and is waiting to see if he will be among the returning pilgrims who now pass by, singing as before. But he is not and she prays with desperation to the Virgin. (This is the tender passage known as "Elisabeth's Prayer".) She refuses Wolfram's offer to escort her and leaves him to confess to the Star of Evening, in the famous romanza to harp accompaniment, what has previously only been hinted—his own love for her. After the song's postlude Tannhäuser comes wearily in and they recognize each other. He tells Wolfram that he has not come to brave the Landgrave's edict but is looking for the path to the Venusberg. He is infuriated by Wolfram's question whether he has been to Rome. He tells him, in a passage of great power drawing on the motives heard in the Prelude, the story of his pilgrimage, the tribulations of the journey, his exaltation on coming into the Pope's presence, his confession, the Pope's reply that never will he gain redemption until his crozier should burst into leaf, his panic-stricken departure. Now he is returning to Venus. He sees and hears the Venusberg at hand, while Wolfram tries to hold him back. Venus is seen stretching out her arms to him. Finally Wolfram utters the name of Elisabeth and at that moment a procession is heard sadly escorting her bier with song from the Wartburg. She is interceding for Tannhäuser at the throne of heaven. Venus disappears, exclaiming that he is lost to her. Tannhäuser is led by Wolfram to the bier and crying "Holy Elisabeth, pray for me" expires. The second party of pilgrims arrive with the news that the Pope's crozier has sprouted in his hand, and Tannhäuser has been redeemed. The Landgrave and Knights hail the miracle and the pilgrims' chorus peals out triumphantly.

Tosca

Opera in three acts. Music by G. Puccini. Libretto by G. Giacosa and L. Illica after V. Sardou. First produced at the Teatro Constanzi, Rome, January 14th, 1900.

SCENE: Rome.

TIME: June 1800.

CHARACTERS:

FLORIA TOSCA *A celebrated singer*	(Soprano)
MARIO CAVARADOSSI *A painter*	(Tenor)
BARON SCARPIA *Chief of police*	(Baritone)
CESARE ANGELOTTI *An escaped prisoner*	(Bass)
A SACRISTAN	(Baritone)
SPOLETTA *A police agent*	(Tenor)
A SHEPHERD BOY	(Contralto)

The fact that this is one of the most popular operas in the repertoire should not blind one to its great merits. It may aim no higher than melodrama but the composer attains all his objectives with his sure sense of the theatre and with his ability to create an atmosphere by purely musical means—the crowd scene in Act I, the music "off" in Act II, and the early morning peace of Act III. The music is in one piece though the vocal parts divide clearly into recitatives and lyrical passages, the former frequently being supported by orchestral material of a melodious nature. The work abounds indeed in melodic fragments which are constantly recalled with pathetic or ironic effect. Their very repetition contributes to the intensity and concentration with which Sardou's play comes over in this passionate, Italianate version.

ACT I

The Church of Sant'Andrea della Valle. After three loud chords denoting Scarpia, which will be heard again and again, Angelotti, a political prisoner who has just escaped from the Castel Sant'Angelo, runs breathlessly in, looking for the hidden key of a certain chapel. The Sacristan enters and goes up to a picture on an easel. After the Angelus has been rung the painter arrives and uncovers a picture of the Magdalen. The Sacristan is scandalized to recognize the features of a lady who has been coming to pray. Cavaradossi, the painter, compares the portrait with a miniature in his pocket of Floria Tosca whose praises he sings in one of the opera's most familiar passages. The Sacristan goes off and Angelotti emerges, thinking the church empty. He and Cavaradossi recognize each other just as Tosca's voice is heard. Cavaradossi gives him food and drink and makes him hide again. The jealous Tosca first reproaches him for meeting another woman whom she thinks she has heard. Reassured, she proposes an assignation for that evening. But when, remembering Angelotti, he asks her to leave him, she sees the portrait and another jealous outburst has first to be assuaged with passionate protestations. All this provides material for a long lyrical duet. Angelotti comes out of the chapel and reveals that his sister (the woman who came to pray) has concealed women's clothing in the church for his escape at night across the frontier, out of the cruel and hypocritical Scarpia's clutches. But Cavaradossi gives him the key to his own villa so that he can get away at once, just as a cannon is fired to announce the discovery of his escape. They leave together, as the Sacristan and a crowd of choristers and others rush in, excited by the news that Bonaparte has been defeated. The sudden entrance of Scarpia and his minions silences them. He has the church searched for Angelotti whose sister's fan is found in the chapel. Scarpia quickly establishes that Cavaradossi has been painting and has given the contents of his basket to Angelotti. Tosca enters, wishing to tell her lover that she must cancel the evening's appointment as she has to sing at the victory celebrations and is disconcerted not to find him. Scarpia, cleverly playing on her vanity and piety, shows her the fan and provokes an outburst of jealous rage. She departs in tears, shadowed by Scarpia's agents. Scarpia is left gloating erotically over his hopes of winning Tosca, as a Te Deum begins and the tolling of bells and the firing of cannon mingle in an exciting climax.

ACT II

Scarpia's apartments in the Farnese Palace. Scarpia is supping. A gavotte is audible from the gala below. Scarpia writes a note to be given to Tosca on her arrival. Spoletta reports that she has been followed to a villa. After her departure the villa was searched without any trace of Angelotti being found. But Cavaradossi has been arrested and is brought in. As the strains of a cantata in which Tosca is soloist drift in at the window Scarpia questions him about Angelotti, but Cavaradossi maintains that he knows nothing. Tosca comes in after her performance. Her lover warns her to say nothing, as he is led off to an adjoining room to be tortured. Scarpia tries in vain to get her to say where Angelotti is hidden. He gives orders for the torture to be increased. Cavaradossi's groans and defiant cries are heard. Finally the doors are opened and Tosca asks her lover if she may speak. He forbids her. But she can bear his cries no more and tells Scarpia that Angelotti is hidden in the garden well. Cavaradossi is brought in faint but proud. Scarpia ensures that he knows that Tosca has spoken and he curses her. Just then news is brought that Bonaparte is victorious after all. This evokes an outburst of triumph from Cavaradossi. Scarpia has him taken away to be executed. When Tosca asks him his price for saving Cavaradossi he replies, in a cantabile passage of sinister passion, that it is herself. To add to Tosca's horror the distant drums of the execution party are heard. Now comes the famous outburst of self-pity ("Vissi d'arte") which is the prima donna's great moment, followed by a vain plea to Scarpia for mercy. They are interrupted by Spoletta who announces that Angelotti has taken poison; all is ready for Cavaradossi's execution. Tosca at last consents. Scarpia says that there has to be a mock execution and instructs Spoletta; Tosca may explain the plan to her lover. At her request he writes out a safe-conduct for them both to leave the country. Seeing a knife on the table Tosca stabs him as he rises to embrace her, exclaiming "This is Tosca's kiss." She re-arranges her hair, piously composes the body with candles at the head and a crucifix on the breast, takes the safe-conduct from the clenched fingers, and cautiously departs.

ACT III

Battlements of the Castel Sant'Angelo. Dawn. Sheep bells and a shepherd's song are heard in the distance. The firing squad bringing Cavaradossi ascend to the platform and he is told that he has one hour to live. He bribes the gaoler to let him write to Tosca but, left alone, is soon lost in a romantic reverie ("E lucevan le stelle..."). Tosca, conducted by Spoletta, rushes to his side and shows him the safe-conduct. She tells him how the night ended and emphasizes that, when the mock execution takes place, he must remember to fall down at the right moment. They look forward in a duet to their future life together. The firing-squad return. Tosca watches light-heartedly as the ritual is accomplished and Cavaradossi falls. But when the soldiers have marched off and she tells him to get up she discovers that he is dead. At this moment news of Scarpia's murder reaches Spoletta and the guards within. She throws herself from the parapet as they rush out to seize her.

La Traviata

(The Fallen Woman). Opera in three acts. Music by G. Verdi. Libretto by F. M. Piave after A. Dumas, fils. First produced at the Teatro La Fenice, Venice, March 6th, 1853.

SCENE: Paris and neighbourhood.

TIME: About 1850.

CHARACTERS:

ALFREDO GERMONT		(Tenor)
GIORGIO GERMONT	*His father*	(Baritone)
VIOLETTA VALÉRY	*A demi-mondaine*	(Soprano)
FLORA BERVOIX	*Her friend*	(Mezzo-soprano)
ANNINA	*Her maid*	(Soprano)
DOCTOR GRENVIL		(Bass)
GASTONE DE LETORIÈRES		(Tenor)
MARCHESE D'OBIGNY		(Bass)
BARON DOUPHOL		(Baritone)

"La Dame aux Camélias", a sentimentalized record of an aspect of contemporary French society, confronted Verdi with a task very different from that presented by the involved melodramas hitherto usually favoured. His reaction to the challenge is seen in his lightening of the textures, especially in Act III, the inclusion of some conventional sections (as opposed to conventional rectiative) and the avoidance, except for the climax of Act II Scene 2, of elaborate ensembles. It appears particularly in the refinement of the melodies, which are nearly all sensitively responsive to the three main characters' emotions; the rumbustious Italianate quality still prevalent in much of "Rigoletto" and "Il Trovatore" is replaced by the mature Verdian sinuosity. The treatment of Violetta herself is interesting. For her party manners Verdi gives her a vocal line of great brilliance, in the bel canto tradition, but in her private life (i.e., her relations with Alfredo) she has melodies of a poignant simplicity. This makes the rôle particularly exacting. In the work as a whole those patches of banality, which had tended to disfigure even Verdi's best scores so far, are refreshingly absent (though the early part of Act II Scene 2 is weak) and it exudes an attractive "period" fragrance.

The Prelude is a short but delicate piece. It begins with a reference to music that will be heard at Violetta's sick-bed and then introduces a passionate phrase from her farewell to Alfredo in Act II.

ACT I

A salon in Violetta's house. A party is in progress. Gastone arrives and introduces his friend Alfredo who, he later tells Violetta, is greatly in love with her. (The opening scene is conversational against two orchestral melodies.) Alfredo sings a brilliant drinking-song (one of Verdi's best-known melodies) which is repeated by Violetta and then by the chorus. A waltz is heard from an adjoining room to which the guests adjourn, but Violetta is suddenly unwell and remains behind with Alfredo. He tells her that he would like to care for her and begins to declare his love in the opening paragraph of a duet which contains a strikingly passionate phrase. Violetta replies, in a florid line, that if he loves her he should leave her, since she can offer only "friendship". Before he leaves she gives him a flower and, to his joy, tells him that he may bring it back when it is dead. The guests now return and, as dawn is breaking, take their leave. Alone, Violetta sings the famous "Ah, fors' è lui", in the first part of which she contemplates, to Alfredo's passionate phrase, surrendering for the first time to true love, but in the second, after a cadenza, sees herself, to a florid melody, devoted forever to a life of pleasure.

ACT II

Scene 1. A country house near Paris. Alfredo has been living with Violetta for three months and sings of his bliss, in the first part of an aria. Hearing, however, from Annina that Violetta has been selling her belongings to defray the cost of housekeeping he determines to go to Paris at once to put their finances in order and, in a cabaletta, reproaches himself. After his departure Violetta comes in and receives an invitation from Flora to a dance which she tosses aside. Then a visitor is announced who proves to be not the expected agent but Alfredo's father who has come to ask her to give up Alfredo. In the familiar opening section of a long duet he tells her that Alfredo's association with her is threatening his young daughter's impending match. In a fine paragraph she stresses what a sacrifice it would mean for her. He continues to plead with her. Finally, in a passage of tender simplicity, she promises to do it for his daughter's sake. Germont is genuinely touched and, in the final section, offers her such consolation as he can, before leaving. Violetta gives Annina a note to Flora and writes a letter to Alfredo, but does not give it him when he returns at that moment. She excuses herself from seeing Alfredo's father whose arrival he is expecting. She weeps, smiles, and leaves him, emotionally calling on him to love her, to the phrase heard in the Prelude. Alfredo is not disconcerted when he is told by a servant that she has left for Paris, until her letter is brought him. His father makes a well-timed entrance from the garden, tries to console him and, in a well-known aria, to persuade him to return to the family home in Provence. But Alfredo fears that Violetta has gone to Douphol and, seeing Flora's invitation, rushes out set on vengeance. *Scene 2.* A salon in Flora's house. The party is in full swing. The Marchese imparts the news that Alfredo and Violetta have separated. Female guests enter dressed as gypsies and tell fortunes and male guests enter dressed as bull-fighters and sing a tale of the bull-ring. Alfredo arrives and sits down to cards. Violetta enters on Douphol's arm and sits with Flora—a soaring phrase indicating her agitation at seeing Alfredo, whose luck at cards is in. He wins at the expense of Douphol who shows signs of tension over Violetta. All go out to supper. Violetta reappears, followed at her request by Alfredo. She begs him to leave for his own safety, fearing a duel. But, jealous, he chooses to misunderstand and when she refuses to accompany him forces her to say that she loves Douphol. Thereupon he summons the whole company, abuses her before them all and throws his winnings at her feet. Amid general horror at Alfredo's behaviour his father, who alone understands the position, enters and reproaches him. Alfredo is contrite. Violetta, recovering a little from her first shock, tells him that he cannot understand the depths of her love for him and an ensemble is built up under her passionate phrases. At its conclusion Germont père leads his son away and the party disperses.

ACT III

Violetta's bedroom. Early morning. A tender little Prelude re-introduces the sick-bed motive and follows it with a sad melody. Violetta in bed awakens and calls to the watching Annina. She leaves her bed. Dr Grenvil visits her with words of hope (which she does not believe), but tells Annina that she has only a few hours to live. She tells Annina to give half the slender contents of her purse to the poor. Left alone, she draws a letter from Giorgio Germont from her bosom and reads it, to a soft reminder in the orchestra of the passionate phrase from Act I. The Baron was lightly wounded in the duel; Alfredo went abroad; but his father has told him all and he is hurrying back. As she looks in the mirror she fears that he will be too late. She sings a sad aria in a minor key, taking farewell from the gay world and longing for Alfredo. A chorus of carnival revellers is heard from the street. Annina comes excitedly in to announce the approach of Alfredo and a moment later he is there. In the first paragraph of the ensuing duet they forgive each other for everything. Then, to a melody of affecting simplicity, they sing of future life together away from Paris. Violetta wants them to go to church to give thanks but falls back too weak to dress. She sends Annina to the doctor with the message that she wants to live again. In a final section of the duet she feels death near, despite Alfredo's words of encouragement. Alfredo's father enters, having done what he promised. Too late, she says, but she is happy to die surrounded by all her loved ones. She gives Alfredo a medallion as a keepsake, with the wish that should he ever marry a "jeune fille" he should let her have it. A very short quintet follows. Then she speaks her last words, against another soft reprise of the passionate phrase, and is pronounced by the doctor to be dead.

Tristan and Isolde

(Tristan und Isolde). Music drama in three acts. Music by R. Wagner.
Libretto by the composer. First produced at Munich, June 10th, 1865.

SCENE: In and off the coast of Cornwall; Kareol, Brittany.

TIME: Legendary.

CHARACTERS:

TRISTAN	*A Cornish knight*	(Tenor)
MARKE	*King of Cornwall*	(Bass)
ISOLDE	*A princess of Ireland*	(Soprano)
BRANGÄNE	*Her lady-in-waiting*	(Soprano or Mezzo-soprano)
KURWENAL	*A retainer of Tristan*	(Baritone)
MELOT	*A knight*	(Tenor)
A SAILOR		(Tenor)
A SHEPHERD		(Tenor)

This huge and intensely serious work is not about love alone; for then much
of Acts I and III would seem too long and there would be substance in the
contemporary critic, Hanslick's jibe about the absurdity that the love in
question should be induced by a drug (whereas in fact Tristan and Isolde
are in love before the action begins and what the potion induces is the
abandonment of all inhibitions). Rather what emerges from Wagner's cloudy
and more than usually turgid verses is the conflict between love and duty
and the conclusion that a love which is felt as transcending all other
obligations can be consummated only in death. It is the most symphonic
of Wagner's operas, with an even closer knit and more dominating
orchestral score than elsewhere, reflecting the inner thoughts of the
characters in what is essentially a psychological and not a romantic drama.
The crucial and most malleable motives are heard in the Prelude and much
that follows can be shown in a close analysis to derive therefrom; but this
is not essential for enjoyment of music of which the primary appeal is
sensuous and emotional.

The Prelude, familiar to concert-goers, introduces leading motives associated
with love and longing. It moves steadily forward to one great climax and

then falls quickly back to the halting phrases with which it began and almost into silence.

ACT I

Isolde's pavilion on board a vessel sailing from Ireland to Cornwall. A young sailor is heard singing of his Irish girl from the mast. At his words Isolde starts up from her couch and prays that the ship be dashed to pieces. Brangäne inquires why she has been distraught since leaving home; but Isolde demands air. Brangäne draws the curtain back and reveals Tristan in the stern looking out to sea with Kurwenal at his feet. Isolde speaks slightingly about him who has "won a bride like a corpse for his lord" and dare not face her. Let Brangäne go to this "peerless hero" (as she has called him) and bid him approach her mistress. This she does but Tristan excuses himself as unable to leave the helm. Kurwenal tauntingly points out that he cannot come as he is escorting her to be the bride of King Marke and adds a reference to Tristan's victory at arms over Morold (Isolde's betrothed), whose head had been sent back to Ireland instead of the tribute which he had come to levy. Brangäne returns to Isolde who narrates how Tristan, wounded in the fight with Morold, had come to Ireland under the name of Tantris to be healed by Isolde's healing arts. She had recognized him and had been about to avenge herself for Morold with a sword when the sick man had looked into her eyes (solo cello) and she had dropped the sword. Now this "hero", despite his protestations of gratitude, has affronted her by returning to escort her to marry his aged uncle, Marke, King of tributary Cornwall. The only solution is that Tristan and herself should die. Brangäne tries to soothe her by suggesting that Tristan has indeed repaid his debt by bestowing her on his royal uncle. Isolde replies that, unloved, constantly to see Tristan would be intolerable and bids Brangäne bring the casket with the magic potions given her by her mother. She rejects the love, and holds up the death, potion. Just then sailors' voices are heard and Kurwenal enters boisterously to tell them to prepare to land. Isolde asks him to inform his master that she refuses to do so unless he first visits her to seek forgiveness for unexpiated wrong. While he is gone Isolde takes farewell of the world and insists that the now desperate Brangäne prepares the death potion. Tristan slowly enters, to a passage of great tension based on a four-note motive which, with the death motive, pervades the following scene. After reproaching him for having been so bound by convention as to have shunned her hitherto, she reminds him how she had nursed him to health and had until now refrained from exacting vengeance for Morold. Tristan hands her his sword and bids her strike him but she proposes instead that they drink reconciliation. Tristan grasps what she has hitherto concealed, adding that he conceals what she does not grasp, thereby indicating that his behaviour has been due to the need to repress his own feelings no less than to convention. Brangäne brings a goblet and they drink in turn, Tristan expecting and desiring death scarcely less than Isolde. But as the music at once tells us, Brangäne has substituted the love potion. Their first words show that they are no longer inhibited, he by honour and she by shame. They have no thoughts for anything but each other, as Brangäne seeks to array Isolde and as Kurwenal, the knights, and sailors hail King Marke who is putting out from shore to greet his bride.

ACT II

A garden in front of Isolde's chamber. The Prelude begins with a motive standing for the hateful day and goes on to depict Isolde's impatience. At the rise of the curtain receding hunting horns of the royal party are heard. Isolde can hear only the sound of a summer night but Brangäne warns her that the hunt is still near. She goes on further to warn her that the world is not as blind as she has now become and that Melot is not to be trusted. But Isolde replies that he is Tristan's friend and begs her to extinguish the torch which is the signal for Tristan to come. When Brangäne hesitates she does it herself and sends her to keep watch on the battlements. Isolde waves with her veil and a moment later she and Tristan are embracing. Now begins the long duet which is the centre-piece of the opera. First come short passionate exchanges which subside into longer passages execrating the day which kept them apart and prevented Tristan from seeing into his own heart. Finally thought of the blessings of the night leads to the love duet proper, the ecstasies of which are momentarily broken while Brangäne, watching from the ramparts, calls in vain, in an exquisite passage, for caution as the night is passing. From night the lovers pass to death and the thought of love-death and (just before Brangäne's renewed warning) we hear a new motive followed, as the music rises to a climax, by another characterized by a turn. Suddenly Brangäne utters a shriek, Kurwenal rushes in with a call to Tristan to save himself, and Marke, Melot, and courtiers are upon them. Melot turns triumphantly to Marke and, introduced by a new motive on the bass clarinet, the King begins a long monologue of sorrowful reproach. Had he not made Tristan his heir and only sent him to woo a bride for himself in deference to his people's wishes? Why has Tristan now betrayed him and wounded his honour? (The markedly thinner orchestral texture may be partly due to the exigencies of writing for a bass but also reflects the desolation of the scene.) Tristan has no answer but turns to Isolde and asks (to tender music recalling the love duet) whether she will follow him to a land of darkness. Isolde assents. Tristan gently kisses her, thereby provoking Melot to draw his sword. Tristan, reproaching his former friend, does likewise and in the ensuing fight falls wounded. A version of the motive of desire which opened the opera is heard in the last six bars.

ACT III

Outside a castle by the sea in Kareol. There is a slow Prelude, the
desolate mood of which is set in the first bar by the open fifths in the
bass and a new version of the motive of desire. The sorely wounded
Tristan sleeps on a couch, watched by Kurwenal. The infinitely sad strain
of a Shepherd's piping is heard "off" (solo cor anglais) and a short exchange
between the Shepherd and Kurwenal makes plain that the former is
watching for the ship bearing Isolde from Cornwall, at the sight of which he
is to play a gay tune. Tristan wakes and is told by Kurwenal that he is in
Kareol, his native land. Tristan speaks of the blessed night of oblivion
where he has been and how only the thought of Isolde has brought him back
into the accursed day. His mind wandering, he asks when she will put out
the light. Kurwenal tells him that, remembering Isolde's healing arts, he has
sent a trusty vessel to bring her to him. Tristan is filled with joy and
gratitude at this news. He yearns unspeakably for Isolde and imagines
the ship to be already near. But the resumption of the Shepherd's sad
strain shows that no ship is in sight. Tristan is now almost delirious,
dwelling incoherently and with increasing vehemence on all that has passed
between him and Isolde till he falls back senseless and Kurwenal fears
that he is dead. But his heart still beats and now, in a quiet passage of
especial beauty, he imagines Isolde sailing to him. At last the Shepherd
signals that the ship is sighted—by playing a gay tune (on the cor anglais or,
if available, a special wooden trumpet). After a moment of anxiety the
ship enters harbour and Kurwenal goes off to meet Isolde. Tristan, in the
utmost excitement, tears off his bandage and rises to his feet. He staggers
to meet the approaching Isolde and dies in her arms. Isolde grieves over
him in another wonderful paragraph and falls senseless on his body.
Kurwenal, who has re-entered, stands frozen with horror as the Shepherd
rushes in to announce the arrival of a second ship. Kurwenal orders the
gates to be closed and defended. When Melot seeks to enter he kills him
and is reluctant to admit Brangäne. In a frenzy he seeks to bar Marke and
his men and is mortally wounded. He dies at Tristan's side. As Isolde
revives Brangäne and Marke try to explain that Brangäne has told the
King about the potion and that he had come to unite the lovers in
marriage. But Isolde does not heed. The familiar "Liebestod" begins
in the orchestra and rises to its great climax near the end, while Isolde,
oblivious of them all, sings in ecstasy over his body, finally sinking on it
in Brangäne's arms. In all this the two motives, the second that with the
turn, heard near the end of the love duet dominate the music; but five bars
before the soft close Wagner seems to underline the opera's meaning by
returning to the motive of longing with which the Prelude had opened
and at last providing a resolution to its chords.

Il Trovatore

(The Troubadour). Opera in four acts. Music by G. Verdi. Libretto by S. Cammarano after A. G. Gutierrez. First produced at the Teatro Apollo, Rome, January 19th, 1853.

SCENE: Biscay and Aragon.

TIME: Early fifteenth century.

CHARACTERS:

COUNT DI LUNA *A young nobleman*	(Baritone)
FERRANDO *Captain of his guard*	(Bass)
LEONORA *Lady-in-waiting*	(Soprano)
INEZ *Her confidante*	(Soprano)
MANRICO *Brought up as Azucena's son*	(Tenor)
RUIZ *A follower of Manrico*	(Tenor)
AZUCENA *A gypsy*	(Mezzo-soprano)

The libretto of "Il Trovatore" is a byword for obscurity and absurdity. The music is in the nineteenth century Italian convention and bears only a decent minimum of relation to characters and situation. It is, on a serious assessment, far inferior to its predecessor "Rigoletto" or its immediate successor "La Traviata". The popularity of the work must be attributed to its immense vitality and the prodigal flow of vigorous Italian melody. This combination of popularity and absurdity must, in its day, have done considerable damage to the cause of opera in countries such as Britain, where there was no strong operatic tradition and one suspects that, of operas that have survived, it must have been this at which W. S. Gilbert was poking fun in "The Gondoliers". The many brilliant arias and duets call for four technically accomplished singers, but there is relatively little by way of ensemble work to test their musicianship.

ACT I

Scene 1. Courtyard of the Palace in Aragon. Armed men are watching for a troubadour whose serenades have aroused the Count di Luna's jealousy. To keep them awake Ferrando tells them (in an aria of unusual

length for a bass) how a gypsy had once bewitched the present Count's younger brother in his cradle. She had been burnt at the stake but her daughter, in revenge, had snatched away the child and its bones had been found in the embers. The old witch's spirit is still abroad.
Scene 2. The garden. Though it is midnight, Leonora lingers in the hope of seeing the unknown young knight whom she recently crowned as victor in a tournament and who has been serenading her. Inez' counsel to forget him launches her on the brilliant second part of her aria in which she speaks of her love. They retire. The Count enters, having seen a light in the window of Leonora whom he loves. But almost at the same time the troubadour appears and begins to serenade her. Leonora emerges and in the darkness mistakes the Count for her beloved, but then, seeing the troubadour, turns to him. When the Count, furious with jealousy, demands to know the intruder's name, the latter declares himself to be Manrico, a rebel. In the ensuing trio the Count challenges him to a duel while Leonora declares that she can never love the Count and that he can kill her if he wishes.

ACT II

Scene 1. A gypsy encampment in Biscay. Dawn. A band of gypsies sing the familiar "Anvil Chorus" in the refrain of which their hammers strike in the rhythm of the music. Azucena follows with an equally familiar aria in which she recalls the horror of her mother's death at the stake. When the gypsies have dispersed for the day's activities Azucena relates to Manrico in some detail how the old Count di Luna had her mother burnt as a witch and how she had stolen his child, heedful of her mother's last call for vengeance. Then she had fainted with emotion and, in delirium, had thrown her own child and not the Count's into the still burning embers. This story, not unnaturally, prompts Manrico to ask if he himself is not then her son, to which she replies that they were but idle words and asks, inconsequentially, if she has not always behaved like a mother to him. Had she not recently nursed him to health after he had fallen in the battle with di Luna? Why had he once shown di Luna mercy in single combat? Manrico describes in a martial passage, which ends softly, how a voice from heaven had stayed his arm. Azucena urges him to be ruthless towards di Luna and he swears to obey her. Ruiz now arrives with an order from the Prince of Biscay to take charge of the defence of Castellor and the news that Leonora, thinking him dead, is about to take the veil. Manrico makes ready to leave forthwith. Azucena tries to restrain him but succeeds in holding him only long enough for a vigorous duet.
Scene 2. The cloister of a convent. Night. The Count and his followers plan to abduct Leonora before she takes the veil. He sings of his love and of his hope in a great two-part aria. A chorus of nuns is heard escorting

Leonora. While the Count and his followers mutter of the impending exploit, Leonora seeks to calm Inez who is saddened by their parting. The Count and his men descend upon her but at the critical moment Manrico and his followers appear. There is an ensemble over which the florid phrases of the joyous Leonora soar. The Count's forces are outnumbered and he is forced to withdraw.

ACT III

Scene 1. The Count's camp before Castellor. Ferrando informs the soldiers of the coming assault and a martial chorus is sung. The Count dreams of snatching Leonora from Manrico's arms before morning. Azucena is brought in, captured by the Count's scouts. Interrogated, she replies (in waltz time) that she is a poor harmless wanderer from Biscay looking for her son. The mention of Biscay leads the Count to ask for news of his young brother, stolen and taken there many years before. Ferrando recognizes her as the child-snatcher and the Count is already threatening to kill her when she calls on Manrico, her son, to come to her aid. The Count seizes, with still greater eagerness, on this opportunity to harm his rival and he condemns her to be burnt at the stake.
Scene 2. Within Castellor. Preparations are afoot for the coming battle, prior to which Manrico is to wed Leonora. He attempts to calm her anxiety for him in a cantabile aria in which he assures her that if indeed he must die, his last thoughts will be of her! Just as the ceremony is imminent Ruiz brings word of Azucena's capture. Manrico resolves to rescue her at once and has time for nothing but the famous aria "Di quella pira" in which it is customary to insert a top C not written by Verdi.

ACT IV

Scene 1. Outside the dungeon tower of the palace in Aragon.   Night. Leonora comes to sing of her love outside the prison in which her lover lies condemned, having been captured in the battle. An unseen choir chants the "miserere". Manrico's voice is heard taking farewell of Leonora in a famous strain and Leonora's sad comments complete a dramatically effective ensemble. In another aria she sings of her resolve to die with him. The Count appears, saying that Manrico and Azucena are to die at dawn. Leonora confronts him and in a long duet pleads in vain with him for Manrico's life. Finally she offers herself in return for his freedom. The Count accepts the bargain and the duet ends in high excitement for both—on Leonora's part because she intends to take her life for her lover's sake.
Scene 2. Inside the dungeon. Azucena lies exhausted, in fear and delirium.

Manrico soothes her and she longs, in a strain of moving simplicity, to return to the peace of her mountains. (This short duet is perhaps the best number in the opera.) Leonora bursts in and bids him save himself. But he guesses the price she has paid and curses her, as Azucena continues to sing of mountain peace. Leonora falls fainting and reveals that she has taken poison. To a truly Verdian phrase she exclaims that she would rather die for him than live for another. The Count enters and there is a short trio before she dies. The Count orders Manrico's instant execution before Azucena's eyes. But she calls out that he has slain his brother and that her mother is avenged.

Les Troyens

(The Trojans). Opera in five acts (two parts). Music by H. Berlioz. Libretto by the composer. Part II first produced (in abridged version) at the Théâtre Lyrique, Paris, November 4th, 1863. First performance of both parts at Karlsruhe, December 5th and 6th, 1890.

SCENE: Troy and Carthage.

TIME: Antiquity.

PRINCIPAL CHARACTERS:

CASSANDRA *A Trojan prophetess*		(Soprano)
PRIAM *King of Troy*		(Bass)
HECUBA *His wife*		(Mezzo-soprano)
POLYXENA *His daughter*		(Soprano)
HELENUS *His son*		(Tenor)
AENEAS *A Trojan hero*		(Tenor)
ASCANIUS *His son*		(Soprano)
CHOROEBUS *Fiancé of Cassandra*		(Baritone)
PANTHEUS *A priest*		(Bass)
DIDO *Queen of Carthage*		(Mezzo-soprano)
ANNA *Her sister*		(Contralto)
IOPAS *A Tyrian poet*		(Tenor)
NARBAL *Dido's Minister*		(Bass)
HYLAS *A young Trojan sailor*		(Tenor)
TWO SOLDIERS		(Baritone and bass)

Despite the work's length Berlioz' long neglected operatic masterpiece was intended to be, and should be, given on one evening if it is to make its full effect although the composer felt obliged to offer it in two parts. The work is planned on an epic scale and this is one of the few operas described in this book to which the old-fashioned term "grand opera" is properly applicable. The form is French-classical, with formal recitatives, arias for one and two voices, mighty choruses, and ballets. But Berlioz has filled much of what are sometimes essentially dramatic tableaux with romantic feeling and his characteristic orchestral colouring and harmonies. The music of Part I leaves an impression of sumptuousness, but that of Part II, especially the middle scenes, has an imaginative and sensitive beauty of its own. While the romantic in Berlioz may linger over Cassandra and Dido, the classicist and admirer of Virgil insists that the subject is the founding of Rome and the point is underlined by repetitions of the Trojan March and the repeated cries of "Italy!"

PART I. LA PRISE DE TROIE (The Capture of Troy)

ACT I

Scene 1. The plain of Troy. The people have emerged from the city, rejoicing and dancing, believing the Greeks gone. They rush off to see the wooden horse left by the Greeks as an offering to Athene. Cassandra enters in agitation. She has seen the ghost of Hector watching on the ramparts and her heart presages disaster to King Priam, her father, and Choroebus, who loves her, but will never live to marry her. But none will believe her. Choroebus comes to her. In an extended duet he tries to calm her while she vainly presses him to escape.

Scene 2. Before the citadel of Troy. The population assemble to give thanks to the Gods in an impressive chorus based on a martial theme with a very characteristic modulation. There is a dance of wrestlers. Then to an extended and mournful clarinet solo, with sad choral comment, Andromache, Hector's widow, enters in silence and presents the small Astyanax to his grandfather, King Priam, and his Queen. Aeneas rushes in with a tale of Laocoön's death. He had hurled his javelin, suspiciously, at the flank of the wooden horse and immediately two serpents from the sea had devoured him. All comment on this appalling event in a big ensemble. Aeneas proposes that Athene be propitiated by their drawing the horse in procession to her temple. Cassandra remains, more desperate than ever, as, to the strains of the Trojan March, the people, deaf to every warning, joyfully drag the horse into the city, and night falls.

ACT II

Scene 1. Tent of Aeneas. Aeneas is asleep; Ascanius, frightened by the noise of fighting, approaches his father's bed but does not waken him. The ghost of Hector appears and tells Aeneas to escape from burning Troy and seek Italy, there to build a great and glorious empire. Pantheus and later Choroebus and his followers rush in with tidings of the armed men pouring from the horse and of death and destruction everywhere. All go forth to do battle.

Scene 2. Temple of Cybele. As the city burns, Trojan women pray to the goddess in a three-part chorus. Cassandra tells them that Aeneas has escaped with a band of warriors and the treasure to Italy where destiny calls them. Choroebus is dead. She urges them to leap from the temple rock to save their honour. Most of them swear to die and, taking up their lyres, sing defiantly. They drive out a small group which has been hesitating. The fire rages more intensely. Cassandra seizes a lyre and sings with the others. The Greek soldiers arrive in search of the treasure and are astonished at the sight. Before they can approach the women Cassandra stabs herself, saying that the pain is nothing. All the women hurl themselves over the precipice or stab themselves. Their last words are of Aeneas's escape and the call "Italy!" is heard.

PART II. LES TROYENS A CARTHAGE (The Trojans at Carthage)

ACT III

A hall in Dido's palace. We see the national celebration of the seventh anniversary of the founding of Carthage by Dido after the murder of her husband, the ruler of Tyre. The people acclaim her in a chorus and she replies in suitable terms in an aria. There are processions of builders, sailors, and labourers, who receive from Dido appropriate awards. Alone with her sister after the ceremony, Anna suggests to her that she should marry again but Dido declares that she remains faithful to the memory of her dead husband. Iopas enters to announce that a strange fleet has been driven ashore and that representatives are seeking audience. Dido, mindful of her own trials, cannot refuse them. Aeneas, disguised as a sailor, and the Trojan chieftains enter to a minor version of the Trojan March and present gifts. Ascanius tells Dido who they are and she welcomes them. But Narbal arrives with news of a Numidian invasion. This leads Aeneas to cast off his disguise and offer the assistance of his band. Dido accepts the alliance and after Aeneas has tenderly entrusted his son to Dido's care, all prepare to follow Aeneas to battle in a stirring final ensemble.

Symphonic Interlude. Virgin forest near Carthage. We hear the wonderful piece of nature-painting known to concert-goers as "The Royal Hunt and Storm" and the scene takes place before our eyes, with huntsmen and Naiads. Dido dressed as Diana and Aeneas as a Warrior take shelter in a cave. Fauns and satyrs are heard crying "Italy!"

ACT IV

Dido's gardens by the sea. The Numidians have been routed but Narbal is uneasy at Dido's dalliance with Aeneas, who is summoned by inexorable fate to Italy. Anna tries in vain to communicate to him her joy at such a match. Dido, Aeneas, and the court now take their places and dances are performed before them, of which the first is musically the most striking. Iopas sings a song in praise of Ceres but Dido can find no pleasure in listening. She feels her resistance to Aeneas to be waning and allows the little Ascanius to draw her dead husband's ring from her finger. This takes place during a charming quintet, which leads (with the addition of Ascanius and Pantheus) to the famous septet (with chorus), as all reflect on the enchantment of the wave-lulled night. Eventually Dido and Aeneas are left alone to sing a beautiful love duet to words suggested by Shakespeare ("In such a night as this"). As they leave with Dido leaning on Aeneas's shoulder, Mercury suddenly appears, strikes Aeneas's shield hanging on a column and calls "Italy!" three times.

ACT V

Scene 1. The harbour with Trojan ships and Trojan tents on shore. Night. Hylas sings of his yearning for his homeland, but falls asleep before he finishes his poetic little song. Two sentries jibe at him. Pantheus and Trojan chieftains give voice to their determination to sail; they fear divine wrath. The shades of the dead haunt them with the cry of "Italy!" The two sentries, who have overheard, express their own preference for remaining in Carthage, where the women are wonderful. Their jaunty little march in a minor key gives an unexpected touch of humour. Aeneas now has an extended scena. He is torn between his duty and his love for Dido, to whom he has broken his intention of departing. Urged by the ghosts of his father and other Trojans, he decides to leave at once without further sight of Dido. The fleet prepare to sail (suggestions of the Trojan March). But Dido rushes distractedly in, full of tearful pleas and reproaches, which Aeneas's protestations of love do not assuage. Finally, as the Trojan March is heard once more and sailors cry "Italy!", she storms out cursing him and Aeneas embarks.

Scene 2. A room in Dido's palace. Dido, no longer proud, begs her sister to send a messenger to entreat Aeneas to delay a short while; Anna points out that it will be useless. Aeneas loves her but is obeying a higher command. Iopas brings news that the Trojan fleet has sailed. After a moment of fury, Dido orders a pyre to be prepared on which she will ceremonially burn all the gifts exchanged between them. Left alone, Dido resolves to die on the pyre. After a passionate recitative she takes farewell of her city and people in a solemn aria, which closes with reminiscences of the love duet.

Scene 3. A terrace overlooking the sea. Priests of Pluto sing a solemn chorus as they take their places round the pyre, while Anna and Narbal utter a curse on the Trojans. Dido mounts the pyre. Then, after proclaiming that her memory will live and one day Hannibal will avenge her, she stabs herself with Aeneas's sword. Before she dies she sees a vision of the Roman Capitol and of the destruction of Carthage. The people sing of vengeance; but the orchestra has the final word with the Trojan March.

Turandot

Lyric drama in three acts. Music by G. Puccini. Text by G. Adami and R. Simoni after C. Gozzi. First performed at La Scala, Milan, April 25th, 1926.

SCENE: Peking.

TIME: Legendary.

CHARACTERS:

PRINCESS TURANDOT	(Soprano)
THE EMPEROR ALTOUM	(Tenor)
TIMUR *Exiled king of Tartary*	(Bass)
CALAF *His son*	(Tenor)
LIÙ *A young slave-girl*	(Soprano)
PING *Grand Chancellor*	(Baritone)
PANG *Lord High Steward*	(Tenor)
PONG *Lord High Cook*	(Tenor)
A MANDARIN	(Baritone)

Puccini's last opera is perhaps his finest, though the total impact inevitably suffers from the fact that he did not live to complete the love duet, which was obviously intended to crown the work, and the final scene. These were completed by Alfano from sketches which were found at Puccini's death. The exotic brilliance of the stage action is reflected in Puccini's music. It remains based on his characteristic cast of melody and is eminently for Italian voices; but the harmonies and textures have been greatly enriched and the whole score is saturated with chinoiserie. While the music of Liù and Calaf is essentially the older Puccini in a more refined form, for Act I with its great choruses, against which the soloists seem to struggle for a hearing and for the Riddle Scene the music is of a subtlety and imaginative power which go well beyond the usual bounds of nineteenth and early twentieth century Italian opera. In particular one may observe the note of fantasy struck in the music for the three Courtiers, Commedia dell'Arte figures in masks, and the skill with which it is blended with that for the other characters—the same problem which Strauss had faced in "Ariadne auf Naxos".

ACT I

A square beneath the city walls. Evening. A crowd listens as a Mandarin reads a proclamation. Turandot will be the bride of a prince who can solve her three riddles, but he who fails will forfeit his life. The Prince of Persia has been unlucky and when the moon has risen is to die on the scaffold. The crowd gloat over this news. Timur, disguised as a beggar, is jostled by them and falls; Liù, the faithful slave, begs for help. At this moment Calaf recognizes his father and there is a moment of joyful reunion, each having thought the other dead at the hands of their pursuing foes. They are lost in the crowd, who sing of their impatience for the moon. At last the moon rises and a procession appears leading the Prince of Persia to the scaffold. The people are moved and call out for mercy. Calaf curses Turandot. She appears (to a phrase in the orchestra constantly associated with her), but with a gesture sends the procession forward. Calaf has been deeply affected by her beauty and Timur and Liù try to get him to leave. As he is about to strike the great gong, the signal that another suitor has arrived, Ping, Pang, and Pong bar his way and try to dissuade him with cynical arguments, gruesomely underlined by the executioner holding up the severed head. Liù adds her entreaties in a famous lyrical passage (with a faint echo of a negro spiritual). But the Prince only urges her, in a short aria, to look after his father, if they are left alone. The music builds up in a sextet with chorus and in a final climax Calaf breaks away and sounds the gong.

ACT II

Scene 1. A pavilion. The three courtiers strike grotesque attitudes and converse about the state of China in an extended trio remarkable for its many changes of mood. They deplore the long train of executed suitors. They wish they were in their country homes. They think with longing of the day when Turandot will at last surrender to love. The music passes without a break to
Scene 2. The big square before the palace with a huge marble staircase in the centre. A crowd is assembling, to a fantastic march, for a State ceremony. Through clouds of incense the aged Emperor is seen on his throne at the head of the staircase. He is bound by a terrible oath which has led to much bloodshed. He seeks to dissuade Calaf who stands at the foot of the stairs, but the latter insists on his right to try his fortune. The Mandarin reads the proclamation again and Turandot makes her entry (to a stately version of her theme). She sings the aria "In questa reggia" in which she sees herself as avenging the rape and death of a conquered ancestress; no-one shall possess her. She too tries to dissuade Calaf from guessing the riddles but in vain. To formal music that shows the strain of the participants she puts the

first two riddles and receives the answers—"Hope" and "Blood". The third is posed (to the same phrase but a semitone higher) and after an agonizing moment, Calaf triumphantly replies "Turandot" and is acclaimed by the crowd. Frantic, she begs her father not to give her to the stranger like a slave, but he replies that his oath is inviolable. When she appeals to Calaf he volunteers to set her one riddle. If she can discover his name before dawn, he will die. (The orchestra anticipates his big aria in Act III.) The Emperor hopes to welcome him as a son at break of day and the Act ends with acclamation of the Light of the Universe.

ACT III

Scene 1. The palace garden. Night. Heralds proclaim Turandot's decree that none shall sleep; on pain of death the stranger's name must be discovered before dawn. In a superb aria (which yet is a reversion to the composer's less sophisticated earlier style) the Prince muses on his secret, which must not be revealed till dawn when the Princess will be his. The three courtiers approach, offering girls, riches, power, if he will but flee and save them from the death which awaits them. The Prince remains unmoved, even when they threaten him. A group of soldiers drag in Timur and Liù. Turandot appears. When she orders Timur to reveal the name Liù says that she alone knows it (to a phrase heard when the trio were united in Act I) and they torture her. When Turandot asks her what gives her such power of resistance, she replies that it is love and adds (in another well-known aria) that Turandot's love will soon be awakened by Calaf. Then she seizes a dagger and stabs herself at Calaf's feet. Her body is borne away, with Timur grieving at her side. Calaf is left alone with Turandot. Ignoring her protests, he tears off her veil and kisses her passionately. She no longer resists and sheds her first tears, conquered by a new fever. She bids him depart with his name unknown but he reveals it fearlessly. The dawn is breaking and trumpets are sounding as the scene changes to
Scene 2. The square outside the palace. Amid general rejoicing Turandot leads Calaf to the Emperor's throne and announces that she knows the stranger's name—it is Love (at which the orchestra recall the phrase to which she had sung that no-one should possess her).

The Turn of the Screw

Chamber opera in two acts. Music by Benjamin Britten. Libretto by M. Piper after Henry James. First produced at the Teatro la Fenice, Venice, September 14th, 1954.

SCENE: A country house (Bly).

TIME: Mid-nineteenth century.

CHARACTERS:

THE PROLOGUE	(Tenor)
THE GOVERNESS	(Soprano)
MILES } *Children in her charge*	(Treble)
FLORA }	(Soprano)
MRS GROSE *The housekeeper*	(Soprano)
MISS JESSEL *A former governess*	(Soprano)
QUINT *A former man-servant*	(Tenor)

This is a cleverly contrived setting of James's macabre tale of two Victorian children corrupted by ghosts, between whom and an initially ingenuous governess, the central character, a dramatic conflict develops. Britten holds together a series of short scenes by the device of basing the whole work on a Theme, heard in and just after the Prologue, of which the linking Interludes are all variations, each serving to introduce a scene which intensifies the horror (or turns the screw). The music is highly atmospheric and responsive to the challenge inherent in unusual material, much of which at first sight seems to defy operatic treatment. The ghost of Quint is given a florid, unearthly melisma, (often supported by the celesta) and the interval of a fourth is freely used to suggest "badness". The school-room scenes are set with engaging wit. To establish the pathos of Miles, the innocent-seeming schoolboy in the grip of evil forces, a boy's treble is virtually essential.

PROLOGUE

The story is introduced in a tenor recitative to piano accompaniment which explains how an "innocent" young governess was persuaded by the charm of a dashing, busy man of the world to take charge of his nephew and niece in the country, on condition that she did not write to, or worry, him at all. At the words "she was to do everything" the Theme is heard on the piano; it rises a fourth and falls a minor third till it returns—or screws back—to its tonic. It is repeated crescendo by the orchestra and leads to

ACT I

Scene 1. (On the Journey). Over an ostinato figure, first fully scored and then for drums alone, the Governess, on the road to Bly, voices her doubts and fears. The words "Oh why did I come?" are sung to a motive that recurs. Variation 1 is a harmonized statement of the Theme.

Scene 2. (The Welcome). The porch at Bly. Mrs Grose and the children await the Governess. Miles and Flora practise bowing and curtseying to harp glissandi. The Governess arrives (the motive from Scene 1 on the violin indicating her state of mind). Greetings are exchanged in a duet with Mrs Grose and the children carry her off. In Variation 2 the Theme is heard in the bass with a bright counterpoint over it.

Scene 3. (The Letter). Mrs Grose gives the Governess a letter expelling Miles from school as an "injury to his friends". The two women are taken aback (Scene 1 motive on the viola); Miles cannot be "bad". Their confidence in him is confirmed by the sound of the children singing "Lavender's blue" outside. The Governess decides to do nothing and Mrs Grose gives her a kiss of support. Variation 3 is warmer in tone with the bird-calls of summer prominent.

Scene 4. (The Tower). In the grounds. Evening. The Governess sings relaxedly of her contentment. But Quint appears for a moment on the tower (to the sound of the celesta). She asks herself in agitation who it can be. (The questioning motive at the words "Who is it? Who?" recurs.) Variation 4 is a grotesque march.

Scene 5. (The Window). The hall. The children ride in on a hobby-horse singing "Tom, Tom, the piper's son". They go out. Before the Governess can follow she sees Quint at the window. She runs after him in vain to the "questioning" motive. To Mrs Grose, who enters, she describes in agitation, over pizzicato strings, the man she has seen. Mrs Grose tells her that it must be Peter Quint the master's former valet. He had been "free" with Miles and with Miss Jessel, the former governess, who had come under his spell and gone away to die. (This narration is prominently accompanied by the cello.) The Governess is shaken by the story and resolves to protect Miles. She is sure that Quint will return though Mrs Grose does not understand. Variation 5 is a sprightly fugue.

Scene 6. (Lessons). The schoolroom. Miles is reciting Latin gender rhymes, to the rhythm of the fugue. He goes on to sing "Malo: I would rather be..." to a sad little tune, almost the Theme's inversion (with a cor anglais obligato), which he has taught himself. Variation 6 continues the tune against bright figuration.

Scene 7. (The Lake). In the park. Flora is having a geography lesson and then settles down to sing a strange little lullaby to her doll, with a wood-wind and harp accompaniment. Miss Jessel appears across the lake and Flora quietly turns away. She goes off to find Miles. The Governess, who has seen Miss Jessel and Flora turn silently away from her, is greatly agitated. Variation 7 introduces the theme on the horn against celesta arpeggios.

Scene 8. (At Night). The garden. Quint calls from the tower in a florid passage based on the motive of Scene 1 and Miles appears, in his nightgown. Quint beguiles him with the seductive imagery of his utterance. Miss Jessel calls to Flora from the lake, and the girl appears at her window, though Miss Jessel is not confident of her power to hold her. The duet of Quint and Miss Jessel works up to a quartet as the children join in and the Theme is heard. The Governess and Mrs Grose emerge and the ghosts disappear. To the former's questions Miles replies, to the fourths of "Malo", "You see, I AM bad."

ACT II

Scene 1. (Colloquy and Soliloquy). Scene undefined. Cadenzas, some suggestive of music already heard and constituting Variation 8, introduce a dialogue between the two ghosts, which underlines Quint's emotional hold over Miss Jessel and the search of each for a victim-companion. Their duet concludes with a powerful unison version of the Theme and repetition of the line "The ceremony of innocence is drowned" (from W. B. Yeats) to a version of the Act I Scene 1 motive. The Governess is now heard expressing her bewilderment in a chromatic arioso. Variation 9 is dominated by the sound of bells.

Scene 2. (The Bells). A churchyard. Over the bells Miles and Flora chant mockingly on their way to church. Mrs Grose is taken in but the Governess sees that they are "talking horrors" and are "with the others". She refuses however to write to their uncle. The two women's voices and those of the chanting children unite for a moment in a big quartet before Mrs Grose and Flora enter the church. In a short conversation, in which the sound of the bells passes to the orchestra, Miles makes it challengingly clear to the Governess that he knows what she knows, leaving her resolved to go away from "this poisoned place." Variation 10 is a little chaconne.

Scene 3. (Miss Jessel). The schoolroom. The Governess finds Miss Jessel at the desk. After a duet in which the latter voices her determination (over mournful triplets), the Governess dismisses her and sits down to write to the children's guardian. She pens the letter to an urgent viola solo and reads it over in an arietta of great lyrical beauty—one of the few relaxed passages in the work as well as a notable addition to the list of operatic letter scenes. Variation 11 is dominated by the bass flute and bass clarinet. *Scene 4.* (The Bedroom). Miles sits on his bed half undressed, singing "Malo" to himself. The Governess enters and in the ensuing dialogue (in which she speaks against bass flute and bass clarinet, he against harp) tells him of her letter and almost extracts a confession from him. But Quint calls to him and the candle goes out, Miles claiming, to the fourths of "Malo", that he blew it. Variation 12 features pizzicato arpeggios and an insistent rhythm heard first in the percussion and then on Quint's voice, tempting Miles to steal the letter.

Scene 5. (Quint). The schoolroom. Quint continues to urge him to take it, as Miles enters and carries off the letter from the desk. In the short Variation 13 the piano makes an entry.

Scene 6. (The Piano). The schoolroom. Miles is strenuously playing a Czernyesque sonatina on the piano while Flora makes a cat's cradle on the floor. The two women admire Miles's playing. The Governess bends over him as he changes to another dreadful piece, while Mrs Grose settles down near Flora and dozes off. Flora slips out unnoticed. When the Governess realizes that Miles has deliberately tricked her they rush off after Flora, leaving Miles triumphant at the piano which continues to be heard into Variation 14.

Scene 7. (Flora). By the lake. The two women find Flora watching Miss Jessel. Flora, in a cheeky rhythm, refuses to admit that she sees anything. Miss Jessel urges her to remain silent. Mrs Grose sees nothing and thinks that the Governess, in her excitement, is not herself. Finally Flora is rude to the latter and is taken away by Mrs Grose. All this makes a spirited quartet. Left alone, the Governess still hears the rhythm of the child's spiteful remarks and feels that she has failed and that "there is no more innocence" in herself. Variation 15 ends with an expressive cello recitativo.

Scene 8. (Miles). Before the house. Mrs Grose, who is taking Flora off to her uncle, has been much shocked by Flora's disclosures during the night. She tells the Governess that the letter to the children's uncle had disappeared. The Governess is left alone to face Miles and the rest of the scene is a passacaglia over a bass derived from the Theme. In a dialogue in a more cantabile style than hitherto she presses him to unburden himself to her, but Quint appears on the tower, and though he admits stealing the letter, he is reluctant, as Quint approaches urging silence, to say more. After a prolonged struggle he shouts "Peter Quint, you devil" and collapses into the Governess's arms. Quint disappears and she thinks she has saved the boy. But after the questioning motive has been heard once more, she realizes that he is dead. "Malo" is heard on the cor anglais and finally is sung by the Governess as a full-throated lament.

Wozzeck

*Opera in three acts (15 scenes). Music by A. Berg. Libretto after
G. Büchner. First produced at the Staatsoper, Berlin, December 14th,
1925.*

SCENE: A small garrison town in Germany.

TIME: About 1835.

PRINCIPAL CHARACTERS:

WOZZECK } *Soldiers*		(Baritone)
ANDRES }		(Tenor)
THE CAPTAIN		(Tenor)
THE DRUM MAJOR		(Tenor)
THE DOCTOR		(Bass)
TWO APPRENTICES		(Bass and baritone)
AN IDIOT		(Tenor)
MARIE *Wozzeck's mistress*		(Soprano)
MARGRET		(Contralto)

*Like "Pelléas et Mélisande", "Wozzeck" is a direct, abridged setting of a
play, though of an unusual one. Both might appear to concede the
primacy of the words; but in fact the position of Berg is less extreme than
that of Debussy in that his music has a highly organized structure of its
own, even though most listeners will not and need not recognize this in
the theatre. For instance Act I Scene 4 is a passacaglia and Act II Scene 2
a fantasia and fugue. If the short scenes, each with its own atmosphere,
and the unassertive music (while the curtain is up) make a slightly
desultory effect, the whole work is pulled together by the brilliant
device of placing a musical climax in the final Interlude and following it
with a much shorter anti-climactic scene. Broadening his style, Berg here
appears to step outside this play about what we should call the "under-
privileged" and address us direct in a compassionate commentary.*

*The music is mostly atonal but with passages in rich post-Wagnerian
romantic style, like Act III Scene 1 and the final Interlude. It is partly
sung, partly spoken, and partly in "Sprechstimme" or rhythmical
declamation. We see the world through the eyes of the half-crazy Wozzeck
and there is at times a deliberate but highly effective distortion of focus
in both words and music.*

ACT I

Scene 1. The Captain's room.   The Captain, whose motive is heard
on the cor anglais at the fourth bar, is being shaved by Wozzeck. He
asks why Wozzeck is in such a hurry.   What should he do with the ten
minutes saved?   He chatters on about Time and Eternity the thought
of which frightens him and the uncomprehending Wozzeck can only
reply "Very good, Sir."   He tells Wozzeck that though he is stupid,
he is a good chap, but without morals; his child has not been blessed
by the Church.   Wozzeck is provoked into reminding him, to his
annoyance, that the Lord said " 'Suffer little children to come unto
me.' Morality is for the rich, not for poor folks like us."   (The words
"wir arme Leut' "[1]are set to an important motive.) The Captain dismisses
him with the admonition that he thinks too much and should not be in
such a hurry.
Scene 2. An open field outside the town. Late afternoon. Wozzeck and
Andres are cutting sticks in the bushes. The latter contentedly sings a
hunting song of folk-song cast. But Wozzeck shows signs of derangement.
He imagines the place to be haunted, is afraid that he hears freemasons and,
when the sun sets, thinks the earth is on fire.   They go home, as the
sound of distant bugles and drums is heard.
Scene 3. Marie's room. She stands at the window with her child, as a
military band approaches. The Drum Major waves to her and she sings a
snatch of the march. Margret, outside the window, makes sarcastic
comments on Marie's interest in soldiers and, after some backchat between
them, Marie slams the window shut and sings a lullaby till the child is
asleep. Wozzeck knocks at the window. He has no time to come in and
talks unintelligibly of what he has seen in the field, showing no interest
when she shows him their child. He rushes away, leaving Marie puzzled and
afraid. "Ach! wir arme Leut ' ", she muses.
Scene 4. The Doctor's study. Sunny afternoon. The Doctor is using
Wozzeck for experiments in dietetics, for a tiny reward. He is indignant
with Wozzeck for coughing. Wozzeck interrupts the Doctor's excited
pseudo-scientific talk by trying to explain that he pays insufficient
regard to individual characteristics. But he gets confused and begins to
speak of his hallucinations. The Doctor tells him that he is going mad and
is displaying a clearly marked "aberratio mentalis partialis, second
species"—a most interesting case. He can see immortality for his theory
and himself. As the scene ends, he makes Wozzeck show him his tongue.
Scene 5. The street before Marie's house. Twilight. The Drum Major
is showing off before the admiring Marie. He speaks of his splendid
appearance on Sunday parades, and roughly embraces her. She struggles
and breaks loose. But he embraces her again and this time she does not,
resist, saying that it is all the same. They go into the house.

[1]we poor people

ACT II

Scene 1. Marie's room. Morning sunshine. She sits, with the child asleep on her lap, admiring herself in her new ear-rings in the glass. When the child stirs, she frightens him into hiding his eyes with a snatch of song about a wicked gypsy, and continues to preen herself. Wozzeck comes in quietly and asks about the ear-rings. She says that she has found them, but he replies that he never found anything in pairs. He notices that the child is sweating and comments that life is all work, even in sleep. ("Wir arme Leut' ".) He gives her the money earned from the Captain and Doctor (to a chord of C major, said to stand for money's prosaic nature). He hurries off, leaving her troubled by her conscience.

Scene 2. A street. The Doctor is hurrying self-importantly but the Captain, meeting him, detains him. He frightens the Captain by speaking of patients who have died and going on to prophesy imminent apoplexy for him. His will be an interesting case on which to experiment. The Captain coughs with excitement as he imagines the mourners at his own funeral. Wozzeck hurries past. They chaff him heavily about Marie and the Drum Major. Wozzeck replies with an outburst of despair. They pretend to be surprised and the Doctor feels his pulse. He dashes away, leaving them commenting on so depressing a phenomenon as himself.

Scene 3. The street before Marie's house. For this scene a chamber orchestra only is used. Wozzeck encounters Marie and speaks elusively of "sin". He asks if "he" had stood there, to which she replies that she cannot forbid people using the street. When he lifts his hand in anger she exclaims that a knife in her body would be better than a hand laid upon her, and goes into the house. Wozzeck is left muttering "better a knife."

Scene 4. A tavern garden. Late evening. Before the curtain rises a rustic waltz has been heard. This is continued by a stage band to which couples are dancing. Two drunken apprentices hold forth about their souls, which stink of brandy. Wozzeck enters and is dismayed to see Marie dancing happily with the Drum Major. He is about to rush on to the floor when the dancing stops and Andres and some of the men sing a hunting song. Andres espies and greets Wozzeck who replies gloomily. The first Apprentice stands on the table and preaches a mock sermon before being carried out. The male chorus is briefly resumed. An Idiot steals up to Wozzeck and exclaims "It may be gay but it reeks of blood." Wozzeck fastens on the word "blood" and murmurs of a red mist before his eyes, as the others all begin to waltz again.

Scene 5. Guard room in the barracks. Night. A wordless chorus paints the snores of the soldiers on their beds. Wozzeck starts up and tells the somnolent Andres that he cannot sleep because his head is full of the scene at the inn, mixed with the image of a flashing knife. He prays. The Drum Major enters, very drunk and boasting of his conquest of Marie. He urges Wozzeck to drink but the latter looks away and whistles. They fight and the Drum Major knocks Wozzeck down before leaving noisily. Other soldiers momentarily stir as Wozzeck sits staring on his bed and exclaims "One after the other."

ACT III

Scene 1. Marie's room. Night. Marie is reading from the Bible (in "Sprechstimme") about the woman taken in adultery, breaking off to relate (in song) what she is reading to her own situation and to pray for mercy. There is some deeply romantic music in this scene (N.B. the exquisite horn solo in the middle).

Scene 2. Forest path by a pool. Dusk. A deep B natural underpins the whole of this scene. Wozzeck is walking with Marie and makes her sit down. He asks how long they have known each other and how long it will continue. He kisses her earnestly. Then as the blood-red moon rises (to a trombone crescendo) the timpani mark his throbbing excitement as he draws a knife and plunges it into her throat. The orchestra dies down as he exclaims "Dead!", and rushes silently away. The transformation to the next scene consists of two tremendous crescendi on B natural in unison, in the first of which the various instruments join successively, while in the second all swell together.

Scene 3. A tavern. Night. A piano strums a quick polka. Wozzeck is trying to drown his thoughts in wine. He dances with Margret and begins to make love to her. She begins a song, but breaks off when she sees blood on his right hand and elbow. (The accompaniment mounts tone by tone.) The dancers crowd round and Wozzeck dashes out, exclaiming "Am I a murderer?"

Scene 4. As for Scene 2. Wozzeck has returned, full of feelings of guilt. He searches for and finds the knife and throws it into the water. The moon, rising red, suggests to him that his secret is known. He wades into the water to wash himself and is drowned. As rising chromatic scales, growing slower, reflect his death throes, the Captain and Doctor come on the scene, having heard enough to suggest that someone is drowning. But they do nothing and the Captain, made more nervous by the red moon and the grey mist (graphically painted) drags the Doctor away.

The ensuing Interlude, a kind of dirge, is ampler and more straight-forward than those before. Beginning with a melody in the bass it works up, using motives already heard, to a great climax, in which "Wir arme Leut' " is heard on the trombones, and suddenly dies away.

Scene 5. The street before Marie's house. Children are playing in morning sunshine. Other children run in with the news that Marie has been found dead. All go off to look. Marie's son, too small to understand, at first goes on playing with his hobby-horse and then rides off after the others. The stage is empty and the music ends indecisively.

INDEX